Rosalie Gardiner Jones
and the Long March
for Women's Rights

G000065747

Rosalie Gardiner Jones and the Long March for Women's Rights

ZACHARY MICHAEL JACK

McFarland & Company, Inc., Publishers
Jefferson, North Carolina

Edited by Zachary Michael Jack

Participatory Sportswriting: An Anthology,
1870–1937 (McFarland, 2009)

Frontispiece: Bain Collection, Library of Congress,
Prints and Photographs Division.

Library of Congress Cataloguing-in-Publication Data

Names: Jack, Zachary Michael, 1973– author.
Title: Rosalie Gardiner Jones and the long march for
women's rights / Zachary Michael Jack.
Description: Jefferson, North Carolina : McFarland & Company, Inc.,
Publishers, 2020 | Includes bibliographical references and index.
Identifiers: LCCN 2020002134 | ISBN 9781476681160 (paperback : acid free paper) ∞
ISBN 9781476639338 (ebook)
Subjects: LCSH: Jones, Rosalie, 1883– | Suffragists—United States—
Biography. | Feminists—United States—Biography. | Women—Suffrage—
United States—History—20th century. | Feminism—United States—History—
20th century. | Women's rights—United States—History—20th century. |
Demonstrations—Washington (D.C.)—History—20th century.
Classification: LCC HQ1413.J66 J33 2020 | DDC 305.42092 [B]—dc23
LC record available at https://lccn.loc.gov/2020002134

British Library cataloguing data are available

ISBN (print) 978-1-4766-8116-0
ISBN (ebook) 978-1-4766-3933-8

Front cover image: Jones smiles broadly as she leads
the second On-to-Albany march out of New York City
on January 1, 1914 (Library of Congress)

Printed in the United States of America

McFarland & Company, Inc., Publishers
Box 611, Jefferson, North Carolina 28640
www.mcfarlandpub.com

For the women of Rosalie's Army
For all those who go the distance
For a cause they believe in.

Acknowledgments

Special thanks to Marc Watkins for permission to quote from Rosalie Gardiner Jones's unpublished diary "Daily Records of RGJ" and for permission to publish Jones's photos from his personal archive, the Marc Watkins Collection.

Wherever possible, and in the absence of complete scholarly monographs dedicated to Jones and her On-to-Washington march, I have constructed this narrative from firsthand or eyewitness newspaper accounts of the New York-to-Washington hike, especially those published in major metropolitan newspapers that sent correspondents to cover the march, including the *New York Times*, the *New York Post*, the *Brooklyn Daily Eagle*, the *Baltimore News*, the *Baltimore Sun*, the Wilmington *Morning News*, and the Washington, D.C., *Evening Star*. Throughout, I have included newspaper accounts published in cities through which, or very near to which, the historic march passed, including such major Eastern cities as New York, Newark, Trenton, Wilmington, Philadelphia, Baltimore, and Washington, D.C. Because the Jones family resided on Long Island, I invoke Long Island newspaper accounts for the kind of local perspectives on Jones and her family that only neighbors can offer. All dialogue has been sourced directly from newspaper quotes. To aid in readability, and in keeping with current editorial practice, *Ibid* has been used sparingly to minimize the number of endnotes.

Table of Contents

Preface:
In the Footsteps
of Rosalie Gardiner Jones

In the early stages of conducting the research that would become this book, I happily took a break from my day job as a professor teaching writing for social change and leadership studies courses to introduce area high school students to Rosalie Gardiner Jones. They listened with open minds as I shared a slip of the incredible social change leader who marched across five states and the District of Columbia in support of women's right to vote. All told, "General" Jones and her army of activist women trudged more than 600 miles in the dead of winter on three separate marches—two from New York City to Albany in 1912 and 1914, respectively, and another, from New York City to Washington, D.C., in 1913. The On-to-Washington march made Rosalie's Army nationally and internationally famous. Once they had learned the rudiments of Jones's résumé, the students were as mystified as I by her absence from their history books.

Early in our time together, I challenged the students to name a leader from the civil rights movement. "MLK!" several would shout before I finished my sentence, followed by a "Malcolm X" from somewhere in the back, and, with an assist from their history teacher, occasionally the Rev. Ralph Abernathy. Okay, I would say, now name me a leader from America's lesser known civil rights movement: the votes-for-women movement of the early 20th century. After a painfully long pause, someone would quietly float the name Susan B. Anthony to nods of distant recollection.

I understood all too well their historical amnesia. Prior to devoting a significant portion of my life to the historical study of voter enfranchisement movements, I knew scarcely more than they did. The question du jour was why—why had we so thoroughly forgotten the foremothers who, through blood, sweat, and tears, won the most sought-after civic right? For the many hundreds of American streets and thoroughfares commemorating the great

1

Martin Luther King, Jr., surely there should be at least as many Alice Paul Avenues, Carrie Chapman Catt Courts, and Elizabeth Cady Stanton Streets.

Of course my students and I had our theories where America's amnesia for its foremothers was concerned, theories that ranged from the ideological—the sexist and chauvinist erasure of women's history—to the conspiratorial and technological. The latter emerged as a plausible theory, because while Americans in the 1960s needed to look no further than their TV screens for appalling images of ballot box violence, intimidation, and suppression, the average American in the Progressive Era knew little of the very real intimidation and bigotry Rosalie's Army faced on its march to Washington in 1913.

Though Jones marched into Washington, D.C., a century before many of my high school charges entered kindergarten, it didn't take long for them to appreciate the star power of a woman who, in addition to leading the longest documented women's rights marches in American history, also earned five degrees, published two books, and ran for Congress—a woman who studied auto mechanics with the Chevrolet Company and earned distinction as the first suffragette to promote equal rights from the seat of an airplane. When I shared with them how General Jones and her right-hand woman, "Colonel" Ida Craft, mustered a woman's army and marched 250 miles to Washington, D.C.—in February, no less—they said she sounded like a righteous social justice warrior. When I revealed that the nation's top newspapers sent reporter embeds known as "war correspondents" to march alongside and document the publicity-rich protest march, the students marveled at the media-friendly design of Jones's campaign. When I confessed that many of the volunteers in Rosalie's Army, daunted by poor weather, illness, and homesickness, dropped out long before reaching Washington, D.C., they said the survivor-style march sounded fit for reality television. And when I projected images of Jones proudly bearing the American flag, they swore she possessed all the poise and beauty of a movie star.

And yet when I signed out of the high school at the end of the day to return to the university, trading in my guest badge for my state-issued ID, I wondered sincerely if the inimitable general and her diehard equal rights army would ever truly breathe the new life they deserved.

• • •

On Labor Day weekend in 2017 an email arrived from the great-great nephew of Rosalie Gardiner Jones. He mentioned that the family had read and appreciated my earlier work for teens on the Albany march and that if my plans ever took me to the greater New York metro area they would be delighted to host. At first I demurred; as a busy scholar and writer, I had no room in my schedule for a visit. Then, shortly before Thanksgiving, he wrote again, this time with an email forward whose subject heading read, "Rosalie

Jones to be honored … pretty incredible!" The email contained a link to press release from New York Governor Andrew Cuomo and Lieutenant Governor Kathy Hochul announcing that the state would dedicate and build a statue of Jones on her native Long Island at Cold Spring Harbor Park. Of the 25 statues currently located on state property, only two, the release lamented, featured women. On Election Day later that November, an image of Jones wielding her trusty megaphone appeared on the blue "I Voted" stickers handed out at polls around New York to commemorate the 100th anniversary of women's suffrage in the state.

Rosalie was back—in bronze, on the backs of hands, and, at long last, front of mind.

Four months later in March 2018, the chance to attend the Votes for Women Centennial exhibit at the New York State Museum in Albany, coupled with the opportunity to meet what remained of the Jones family, proved too enticing to resist.

• • •

When finally I sat down with Rosalie's great-great-nephew Marc and his father David in Marc's handsome home in New Jersey, David made it clear that Rosalie, a great-aunt he had grown up next door to, had not been an easy woman to love in her dotage. She had poorly handled the family's financial legacy, frittering away one of New York's larger fortunes; she had alienated friends and neighbors alike with a contrarian bent and a willingness to pursue her rights in court.

Later that same day, Marc ushered me into his historic home's walk-up attic, rolling up his sleeves to help search through the dusty boxes that constituted the family archives. He was eager to have someone with whom to share these forgotten ancestral relics that had lately hummed with new cultural resonance. Our search led us first to the memorabilia of Mary Gardiner Jones, Rosalie's niece and the nation's first female trade commissioner of the Federal Trade Commission, a strong feminist and lawyer like her aunt. Moments later, as we dug through an especially dusty box that contained several sheaves of typed records from the mid–1940s to the mid–1950s that together constituted Rosalie Jones's only extant diary, an entire electrical circuit went dead to startled cries from Marc's family below. Undaunted, we dug on.

Several days later I found myself in Albany queuing up with New York schoolchildren giddy with Spring Break fever to visit the Votes for Women centennial exhibit at the New York State Museum. The exhibit, created in partnership with the New York State Archives and New York State Library, had been one of the most popular in recent memory. Making my way past a series of New York suffrage banners from 1917, I located a photo of Jones dated March 1913—the month her women's rights army marched triumphantly into

Washington after 250 miles of arduous wintertime hiking. In it she holds a bouquet of roses and smiles becomingly for the camera in a modest cloak. Hung on the wall immediately beside the captioned photo was the famous suffrage scroll the general had carried on foot 175 wintry miles to Albany in 1912 through the sleet and snow and rain of a New York winter. Beautifully hand-lettered—legend has it by Jones herself—the scroll maintained its luminosity more than a century later, the ink of its signatories—fixtures of New York suffrage from Harriet May Mills to Nora Blatch de Forest to Mary Garrett Hay—still seemingly fresh. Seeing the illuminated scroll for the first time in person, I was struck by a telling omission: Jones herself had not signed the scroll with which she had so faithfully hiked, fancying herself a humble pilgrim-messenger bearing a message larger than herself.

I took a second tour back through the Votes for Women centennial exhibit before leaving Albany that day. I wanted to confirm that among all the celebratory banners hung from the ceiling honoring influential New York women from Gloria Steinem to Shirley Chisholm to Hillary Rodham Clinton, I had not somehow missed the banner rightfully belonging to Rosalie Gardiner Jones.

I had not, though many of the curated objects in the women's suffrage centennial led back to Rosalie Jones, including the Spirit of 1776 wagon displayed in the lobby. Jones's own yellow suffrage cart, the one in which she had toured across Long Island and Ohio, had served as the inspiration for the Spirit of 1776 wagon piloted by Edna Buckman Kearns in its July 1913 trek across Long Island. And there were still more connections between Jones and the celebrated suffrage wagon, which had once been owned by Jones's relatives.

Once more the suffrage general had slipped away, disappearing into the mists of history while escaping the full weight of her historical legacy even in this, the long-awaited exhibit marking the 100th anniversary of the very vote she helped win for New York women. Still, there were signs of growing awareness—not just the Votes for Women centennial exhibit in Albany but also the plaque unveiled by town officials in Huntington, Long Island, at the corner of Wall and Main Streets. There, Rosalie's anti-suffragist mother had famously stepped in front of the Spirit of 1776 wagon, refusing to accept its use for a cause she considered unpatriotic. Titled "Suffrage Rally," a newly commissioned plaque read: "On this site in July 1913 a thousand people witnessed anti and pro suffragists clash over 1776 wagon used as symbol of votes for women." Five years earlier, both chambers of the New York State Legislature passed a resolution declaring July 1, 2013, as the "Spirit of 1776" Wagon Day.

Before catching my flight home I decided to make one last homage, an eleventh-hour trip to visit Jones's gravesite at St. John's Episcopal Church in Laurel Hollow on Long Island. The cemetery sits atop a high hill overlooking the little white chapel where Rosalie married in late winter of 1927, tucked away in a mossy copse of trees overlooking a placid lake. Though it had snowed several days before my visit, mine were the first footprints on the steep incline to the carefully tucked-away family plot.

No sign or registry told me where to go, but I knew somehow, and before long I stood before her marbled gravestone—simple, unadorned, and with no epitaph beyond names and dates of birth and death. I expected to find an offering laid in the snow—faded flowers or perhaps some other token of thanks left by a disciple who, with difficulty, found her way here to thank a foremother for her sacrifice and vision. Finding none, I resolved to leave something, though as I reached my hands deep inside my empty coat pockets, I realized I had nothing worthy of Jones's legacy.

I would leave her a book instead.

What follows is the first-ever book-length biography of one of America's original social justice warriors. In it, I attempt to capture the news value, novelty, and brazen courage that attracted embedded reporters by the dozens to participate in Rosalie's historic women's rights march. The narrative structure I deploy is not artifice or aesthetic contrivance but an organic representation of the day-by-day, step-by-step nature of the two-week odyssey— the pilgrimage—undertaken by these intrepid women activists. For them, each day's march of 15, 20, or 25 miles must have felt like a new chapter in a long-running drama marked by impossible plot twists. As the leader of the votes-for-women army, Jones naturally serves as protagonist, but I often prefer the appellation Rosalie's Army instead, for this was a collective effort made by self-styled soldiers for the cause.

Wherever possible, and in the absence of dedicated scholarly monographs on Jones and her On-to-Washington march, I build my account from firsthand or eyewitness newspaper coverage of the New York-to-Washington hike, especially those published in major metropolitan newspapers that sent correspondents to cover the march, including the *New York Times*, the *New York Post*, the *Brooklyn Daily Eagle*, the *Baltimore News*, the *Baltimore Sun*, the Wilmington *Morning News*, and the Washington, D.C., *Evening Star*, among others. I have included newspaper accounts published in cities through which, or very near to which, the historic march passed, including such major Eastern metros as New York, Newark, Trenton, Wilmington, Philadelphia, Baltimore, and Washington, D.C. As the Jones family made its ancestral home on Long Island, I invoke Long Island newspaper coverage for the kind of local perspectives on Jones and her family that only neighbors can offer. All dialogue has been sourced directly from newspaper quotes.

Rosalie Jones led a uniquely long and varied life as a reformer and activist—long enough, in fact, to be largely forgotten when she passed away just six weeks shy of her 95th birthday in 1978. Because Jones achieved the pinnacle of her fame on the New York-to-Washington, D.C., March of 1913, I zoom in on the years 1912 to 1914, during which Jones marched many hundreds of miles, as a focal point. I have avoided the temptation to end the book in Washington, D.C., in March 1913 at the height of Jones's glory, hoping to avoid the folly of biographers writing about luminaries who achieved their greatest notoriety and acclaim while young. Too often they neglect to follow that original impetus through to its metamorphosis into old age. Instead, I conclude the book with several substantive chapters covering Jones's experience from 1917, when women earned the vote in her home state of New York, to the end of her life, giving readers a panoramic view of the general's life after she effectively retired from her post as America's most beloved suffrage general.

Let the march begin.

Introduction:
Rosalie's Army Marches Anew

It wasn't just the election of President Donald J. Trump in 2016 and the defeat of Hillary Rodham Clinton that caused women's rights activists to reconnect so powerfully with pioneering votes-for-women activist Rosalie Gardiner Jones. In January 2017 hundreds of thousands of voters, indignant at what they considered a stolen election, mobilized across America for the Women's March on Washington to demand the attention of a president-elect they felt certain did not respect their rights.

In 1913, that president was Woodrow Wilson, a promising Democrat who had proven lukewarm on the prospect of passing a constitutional amendment guaranteeing American women the right to vote. Wilson's vacillation caused votes-for-women advocate "General" Rosalie Jones to vote with her feet, mustering a women's army for a harrowing 250-mile wintertime march from New York City to Washington, D.C., carrying a message from the National American Woman Suffrage Association (NAWSA) for in-person delivery to the new president. Meanwhile, NAWSA's Alice Paul planned a protest parade for Wilson's inauguration day, only to be assigned the day before, March 3, as a consolation date.

Scarcely more than 100 years later, organizers of the 2017 Women's March on Washington heard history's rhyme all too well as they encountered a slew of similar bureaucratic obstacles—denied and delayed permits, last-minute date changes, a disdainful or at least dismissive president—in their efforts to send the strongest possible message to the nation's chief executive regarding the protection of women's rights. Just as they had in the winter of 1913, women in 2017 boarded trains and chartered buses by the hundreds of thousands for the journey of a lifetime to the nation's capital, where many learned for the first time of their forgotten foremother of 1913: a 20-something, raven-haired visionary with the moxie to march 250 miles to the capital carrying an audacious message for the presumed leader of the free world.

In the days before President Trump's inauguration Rosalie Jones marched anew.

7

Around that same time newspapers around the nation asked if I might provide their readers with historical context on the dramatic protest march planned for Washington, D.C. I had studied the perils women of the Progressive Era faced, in particular when lacing up their boots to hike for their rights, as well as written the first book-length treatment of Jones, a lengthy work of young adult nonfiction that had made the ABA's list of Best Books for Young Readers the year before. As a professor teaching writing for social change courses as well as a scholar of social justice narratives, I knew the obstacles Jones encountered proved all too common for those determined to pursue equal rights. On their 1912 march from New York City to Albany, for example, Jones and her second-in-command, "Colonel" Ida Craft, faced heckling, attempted kidnapping, and makeshift explosives aimed in their direction. While marching from New York to Washington, D.C., several months later in February 1913 they encountered more of the same. When Jones finally joined Alice Paul, Inez Milholland, and other votes-for-women luminaries for the national women's rights march up Pennsylvania Avenue on March 3, 1913, the demonstrators faced still worse—verbal abuse, public violence against women, a protest parade disrupted by male mobs, and a Washington, D.C., police force that activists later proved conspired to leave the protestors vulnerable.

I choose the title "Men Fear When Women March" for one particular op-ed that ran in the *San Francisco Chronicle*. In it I wondered aloud why it is that when women march, military-style and en masse, they tend to meet with ideological if not physical violence, as Jones and her sister suffragettes did in 1913. Is it women's displays of physical and intellectual strength that men historically fear, or women's sisterhood and solidarity? In 1913, masculine fear of mobilized women mustered to march for their rights resulted in street violence in Washington, with more than 100 marchers hospitalized, and a public outcry that ended in an eleven-day congressional inquiry that helped secure congressional passage of the 19th Amendment six years later in 1919. Could it happen again? the opinion editors at the *Chronicle* asked me. Could women suffer brutality and bodily harm in the streets of Washington, D.C., in 2017 simply for daring to act on their convictions?

Ultimately I reached a sobering conclusion: While the women marching against the policies of President Donald J. Trump did not expect to be greeted with violence on the National Mall, they could not be assured of an entirely peaceful reception either. History reminds us that Rosalie Jones and her On-to-Washington marchers of 1913 likewise failed to anticipate the mob violence they faced. Too often we have doubly failed those who dare to demonstrate for their civil rights—both in perpetuating a system whose inequities demand that such protestors take to the streets to be heard and in failing to protect them when they do so.

I hope this first-of-its-kind chronicling of the historic achievements of Rosalie Jones and her army of marchers helps right, in some small way, those enduring wrongs. Here is the untold story of a heroic yet flawed women's rights activist who, in addition to leading America's longest and most arduous women's rights marches, barnstormed her way into gubernatorial inaugurations, met with U.S. presidents, earned five degrees, published multiple books, and ran for Congress. Had her achievements occurred in an era of television or social media, Jones's star would surely have shone forever in the pantheon of social justice greats; as it was, she lived out her remaining decades quietly invested in the local dramas of her native Long Island and New York City homes, a passionate witness to perceived injustice in neighborhood, district, and borough.

That is how the story of General Rosalie Gardiner Jones ends, at the time of her passing in January 1978, 65 years after the 29-year-old suffrage general first announced her historic New York-to-Washington march. The story ends with Jones, a month shy of her 95th birthday, belatedly recognized in obituaries in the *New York Times* and elsewhere as the proto-feminist and civil rights activist-pioneer she always was.

But the real story begins in early 1913 with a visionary march for social change and the mobilization of a social justice warrior whose daring exploits are utterly unique in American women's history.

The remarkable story of Rosalie Jones and her women's rights army begins, as all stories must, with first steps.

1

Rosalie's Army

"We have come into a great and wonderful time. For the first time in the State of New York a real suffragist sits in the gubernatorial chair."[1]

Carrie Chapman Catt stared resolutely into the crowd of 3,000 suffrage supporters packed into the opera house at Brooklyn's Academy of Music building for a gala night of speeches. "For many years [Governor] William Sulzer has been an outspoken advocate for the cause. For the first time every political party in the state has endorsed our fight."

Catt could afford to be confident. On this auspicious night the prospect of women earning the vote in the most culturally influential state in America enjoyed its most promising hour yet. Activists had snapped up every seat in the auditorium, determined to hear Catt's every word. If dollars contributed to the cause served as any indicator, New York's suffrage sentiment soared. The evening thus far had yielded 60 to 70 pledges for the votes-for-women cause, and more than $3,000 had been raised for a campaign to educate voters. Three thousand dollars couldn't completely fund the fight, but the dollars— equivalent to six of Henry Ford's new Model T Runabouts—still represented a substantive down payment on social change.[2]

The stars of the movement shone at the gala event, including Catt, a former National American Woman Suffrage Association (NAWSA) president, and Dr. Anna Shaw, its current executive. Still, no star burned brighter against the backdrop of the evening's electrifying speeches than the one belonging to the movement's new hope, suffrage "General" Rosalie Gardiner Jones.

Only a year earlier few activists outside New York had ever even heard of the 29-year-old president of the Nassau County NAWSA branch who had recently returned from leading a grueling women's protest march from New York City to Albany. And now, less than a week after her triumphant return from the state capital, the suffrage general once again stood at the center of the night's biggest news. Jones and her second-in-command, "Colonel" Ida Craft, had just announced that they would be leading another winter hike that would "dwarf the [march] on Albany,"[3] leading a new women's march for equality from Manhattan to Washington, D.C., in time for Woodrow Wilson's inauguration in early March. Once in Washington, Rosalie's Army would join what organizer Alice Paul hoped would be the largest women's rights demonstration ever, with as many as 100,000 women gathering in the nation's capital in defense of their civil rights.

Less than two years earlier in June 1911 an estimated 50,000 suffragettes led by "General" Flora Drummond had marched five miles from Westminster Bridge in London to Kensington.[4] Costumed as powerful women such as Catherine of Aragon, Mary Queen of Scots, and Queen Victoria, marchers in the British suffrage pageant had captured the popular imagination while

Rosalie Jones poses with the American flag while Ida Craft holds a poster advertising the suffrage mass meeting at the Brooklyn Academy of Music (Bain Collection, Library of Congress, Prints and Photographs Division).

helping to attract media attention to the cause. The proposed march would be 50 times as long and many times more physically demanding. Rather than march through the paved city streets at the height of summer, the American suffrage general would guide her women's army cross-country in the dead of winter. Rather than ride on horseback in full military regalia, as was the habit of General Drummond in Britain, Jones would lead her pilgrimage with both feet firmly on the ground while dressed in a modest brown cloak. If completed, her On-to-Washington hike would become the longest women's rights march in American history.

Rosalie's Army would leave New York City at approximately 8:45 a.m. on or around February 10 and march through New Jersey, Delaware, Pennsylvania, Maryland, and, finally, into the District of Columbia. Soldiering across five states and the District of Columbia in just over two weeks would put the so-called Army of the Hudson in Washington, D.C., on March 1—two days before the giant national suffrage procession planned for March 3. Though the exact details of Jones's and Craft's second suffrage crusade had yet to be announced, the news sent activists scrambling for their checkbooks.

Separated by more than 20 years, Jones and Craft seemed an odd intergenerational pairing at first. Already in her early 50s, Craft was a seasoned and sanguine veteran of suffrage campaigns, while the idealistic Jones was a relative newcomer. The superficial differences between the two were perhaps best captured by their disparate wardrobes for the night's big event. Jones had come to hear Catt and Shaw speak wearing the type of gown expected of a young and beautiful New York socialite. By contrast Craft had come garbed in the weather-beaten marching clothes she had donned on the difficult December march to Albany. Unsmiling and resolute, the colonel carried the same birchbark walking stick on which she had leaned for the duration of their previous march up the Hudson Valley.

It had been the talkative colonel rather than the more understated general who had earlier in the day relayed to an eager press corps an outline of the impending march. One hundred women would leave exactly one month and one day after the night's big fundraiser at the Academy of Music. Roughly 100 more would join up en route. General Jones would be leaving the following day to chart a course for the historic suffrage hike, whose rallying cry would be "On to Washington!"[5]

The *Brooklyn Daily Eagle* couldn't help but boast about its contribution to the cause the day after the gala. "The abstraction of human rights has never been a matter of indifference to Brooklynites," crowed the editors, adding, "the best ways of establishing human rights have always been as hotly discussed here as in New England."[6] Suffrage, the paper pointed out, had shone at the Academy of Music gala event, and Brooklyn could be proud of its host role. Indeed, it had produced a remarkable human resource crop of votes-for-women workers, whose ranks included not just the well-seasoned Craft but also younger marchers who had claimed the borough as their home: most notably lawyer and frequent suffrage parade leader Inez Milholland as well as emerging activists such as Phoebe Hawn and Minerva Crowell. Of late, Jones, who had been residing in the area when she wasn't staying at her family's estate on Syosset, Long Island, had completed her bachelor's degree at Adelphi College in Brooklyn.

In addition to sharing a neighborhood, Jones and Craft were more alike than most casual observers knew. Both came from monied families, allowing them time to grow both expert and ardent in their activism.[7] Both had long defied well-heeled, ardently anti-suffragist mothers who publicly opposed their daughters' positions. Both Jones and Craft were fiercely loyal to those who reciprocated their loyalty, while being capable of holding endless grudges against those who failed or betrayed them. Their deep underlying similarities, counterpointed by the positive differences by which they avoided needless duplication, made them ideal running mates, the kind that gave confidence to those funding the cause.

On hearing Craft's announcement, suffrage leaders in Washington, D.C., hung purple, green, and white banners at their national headquarters at 1420 F. Street. "That the suffragists were jubilant is putting it mildly," wrote the *Washington Post*.[8] Not only would Rosalie's Army be coming but a permit allowing the women to march up the entire length of Pennsylvania Avenue on March 3—the day before President-elect Woodrow Wilson's inauguration—had been issued. The secretary of the treasury, the speaker of the House of Representatives, and the president pro tempore of the Senate had each signed off on their approval to use the space outside of their respective buildings as gathering spots for tens of thousands of progressive women from every corner of the United States to make known their call for enfranchisement.

Additional details of the votes-for-women parade trickled out. A large contingent of D.C.-area schoolteachers would cancel classes and walk the parade route in support of women's right to vote. Washington, D.C.-area women's rights activists skilled in horsemanship would ride, and platoons of women would march alongside. The *Washington Times* called the event a "monster pageant" and promised readers the spectacle of "platoons of petticoated cavalry leading the marchers up Pennsylvania Avenue."[9]

Immediately after the gala event at the Academy of Music, Jones left New York for Norfolk, Virginia, where she hoped to recruit troops for her women's army. She sought five women from each of the states through which she and Craft planned to march. "I want you to understand," she told reporters, "that there is a distinction between the suffragette and the suffragist. The former is one who wants to get votes for women and works for it. The latter is one who thinks about it, and hasn't the time to work for it."[10] The definition belied her ever-growing frustration with the bureaucratic arm of the votes-for-women movement to which she had lately brought mass appeal. Less than two weeks earlier, General Jones, Colonel Craft, and "Surgeon General" Lavinia Dock had marched halfway across the state of New York to deliver to Governor-Elect William Sulzer a message jointly crafted by the New York City suffrage societies. As her army waited for the most opportune moment to approach the state's soon-to-be-chief executive, the elder bureaucrats in the movement had raced to meet the governor-elect themselves, lest the heroic exploits of the suffrage pilgrims garner undue attention. The *Press and Sun-Bulletin* in Binghamton, New York, wryly noted Jones's meteoric popularity in observing that a statue of Joan of Arc would soon be erected in New York City. "This is unfair," the editors opined, tongue only somewhat in cheek. "Why crowd Joan in ahead of 'General' Rosalie Jones?"[11]

After marching nearly 175 wintry miles, the 11th-hour chastening from New York suffrage leader Nora Blatch de Forest and others in the movement's bureaucratic wing had felt like a slap in the face to the On-to-Albany marchers, sufficient to make Jones wish to distance herself from its dignitaries. However, the national momentum the march on Albany had created had been too much for even the general to refuse. Because of it, Jones had achieved a difference-making kind of celebrity, though already that celebrity threatened to overshadow quieter work accomplished by others. Votes-for-women advocates took it as an article of faith that the cause was greater than any single soldier fighting for it, even if, and when, that solider was a general on a meteoric path to stardom. In early December Jones had been a marginal player who had needed the endorsement of the Manhattan suffrage societies to make her votes-for-women pilgrimage to Albany. Less than six weeks later, after the story of the hike to Albany had caught on with New York's newspapers of record and been picked up by wire services across North America, her star threatened to outshine the important legislative action and lobbying efforts undertaken by more deskbound, less charismatic strategists.

Many Americans were charmed by newspaper stories of the indefatigable general who stood scarcely more than five feet tall but possessed the mettle and the moxie to march 25 miles through snow and ice. Though she had come from money, Jones, one of six children of conservative Long Island parents Mary Elizabeth Jones and Oliver Livingston Jones, had charted her own course in life, lately forgoing the privileged gaiety of the debutante for the life of the activist. As a young woman she had raised chickens to pay for a daring solo trip across America and later traveled to the United Kingdom, where she rejected the violence of the British suffragettes while still thrilling to the courage and drama of their cause.[12] She had overcome a powerful fear of public speaking, proving that the race was not always to the swift and that courage required deeds as well as words. She delivered her first votes-for-women speech in Roslyn, Long Island, to a hostile crowd in an event sufficiently trau-matic for the shy young woman to consider running from the cause entirely. Still smarting from that early rejection, she summoned her courage to join forces with votes-for-women icons Harriot Stanton Blatch and Alva Belmont to speak at the corner of Wall Street and Broadway in New York City in 1911, where angry crowds threw eggs and tomatoes at them.[13]

Lately the public's anomalous sympathy for Jones as a suffragette had created a growing rift between the youthful conscripts in her equal rights army and the older hands working behind the scenes to influence legislation in Albany. "General Jones Rejoices," trumpeted the *New York Tribune* of the New York state senate's posting of a bill that would put the suffrage ques-tion before the people in a referendum set for 1915. Directly below "Jones Re-joices," however, ran the subheadline: "But old campaigner says that 'Rosalie is young.'"[14] The "old campaigner" in question was Mary Garrett Hay, chair of the New York City Woman Suffrage Party. By 1913 Hay and other elder activists had been toiling in the movement for close to 40 years and had good reason to regard the senate bill with caution. Hay expected the bill to pass in a matter of weeks, while realizing that the larger battle was only just beginning. "It is work, work, work for the suffragette until 1915," she told the press.

Jones's unbridled joy at the legislative breakthrough contrasted sharply with the cautious response from higher-ups. "Isn't it wonderful to get some-thing for once without slaving for it on bended knee," she enthused, though she neglected to mention that her army had, quite literally, slaved for it the previous month, trudging 175 miles through cold and snow to Albany to deliver the suffrage message to the governor. With trademark humility, the general downplayed her crucial role in winning the legislative victory. "[We] kids haven't the sense for legislative work," she remarked, echoing the elders in the movement.

At the office of the Woman's Political Union in New York City, Nora De Blatch Forest, who had allegedly endeavored to steal Jones's thunder in the climactic moments of the march on Albany, readied herself once more to dampen the general's enthusiasm, pointing out that the bill's loaded language might sabotage its prospects. "The reason we were so angry when we heard the bill was read [in the Senate] with 'every citizen of the age of twenty-one' was because it is a moot point if women are citizens.... No, we wanted the law to read 'every citizen regardless of sex. Then there would be no trouble,'" Blatch explained, parsing the bill's problematic language for reporters. An-other activist put a still finer point on the troublesome wording. "That is one thing," granted Mrs. A.F. Townsend, "but another is the great objection we have to letting illiterate foreign-born women who have been here only a few minutes vote.... Oh, the wording of this bill is a very serious matter. It lost us the vote once. It will try to do it again." While Jones had rejoiced at the bill's reading in the statehouse, gushing that she was absolutely "tickled," Blatch had replied more carefully. "Yes, we're happy—that is, we're happy if the bill is right. We aren't crowing, though, until we've seen it in print and checked on every comma and semicolon."

Did celebrating a real breakthrough for women require dotting every "i" and crossing every "t" on the proposed New York suffrage bill? Jones didn't think so. The march to Albany had taught her to savor victories when they came, and why not? For the long-distance protest marcher, victory seemed, quite literally, forever just around the corner. Jones had already led one historic suffrage pilgrimage, earning a direct audience with the governor, and was now set to lead her army on a march that would no doubt be the longest women's rights march in American history—approximately 250 miles from New York City to the nation's capital. Even fleeting joy served as a partial remedy to the near-continuous setbacks, detours, and defeats expected in a reform movement.

Already the risks of Jones's second, longer march were mounting. The first risk was to the general's physical and mental health. Overtired from the 175-mile December march on Albany, and burdened by her newfound fame, Jones had found it necessary to book a private train car for her recruitment trip to Norfolk, Virginia. The private car would allow her well-earned rest and a moment away from a press corps that had lately followed her every step. Thanks to the steady stream of coverage produced by the "war correspondents" embedded in the army's December march, her name had become iconic in the northeast.

The newspapers were now reporting a new risk to the marchers: a serious outbreak of smallpox in the area through which Rosalie's Army proposed to hike.[15] New Jersey's state board of health had taken emergency precautions, ordering vaccinations from Jamesburg all the way to the Jersey shore to prevent an epidemic. Walking 250 miles in wet woolens in the dead of winter all but invited the horrors of influenza, bronchitis, and even pneumonia, but smallpox was something else entirely. Jones and Craft were certain to face potentially life-threatening weather. Southeastern Pennsylvania winters had once nearly vanquished Washington's Army of the Potomac at Valley Forge, and they could just as well halt the progress of Jones's Army of the Hudson. Average daytime highs in mid–February hovered around 40 degrees in the region, with nights often plunging into the teens with wind-chills below zero. It was one thing, Jones knew, to walk outdoors on a calm, sunny, 45-degree day but quite another to march 25 miles nonstop in freezing temperatures that could bring even the most seasoned soldiers to their knees.

For the moment, the general occupied herself with the challenge of recruiting for a trip whose physical and emotional risks were all too real. In New York, Colonel Craft had already promised the press 200 women hikers. And yet on January 11 Jones left Norfolk for Washington, D.C., having made only the smallest progress toward those recruitment goals. Only the day before she had secured a modest pledge from the president of the Norfolk Suffrage Society, who with her young niece and six others, would walk to Washington, D.C., in time to join the suffrage pilgrims in the mass protest parade scheduled for March 3.[16] Jones needed more than warm bodies willing to hike for half a day, however: She needed loyal foot soldiers resolved to walk multiple days and to recruit to her platoon proven leaders capable of solving logistical dilemmas in the field. She needed strong women with thick skins, having confessed to the *Washington Herald* that the biggest obstacle to recruiting was women's fear of the ridicule they might face for standing publicly for what they believed in.[17]

During the previous campaign to Albany, Jones had availed herself of the services of Milwaukee journalist-activist Jessie Hardy Stubbs to deliver the podium-thumping speeches crowds expected of the suffragettes. "The hikers are often too tired to be in good voice," newspapers explained of the need for an orator-in-chief.[18] Upon her arrival in Washington, D.C., Jones announced that her friend and fellow suffragette Jeannette Rankin of Missoula, Montana, would serve as the army's official speaker. Two years earlier, Rankin had become the first woman to speak to the Montana legislature on behalf of suffrage, and lately she had served as a field secretary for NAWSA. In making her surprise announcement Jones offered few details of Rankin's appointment. Certainly, Rankin's home state of Montana figured prominently in the NAWSA war map—a document listing the states in the order in which the organization hoped they would grant full suffrage. As the map's designer, Mary Ware Dennett, put it to the votes-for-women faithful: "Please don't waste all your time and money converting your own state…. There are twenty-three states that can get it [the vote] in 1914."[19] Among the hopefuls for 1914 were two of the six states through which Rosalie's Army would march—New Jersey and Maryland—and several other nearby New England states, including Massachusetts and New Hampshire. New York, Virginia, and Pennsylvania could fall before votes-for-women forces in 1915 if only influential suffragists in New York possessed the moxie and daring to campaign beyond the borders of their home state.

The message Carrie Chapman Catt, Jane Addams, and Anna Howard Shaw intended to deliver at the NAWSA meeting in February aligned closely with the raison d'être behind Jones's impending invasion of New Jersey, Pennsylvania, Delaware, Maryland, and the District of Columbia. If the suffragette march and the subsequent protest parade in Washington succeeded in converting even a fraction of the fence-sitters living in the states targeted in Dennett's war map, Rosalie's Army might well become the single most influential campaign in the enfranchisement fight to date.

Initial expectations for Jones's previous New York-to-Albany march had been low. Even after its completion Nora Blatch de Forest had unfairly framed the history-making women's march as merely a "picturesque thing to do."[20] Now, just as suddenly, NAWSA had made the On-to-Washington hike and national suffrage procession that would follow the center of a two-year strategy they hoped would yield the ballot in some 23 states.[21]

• • •

While Jones consulted with national headquarters in Washington, D.C., in New York City Colonel Ida Craft kept the newswires humming with a steady drip of newsworthy revelations. Craft had learned from preparations made for the On-to-Albany hike that fashion would be foremost on the minds of potential enlistees—not high fashion but fashion fit for the field. The long skirts expected of stylish women on the board avenues of New York City would simply not work on the muddy and rutted roads awaiting marchers in states like Maryland. Craft's problem-solving mind had begun working on the fashion dilemma even on the way to Albany. Shorter skirts, she believed, were the only reasonable option for walking great distances, coupled with something she called "hikers." The *New York Tribune* registered confusion as to what such a novel fashion might entail. Whatever "hikers" were, the newspaper reported, Craft was having prototypes made patterned after those she had worn on the previous campaign. That particular effort had ended badly for marchers who had ignored Craft's insistence on march-appropriate clothing. "Many a one who left New York [for Albany] fresh, young, and vigorous," the *Tribune* opined, "was mustered out a total wreck."[22] If Craft had her way, the rallying cry for the coming march was to be "No more silk ruffles. Give us hikers!" To stay warm, Jones's lieutenant would wear a gender-bending uniform consisting of a men's Norfolk shooting jacket and a brown corduroy skirt with "hikers" underneath that resembled men's knickerbockers.[23]

Since learning of the coming hike, curiosity-seekers had flocked to suffrage headquarters in search of details, though few had signed on to the march as of yet. As Craft rallied troops in Manhattan, from Jones in Washington came a telegram with the rudiments of an itinerary:

> Arrive Philadelphia, Saturday evening, February 15
> Arrive Wilmington, Tuesday evening, February 18
> Arrive Baltimore, Wednesday evening, February 26
> Arrive Washington, D.C., Sunday evening, March 2.[24]

New York suffrage chief Hay announced she would not be joining the cross-country trek. "February is the worst month in the year," she explained to reporters, "and the roads will be in awful condition.... I'll go down to Washington for the [suffrage] parade, but I'll go by train, thank you." Indeed,

Hay and her staff at the Women's Political Union faced a more immediate deadline: an enormous suffrage ball that would bring women by the thousands to the Seventy-First Regiment Armory—an orange brick behemoth on Park Avenue capacious enough to hold a small city of suffragettes. While Jones had hastened out of town to map the upcoming marching route and scout advance lodging for her troops, Craft and the other members of the Albany hikers had stayed behind in New York to drum up new recruits and fundraising dollars. "Everybody who was expected to came, all their friends, and then some others," the *New York Times* reported of the suffrage ball at the Armory, adding: "there were 5000 people on the floor and in the big galleries. Even the Albany hikers were there, every one of them, except General Rosalie Jones, who is away prospecting for the February hike to Washington."[25]

The legend of Rosalie Jones had sufficiently lodged itself in the minds of Washingtonians that many expected her to show up wearing her suffrage pilgrim's cloak and carrying her trademark birchbark walking stick. Instead she had arrived in a Pullman car. While her visage was instantly recognizable to many newspaper readers in New York state, many in the nation's capital registered surprise on seeing her for the first time. The *Washington Herald* remarked: "This young woman who earned the title of 'general' is of the type that may be seen any afternoon in the autos that thread F. Street and Connecticut."[26] The *Evening Star* described the equal rights leader as a woman of about 30, an "autumn-leaf maiden" with "hazel eyes, brown skin, and russet freckled cheeks." She was of "womanly" build and voice, the *Star* assured its readers, adding, "She is for all her life, whether she ever fulfills her destiny or not, a wife and mother." Pro-suffrage newspapers like the *Evening Star* were often at pains to emphasize the beauty and femininity of marchers, who were thought by anti-suffragists—"Antis" for short—to be "unsexed" by their physical prowess and supposed radical views. Indeed, in one popular song of the era, titled "The Hiking Suffragettes," composer Mrs. E.S. Fitch dismissed the marchers as androgynous "he shes" rather than true women.[27]

In part to diffuse such preconceived notions, Jones sought to introduce herself to Washingtonians in the most plainspoken manner possible. "I have been a suffragist ever since I was born," she told the *Herald*, "but I never knew it until about three years ago. Then I became interested in some of the suffragist clubs of New York. But I did no active work. I did not know there was any active work to be done, or any need for it." Upon being asked what she had been doing prior to her conversion to the cause, the general replied that she had not spent her early and mid–20s attending college, as had many of her peers. "I just did the things most girls do," she told them, "went out in society, traveled in Europe, and that sort of thing. That was the only training I ever had in the suffrage cause."

The comments were vintage Rosalie Jones—brief, straightforward, honest to a fault—and yet they exemplified critiques of the young leader offered by some of the elder suffragists, whose comments sometimes implied resentment at what they perceived to be Jones's unearned fame. Still, many of the veteran stateswomen, dubious of her late arrival to the movement, had themselves not started in the cause until they were well into their 20s. Then, too, the general's comments about her pedestrian past downplayed the serious work in the field she had already accomplished by early 1913—efforts that went well beyond behind-the-scenes paper-pushing and afternoon teas. Earlier in May, Jones had taken a family pony cart and, along with her friend and fellow suffragette Elisabeth Freeman and a horse dubbed *Suffragette*, turned it into a suffrage wagon to canvas her native Long

Rosalie Jones, age 12, dated March 1895 (Marc Watkins Collection. Reprinted by permission of Marc Watkins).

Island. Seven years Jones's senior, Freeman had quickly become her mentor. As a child Freeman had immigrated from Britain to Long Island with her single, working mother and, over time, had established an enduring friendship with Rosalie.[28] When Jones and Freeman undertook their Long Island suffrage campaign together, Freeman had recently returned from a six-year stint working for the militant British suffragist Emmeline Pankhurst as organizer and speaker for Pankhurst's Women's Social and Political Union and, as such, was able to inform Jones of momentous votes-for-women happenings in the United Kingdom, including a long-distance suffrage march from Edinburgh to London led by Florence Gertrude de Fonblanque. De Fonblanque's march had likewise involved a horse-drawn cart, though its six thru-hiking suffragettes had failed to obtain the hoped-for press coverage. In fact, Fonblanque's epic journey had been called a mere "long walk" by *The Times* of London, a national newspaper of record that mostly saw fit to ignore the inroads made by the British marchers.[29]

That summer Jones took still more dramatic action for the cause, shipping the family's wagon to Cleveland, Ohio, where men would cast their ballots on the votes-for-women question in a statewide referendum.[30] Well before her December hike to Albany, New York, captured the national imagination, Jones made headlines in the Buckeye State, where she and Freeman costumed themselves in old-fashioned white dresses and lacy caps with yellow "Votes for Women" bags full of pamphlets slung over their shoulders.[31] In late July the *News-Journal* in Mansfield, Ohio, ran the headline "Leave Mansfield in Yellow Wagon—New York Suffragettes Depart from City After Week of Local Activity."[32] That article, and several others like it, relayed the story of how Jones and Freeman had been piloting their "one-horse vehicle" loaded with 40 pounds of suffrage literature across the state, moving to Cleveland to establish a headquarters for their statewide advocacy tour.

By the end of August Jones and Freeman had arrived on the last leg of their 1,200-mile wagon tour, appearing in Elyria, Ohio, on their way back to Cleveland. They stopped long enough to share their confidence with local newspaper reporters of the ultimate passage of the state's votes-for-women amendment. "I don't believe we have encountered a single farmer who is opposed to the amendment," Freeman told reporters, "and the men in the mills and the factories promised us they would remember us when they marked their ballot."[33] If approved, the amendment to Article 5 of the Ohio Constitution would delete the word "male" in the first line and insert the words "or she" to solve the dilemma posed by the existing "he" gender pronoun. The revised wording would read: "Every citizen of the United States of the age of twenty-one years, who shall have been a resident of the state for one year next preceding the election, and of the county, township, or ward in which he or she resides such time as may be provided by law, shall have the qualifications of an elector and be entitled to vote at all elections."[34]

Whether Jones and Freeman felt obliged to project confidence or were merely being politically naive, their trust in the electorate proved misplaced,

Rosalie Jones (left) and Elisabeth Freeman pose with their suffrage wagon in Ohio, spring 1912 (Marc Watkins Collection. Reprinted by permission of Marc Watkins).

as Ohioans rejected Amendment 23 by more than 15 percentage points, with nearly 600,000 votes cast.[35] Wisconsin's all-male electorate likewise rejected the idea of granting women the vote. When canvassed before the referendum, many male voters pledged support, but many of those "yesses" had turned to "nos" at the ballot box.

Had the same phenomenon—public shows of support and private, ballot-box doubts—been manifest in the Army of the Hudson's December march on Albany? In the District of Columbia, Jones's comments to the *Washington Herald* concerning her recently completed trek echoed the confidence she and Freeman expressed that previous summer in Ohio. "All the way from New York to Albany," she told them, "we had not the least trouble.... Everywhere we received applause and never ridicule. As we marched along people came out to their gates and offered us refreshments and encouragement."[36] Their epic adventure, which saw the so-called suffrage pilgrims attending high teas and charity balls in addition to hiking as much as 24 miles a day, had been, as Jones put it, "a serious movement with a jolly side."[37] In any case the general maintained that her previous long-distance march had been uniquely successful in reaching rural and small-town voters. "We reached ... two classes that would never come to a suffragette meeting in a hall.... Nobody wants to sit around a couple of hours listening to a dry discourse," she maintained, "but they will stop to watch a band of women marchers and listen to a street corner meeting." The On-to-Washington march, Jones intimated, would feature similar impromptu meetings held at country crossroads, small-town churches, and courthouse squares along their 250-mile route to Washington.

On the way to Albany, farmers and townspeople had kindly supplied Jones and her suffrage pilgrims not just with lodging but with water and milk and tea and other rations. But they had also aimed shotguns in the marchers' direction and launched explosives in the vicinity of the votes-for-women army.[38] Some bystanders had ignored them; others had openly disagreed with them. Whether due to popular opposition or merely the arduous physical nature of the journey, of the hundreds of hikers who had walked alongside Jones at various times on the march to Albany, only five had marched the entire way. That, Jones now explained to the *Herald*, had been the intention from the beginning. "It is true there were only five of us at the finish but there were only six at the start pledged to go on through to Albany. We had about thirty-five with us when we left New York City, but they were not pledged to go through." This time around, Jones predicted, troop numbers would swell as the Army of the Hudson approached Washington, D.C.[39]

At the end of the planned On-to-Washington hike Jones would be given a prominent position in the massive suffrage protest parade her troops would join at the end of the army's proposed 18-day slog. Still, the details of just how the famous, and infamous, Rosalie's Army would merge with the mother of all equal rights parades remained unclear. Already NAWSA had distanced itself from some of the views and opinions expressed by Jones on her January 11 visit to Washington, D.C. Among the more controversial comments the general made during her short stay in the capital were those concerning her stance on suffrage in the District of Columbia, where she believed women should be granted the vote even though D.C. was not officially a state. Jones's definition of a suffragist also rankled higher-ups in the movement. She had taken great pains to explain to anyone who would listen that "a suffragist is a woman with a wishbone, but a suffragette is a woman with both a wishbone and a backbone."[40] On the previous day in Norfolk, Virginia, the general had floated an alternate definition: A *suffragist* was one who "thinks of votes for women" while a true *suffragette* was one who "gets out and works for it."[41] To the many hardworking women's rights activists who had not marched for the cause, and never would, the general's sentiments sounded disrespectful.

Jones's sentiments on marriage and engagement also may have vexed NAWSA. On the march to Albany at least one of Rosalie's prized recruits, college student Gladys Coursen, had accepted a "three-month probationary engagement" from a wealthy reporter from Poughkeepsie by the name of Griffith Bonner.[42] The reaction to a nascent engagement within Rosalie's Army had been decidedly mixed. On one hand the announcement made great fodder for the journalists, nicknamed "war correspondents," following the march, adding a love story to the already engrossing quest narrative the suffrage faithful had commenced with their long-distance pilgrimage. The Christmas-day engagement had reminded readers across the nation that suffragettes could fall in love and desire marriage as readily as could other women, a realization that helped combat the enduring public image of them as cold or loveless. On the other hand engagements inevitably distracted from the cause, generating headlines more worryingly traditional—young woman sacrifices personal goals for love—than progressive.

Presumably, in giving Coursen's engagement her blessing during the Albany hike, Jones had hoped to show that love of a romantic partner and love of a cause were not mutually exclusive. And now, in speaking with the press in the nation's capital, she reaffirmed that philosophy. If it happened that one or two of her marchers became engaged on the forthcoming march to Washington there could be a silver lining in terms of recruits, Jones explained, "for the would-be husbands [would] feel constrained to … march with us."[43] No, the general concluded, she was not overly anxious at the prospect of romance-inspired desertions from her ranks. "The girls who march in this army are all good soldiers," she assured the doubters. "They will not desert but rather will they convert."

The mostly male reporters quizzing Jones in the nation's capital were eager to learn the particulars of the women who had pledged themselves to march. One made inquiries concerning what he called the "charms and qualifications of the suffragette army" and, on hearing them, reported to his readers a sexist catalogue of allures that included "blondes and brunettes, girls with blue eyes, girls with snappy black eyes, girls with brown eyes—coy girls, dashing girls, all kinds of real nice girls." Reporters could expect some "marriageable girls" on the march, a term which at least one reporter translated to mean "good suffragettes, good housekeepers, and withal strikingly beautiful girls"—"marrigettes," he called them, marching in a "marriageable army." A sidebar titled "Suffragettes' Plan" conceded that while Rosalie's Army would be dressed modestly as penitent pilgrims in long brown cloaks, underneath their robes they would be wearing enticing "hikers"—that indescribable garment favored by Colonel Craft that one newspaper described as "a cross between bloomers and a ... gown" at which "the [Plymouth] Pilgrims would have looked askance."[44]

As much autonomy as Jones and Craft had secured for themselves as general and colonel, respectively, both nevertheless answered to Alice Paul, the organizer of the national suffrage procession in Washington and a formidable young leader within NAWSA. Two years Jones's junior, Paul had already earned a master's degree and been jailed on three separate occasions in Great Britain for civil disobedience in the militant suffrage movement led by Emmeline Pankhurst. For Paul, the march of Rosalie's Army was only one part, albeit a highly visible one, of a larger national campaign for a constitutional amendment giving women the right to vote.[45] Paul wanted Jones's march to represent more than publicity for the cause and pressed her to seek signatures on a petition for a constitutional amendment enfranchising women.[46]

During her meeting with Jones in Washington, D.C. Paul reaffirmed those priorities, shifting the focus from the well-publicized march to the upcoming protest parade in D.C., which would feature

Alice Paul in academic robes, 1913, likely after earning her PhD at the University of Pennsylvania (Library of Congress, Prints and Photographs Division).

suffragettes on horseback led by Inez Milholland. The statuesque New York suffrage lawyer had served as a herald on horseback for both the New York City and London processions and in so doing had become a parade mainstay and popular attraction. With platoons of mounted "petticoat cavalry" and divisions of protesters marching behind like foot soldiers, Paul's planned procession would mirror the martial pomp popularized by the New York City suffrage parades of recent years. A year and a half before Jones announced the On-to-Washington march in Brooklyn, the military styling of the Women's Political Union parade from 5th Avenue and 59th Street in New York City to Union Square had prompted an unexpectedly strong turnout of 10,000 spectators and 3,000 marchers. Pledge cards sent to would-be participants included not just blanks for "Name of Marcher," "Occupation," and "Address" but also an evocative description of the triumphalist moment marchers could expect to join:

> To the beat of martial music.... Our woman trumpeter awakes us to our duty to bear our share in the march of progress as in their time did our pioneers. Our trumpeter speaks to us in clarion notes of the noble sacrifice and worthy achievement of the women of every land through the ages. They braved all things and we harvest the fruit of their pain. Our trumpeter calls to us to march ever forward, honoring the women of the past, dedicating ourselves to the women of the future.[47]

Like its predecessor in New York City the March 3 votes-for-women demonstration in D.C. would be peaceful and nonviolent despite its martial theme.

After meeting with Paul, Jones traveled next to Paul's hometown, Philadelphia, by way of Baltimore, having secured 30 pledged recruits thus far on her journey. Baltimore itself had been hot and cold on the idea of the proposed march, though Jones hoped to lessen the city's ambivalence by meeting with her lieutenant there, Mrs. Charles Keller of the Just Government League. Some would-be hikers lost interest on learning of the physical discomforts the march entailed, but Jones won over a handful of the skeptics before catching her 1 p.m. train for Havre de Grace, Maryland.[48] "Buzzing with discussions of her plans," the city pledged 10 women to march the two-day, 40-mile leg from Baltimore to Washington, D.C.

By the time Jones's train rolled into Wilmington, Delaware, later that same day she had tallied seven new recruits from her brief stopover in Havre de Grace. Now she hoped to find five more enlistees in Wilmington.[49] The general was up early the following morning for a meeting with the local suffragettes at Clayton House, a lavish five-story hotel with a mansard roof said to offer the best lodging in the state. Taking into account the recently pushed back departure date of February 12, Jones told supporters that her army would arrive in Wilmington on February 24. Glad as the city was to host the famous general, Wilmington's *Morning News* ran an editorial urging the municipality to do better than supply five recruits. "Her figures are entirely too low," the newspaper declared, exhorting its readers. "Surely from the number of earnest suffragists in Delaware ... more than five can be enlisted who would make the 'hike' from this city to the national capital. The march of the forces of General Jones is one of the most picturesque movements yet attempted by the suffragists, and Delaware should be part of it."[50] The editors promised Rosalie's Army would be given a cordial welcome when they reached the metropolis at the confluence of the Christina and Brandywine Rivers. Meanwhile, Wilmington's *News Journal* took a more sanguine approach to the question of whether the city's equal rights activists would sign-up for the long-distance march, writing, "We are of the opinion that most of them will prefer to go to Washington by the speedier and far more comfortable means of railroad trains."[51]

By Friday, January 17, Jones was in Philadelphia perfecting her evolving pitch—not only would enlistees enjoy the satisfactions of marching for a good cause but they would also benefit from greater physical fitness. "I can guarantee that every woman who takes the trip—joins the grand hike—will look much younger when she gets through than when she started," Jones assured would-be conscripts in the Quaker city.[52] As if to reinforce this message, the *Morning News* in Wilmington described the general as "youthful, slender, and altogether charming," adding, "It seems there are to be short-distance hikers and long-distance hikers ... of these go-the-limit hikers there are at present enlisted five from Connecticut, six from New York, eight from Maryland, and eight from Virginia." All hikers would be welcome, whether for "a day or two, or a week, or only a few hours will serve to show the spirit in the heart of the suffragette, even if the flesh be weak."[53]

Before leaving Philadelphia, Jones floated an even bolder scheme—one that she hoped would kickstart fundraising. The idea came in the form of a mandate: "either hike or pay the expenses of a substitute."[54] Those who didn't care to join the demonstration could now "show their interest in the cause by getting someone to take their place, and pay all the expenses," she suggested. Several of the city's wealthiest activists took Jones up on her offer, agreeing to pay for a surrogate to spare them the sore feet and tired legs of the true suffrage pilgrim.

• • •

The *New York Times* reported Jones's attendance at the wedding of Mary Livingston Delafield, a relative on her mother's side, later on the same day that Jones left Philadelphia, but otherwise the general appeared ready to let others occupy the spotlight.[55] Her reconnaissance journey, nearly 10 days in length, had taken a toll on her already depleted supplies of energy. During her absence, votes-for-women advocates in New York had been dealt a blow when the proposed suffrage amendment bill they had so recently cheered had

"Such Is Life," Maurice Ketten, January 24, 1913, *Washington Times*.

been held up in the Senate. Senators had begun to parse the flawed language of the proposed amendment, noting that, if passed as written, certain women, including foreign-born women who married American citizens, would enjoy voting rights that exceeded those enjoyed by some men.[56] And yet there had been victories, too, while Jones canvassed four states in search of enlistees in her women's army, including an overwhelming vote in favor of a future suffrage clause in the constitution of South Dakota, where the proposed amendment met with only two opposing votes in the senate.[57] And in Michigan, where suffrage had recently been defeated amid accusations of voter fraud, the governor announced the votes-for-women question would once again be put before the people in spring elections.[58]

Rosalie's Army galvanized sentiments on both sides of the votes-for-women debate. Coincident with Jones's visit to Philadelphia, Antis had denounced her long-distance march, expressing resentment at the five pledged recruits she had secured in the city. One prominent member of the Pennsylvania Association Opposed to Woman Suffrage issued a statement that read in part, "the constant aim of the suffragettes seems to be publicity, and that certainly is unwomanly. It makes one sick to see the eagerness with which some of the women are courting publicity as well as votes."[59]

On January 18, Montclair, New Jersey, hosted a debate between pro- and anti-suffrage voices billed as a battle royale, and the event didn't disappoint. While suffragists were generally better organized than Antis, votes-for-women backers were often portrayed by the press as a minority faction. In a New York Constitutional Convention five years earlier, suffragists had presented 175,000 signatures compared to zero on the Anti side.[60] As Rosalie's Army achieved ever more publicity for the pro-vote cause, the debate in New Jersey turned ugly. Fists were raised and fisticuffs were narrowly avoided in an event described as "disgraceful and shameful." In the end, suffragist Flora La Follette, daughter of U.S. senator from Wisconsin Robert La Follette, and anti-suffragist A.G. George had to be escorted from the venue well after midnight for fear of those who might further "insult or abuse" them.[61]

On January 20 pro- and anti-voices met once again for a sharp debate in New York City, this time at the Metropolitan Temple. Representing the Antis, Charlotte Rowe warned that suffrage would inevitably lead to a nation with a First Husband rather than a First Lady. "What kind of a man will such a woman's husband be?" Rowe asked from the bully pulpit. "One wonders what he will be doing when his wife is battling with the Senate.... Will he sit at the end of the table and pour the tea? Will he have to retire at the proper time with the wives of the diplomats? Will this weak man in the end revolt and ask for votes for men?"[62] Rowe worried aloud at the alleged hypocrisy of women who wanted some of the rights of citizens while distancing themselves from less desirable civic responsibilities. "I saw the men returning wounded and sick from the Spanish War," she told the audience. "Were the women heckling for equality then? They were probably down on their knees thanking God for brave men. Equal suffrage is a repudiation of manhood." Elisabeth Freeman, General Jones's partner in the unsuccessful campaign to win women the vote in Ohio and a labor activist in her own right, countered on behalf of the equal rights contingent, promising that just as working-class men had used the ballot as a means to achieve civic empowerment and social betterment, so too would enterprising women, once enfranchised.

Meanwhile, in Wilmington, Delaware, a city energized by Jones's recent visit, activists gathered to learn how best to deal with the public confrontations likely to result from the arrival of Rosalie's Army. They invited Ella Reeve Bloor, a leader of the votes-for-women campaign in Ohio, to prepare them for the battle ahead. "There might be some criticisms and sneers if they'd go into the street," Bloor cautioned, "but when you get the strong conviction that it is your right and your duty you won't mind."[63]

That, at least, was the sentiment on which the fate of Jones's forces now depended: strength of inward conviction sufficient to overpower the slings and arrows of outrageous fortune. After all, what fighting army could be more formidable, and more indomitable, than one whose every step was propelled by a sense of righteousness?

2

General Jones
Prepares for War

Rosalie Jones returned to New York to considerable fanfare. The January 21 edition of the *New York Times* declared the recruiting trip made by the "little general" to be a "suffrage triumph."[1] So much in demand had Jones been, the newspaper stated, that her throat was sore from the surfeit of interviews and speeches. "Everyone is prepared to receive the pilgrims with joy and gladness along the route," the *Times* claimed in an article whose triumphalist tone suggested a rewritten press release.

With the beginning of the votes-for-women pilgrimage scarcely more than a few weeks away, more complete details of the impending march were released. Women would be invited to join Rosalie's Army for an hour, a day, or a week—whatever time they could spare. A suffrage pilgrim uniform had been readied for purchase for the "low price of $2" and included a cloak and hood, knapsack, and walking stick. Participants were encouraged to bring their own first-aid kits, since "Surgeon General" Lavinia Dock of the march on Albany would not be along for the entirety of the On-to-Washington march. First-aid, the announcement noted, should include absorbent cotton, medical tape, and a roll of gauze. Soft leather shoes with rubber heels and warm socks were strongly recommended. The projected itinerary would take the Army of the Hudson across five states and the District of Columbia in two and a half weeks of marching:

> Leave Hudson Terminal Station, New York City, February 12
> Reach Elizabeth, New Jersey, February 12
> Reach New Brunswick, New Jersey, February 13
> Reach Trenton, New Jersey, February 14
> Reach Bristol, Pennsylvania, February 15
> Reach Burlington, New Jersey, February 16
> Reach Philadelphia, Pennsylvania, February 17
> Reach Chester, Pennsylvania, February 18

Reach Wilmington, Delaware, February 19
Reach Newark, Delaware, February 21
Reach North East, Maryland, February 22
Reach Havre de Grace, Maryland, February 23
Reach Abingdon, Maryland, February 24
Reach Chase, Maryland, February 25
Reach Baltimore, Maryland, February 26
Reach Laurel, Maryland, February 28
Reach Washington, D.C., March 1

While the marching suffragettes had their evening gowns and afternoon tea dresses shipped to them en route on their December hike to Albany, this time there would be no such fineries. Evening dresses and showy hats would be "strictly barred."[2] Pilgrims sojourning for the cause would be allowed a single small piece of luggage, which would be carried from town to town via the army's baggage car driven by Alphonse Major. "Gentlemen pilgrims are welcome to enter the ranks commanded by General Rosalie" one clause read, implicitly emphasizing the need for male marchers to submit to Jones's authority in advance.[3]

The *New York Times* reported that Dr. Ernest Stevens of the Men's Walking Club of Philadelphia would join Rosalie's Army in that city and walk on to Washington. In a show of solidarity he would be wearing the regulation pilgrim's cloak for women, which cost one dollar. Women's hats made of white canton flannel with a yellow suffrage button in the center and a yellow cockade on the side would be made available to women marchers for 49 cents.[4] Colonel Craft would sport a costume of her own invention—the many-pocketed men's Norfolk shooting jacket, short skirt, and self-styled "hikers" the *Washington Herald* described as a "singular garment" and a "combination of a short sheath gown ... with an undercurrent of bloomers."[5] The short skirt would feature a high side split for ease of movement. "The bloomers, of course, are worn underneath," the write-up hastened to add. General Jones, meanwhile, would wear the brown hooded pilgrim's cloak that had become her trademark.

A few short days after returning to New York City, Jones took to the road once again, this time to Albany for what the general and the suffrage leaders accompanying her were told would be the passage of the suffrage amendment at the New York statehouse. Instead, they were once again met with disappointment when the Assembly abruptly adjourned due to a "misunderstanding" between the leaders of respective chambers who had failed to reach concurrence on the bill.[6] Ultimately, the amendment "in the shape desired by the suffragists" had been passed by the senate 40 to 2, though the debate in that chamber, minimal as it was, suggested many as-yet-unvoiced reservations at the prospect of fully enfranchised women. "Instead of giving the right to vote to women wholesale," an exasperated Senator Elon Brown, minority leader in that chamber, told his colleagues, "we should restrict the right of ignorant men to vote." In the end, Brown, a Republican, summarized the practical views of the all-male senate in saying, "I'm not willing to live the rest of my life in antagonism of women. I'd rather have suffrage than war."

If there was a silver lining to the bill's tabling, it was that such setbacks inevitably spurred activists to action. If a bill lacked subscription or the right amount of public support, many within the movement reasoned, it must be because inadequate pressure had been applied to lawmakers or because the sort of publicity likely to win public favor had been lacking. From recent stinging defeats in Ohio and Michigan, for example, had been born the idea of the grand, military-style suffrage protest parade planned for the day prior to Woodrow Wilson's inauguration, an event whose creativity and complexity grew with each passing day. Jones and her pilgrim band would be "foremost among the ranks of marching suffragettes" in the March 3 protest now projected to include "Ten to twenty thousand women on horse, afoot, riding on floats, in ... cars, with pennants and banners waving down Pennsylvania Avenue past the very doors of the White House."[7] Paul had successfully petitioned the War Department for use of the Treasury Building grounds for a portion of the procession, whose stated goal was to promote the need for an amendment to the Constitution granting votes for women.[8]

Most recently had come word that six golden chariots drawn by milk-white steeds of the kind featured in *Ben Hur* would be entered in the parade by Baltimore suffragists. Still more controversial was this claim made by an unidentified official at suffrage national headquarters: "In chains behind our chariots we may parade some of our unfair critics."[9] Of late, plans for the procession had expanded to include a suffragette impersonating Joan of Arc on horseback leading four squadrons of "petticoat cavalry" and a "gray-haired woman of seventy," Rebecca Linton of Philadelphia, scheduled to march with her six daughters, all of them suffragists. The pageant would include a tableaux or allegory enacted on the steps of the Treasury Building, with the famous soprano Lillian Nordica tentatively scheduled to play the role of Lady Columbia and the "five virtues of womanhood"—Justice, Liberty, Charity, Peace and Hope—each to be played by a "widely-known actress."[10] More spectacular still—a report had surfaced that daring test pilot Bernetta Miller—only the fifth woman in the U.S. to have earned her pilot's license— had been commissioned to fly low over Pennsylvania Avenue, generating the memorable, tongue-twister of a headline, "Women Plan Plane Swoop."[11]

Of the Washington, D.C., protest parade's many attractions, Rosalie's Army was to be front and center. In the District of Columbia preparations had already begun in earnest, though the army itself had yet to muster. Training brigades marched across the city in rehearsals for the coming event. Women government employees would be granted a half-day holiday if they notified their supervisor of their desire to take part.[12] March 3 was to belong entirely to the nation's women, though from NAWSA came word that the organization had not been invited to participate in Wilson's inauguration ceremony on the following day, March 4, and did not desire to do so. Rosalie's Army, the association dictated, would also not take part in Wilson's inauguration. Head of the publicity committee Helen Gardener had made it clear that the society she represented was non-partisan and would not participate even if they had been invited.[13]

As if in preparation for the political battle ahead, Jones attended yet another of the series of debates between equal rights for women advocates and their adversaries, this one sponsored by the Republican Club of New York. For the first time in its 35-year history the club's toastmaster began his remarks with the term "ladies." Jones was far from the only high-profile woman in a room that included New York suffragette lawyer Inez Milholland and journalist and suffragist Ida Husted Harper, author of *History of Woman Suffrage*. The room bristled with tension. Harriet May Mills, president of the state suffrage society, advocated the votes-for-women viewpoint, while Bertha Lane Scott represented the Antis. The Republican luncheon crowd was mostly against granting the vote, but as Jones watched from her seat, Mills successfully lodged a persuasive point: that women voters would clean up the graft and greed plaguing government. However, Scott fired back, "I have myself within a year seen two perfectly honorable ladies, women who could be absolutely trusted … usurp the control of their organizations by methods that could hardly be outdone by Tammany Hall."[14] Mills's partner in the debate, Alice Chittenden, echoed those sentiments, adding, "Once in politics women will lose their present perspective. They will play the game just as men play it, no better and no worse." In fact, Chittenden maintained, pointing to the "hysterical force" and violent tendencies of the English suffragettes, they might not play the politics game as well.

Gertrude Foster Brown, incoming president of the state suffrage association, countered that women were not trying to imitate or duplicate men but were instead simply trying to fulfill their own destinies. "We don't want to do his work or interfere in his affairs," she explained to the audience. "We want to do our own work, the work we have always done…. There is a vast fund of energy and ability in American women going to waste. There are millions of us who, when our private duties are done, have some time we could give to the state and social service. It is useless to tell us to go into charity work when you deny us the fundamental responsibility. We are discouraged at the outset. Public spirit is stifled in women." Brown saved her most persuasive point for last—namely that the corruption plaguing the state of New York might be an indirect result of mothers with unrealized personal potential. "Men inherit from mothers as well as fathers," she reminded the male luncheon group. "If we want honest, courageous, capable energetic men we must have honest, courageous, energetic and responsible mothers."

Jones's thoughts must surely have turned to her own mother, whose ambitions had been featured that very day in the *New York Times*, though not in the ways Rosalie might have hoped. Mary Elizabeth Jones was one of New York's best-known Antis, and also one of its most wealthy and conservative. While the *Times* write-up chiefly concerned the sumptuous, red-tile roofed, concrete colonial mansion Mary and Oliver Jones were building on their family's 1,000-acre Long Island estate, the focus on the home's opulence would not be helpful to the younger Jones's attempts to represent herself as the leader of a down-to-earth women's army.[15] Still, the daughter of Mary E. Jones had become accustomed to newspaper features like this one—pieces meant to stir up the long-burning and very public controversy between herself and her mother and, quite possibly, to undermine her own credibility as a leader of the people.

In Washington the 10 Baltimore women who had signed on to march with Rosalie's Army from that city undertook scrimmages of their own, taking an "unwonted amount of exercise" in an attempt to get into shape for the walk to the capital.[16] General Jones's chief "lieutenant" there, Mrs. Keller, had begun carrying a pedometer with her during practice walks with her husband, Dr. Charles Keller, following behind in the car. At the end of two miles, newspapers reported, she was "not exactly weary, but consented, nevertheless, to a ride the balance of the way to the suburb." Even the governor of Maryland, it appeared, would need to ready himself for the coming march of the suffragettes. NAWSA's Dr. Anna Shaw and nine other activists barnstormed his office with banners flying and cornets blaring. Governor Foss couldn't promise Shaw and her followers that he would meet their demands to send a pro-suffrage letter to the Maryland legislature, but he was willing to go on record as supporting the cause.[17]

A spirit of readiness swept through New York City, with newspapers reporting the curious sight of what they called a "gypsy camp" sprung up in Central Park West along the lake.[18] On further inquiry reporters had learned that Rosalie's Army had begun what it called a "preliminary 'experience' before the votes-for-women tramp." Jones had led 10 of her infantrywomen and one man, "commissary wagon" driver Edward Van Wyck of Brooklyn, to the open-air picnic pitched under an oversized yellow banner that read "New York to Washington 1913."[19] So many onlookers flocked to the Central Park to watch the marchers try out their new boots that mounted police summoned to examine Jones's permit were forced to remain on-hand for crowd control.[20] Colonel Craft presented the permit to the general with a sharp salute. Once satisfied with the gathering's legality, policemen and pedestrians alike paused to watch the commander-in-chief of the "female army" lead her troops in maneuvers of "quickness and precision." Passersby quickly joined in, snapping pictures of the novel event from "every tree and apartment house within range."[21] Eleven of the would-be marchers, with their pilgrim's cloaks worn over top of their gypsy garb, took a break from war preparations to pose for photos on a patch of grass that looked almost spring-like. The weather had been sufficiently warm that winter that the shallow ponds of Central Park remained closed to ice skaters.

The pictures served the dual purpose of satiating New York media hungry for images of the marchers while also serving as a fundraiser for the cause. Cameramen snapped shots of the photogenic Jones and Mary Boldt for picture postcards the pilgrims hoped to sell to defray expenses on the way to Washington. Uncharacteristically, Jones agreed to pose individually for a page-one photo, smiling big for the camera as she held aloft a banner that read "Hear ye, Votes for Women Pilgrimage, from New York to Washington, 1913"[22] The gypsy camp motif served not just as an inventive public relations spectacle but also as an occasion to more fully introduce members of Rosalie's

Rosalie's army of pilgrim hikers pose in Central Park. Photograph published February 11, 1913, though taken February 10. Left to right (rear row), Hettie Graham, Marie Louise Burge, May Bell Morgan, Olive Schultz, Evelyn McCullough. Front row, Elisabeth Freeman, Ida Craft, Mary Boldt, Rosalie Jones, Martha Klatschken, and Mary Baird (Marc Watkins Collection. Reprinted by permission of Marc Watkins).

Army that had recently joined with intentions of walking all the way to Washington—Mary Baird, Mary Boldt, Elisabeth Freeman, May Bell Morgan, and Martha Klatschken. The latter, standing less than five feet tall, had been dubbed the army's "Little Corporal" for her Napoleon-esque stature.[23]

Corporal Klatschken would oversee the fundraising for the march. She had given up a lucrative job as a stenographer at a firm in downtown New York City when, as friend and journalist Eleanor Booth Simmons put it, "she asked herself why should she enrich a Wall Street money-maker … when she was burning to give that all to suffrage?"[24] Klatschken had promptly quit her job, taken a small room above suffrage headquarters on East 34th Street, and proceeded to tackle all the small, thankless jobs others in the movement thought beneath them. "I have a vision of her," Simmons recalled, "a little, short,

One of the picture postcards signed by marchers to fundraise for the cause. This one, showing Jones in formal dress, is signed "Votes for Women, Rosalie G. Jones" (Marc Watkins Collection. Used by permission of Marc Watkins).

plain girl marching up the steps of Mrs. John Jacob Astor's 5th Avenue mansion and handing suffrage leaflets to the utterly flabbergasted but still conventionally correct butler."

The gypsy camp stunt likewise offered the chance to introduce Freeman, the avowed British militant who had previously traveled 1,000 miles with Jones across Ohio. The yellow suffrage wagon she had driven that summer in the Buckeye State had now been repurposed as a gypsy wagon. The suffragettes staged Freeman's introduction with true theatrical aplomb in a dress rehearsal the *New York Tribune* described as if setting the scene for a Broadway play, noting "a rustling in the bushes, a flash of red and yellow against the somber background of pond and wintry woods and a gypsy girl leaped into the circle." Freeman played the part of the "gypsy maid" come to tell the fortune of Jones, who submitted her gloved hand for the gypsy's would-be palm-reading. As the photographers obligingly snapped photos, Freeman, with much melodramatic whispering and murmuring, prophesied that Jones would soon "be going on a long journey" and afterward volunteered to tell equally accurate fortunes for any bystander willing to greet the marchers in person and pledge 10 cents to the cause on the way to Washington.

With little explanation the 36-year-old Freeman had replaced Jeannette Rankin as the marchers' official speechmaker. Wearing a red and yellow dress with a checkered bandana and long braids,[25] Freeman explained to puzzled members of the press covering the event that just as gypsies had once traveled with pilgrims to avoid undue persecution, so would she now travel with Rosalie's roving band.[26] In assigning an official role to a known militant suffragette from Britain, Jones walked a dangerous line. Deeply desirous of Freeman's help in driving the horse-drawn suffrage wagon and her assistance in making speeches, and yet eager to distance herself from the violence with which Freeman had been associated overseas, the gypsy theme would reinforce the ideological difference between American suffragettes—the generals in charge in this instance—and the foreign British militant traveling as their guest. If the public was meant to view Jones as a modern-day George Washington and her band of woman soldiers as a latter-day Continental Army, then, by extension, Freeman, as a British citizen, could have no place in the marching brigade except as a tagalong. For Jones, the little wagon Freeman planned to drive carried baggage of a more symbolic sort. The pony cart had belonged to the conservative ancestors of her archconservative, anti-suffragist mother. Despite her well-publicized opposition to her daughter's cause, Mary Jones had agreed to lend the wagon to her daughter for Rosalie's first votes-for-women campaign that summer. "That little yellow cart," Freeman vowed to reporters, "is going to last until Rosalie and I get the vote."[27]

Just as she had in advance of the Albany campaign, Mary Jones had gone directly to the press to publicly break with her daughter's politics and to express her doubts about the feasibility of her latest pie-eyed project. Mary Jones confidently predicted that when Rosalie's Army reached the awful roads between Wilmington and Baltimore, they would be sorry they had ever undertaken the trip. While the Wilmington newspapers took exception to the slight against their roads, calling the general's mother "a woman of the old school," they did concede that the soupy condition of the route from Elkton, Maryland, to Washington, D.C., could pose a serious threat to the army's progress.[28]

While the Army of the Hudson staged their gypsy encampment in Central Park, suffragists at the national headquarters in Washington arranged a newsworthy spectacle of their own, organizing a street meeting attended by more than 200 men and women despite heavy snow. There, canny protestors managed to generate the attention-getting headline "Suffragists Brave Police" by pinning suffrage buttons on stern policemen who had shown up to prevent the buttons' unpermitted sale.[29]

• • •

"Real Winter Is Coming." The page-one headline on the first of February chilled suffragists up and down the Eastern Seaboard.[30] January had brought uncharacteristic warmth, and January 31 had shattered previous record highs by a shocking 11 degrees. "Weather Man Fears Ice Shortage Here," announced the headline in the *New York Times* on January 26, describing the warmest January on record in New York City, with average daytime temperatures of approximately 44 degrees.[31] The Hudson River had not yet frozen over, and for the first time since 1874, ship traffic moved freely up and down the river well into early February. Now New York would "have its first real touch of winter," with storm advisories forecasting accumulating snow, deep cold, and gusty winds.

And there was worse news still, an apparent death-knell entombed in the headline: "Gloom in Suffrage Camp. Hear Gen. Jones Has Broken Down."[32] After smiling gamely for the cameras just two days earlier in Central Park, Jones had gone missing, and rumors had spread that she was ill. The *Times* heard "gasps of consternation at suffrage headquarters" when activists there learned that their indomitable general had suffered a nervous breakdown. The *Washington Times* likewise reported that Jones was suffering from "over-work" and was "on the verge of a breakdown" and had subsequently returned to the family estate near Cold Spring Harbor, Long Island, to rest.[33] The news service claimed that Jones would return to lead the march scheduled to begin February 12, while the *Times* asserted that she had been incapacitated and had appointed Colonel Craft to lead in her stead. Word of Jones's plight reached Washington, D.C., as suffragists there converged on the capital to testify in favor of a proposed amendment to the Constitution allowing women to vote for members of the House of Representatives. Suffragists and representatives bound for the Capitol building had found themselves aboard the same train on which at least one suffragist tried an alternate tact: sitting on the lap of Representative Sereno Payne of New York. By the time the resulting hubbub had quieted down, the lap-sitting suffragette had earned one more vote for the cause.[34]

In Britain suffragettes had all but given up on the strategy of leveraging feminine allures to win converts to their cause, choosing instead to add a more potent weapon to their arsenal: the slingshot. A weapon of choice, they used it to break windows with lead discs stamped with the message "Votes for Women." The lead shot had yet to cause any fatalities, but doctors testified that the projectiles were capable of killing.[35] Already the British militants had made a concerted attack on Dublin Castle and bombarded the home office in

London.[36] Suffragette Lenora Cohen had used a hammer to smash the glass case in the jewel room at the Tower of London. Fears of similar attacks had prompted the closing of multiple royal palaces, including those at Kensington, Hampton Court, and Holyrood.[37] Special precautions had been taken at the National Gallery and the British Museum as well. Golf courses had lately been targeted by creative militants who had torn up putting greens in Birmingham and burned the words "Votes for Women" into putting greens with acid.[38]

In London suffragettes kept shopkeepers and police on edge by smashing windows, tampering with the mail, and doing prison time for acts of violent resistance. Hunger strikes had become the norm among the imprisoned

A BUSY DAY FOR AN ENGLISH SUFFRAGET

An unsigned cartoon, titled "A Busy Day for an English Suffragette," that appeared in the *Wilmington Morning News* on March 6, 1913. The cartoon shows a militant suffragette breaking windows, tampering with the mail, poisoning soup, then going home to dream of causing more mayhem.

suffragettes led by Flora Drummond, who, when called before a magistrate, declared, "It is now war to the knife."[39] In Scotland warring suffragettes had raised "pandemonium" in disrupting an appearance by Prime Minister Herbert Asquith in the city of Dundee.[40] The militants had shouted "traitor" at the premier until police had been forced to eject the protestors from the ceremony. One suffragette had leapt over the front of the gallery and been saved from a fatal 20-foot plunge into the crowd below by men who had "seized her by her skirt and held her suspended." Indeed, suffragettes had struck such fear into the populace that special religious services had been arranged at Westminster Abbey and St. Paul's Cathedral for those who wished to pray for an end to the violence.

Officially, American suffragists disavowed the anarchic violence of the British movement, and yet already the actions of women willing to bomb, burn, and maim for the righteousness of their cause had yielded results in the United Kingdom. In London the British Labor Party had declared itself for suffrage, if not for ideological reasons then for practical ones. Britain's labor unions accounted for nearly three million votes,[41] and the suffragists' ability to link their demands for equity with the larger dispossession and marginalization felt by the working class had energized the women's campaign.

While America's suffrage leaders resisted the extreme measures of their sisters in the United Kingdom, the rise of the military metaphor at the heart of Rosalie's Army, coupled with the uniformed women on horseback slated to lead the suffrage demonstration in the capital, moved the needle in the direction of militant action. Indeed, on the same day news ran of the Labor Party's historic allegiance to the votes-for-women cause, New York newspapers reported that General Jones would outdo General Washington in crossing the Delaware River not just once but three times on her upcoming journey. Before disappearing from public view with her mystery illness Jones had been quoted as saying, "We expect to rival the Continental Army in history-making."[42] Meanwhile, four women on horseback dubbed "Paul Revere suffragists" would, they claimed, be "heralding the way of 'General' Rosalie Jones's pilgrims from New York to Washington."[43]

While such grandiose analogies struck some patriots as hyperbole if not heresy, comparison between generals Washington and Jones had merit for many suffragists. The wintry march Jones was scheduled to lead would be many times the length of Washington's to Valley Forge and in conditions no less favorable. While many pointed out that the suffragette march did not involve the life-and-death exigencies of Washington's campaign, Jones's defenders disagreed, arguing that, like true patriots, a brave few among the legions of votes-for-women activists would rather suffer the extreme hardship of a long march in the cold, or even death, than go on living without the rights and liberties their citizenship earned them. Thanks in large part to explosive growth in the American newspaper industry, Jones's history-making march on Washington would generate many thousands of times more column inches than had the march of the Continental Army. Still, the hyperbole many Americans read into the comparison between "General" Jones and General Washington highlighted an ongoing struggle for historical legitimacy. Where votes-for-women activists saw the need for a true revolution to achieve their civil rights, many men saw high comedy in the fanciful notion that a group of mostly well-to-do white women would masquerade as a bona fide army. Likewise, America's newspaper editors struggled to reconcile the disparate tones of the On-to-Washington march—one deadly serious, the other fun-loving and adventurous.

As Jones allegedly convalesced at home on Long Island, the *Washington Post* reported on one eccentric plan underway in Washington, D.C., to thwart the women's vote. In "virtually every college in the capital" male students had been discovered conspiring in a plot to release rats and mice to disrupt the coming women's suffrage parade.[44] The conspiracy had been discovered after "an unusual demand for rodents" had been recorded and was purported to include college men stationed at every corner along Pennsylvania Avenue ready to release baskets or bags of mice and rats—some 1,000 of the vermin in all.[45] On learning of the plot, suffragist leaders had appealed to the capital police for protection only to be told that no arrests could be made until, and if, the rodents were actually let loose in the streets. Still, the potential for the prank to cause mass panic gained the attention of Cuno Rudolph, president of the board of commissioners of the District of Columbia. "The plan must be nipped in the bud," the commissioner declared. "The women have a perfect right to march through the streets and this right must be safeguarded."[46] Young men would be young men, the commissioner allowed, but these particular young men had gone too far. He recommended referring the matter to Dr. William Woodward, the district health officer, who "had a fund for exterminating rats" and who had "better get busy" if he hoped to head the college boys off in time.

In Chicago another well-known suffragette, physician Dr. Mary Edwards Walker, found herself inspired by the historical moment to continue her own long-running protest. A recipient of the Medal of Honor for her service as a surgeon in the Civil War, Walker had once again been arrested for dressing as a man in what, for her, constituted an ongoing protest against the tyranny of dresses and petticoats. Dr. Walker's preferred manner of dress was not dissimilar from the controversial marching uniform selected by Colonel Ida Craft—a shorter skirt with something like men's knickerbockers worn underneath—though occasionally Dr. Walker would opt for a gentlemanly top hat and waistcoat to accessorize her gender-bending ensemble.[47] While

Craft's marching bloomers had yet to debut on the streets of New York City and Newark, authorities in Chicago had hauled the distinguished Dr. Walker in for her wardrobe, citing charges of unlawfully masquerading as a man.

• • •

On February 2 Ida Craft surprised the press in announcing that Jones would in fact lead the march. When asked directly whether the general had suffered a mental collapse from overwork, Jones's lieutenant offered a revisionist narrative, replying, "She was not in fact ill at all, only taking some time to give her beloved suffrage wagon a fresh coat of yellow paint."[48] When she was not painting, Jones had been making more cloaks for the pilgrim army to wear, Colonel Craft insisted, adding, "She is as fit as possible, and she will be in the pink of condition when the army starts off on the birthday of one of the suffrage heroes, Abraham Lincoln." The *Times* appeared to take Craft's declaration with a grain of salt, adding with a note of irony that the suffrage wagon Rosalie had been given by her mother might have "anti-suffrage proclivities, having originally belonged to anti-suffrage half of the General's family."

Despite Craft's reassurances, the uncertainty over Jones's participation in the rapidly approaching march persisted well into early February. Under the heading "Rehearsing for the Hike," the *Baltimore Sun* ran a photo of four key members of the regular army, noting in the caption that Craft would lead the hike if General Jones "should be incapacitated."[49] Mary Boldt, May Morgan, Ida Craft, and Lavinia Dock posed for the photo instead with walking sticks and knapsacks for props. While the picture lacked the star appeal it might have enjoyed with the photogenic general as standard-bearer, the presence of "Surgeon General" Lavinia Dock, a well-known nurse and author who had hiked the length of the pilgrimage to Albany, and Morgan, a professional suffrage organizer, suggested the acknowledged need for a proxy of gravitas. To lose Jones would deal a staggering blow to the movement.

The promising fundraising campaign now underway depended in large part on the general's charisma, credibility, and celebrity. The reading public who had eagerly followed newspaper accounts of her courageous feats on the march to Albany found her to be both a heroic and a sympathetic figure. Small of stature, quiet of voice, and attractive in appearance, Jones did not fit the public stereotype of the angry or shrewish suffragette. The public had responded positively not only to her stalwartness—she had completed the On-to-Albany march despite serious illness and attempted abduction by the Jones family doctor acting on the orders of Rosalie's anti-suffragist mother— but also to her status as a reluctant hero with a life beyond the movement. On the way to Albany Jones had been one of the few pilgrims to reliably dance in her gown at the various fundraising galas, even after days in which she had led 20-plus-mile hikes in freezing temperatures. In Poughkeepsie she had ice skated with the teenagers of that town and later sledded with children, and the public respected her for such displays of humility and humanity. Like other American generals, including Washington, Jones clearly longed for a private life away from the greater cause for which she nevertheless felt compelled to fight.

Fundraising for the suffrage hike had continued apace, with Philadelphia outpacing even New York City for pledges of financial aid.[50] "Women are digging deep in their pocketbooks to support women suffrage," led the story in the *Philadelphia Inquirer* detailing the special train commissioned to take that city's delegation to Washington, D.C., for the March 3 protest parade. "News received here from Baltimore and other points along the route, as well as from Philadelphia indicate that General Jones is to have a real army this time, which will create a stir when she arrives in Washington." On the same day, the *Evening Times* in Trenton, New Jersey, ran the page-one headline "Suffragists to Invade Trenton" in advance of an important suffrage hearing in the New Jersey State House.[51] Twelve women had now pledged "to walk every step of the journey" on the march to Washington that would now begin, appropriately enough, on Lincoln's birthday. The advent of Rosalie's Army in Trenton promised a thrilling week of suffrage-related meetings and debates capped with the projected arrival of the general on Valentine's Day.

A triumphant script had been written in advance, though the question remained: Would Rosalie Jones be well enough to lead her army?

3

Mustering in Manhattan

Rosalie Gardiner Jones lowered her megaphone, climbed down from the bench upon which she had been standing, and stood, exasperated, at the Hudson Terminal on Fulton Street in Manhattan. It was Wednesday morning, February 12, and Jones and an estimated 50 sympathizers had grown impatient waiting for the last of approximately 16 marchers who had pledged to hike the entirety of the day's 15-mile trek to Metuchen, New Jersey.[1] Around her hummed the usual Wednesday foot traffic in a building that accommodated nearly 700,000 commuters a day but had surely never given quarter to a suffragette army on the move to Washington. Directly above where General Jones and Colonel Craft waited for the subway car that would take them across the Hudson River to Newark stood the 22-story skyscraper that billed itself as the largest combined office building and railroad terminal in the world.[2]

Rosalie's Army had been scheduled to arrive in Newark at 9:10 a.m. that very morning, but the missing solider was the sort for whom one waited.[3] Helen Hoy Greeley was a practicing lawyer, an elected officer of the Woman Suffrage Party in Manhattan and the Bronx, and an important legislative lobbyist at the statehouse in Albany. When Greeley finally arrived, she explained that she had been delayed in an effort to powder her face, generating the unfortunate headline "Suffrage Army Start Delayed by Shiny Nose."[4]

This was certainly not the first-day publicity for which Jones and Craft had hoped.

The tardy marcher was the very same who had stepped in to fill the weary general's shoes on a New York City suffrage bus tour two days earlier. Greeley had arranged for a double-decker bus to pick up the suffrage pilgrims at the 5th Avenue headquarters and parade them through Manhattan, waving banners and chanting slogans as suffragette Rose Sanderman, clad in a fashionable fur coat, blew the cornet.[5]

The bus tour had been destined for Madison Square Presbyterian Church on the corner of East 24th and Madison Avenue, from whose famous pulpit social reformer the Reverend Charles Henry Pankhurst had helped

Elisabeth Freeman atop the double-decker bus as it tours through Manhattan. The banner beneath reads "Votes for Women" and advertises 800 free tickets to hear Jane Addams speak at Carnegie Hall on February 17, 1913. The photograph was taken February 10 (Bain Collection, Library of Congress, Prints and Photographs Division).

Rose Sanderman (holding cornet) and Freeman (right) smile for the camera on the suffragettes' Manhattan bus tour, February 10, 1913. Mary Boldt (back left) looks on (Bain Collection, Library of Congress, Prints and Photographs Division).

bring Tammany Hall to justice. There, Jones and her army had disembarked for photos on the steps of the beaux-arts church as Greeley issued orders to move out onto the streets to distribute suffrage literature and to collect donations for the cause. Craft, not Jones, had made the day's speeches from atop the chilly bus. The predicted cold snap had the city in its stranglehold, leaving the frost-nipped protestors to resort to caps, mittens, and heavy sweaters in a dress rehearsal for the more difficult conditions to come.[6]

At least one reporter had remarked on Jones's early departure from the bus tour that day and had been given an official if not unconvincing expla-

The marchers pose on the steps of the Madison Square Presbyterian Church on the corner of East 24th and Madison Avenue. In this photograph from February 10, 1913, marchers are shown holding placards naming the states where women could vote or where referenda had been held on suffrage amendments. In the front row, left to right, Martha Klatschken holds the placard for Ohio; Mary Boldt displays Utah; Ida Craft represents Colorado, and Elisabeth Freeman holds Oregon. At center Rosalie Jones displays a banner that reads "Ye Votes for Women Pilgrimage from New York City to Washington D.C. 1913" (Bain Collection, Library of Congress, Prints and Photographs Division).

nation: The general had needed to leave early to travel to Newark, where she would confirm that the yellow suffrage wagon she had painted and deployed there was in full readiness. Doubts persisted concerning Jones's stamina for the crusade ahead.[7] The general had, in fact, traveled to Newark two days earlier to check on the condition of the old family pony cart that would soon be pressed into service as an "ammunition wagon" for the pilgrims' suffrage buttons and literature, and that had already covered 1,000 miles in the previous summer's campaign in Ohio.[8] She had returned to Newark the following day as well, this time in freshly fallen snow, in search of a horse to pull the wagon to be driven by Elisabeth Freeman. Whether by luck or by good judgment, she had found a draft horse promptly dubbed Lausanne. The mare, it was said, had been selected not for "fairness of foot or fairness of form" but for its stubbornness and "staying quality and known devotion to the suffragette doctrine."[9] Purchased for less than 60 dollars, Lausanne became known as the "bargain horse."

Now, as the last of the marchers assembled in front of her at the Hudson Terminal, the general climbed atop a bench and blew her whistle. The army was now a full half hour behind their appointed rendezvous time with Freeman and Lausanne at the Newark Terminal on the other side of the Hudson River. "Get your tickets to Newark," Jones shouted to her soldiers over the din of commuters and a few hecklers massed at the subway platform.[10] "Remember, we are going through. Let those who fall out return ... our motto is 'On to Washington!'"

The boo-birds had begun to roost in increasing numbers in the days leading up to the day's mustering out, beginning with the suffragette bus tour, during which marcher Mary Boldt had been so thoroughly verbally assaulted by an Anti that police had had to intervene on her behalf.[11] Yet both pilgrims and press corps were determined that the long-awaited march begin; as one newspaper put it: "No matter how the [New] Jersey populace jeers and the tender feet ache in the red mud, it's on to Washington."[12]

Far outnumbering the day's scrum of reporters and hecklers were the onlookers who had turned out to witness history. Traveling with the suffragette army as a war correspondent, journalist Emilie Doetsch wrote: "In addition to the hikers and their enthusiastic support, the latter numbering about 200, the station at New York was crowded with thousands of curious folk who came merely to see the show. Some took the whole thing as a joke and smiled in amusement or good naturedly chaffed the pilgrims. On other faces was pictured frank amazement and looks of incredulity that such things should be."[13] To Doetsch, the battle-weary general appeared fully rested, "fresh and bright" for commanding her army with "eyes aglow and cheeks rosy with animation and excitement." Boldt, tall, young, and lithe, likewise impressed reporters with her fitness, telling the press corps that she was a practiced walker, golfing 72 holes in a day during the summer without the slightest hint of fatigue.[14]

At the Hudson Terminal war correspondents were said to outnumber marchers, so great was the media appetite for the journey ahead.[15] The journalists who had shown up at Fulton Street itching for headlines found themselves gifted with controversy from the start. Colonel Craft had refused the general's initial order to purchase a subway ticket to Newark, arguing that if theirs was to be a true march, they ought to walk the initial miles out of Manhattan across the Brooklyn Bridge. Jones countered that the soft roads in the New Jersey meadowlands were sufficiently flooded that they had no choice but to take the tube to Newark. The *Brooklyn Daily Eagle* agreed, remarking "that if the Hudson had been frozen over and the Hackensack Meadows penetrable, this modern-day Joan of Arc and her loyal pilgrims would have started right from New York."[16] Still, Jones's logic failed to persuade Craft, who maintained that riding the initial miles betrayed the walking-only policy the army had made in advance. As a face-saving compromise, she suggested the troops march through the rail cars as the compartments moved forward on the short ride to Newark. When Jones refused to issue such an impractical order, Craft insisted that she would walk on her own and made three complete journeys through the train before the indignation of the other passengers and the conductors ended her protest of one.[17]

In the past, Craft's deeply dogmatic nature had been a double-edged sword for Rosalie's Army. On one hand, the On-to-Albany campaign had demonstrated that the suffrage veteran would never hesitate to confront a bully or stick up for the downtrodden. On the other, Craft had appeared all too eager to take command of the march when, for example, Jones had been threatened with abduction by those loyal to her anti-suffragist mother.[18] The colonel, too, was known to be a stickler for keeping plans and predictably revolted whenever her general suggested adding or subtracting a stop or skipping a planned speech or street meeting for the sake of efficiency.

Largely unheralded as second-in-command, the characteristically unsmiling, bespectacled Craft had begun to edge out from underneath Jones's shadow. As if by design, she had begun making headlines of her own—not just as the anointed replacement, should the younger leader falter, but for her single-minded determination to march to the beat of her own drummer. Already she had deviated from the rest of the suffrage pilgrims in designing and publicizing her own hiking uniform. Openly solicitous of the media in ways Jones was not, Craft had once again made headlines in the previous day's newspapers with the announcement that she would carry a pedometer. The news caused the *New York American* to opine, "If it behaves itself it will have an interesting story to tell when the long pilgrimage is ended."[19] Though her public comments were more expansive than Jones's, Craft failed to elicit the same respect shown the general by the press corps, perhaps because she showed little of Jones's ability to laugh at herself or at circumstance.

Beyond Craft's intransigence, however, the morning's short subway ride came off without a hitch, as Jones and the last of the marchers rode the 9:12 a.m. to Newark.[20] Once disembarked, Rosalie's Army formed a line in Newark's Military Park, a town commons that had been used for hundreds of years as a training ground for soldiers. An estimated 1,000 spectators and well-wishers turned out to greet the marchers on a frigid morning with ice and snow still on the ground.[21] Jones declared to the crowd, "We're walking for humanity."[22] "Surgeon General" Lavinia Dock had come ready to remind New Jersians just how backward the East was where women's rights were concerned. She wore a United States map showing the handful of Western states where women had already been granted the right to vote. Meanwhile, marcher Elizabeth Aldrich wore a sign that read, "I was a voter in California. New York had better get busy."[23]

Wearing her highly identifiable houndstooth Mackinaw hat, "Colonel" Ida Craft delivers a speech from atop the Olive Schultz suffrage touring car (Schultz is pictured at right). The Library of Congress dates the photograph 1910 to 1915, though context strongly suggests a more precise dating of February 12, 1913, in Newark, New Jersey (Bain Collection, Library of Congress, Prints and Photographs Division).

Milton Wend, a senior at Union College and son of marcher Catherine Wend, blew his bugle, and the 40 or so day-marchers who had pledged to walk with the army from Newark to nearby Elizabeth, New Jersey, readied themselves for the cold trek ahead. Craft seized the moment to climb atop the scout car driven by Olive Schultz and, with some difficulty, shouted over the hubbub of hecklers making "noises deep down in their unsympathetic throats." "We are marching to Washington," she bellowed into a biting wind blowing in from the Hackensack River, "and we will go every foot of the way. How many of you who sneer would do it—could do it? We would even have walked through the tube, rather than ride, if we had been able to get permission."[24]

Craft insisted that a new millennium would never come without universal suffrage for women and would have gone on talking had Surgeon General Dock not cautioned her against the danger of frostbite. The thermometer that hour in New York City hovered around 15 degrees with a gale-force northwest wind blowing at well over 35 miles per hour, creating a wind chill factor near 10 below zero.[25] Temperatures further upstate were forecast to drop to an air temperature of 20 below zero in sections of Orange and Sullivan Counties in New York.[26]

Once Craft had finished, Jones called roll, and the Brooklyn contingent of the army—Craft, followed by Phoebe Hawn and Smith College graduate Minerva Crowell—marched to Jones's side.[27] Craft had been a stalwart since the march's inception, while Hawn and Crowell had been more recent recruits. Crowell had joined up only the day before, at the 11th hour, moved to march by the coverage of the Army of the Hudson in New York City newspapers. In addition to Jones, Craft, and Lavinia Dock, roll call for the Army of the Hudson now included Olive Schultz in the scout car, Corporal Martha Klatschken, Bugler Milton Wend, Johannes Meyer, Elisabeth Freeman, Mary Baird, Mary Boldt, May Morgan, Catherine Wend, Elizabeth Aldrich, and Phoebe Hawn. Newspapers listed Crowell, Flora Cornelia Allyn, and Celia Gaffney as new "raw recruits."[28] Several journalists who intended to be thru-hikers also joined the army in New Jersey, including Constance D. Leupp, daughter of former Commissioner of Indian Affairs Francis Leupp. Emilie Doetsch of the *Baltimore News* would tramp alongside the pilgrims for the duration. Ethel Lloyd Patterson, the youthful special correspondent for the *Evening Star* in Washington, D.C., had come all the way from the nation's capital with the intention of reporting every step.

In addition to Bugler Wend, two men—the unofficial poet and historian of the march, Dr. Ernest Stevens, and E.S. Lemmon—had pledged themselves as thru-hikers. Together, the male thru-hikers in Rosalie's Army made for an eclectic lot. Physically fit and well over six feet tall, Wend was a vegetarian and a gifted musician attending Union College in Schenectady, New York.

"General" Jones, holding the American flag, leads the suffrage hike from New York to Washington, D.C. The Library of Congress does not date the photograph more specifically than February 1913 or identify the marchers beyond Jones and Craft. However, context strongly suggests a more precise dating of February 12, 1913, in Newark, New Jersey. The resolution of the photograph is sufficient to identify marchers Ida Craft (third from left), Lavinia Dock (wearing a map of the U.S.) and Martha Klatschken (sixth from left) (Bain Collection, Library of Congress, Prints and Photographs Division).

Dr. Stevens, of Philadelphia, would serve as the hike's unofficial chronicler. A renaissance man, he was said to be under contract with a magazine to write the story of the march, though he would not say which. Dubiousness over the doctor's claims only compounded when reporters learned that he also claimed to be giving "a series of lectures across the southern states and in the West Indies" upon completion of the historic journey. A nature enthusiast forever in search of inspiration on fresh-air hikes, Stevens also fancied himself a nature poet.[29] Like Stevens, Lemmon considered himself a "real hiker" and had therefore been assigned the unofficial role of "pilot" of the expedition. A New Yorker and a pastor's son who claimed Harford County, Maryland, as his birthplace, Lemmon amused the war correspondents with his insistence that his name be pronounced in the French fashion "Lem-mon" with the accent on the "mon."[30] "He scorns to be identified with plain lemons," one reporter quipped. While not listed as a thru-hiker, Brooklyn Boy Scout magazine editor Norman Sper, rumored to be the youngest magazine editor in the country at 17 years old, would accompany Mary Boldt as a kind of personal escort. Additionally, two men from Brooklyn would serve Rosalie's Army in important behind-the-scenes supporting roles. Edward Van Wyck, alternately identified as the "advance agent of the hikers"[31] and the "husky baggagemaster"[32] would serve as the general's Jack-of-all-trades, while Alphonse Major would drive the automobile serving as the "commissary wagon" as he had in the December march to Albany.

Just before 10:00 a.m., Brooklynites Craft, Hawn, and Crowell saluted and declared in union, "I have the honor to report, General, that the army is ready to move."[33] Jones returned their salute, raising the megaphone once more to her lips. At her word, one reporter wrote, the soldiers "fell into line as the stirring note of the bugle smote the frosty air, and the much-heralded march was on."[34]

Jones, holding an American flag, walks behind the Buick scout car driven by Olive Schultz in this photograph taken in Newark, New Jersey, on Broad Street, just north of West Kinney Street, on February 12, 1913 (Bain Collection, Library of Congress, Prints and Photographs Division).

First came the mounted policeman led by a lieutenant with a yellow votes-for-women banner strung from his saddle, followed by eight mounted men to ensure the safety of the hikers. Next came the scout car driven by Schultz, followed by the yellow horse-drawn wagon driven by the army's official "gypsy" spokeswoman, the English suffragette Freeman. Next marched General Jones and Colonel Craft, followed by a line of women marchers a full city block long. Roughly 100 of the day-marchers in Rosalie's Army had come from the ranks of New Jersey suffragists; others had traveled from a dozen other states to ensure that the long march got off on the right foot. Newark, one reporter wrote, was already in "festive attire" for the occasion of Abraham Lincoln's birthday, but the holiday "would have to share honors with the would-be emancipators of women who trudged along over the ice-covered roads."

The historic march had begun in marching gear described as "terribly and wonderfully made,"[35] with one newspaper opining that Newark had surely never seen "such an array of femininity and costumes."[36] Another titillated its readers, suggesting that "under their jaunty walking skirts" the suffragettes sported "sassy-looking bloomers."[37] At least 15 of the most serious marchers wore their standard-issue pilgrim's cloak, a brown flannel wrap war correspondent Ethel Lloyd Patterson described as long enough to drag through the mud and slush. When the wind caught the cloaks, they blew out straight behind the marchers, "pulling at their unfortunate wearers' throats."[38]

Craft wore a men's Norfolk shooting jacket having "more pockets and larger ones than any woman has enjoyed in the last twenty-five years."[39] Many of these she had filled with bandages and balms for the journey ahead. To accessorize her Mackinaw coat she wore a checkered Alpine hat, and in place of the customary long dress and petticoat the second-in-command wore her prototype short corduroy skirt with "hikers" underneath. Finally, as the pièce de résistance, she donned a pair of auto goggles with heavy rims to blunt the arctic winds gusting through the city.[40]

Spectators lined the street for miles to see the pilgrims, offering the "plaudits of thousands."[41] "It is doubtful whether any of the good people of Newark got their [lunches] today," war correspondent Doetsch wrote of the housekeepers and shopkeepers who lined the road for miles to watch the marchers pass.[42] Mothers, fathers, and children who had the day off from school in honor of Lincoln's birthday crowded the streets to catch a glimpse of Rosalie's Army.[43]

The predicted cold snap now gripped New Jersey, and as the hikers plodded southward out of Newark, they struggled to keep warm in temperatures near zero. Near the historic Lyons Farm Schoolhouse at the intersection of Chancellor and Elizabeth Avenues, a Good Samaritan greeted the platoon of

Jones leads her marchers through the icy streets of Newark, New Jersey, on February 12, 1913 (Bain Collection, Library of Congress, Prints and Photographs Division).

activists with a dozen warm hardboiled eggs. She gifted one to each member of the standing army with instructions to hold it in their palms for warmth.

After a brisk march south on the frozen roads, Jones ordered her troops to a stop at the Macdonald residence, where hot coffee and sandwiches were served for fortitude on the way to the army's next stop in Elizabeth, New Jersey. As the troops approached that city, members of the New Jersey National Guard in full uniform stood at the curb, saluting as the general passed. "Here come the women!" the citizens of Elizabeth shouted as the column of female soldiers moved past them, and Jones, in her trademark pilgrim's cloak, returned the salute. Once in town the hikers paused for a reception at the Elks Club, posing for photographs in front of a giant elk statue as tall as any two of the marchers put together. Mary Boldt climbed atop the pedestal, laying her Alpine walking stick across the great beast's back. The members of the army wore the votes-for-women messenger bags in which they kept their ammunition—the suffrage literature and fundraising postcards they pledged to distribute along the way—slung over their shoulders.

Though it was bitterly cold, even the most reticent of the hikers wore a bright smile for the camera. Most still wore their pilgrim's cloaks, the "picturesque brown monk's cowls and hoods" that served as their calling card.[44]

Craft had removed hers, draping it across her forearm in a Napoleonic pose for the photographers. Behind the pilgrims, men in flat caps crowded into the frame, eager at their chance to nudge their way into history. The mood on day one was one of "jaunty confidence," with the pilgrims sharing a sense not of invincibility but of feasibility, aided in part by the comforting presence of Surgeon General Dock, who could do anything from "cure a blister" to give a "hot mustard bath." Of the 13 women thru-hikers listed in the media roster, only three—Jones, Craft, and Dock—had marched all the way to Albany months earlier, and their prior experience likewise lent a sense of surety to an otherwise uncertain and dangerous venture.

Colonel Craft had ensured the commissary wagon automobile driven by Alphonse Major with an assist from Edward Van Wyck had been well-provisioned. Its contents were:

> 20,000 suffrage leaflets
> 20,000 picture postcards of the suffragettes
> 300 copies of *Woman's Journal*
> 300 votes-for-women buttons
> 300 malted milk tablets
> 5 megaphones
> 20 cakes of foot soap

Buoying the pilgrims' confidence still further, three vehicles would motor out in front of the army, including the vehicle owned by Major that had traveled with the faithful pilgrims on their first campaign to Albany. A wealthy businessman who had made his fortune in the cement company that bore his name,[45] Major was too advanced in years to trudge the long miles to Washington, but he was determined to accompany the marchers each and every mile by car. A second vehicle, this one driven by Olive Schultz, would serve as the official scout of the expedition.[46] After driving her Buick touring car the length of the On-to-Albany campaign, Schultz had earned the complete confidence of the suffrage establishment.

Meanwhile, a third "vehicle," the famous suffrage wagon that had accompanied Jones on earlier campaigns, would be filled to the brim with votes-for-women literature, picture postcards, and buttons, piloted by official speaker Freeman. Jones's Army of the Hudson would be well fed, as Mrs. O.H.P. Belmont had volunteered to provision each marcher with three chocolate cakes and plenty of malted milk, at least for the first three days of the historic trek.

In New York, Jones's image had become commonplace thanks to widespread newspaper coverage of the march on Albany. But in Elizabeth, New Jersey, and elsewhere along the opening-day route, many spectators were seeing Jones for the first time. The sight of women marching en masse for their own political rights was a novelty for New Jersians, as it was, apparently, for politicians in Washington. Only one day earlier a story in the *New York Times* headlined "Bars Women from Parade" carried the news that a definite announcement had been made by the committee in Washington planning President Wilson's inaugural.[47] There would be no women representing colleges, or any women representing any organizations at all, in the president's inaugural parade. Women, if they wanted to parade, would have to content themselves with their own procession on March 3.

By early afternoon, as the sun came out and the Army of the Hudson pressed toward their destination at Metuchen, New Jersey, the ice and snow melted away to exactly the mix of mud and slush that made marching most difficult. The cold breeze stiffened. Of the 50 or so marchers who had hiked the first handful of miles, many were now imploring Jones to stop short at Rahway, New Jersey, to spend the night.[48] Five miles from Metuchen, three of the hikers revolted, insisting that they could not go a step farther. Jones refused, saying plainly that the army must push on; defectors and dropouts could return to Rahway on their own if they wished. Well into the afternoon the general urged stragglers to keep pace. Throughout most of the march to Albany, Jones and Craft had walked out front of their infantrywomen, but as evening approached in New Jersey they were forced to drop to the rear of the column to urge them forward.

By the time the Army of the Hudson finally reached the Hillside Hotel in Metuchen at 6 p.m., darkness had fallen, and Hetty Wright Graham collapsed as she crossed the threshold into the old inn.[49] Surgeon General Lavinia Dock raced to her side and revived her, but Dock herself had caught a cold earlier in the day. The army ranks now numbered a mere 16 soldiers, down from the estimated 200 suffragettes who had marched in Newark that morning. As the first day's march wore on, newspapers reported that dozens of hikers "unostentatiously left the ranks and sought warmth indoors, and then confessed themselves deserters by boarding trains for their homes."[50] Another grimly concluded, "I do not think many of the women will stand the ordeal. Not if the march is constituted along the lines Gen. Jones has planned."[51]

The headlines awaiting the suffrage pilgrims on their first night suggested a wide difference of opinion regarding the efficacy of the day's march. In Pennsylvania, where the army would march after leaving New Jersey, the *Bradford Era* ran with "Rosalie and Her Army Hope to Win in a Walk," but far more ominous headlines intermingled on page one of the *Era* and elsewhere, including the macabre "Blood Flowed Freely in the Streets of Mexico City."[52] In the capital city, rebel and federal forces had battled with machine guns and artillery for seven straight hours. Meanwhile, in Charleston, West Virginia, American generals were waging war against unrest at home, attempting to subdue rioting miners whose violent protests had lately rocked coal country. Fifty-one protesters currently awaited trial for rioting, shooting to kill, carrying firearms, and attempting to dynamite trains.[53] In New York, the Associated Press reported that 24,000 firemen working on 54 railroads east of the Mississippi and north of the Ohio Rivers had threatened to strike for higher pay and better working conditions.[54] If the railroad failed to meet their demands there would be service disruptions up and down the East Coast at exactly the time that tens of thousands of women seeking justice of their own would be trying to reach the March 3 suffrage parade in Washington, D.C., and a once-in-a-lifetime chance to join Rosalie's Army as it marched through the streets of the capital. In the midst of it all, one small but determined army uniformed in brown cloaks carried 20,000 votes-for-women leaflets with which "they hoped to capture all enemies along the way."[55]

Not long after arriving at the Hillside Hotel, Jones fielded a telephone call from an angry woman demanding her journalist husband be returned to her at once. "I'll thank you to send my husband right back home, Miss Jones," the woman said on the line from Newark. "He has no business running off with a lot of crazy women, and if he isn't home in three hours I am going to put the police on to the whole lot of you and…"[56] Jones hung up before the woman on the other end could complete her threat. "If her husband is with us it is a plain case of butting in, for we don't want men in line," she said. "We particularly asked the newspapers to send women reporters along instead of men."

While more than a dozen reporters had trudged alongside Jones and her equal rights crusaders for the duration of the first day, considerably less than half of those were women. It wasn't exactly true that Jones didn't want men on the march but that men, drawn by the allure of marching with an army made up mostly of younger, athletic women, had already begun to infiltrate the ranks. That very night one of the men who had joined the march in Elizabeth had been thrown out of the hotel for public intoxication. By the end of its first day, Rosalie's Army already faced a growing dilemma: how to avoid becoming a victim of its own sensational popularity.

That popularity had also created a pressing logistical dilemma as the smaller villages such as Metuchen, with a population of approximately 2,500, could not accommodate the sudden influx of visitors. On her first night on the march, Ethel Lloyd Patterson of the *Evening Star* gave her readers back in Washington, D.C., the real scoop on the challenging circumstances and accommodations of the nascent march:

> The rooms ran short, and we found it necessary to adopt that unfortunate contingency known as "doubling up."
> The night was passed with two or three pilgrims in each room. And how cold it was! There seemed to be no steam nor heat of any kind in the country inn. These

things are not well for women who must march twenty-one miles…. Also they are not well for one who must write the record before she may sleep.

Quite frankly, I admit I am very tired. Perhaps I shall harden to it. No particular part of me aches. I am just tired all over. Fortunately, my clothing keeps me warm. I have not suffered from the cold as yet, and I still wear the bunch of violets given me by the man I left behind me.[57]

4

A Rough Road in New Jersey

Every march needed a rallying cry, and to the delight and consternation of suffragists, Alabama Congressman "Cotton Tom" Heflin had stepped blithely into the role. Approximately one week before Rosalie's Army marched out of Newark, Heflin had delivered a rabble-rousing speech in Falls Church, Virginia, in which he claimed, among other things, that the general and her army—indeed all the women who planned to march in the votes-for-women procession planned for March 3 in Washington, D.C.—might just as well stay home in the kitchen. Ever since, the most ardent supporters of women's rights had been "calling for [the] Alabaman's scalp."[1]

Cotton was already a legend in the House of Representatives, though mostly for the wrong reasons. As a consequence of death threats made against him for bigoted comments made earlier in his legislative career, Cotton Tom now carried a pistol and frequently wore a 10-gallon hat to deliver his bombastic speeches. By the time he delivered his infamous women-should-stay-home speech, Heflin had already been indicted on three counts of assault against a black streetcar passenger, repeat offender Louis Lundy, whom he claimed had insulted him, as well as exchanged fisticuffs in the street with the driver of a speeding car.[2]

Some called Heflin a hero and the epitome of Southern manhood, others an arrogant, bigoted fool with a fragile ego. In any case, the controversial congressman appeared destined to run afoul of suffragists, who immediately seized on the comments he had made in Falls Church, calling him a "cave dweller" and the "Beau Brumell of the House of Representatives"—the latter a reference both to Heflin's dandified dress and to his reputation as a braggadocios leader.[3] Suffragist Genevieve Bennett Clark, wife of Speaker of the House Champ Clark, wasted little time in chastening her husband's congressional colleague, opining, "No party can afford to slap in the face of more than 1,000,000 voters." Clark's sister, Anne Hamilton Pitzer, of Colorado, added, "We suspect that reduced to its lowest terms, this attack of Mr. Heflin's, which looks on the surface like the adoration of womanhood, and the beautiful spirit of chivalry, is the growl of the caveman, who desires absolute ownership of his most valued beast. But woman is coming out of the cave." In Cincinnati, women's rights activist Anita Hall had announced that she would attend the upcoming equal rights march in Washington dragging a literal ball and chain to demonstrate society's imprisonment of women's aspirations for political participation.[4] Cotton Tom had become the movement's favorite scapegoat and straw man rolled into one.

The *Chicago Daily Tribune* reported that the much-loved, much-hated representative from Alabama had "stirred up a veritable hornets' nest,"[5] and the day's news from Regent's Park in London only increased the buzz—suffragettes there had burned down a building, leaving behind the words "Votes for Women" scratched into the gravel.[6] Heflin registered amusement both at the caveman accusations and at subsequent invitations for a public debate on the question. "I have been having lots of fun out of the suffragists," he told the *Washington Post*, adding, "but I am afraid I haven't time to debate them."[7] However, the resulting controversy proved sufficient for Heflin to issue a clarification of his earlier comments, telling the press, "My speech at Falls Church has been more or less twisted, for I did not attack them for their procession, but for their action in chasing over Washington making speeches from automobiles. I think they could do much more at home." In an attempt at magnanimity he conceded that there were at least some fine women in the movement and that men were often to blame for suffragist stirrings "because they do not look after their womenfolk as they should, and do not provide for them properly."

News of Heflin's latest provocations greeted General Jones and Colonel Craft as they woke early for the long day's hike to Princeton. The cold of the drafty old hotel had disturbed Jones's sleep, and she had awoken not with an extra blanket pulled over top of her, as she had thought, but covered up with a suffragette banner that read "Criminals and the Insane Can't Vote, Neither Can I…"[8] The day outside the general's window dawned clear and bitterly cold.

By 9 a.m. Jones and Craft had their weary army of 16 mustered and moved out. The distance to be covered by the day's march looked especially daunting, as earlier drafts of the schedule had Rosalie's Army overnighting in New Brunswick some six miles distant.[9] Now what had originally been planned as a 16-mile hike from New Brunswick to Princeton had turned into a 20-plus-mile trudge on slushy, muddy roads softened by warming temperatures. Allowing for a stop at Rutgers College in New Brunswick, where Rosalie's Army was scheduled to meet with students and lunch with the president, they would do well to make Princeton by nightfall.

By the time the army completed the six-mile hike from Metuchen to New Brunswick, blisters, intense cold, and cramped feet had caused three more desertions, with the ranks of the regular army now reduced to 13.[10] The newspapers reported that the pilgrims looked forward to Rutgers with uneasy anticipation, and it was true; unlike the all-woman Vassar College in Poughkeepsie, where Rosalie's Army had made a triumphant visit on their way to Albany in December, Rutgers was an all-men's school, and as such, the army could expect some jeering. Olive Schultz, traveling out front in the scout car, had seen to it that the students knew in advance that the army was coming, and the subsequent turnout didn't disappoint.[11] Despite temperatures hovering around 10 degrees, an estimated 400 to 600 students massed at the edge of campus, sending up the cry, "General Jones is coming!" Shortly thereafter the Rutgers alma mater song, sung by a growing chorus of voices, split the chilly air:

> My father sent me to old Rutgers,
> And resolved that I should be a man;
> And so I settled down,
> In that noisy college town,
> On the banks of the old Raritan.
> (*Chorus*)
> On the banks of the old Raritan, my boys,
> where old Rutgers ever more shall stand,
> For has she not stood since the time of the flood,
> On the banks of the old Raritan.[12]

There was no place for women in the lyrics of the 1873 alma mater, still the young men of Rutgers could appreciate a well-drilled army. Many had come dressed in their cadet uniforms to greet Jones's troops. The general issued the order to fall in line and the cadets obliged, forming a long procession that looked partly like a carnival and partly like a military column. As they approached the gates to the college, the procession devolved into something more like a mob, the bodies of the giddy cadets hemming in Jones and her officers until there was no way out. So great was the jostling and pushing that members of the army, hoping to take photos of the momentous event, were forced to stow their cameras for safety.[13]

Jones had promised that she would leave most of the speechmaking to Freeman on the march, but for the men of Rutgers College she made an exception, asking Craft and Morgan to give short open-air speeches.[14] When they were through, the general stood atop an automobile to thank the Rutgers faithful for the warm if not overzealous reception, while the opportunistic Craft darted in and out of the teeming crowd to distribute suffrage buttons and pamphlets.[15] Showing off a lucky horseshoe she had been given by a sympathizer, Jones told the crowd that she had never heard such cheering in her life and enjoined the Rutgers faithful to channel a portion of their energy into the forming of a men's league for women's suffrage on campus. She joked that she had enjoyed the reception so thoroughly that she hoped to join the all-male college one day.

As a culmination to her visit, Jones met college president William Henry Steele Demarest, a reverend who had grown up in New York and was known to be sympathetic to the cause of women in higher education. Rosalie's Army's used New Brunswick as a launch point for an even bigger trial balloon involving a New Jersey college president; once in Princeton, they announced, they would seek out President-elect Woodrow Wilson, the former Princeton University president who would assume duties as the nation's chief executive in a mere few weeks.

Enthusiastic students escorted the Army of the Hudson out of campus and up George Street to the Hotel Klein, a 50-room, four-story brick landmark near where the Albany Street Bridge crossed the icy Raritan River.[16] On Albany Street the citizens of New Brunswick gathered for their first look at the acclaimed general and her troops. The cold wind blew down the river from the northwest, filling the yellow suffrage banners like sails.[17] As Rosalie's Army crossed the bridge, a veritable swarm of locals surged toward a "strikingly attractive and athletic young woman whose commanding demeanor betrayed at once that she was the generalissimo of the army of feminine political revolution." At the rear of the procession came 6'2" Milton Wend, the army's trumpeter, walking alongside 4'11" Corporal Martha Klatschken, causing clever reporters to call the army's rear guard "the long and the short" of Rosalie's Army. Warmed now by a brief respite of fire, food, and friendship at the Hotel Klein, Princeton, some 16 miles distant, seemed more reachable than before. Jones called roll and received 13 replies, down from 16 the previous night.[18]

Sobered but otherwise undaunted, Rosalie's Army set out at 1 p.m. toward Princeton. Assuming a brisk walking pace and no unforeseen delays, it appeared as if they would be marching into the university town by streetlamp rather than sunlight. Additional concerns now occupied Jones and Craft, as the *New York Post* reported an unusual student tradition at the Ivy League university that forbade anyone other than students from marching down Nassau Street into the heart of campus. The marchers were said to be "in danger of bringing down upon themselves the wrath of the undergraduate body through the violation of Old Nassau's most sacred traditions."[19]

As the dinner hour approached in Princeton, Olive Schultz, who had motored ahead in her scout car, began to grow worried and returned along the road to New Brunswick to ascertain the army's whereabouts.[20] When finally she found them it was nearly 7 p.m., and the marchers were still more than two miles outside the city limits. Schultz found Jones and Craft in good health, but several of the other marchers, including Mary Baird and May Morgan, had been forced to drop out of the march not long after the army had left New Brunswick and had carried on to Princeton by train, arriving in advance of the main guard. Corporal Klatschken, meanwhile, had struggled mightily, falling a full quarter-mile behind Jones and Craft at the front of the column. Schultz offered Klatschken a lift into town, but the stalwart corporal refused the ride on principle.

Thanks to a short cut taken en route, Boldt arrived at approximately 6 p.m., a full hour ahead of the main marching column lead by Jones.[21] Classes had been dismissed for the occasion, and Mary Boldt, perhaps mistaken for Jones, was met by nearly 300 students who picked her up and carried her to the porch of the inn despite her angry protestations. The students rushed her and, in their enthusiasm, "half carried her, half dragged her fully a half mile through the streets of the village."[22] Boldt was said to be "crying from anger and fright" before local police rescued her.[23] Elisabeth Freeman likewise suffered from the students' overexuberance, as the Princetoners lifted the suffrage cart from its wheels, hijacking the wagon as it entered town and leaving Freeman to lead Lausanne on foot.[24]

Arriving later, General Jones and Colonel Craft were mobbed in a more good-natured siege of curious students demanding a speech. Jones offered her weary greetings from a rocking chair on the front porch of the inn, leaving the fuller-throated speechmaking to Freeman, who rallied the Princetoners until nearly 9 p.m.

The raucous joy of the evening rally helped chase away memories of a day marked by difficulty. Baird and Morgan had to ride into Princeton, so grim was their condition, while Klatschken arrived at the hotel in a state of exhaustion so severe she had to be helped to her room. Along the cold muddy roads of northeast New Jersey, the army had met with considerable opposition and indifference from those they had attempted to convert. They had encountered African American women too busy in the role of caregiving and housekeeping to dare ask for the vote and an elderly woman in Livingstone Park, New Jersey, who had curtly informed the general that Jones and her band of unruly women ought to be home mending their husbands' clothes instead. At one point on the march to Princeton, spirits had fallen so low Jones had asked male hiker E.S. Lemmon to compose a marching song to buoy their spirits. Lemmon's verse went:

> Hark! Hark! the dogs do bark
> The suffragettes are coming to town.
> Trimmed in yellow and dressed in brown.
> Telling the tiding all around
> We must have votes for women.

It was a silly little ditty, but for the few moments that it hung in the air it helped the suffrage soldiers forget the cold nipping at their heels.

For Jones, the end of the day at Princeton meant two pitchers of hot water for a scrub in her room, a moment away from the crowds, and a review of the public relations disasters that would be reported in the next day's newspapers—not just the struggles of Klatschken and the ailing marchers who had to ride to Princeton but also the forced retreat due to illness of one of the oldest marchers, "Surgeon General" Lavinia Dock, who would soon turn 55, and seasoned suffragist Hetty Wright Graham, who had to be helped into Metuchen, New Jersey, the night before. Jones had been forced to order both back to New York City for the sake of their own health.[25]

"Two Quit at Princeton," the *Pittsburgh Post-Gazette* trumpeted with what seemed barely disguised glee, while the *New York Times* relayed an even more embarrassing episode wherein marcher Elizabeth Aldrich, who had collapsed earlier in the day from exhaustion, had appeared to spot a sun-bonneted woman in the distant fields and run to give her suffrage literature, only to discover that the potential convert was in fact a scarecrow.[26] The embarrassing detour had cost the army nearly a half hour and had been witnessed—with relish—by the corps of mostly male war correspondents hoping for exactly such story fodder.

Written by one of a relative few female journalists consistently covering the march, Ethel Lloyd Patterson's dispatch for the *Evening Star* omitted mention of Mary Boldt's alleged manhandling, focusing instead on Boldt's popularity with students. While the majority of reports filed in Princeton that night focused on Boldt, Baird, or Morgan, Patterson worried more over the condition of Jones, who had taken a full hour to march the last two miles into Princeton. "There was a grim look about her mouth as she came into the arc of the light made by the inn's lamps," Patterson noted. "At dinner she ate very little … and … tottered slightly. Should she give out the army would go to pieces at once. She is quiet but she is an ever-present force. The other women lean on her."[27]

• • •

The following morning the newspapers hummed with word of Boldt's controversial run-in with the raucous student body of Princeton. Now Dean of Faculty William Francis Magie, himself a proud Princeton graduate and longtime physics professor, rushed to release a statement to the press, lest the reputation for gentlemanly civility of his alma mater be tarnished:

> Certain reports which appeared in some of the newspapers this morning that Mrs. Boldt had been ill-treated by Princeton students were of such a nature as to call for an investigation. I am assured by students in whom I have confidence that Mrs. Boldt was not insulted, nor was she jostled or interfered with intentionally in any way, and that the report that she was injured or exhausted by the treatment that she received is false.[28]

Earlier that morning, as Rosalie's Army had prepared to march out of Princeton, Boldt had been tapped for a no less important public relations mission: to lead a secondary march to the private Princeton residence of President-elect Woodrow Wilson, where she hoped to broker a brief private meeting between Jones and the president-to-be. The high-risk plan went against Jones's earlier inclinations—to save a potential meeting with Wilson until nearer to his inauguration on March 4 in Washington, D.C.—but Craft and Freeman viewed the prospect as opportune. A side-march would help rewrite Boldt's narrative, revising it from helpless hiker to intrepid young leader. Second, Boldt's request for a meeting could serve as an invaluable trial balloon. As a Democrat from a northeastern state, Wilson was assumed to be open to the possibility of future suffrage, and the side-march could help test his willingness to publicly support the cause. If Wilson so much as greeted Boldt at the door, it would be hailed a victory for the votes-for-women movement and a harbinger of better prospects to come in the new administration. If the president-elect turned Boldt away, that could be a public relations boon, too, building sympathy for the pilgrims' cause in the press. Any meeting between Jones and Wilson could be pitched as a conversation between two proud and principled leaders on equal footing.

The morning had already turned sunny by the time bugler Milton Wend blew reveille outside Wilson's mansion, and the estimated 50 Princeton students who followed Boldt to the door answered with the Princeton yell.[29] Boldt, standing tall with the hood of her plain brown cloak drawn up tightly around her face, cut a strangely incongruous figure against the backdrop of Wilson's home at 25 Cleveland Lane. Since New Jersey lacked an official governor's mansion, the Tudor home had become the de facto executive residence. Unfortunately, the "governor's mansion" was missing the governor when Boldt knocked on the door to discover that Wilson had left the previous night. Among the many risk–reward scenarios entertained by the army's commanding officers, this—Wilson's sudden departure—had not been prominent among them. Had Wilson left town in anticipation of the army's arrival? Several months earlier, William "Plain Bill" Sulzer had run for governor of New York as a pro-equal rights man of the people, yet after pledging to be in New York City to see Rosalie's Army off on its way to Albany, he, too, had found an excuse to leave town.

With Wilson gone, the challenge before the On-to-Washington army was to make good time in the day's fair weather. The blustery conditions of the first two days had generated headlines that made the army look weak—mass desertions, marchers lost in darkness, multiple collapses. By contrast, the march to Trenton could help reemphasize the women's strength and stamina. Aided by the excellent roads between Princeton and the New Jersey capital, Rosalie's Army reached the city by 2 p.m. They arrived so early, in fact, that they were already in town greeting schoolchildren by the appointed hour when the local suffrage contingent had planned to meet them on the outskirts of the city.[30]

Even the army's horse, Lausanne, arrived in Trenton feeling its oats. A day earlier, Rosalie had sought the opinion of a veterinarian as to the animal's fitness for the remainder of the journey. Today, the army's bargain horse from Newark gamboled and frolicked like a foal, so much so that it appeared at times as if it might run away with Freeman at the reigns of the ammunition wagon loaded with pamphlets and buttons. Jones chalked up the mare's giddiness to enthusiasm for the cause, though the press proved less than impressed with the ragtag arrival of the army in Trenton in their mud-colored pilgrims' cloaks. "Their approach," observed the *New York Times*, "might be described as the coming of a thin, very thin, brown line."

The army had now tallied approximately 55 miles on foot, and the wear and tear had begun to show as the pilgrims walked stiffly to the drugstore to stock up on foot balms and lotions. "There has been no high-brow conversation this afternoon and little abstract discussion of the suffrage cause," noted the *New York Post*.[31] Instead, the proper application of surgeon's plaster, the most successful methods for treating blisters, and the value of raw potatoes when applied to ankle sprains dominated the pilgrims' conversations. As one of the war correspondents hiking along with the marchers summarized it: "Last night, one big blister … one overwhelming, overpowering muscle and spirit-paralyzing ache."[32]

A few of the recruits were in such pitiable shape that more desertions were expected. Corporal Klatschken suffered acutely, having arrived an hour behind Jones and the rest of the army, suffering from swollen and frostbitten feet so debilitating the *Brooklyn Daily Eagle* declared the "tiniest pilgrim" in the army "could not possibly hold out much longer."[33] All agreed the corporal's gutty march to Trenton had been nothing short of an act of "heroism."[34] Excluding Freeman, who had been "brought along not to walk, but to talk," the roster of the army in Trenton included just nine women thru-hikers: General Jones, Colonel Ida Craft, Elizabeth Aldrich, Augusta Righter of Newark, Mary Boldt, Catherine Wend, Corporal Martha Klatschken, Minerva Crowell, and Phoebe Hawn. The word "decimated"—to lose one in 10—had often been applied to beleaguered armies, but in this case the boot seemed to fit. Of an estimated 200 activists that had swelled the ranks of the On-to-Washington army as it had left Newark, fewer than 10 percent now remained.

Klatschken wasn't the only brave soul marching against steep odds. Less than 24 hours after her alleged mistreatment at Princeton, Boldt was undertaking the improbable—traveling back to the lion's den to speak with the very students whom the newspapers claimed had manhandled her. Given her indignation, the motivation for Boldt's decision remained unclear. Had Jones and Craft directed her to make peace for the sake of public relations? Had they been afraid that the image of Boldt forcibly kidnapped by male students would make the marchers seem weak instead of accurately portraying the seasoned suffrage soldier Boldt was becoming? In any case, the rapidity with which Dean Magie had sought to snuff out the more salacious rumors of her treatment, coupled with her unexpected decision to return to Princeton, suggested an eagerness to reframe the narrative.

After Rosalie's Army had made the comparatively short 11-mile hike from Princeton to Trenton, Boldt motored back to campus to lead a parade of more than 300 students, delivering a speech to her admirers and raffling off her pilgrim's cloak in support of the cause. First-year student C.E. Eager won the cloak, but before he could appreciate his windfall, students tore the coat to shreds and pinned the remnants to their lapels in zealous support of the cause.

Boldt was tireless with a seemingly unlimited appetite for hiking, but back in Trenton the rest of the pilgrims counted their blessings for the day's light march. "Another tramp of twenty-five miles and the suffrage pilgrims would give up the ghost," one war correspondent-hiker quipped. "As for me, I am sure even the ghost I would give up would have a pain in its back."[35]

5

Love and War

Ida Craft was not a happy hiker. Though the day's relatively short march from Princeton had been on the flat Trenton turnpike, and though, aided by improving weather, the miles had been "a mere snap of the finger for Rosalie Jones," an old dilemma troubled the colonel's conscience.[1] It was Valentine's Day—a dubious holiday in any case, Craft felt, and even more so on a suffrage march, where, she had earlier warned, there should be no room for romantic entanglements. Craft had "put the ban on romance," one reporter noted, adding, "Not that the 'Colonel' disapproves of love, but, in her opinion, [that] there is a time for love and a time for hiking, and this is time for hiking."[2]

Even the recalcitrant Craft could acknowledge that there were many different kinds of love—love of cause, love of country, love of comrades as brothers and sisters. All of these existed within the ranks of the Army of the Hudson. What need could the marchers possibly have for romantic love on a two-week march? Wasn't the high adventure of their pilgrimage romance enough?

And yet love arrived by the mailbag in Trenton. Among the day's haul were dozens of valentines—including one from a "Brooklyn Admirer" that arrived for Craft. Jones received many valentines, including one signed "Your slave."[3] Boldt received a hand-drawing from her husband John showing his wife riding in an automobile with Cupid fluttering nearby.[4]

It was the advent of puppy love, more than proven love, that worried Craft, as the youngest female member of the army, 18-year-old Phoebe Hawn of Brooklyn, had indulged just that. To the colonel's consternation the headline in that afternoon's *Philadelphia Inquirer* read, "Cupid in Ranks of Suffragettes," followed by the summary headlines "Princeton student leaves books to woo youngest of hikers" and "He is lured on march and will get an answer in Philadelphia."[5] The disconcerting captions proved eerily similar to those generated by the unexpected engagement of hiker Gladys Coursen to reporter Griffith Bonner on December's hike, when New York reporters tantalized readers with headlines reading "Romance Thrills Suffragettes on March to Albany"[6] and "Romance Stirs Suffrage Ranks."[7] While love stories made for good news copy, Craft felt they detracted from the mission.

Whether Hawn had indeed "lured" the male college student, as the headlines claimed, remained unclear, but Princeton first-year W.W. Cator had been identified as the "college boy" in question.[8] Cator suffered from what the newspapers diagnosed as a "bad case of love at first sight." He had been one of the thousands of Princetoners who had attended the raucous rally on the night of the pilgrims' arrival there and had awoken early the next morning to give the marching suffragettes a proper send-off. Dazzled by the sight of Hawn among the hikers, he had asked if he might accompany her on the day's hike, and by the time the army reached the outskirts of Trenton he had reportedly asked for an engagement. Initially, Hawn believed Cator's proposal to be a Valentine's joke, but the young man had persisted, and Hawn promised that if he would hike with the army to Philadelphia, she would give him an answer there.

As the youngest of the marching suffragettes, the attractive Hawn had earned the nickname "Brooklyn Baby." In Princeton she had sold autographed picture postcards of herself with proceeds to benefit the cause, and again in Lawrenceville, where the Army of the Hudson had stopped to speak briefly to the boys at the Lawrenceville Academy. The academy was one of the oldest and most prestigious in America, and, true to form, Craft had delivered a serious speech to the cadets, asking them to grow up to be the kind of men who would support equal rights for women. While some of the students appeared to understand the gravity of the message, others seemed more excited by the beauty of Hawn and stage actress hiker Elizabeth Aldrich.

In a full-page spread, the *Washington Post* had dubbed Aldrich "the beautiful girl suffragette" while extoling her pedigree in the movement; she was the great-granddaughter of the renowned Quaker suffragist Avis Keene and an actress of considerable promise.[9] The plan to sell picture postcards to raise funds had been announced weeks earlier at the photo shoot in Central Park, and, to date, Hawn and Aldrich had been the two biggest draws, raising "shekels galore" for the cause.[10] At the Lawrenceville Academy the giddy boys had engaged in a simulated war dance, joining hands to form a circle around Jones, Boldt,

The seldom-photographed Quaker activist-marcher Elizabeth Aldrich is shown here in a 1913 photograph run in the *Salt Lake Tribune*.

and Hawn.[11] Another contingent of young men had stolen the yellow ammunition wagon from Freeman, driving it wildly around the grounds of the school while Freeman gave chase. The students of Lawrenceville Academy then kidnapped Hawn, taking her away as if she were a spoil of war while simultaneously cheering her for a solid 10 minutes.

The boys of the military school had fallen in love with the famous suffragettes; their war dances and wagon captures and silly songs served as their juvenile way of showing it. Were the men of New Jersey, a state which had yet to grant women the right to vote, really all that different in their affections, or were they likewise prone to mischief and silliness before the thing that they did not understand but by which they were nevertheless wholly intrigued?

Valentine's fever had clearly caught on among the suffragists of Baltimore, too, who loaded up in a wagon drawn by four white horses and left the Just Government League headquarters on a public relations campaign inspired by Cupid's holiday. Suffragettes handed out valentines up and down Charles Street—to shopkeepers, to city employees, and to the mayor himself.[12]

• • •

Journalist Emilie Doetsch was in love with the movement—so much so that the young reporter had convinced her editors at the *Baltimore News* to send her on the march as war correspondent.

Doetsch had graduated from Goucher College and the Baltimore Law School.[13] In pitching the idea of covering the women's march on foot as one of the few female war correspondents, Doetsch, a spirited suffragist herself, might have worried that her own love of the cause might lessen her objectivity or that she might become caught up in the romance of the hike.

Her second dispatch, datelined New Brunswick, New Jersey, February 13, opened with an unusually self-conscious line: "Being an impartial observer, I suppose I shall have to report it," she wrote, as if willing herself toward an objectivity she did not naturally possess.[14] By her third dateline in Trenton on the evening of Valentine's Day, Doetsch had fallen further in love with the cause, as evidenced by the exuberance of a dispatch that read, "Alas, poor suffragists! Alas, poor hikers! Last night one big blister; this morning one overwhelming, overpowering muscle and spirit-paralyzing ache." In the second paragraph she reiterated the difficult promise she had made to her readers "not to lapse into either poetry or argument."[15] Unlike most of the male war correspondents, Doetsch considered herself both a marching suffragette and a professional journalist on assignment. Rather than drive ahead to the next town to await Rosalie's Army, Doetsch insisted on sharing every step with them, though she had thus far stopped short of calling herself a regular member of the army in print. Already, her head-over-heels embrace of the

On-to-Washington hike had sewn professional resentment if not personal ridicule among the more seasoned male journalists. In one story identifying the marchers by name, the *New York Times* added that there was at least one writer who "insisted that she should be listed as a hiker."[16]

Doetsch's first two headlines bristled with poetry and personality; her headline from the previous day had read, "Hairpins Fall Along Path of Heroes of 1776," followed by "Suffragette Hikers Today One Big Ache." Already, her insistence on walking every mile in the hikers' shoes had lent to her reportage an admirable exuberance coupled with a clear-eyed realism that could only be captured by a woman who had experienced the pangs of marching. She had freely used the word "heroes" in both of her first two headlines and subheadlines to describe the marchers. In her second dispatch she waxed still more poetic, opining: "A hike may be a hike. Or it may be a pilgrimage. According to whether you're a high-brow pilgrim or a low-brow hiker. But it's martyrdom all the same."[17] On the Valentine's Day hike to Trenton, Doetsch yielded more fully to the whimsy of the occasion, devoting several paragraphs to the particular pining of Ernest S. Stevens, the "man-hiker" from Philadelphia and a bachelor who, she wrote, "makes no secret of it." Stevens, elsewhere called "the most eligible bachelor in the army," had become the unofficial historian and poet laureate of the On-to-Washington hike and had so thoroughly given himself over to the cause that he had insisted on wearing the pilgrims' cloak worn by the women. Of the titillating possibility of romantic intrigue between a hiker and the very poetic Mr. Stevens, Doetsch reminded her readers of Craft's ban on romantic liaisons among marchers.

Meanwhile, Elizabeth Aldrich had waited until the army's arrival in Trenton to make a big announcement of her own. She had been a stage actress, and it showed in her flair for the dramatic. In Trenton she gathered her fellow hikers together to announce that she, too, had received a marriage proposal on the day's hike. Ever the thespian, she waited for the ensuing hubbub to die down before explaining that a well-to-do farmer, after walking with her long enough to convey both his wealth and his loneliness, had offered his hand in marriage and $100,000 for her troubles. Wearing a smile, Aldrich informed her sister suffragettes she had politely declined.[18]

And what of the romantic spirit that moved women to walk 250 miles in frigid weather? At Trenton, Rosalie's Army had been jeered from second-story windows.[19] As they marched down the streets of the state capital they found themselves ridiculed by schoolchildren and hooted at by gangs of men at the corners until at one point, "trouble looked certain." Policemen had moved in then, just in the nick of time.

New Jersey had once been a crucible of the American suffrage movement, but now the On-to-Washington army faced outright hostility. New Jersey women had been allowed to vote in some legislative and local elections as early as 1797.[20] In December of 1858 suffragist Lucy Stone had protested against taxation without representation. In the city of Orange, not more than 60 miles from where the suffragists now readied for an evening of fiery speeches at a Trenton theater, Stone had penned her famous letter to the local tax collector that read, "Enclosed I return my tax bill, without paying it. My reason for doing so is, that women suffer taxation, and yet have no representation, which is not only unjust to one-half of the adult population, but is contrary to our theory of government."[21]

Love of cause abided even the threat of violence and imprisonment—this was suffragette creed and the reason why Doetsch and others did not linger long over the irony that New Jersey, which had given original impetus to the movement, had now been labeled as the state "most antagonistic to the cause."[22] Attempting to capture for her readers back in Baltimore the spirit of solidarity she felt in the suffrage army, Doetsch resorted to poetic prose:

> A hike waits for no one. It is very much like time and tide in that respect. Your face may be chapped to the roughness of parchment, your feet may refuse to go into your shoes, your heart may grow cold at the thought of twenty miles of endless road. But when 9 a.m. arrives and Bugler Wend gaily bugles the reveille and "General" Jones says, "Forward March!"—off you go! Yours not to reason why; yours but to do and hike.[23]

Still, for all their physical ailments, affairs of the heart may have been a bigger pain for Colonel Craft as night settled over Trenton. According to published reports, Hawn had promised her would-be fiancée an answer to his proposal in Philadelphia, and that city loomed just two days away. Now that the newspapers had broken the story, Hawn was reported to have confessed a bigger worry: that as soon as her parents read the headlines they would not allow her to return home when the march was done.

Love, Craft knew, could make an army, but it could unmake one just as well.

• • •

All eyes were now on Philadelphia, but before the On-to-Washington army could reach the City of Brotherly Love they first had to reach Burlington, New Jersey, some 16 miles distant. The Quaker town on the banks of the Delaware River had been a provincial capital long before New Jersey had become a state, but for Rosalie's Army, Burlington would be a staging ground. Fewer than 9,000 people lived there, meaning no elaborate events would be required of them. Instead, Burlington promised a chance to marshal their forces for the march on Philadelphia.

Thus far, New Jersey was proving something less than the suffrage stronghold the army had hoped it would be. When meeting passersby on the side of the road, they had fallen into the habit of first asking if they were a suffragist. So when Jones asked the by-now-ritual question of a young woman early on the day's hike to Burlington, and the young woman in question failed to comprehend, the general tried again. "What I mean," Jones asked, "is what are you going to be when you grow up?"[24] To her chagrin the girl answered "washerwoman" before unceremoniously departing. Thankfully, not every reply was as disappointing. Later, coming upon a married Quaker woman, Jones had asked the same are-you-a-suffragette question and was heartened by a more affirmative reply. "Dear child," the woman replied, "don't you know every member of my sect is. It's one of the first tenets of my religion that men and women are equal and should be in everything."[25]

At Crosswick Creek, just north of Bordentown, Jones stopped to consider crossing the Delaware River. She ordered the army off the road to a point where the wide tributary turned into a wetland that emptied into the Delaware and stopped there to weigh the risks.[26] What looked to be a firm layer of ice had formed over the still waters of the wetlands, but the ice pack over the swiftly flowing river adjacent appeared far less solid. Jones badly wanted to make a dramatic crossing, something to demonstrate that the votes-for-women movement was "as of much importance to the country … as General Washington's celebrated crossing of the Delaware." The pilgrims cheered that particular sentiment, with one male hiker saying that he "hoped General Jones and General Washington would go down in history together." Once again, however, discretion proved the better part of valor, and the general held off. Lausanne alone surely weighed more than a thousand pounds, and the yellow pony cart stocked with pamphlets, postcards, and provisions would surely double the burden.

Not far south of Crosswick Creek, the army encountered another elder turned out to witness history, this one a gray-haired man leaning over a rail fence on an otherwise lonely section of road. He held a dirty piece of paper on which he appeared to be writing. Jones slowed the march to offer him a votes-for-women pamphlet. "You came too soon," the old man told her. "It's not ready yet." He had been penning a poem for the occasion but had not yet finished the last line, he explained, reading aloud to Rosalie's Army what he had written thus far:

> Oh, the suffragettes are coming
> They are coming down the pike,
> Ma's got her bonnet on,
> She's ready for the hike.
> They are heating up the countryside,
> Starting buds upon the trees…

When the man paused in the middle of his poem, Jones suggested, "They are coming down the breeze," as a final line, but the man was still unhappy with the rhyme. As the army resumed its march he was still muttering possibilities to himself—*fleas, breeze, sneeze*—when the last line of his improvised verse hit him with the strength of epiphany:

They are spoiling all the cheese.

The pilgrims couldn't help but be amused, unsure whether their warmth had proven to be the spoiler of the man's improvised verse or merely the pungency of their cause. Lucy Slimm, a mother the marchers encountered on the roadside shortly thereafter, seemed to favor the latter interpretation. Moved by the sight of General Jones and her women's army, Mrs. Slimm's 13-year-old daughter, Marion, asked to join the march. Jones encouraged the young woman to walk with the pilgrims for a short distance. "She is going to do nothing of the sort," Mrs. Slimm countered, telling the marchers, "Go home and mend your husbands' clothes."

Near Bordentown, seven miles from Trenton and 10 miles short of Burlington, the army marched into Bordentown Military Institute, where they had been invited to lunch with the young cadets. A full military brass band heralded their arrival. Freeman, twice jailed in Britain, impressed the young men by walking up and down the military grounds "with an erect military carriage and a heavy gun on her shoulder." She displayed "an ominous skill" in handling the weapon.[27] As the pilgrims lunched with the youthful cadets and their commander, an almost unbelievable occurrence interrupted the military school luncheon. Without warning, a band of Princeton college students burst into the military institute and kidnapped Hawn's would-be fiancé William Cator.[28] The Princeton faculty had been displeased with the negative press coverage of Cator's impulsive behavior and had evidently sent a delegation of students to bring him back. Colleges and universities were forced to deal with elopements and engagements on a regular basis. That very day in Harrison, Virginia, the state teacher's college had expelled a young woman for eloping with a young man, an action they deemed in violation of the university's honor system. Nineteen-year-old Lilian Campbell had made a rope of her bedsheets and, tying it to her bedpost, lowered herself 15 feet to the ground and into the arms of 21-year-old Thomas Berry.[29] Conspicuously missing in the newspaper coverage of Cator's dramatic abduction was the reaction of Hawn herself, a curious omission which suggested that the newspapers may have exaggerated the couple's romance and were now understandably anxious at quoting a version of events that might call their reportage into question. "Romance," the *Philadelphia Inquirer* confidently declared, "lies buried."[30]

After the high drama of the capture at the military institute, Rosalie's Army marched across the military grounds into the town of Bordentown, where a crowd of 1,500 turned out in a town of scarcely more than 4,000. Jones delivered a speech from what was once the front doorstep of Delia Stewart Parnell, the American wife of Irish national Charles Stewart Parnell and one of the America's first advocates of suffrage. The Army of the Hudson then made one more homage before they set out for their night of rest and recovery in Burlington, sending their regards via telegram to New York City, where the Women's Political Union of New York was throwing a dual birthday bash at the Hotel Astor for two of New York's greatest suffragists, Susan B. Anthony and Harriot Stanton Blatch, daughter of the pioneering women's rights activist Elizabeth Cady Stanton. Stanton had been an author of the Declaration of Sentiments adopted in the Seneca Falls Convention of 1848, a document whose statements had served as the suffragist esprit de corps ever since.

As the army marched toward Burlington on the eve of their advance on Philadelphia, the litany of Stanton's complaints and protestations of 1848 seemed sadly contemporary. "The history of mankind is a history of repeated injuries and usurpations on the part of man toward woman," Stanton had written, adding, "having in direct object the establishment of an absolute tyranny over her."[31] Number one on Stanton's list—that women had never been permitted to exercise "her inalienable right to the elective franchise"—was the very transgression that now fueled the army's march across New Jersey.

Less than 70 miles from the Maryland border, Burlington, observed the war correspondent following the march for *The Sun*, was "the first town in line of the march to begin to show distinctively Southern characteristics," including "negroes on the streets" and "low rambling porches reaching out over the dirt sidewalk [that] give the streets a different air."[32] Given the difficulties Rosalie's Army had been led to expect south of the Mason-Dixon Line, "distinctively Southern" might as well have been code for trouble.

The town was said to have "woken from its lethargy" at the coming of the pilgrims. Women wearing white furs and feather boas crowded the sidewalks in the spring-like weather, lending the town a gala appearance that contrasted sharply with the disorder in the streets as curious crowds gathered to meet the famous visitors. In Burlington, as in Trenton, the army encountered a considerable amount of ridicule and derision among otherwise enthusiastic crowds numbering in excess of 1,500. As it entered town, citizens lined the roadside to "cast jibes at the heroines." The insults increased in frequency as the marching suffragettes began to break ranks, "and the temper of General Jones and her escorts was not angelic when Burlington was reached."[33] Burlington's mayor, however, was in high spirits, sending a local Boy Scout troop to deliver a letter to the marchers that read: "It gives me great pleasure to assure you and your comrades on this historic march that a hearty welcome awaits you in the most historic town in New Jersey. It will be an honor to write in the annals of the city the fact that you have made a visit to us in this city."[34] Buoyed by the mayor's offer of a key to his city, the troops marched as planned to the town theater, in front of which they delivered votes-for-women speeches only to be shouted at once again. When a suffragette suitcase fell to the ground and burst open outside the hotel, the crowd caused a small riot as they pushed forward to catch a glimpse of its intimate contents.[35]

Burlington proved something of a bitter pill to swallow for the suffragettes, who had intended to cross the Delaware at Trenton to much fanfare, only to discover that transporting their horse, Lausanne, and the suffrage wagon would have proven impractical. The day's alternate route, hugging the New Jersey side of the Delaware River, presented the marchers with a grind of 18 miles over roads that alternated between pavement and "ankle-deep … mud."[36] Just north of Burlington, in the small working-class town of Roebling, Jones and her troops had attempted to address a gathering of factory workers and their wives, only to be "thoroughly ridiculed."[37]

The need for recuperation perhaps explained why the entire hotel lobby soon reeked of what one reporter described as "vile-smelling but soothing pain annihilators."[38] Most of the marchers went immediately to their rooms on checking in to the hotel, bandaging badly blistered feet and wrapping them in liniments. The suffrage flag, one marcher joked, would do well to depict a bottle of witch hazel pictured against alternate bands of black and blue bruises. Rosalie's Army could hardly be blamed if it "wanted nothing more that night than to retire early at Burlington."[39] There was, one reporter noted, a "cavernous demand for food and heat and bed" as the army attempted to fortify itself for the following day's invasion of Philadelphia.

The declining condition of the army as it arrived in Burlington spurred the *Evening Star*'s Ethel Lloyd Patterson to question the necessity of the hike itself, and, in so doing, to offer portraits of the courage of individual hikers struggling valiantly not to give in.

> Really, this suffrage is not funny. There is something almost tragic about it. The army struggles on … limping, going more and more slowly, spurred to the task by pure grit. Mistaken, if you like, but grit. Jaws set, vertical line between the eyes, shadows beneath them, and for what? Does it all really mean anything? Will it really do any good?…
> Each person who sees this band of bowed, brown-clad women pass must ask himself these questions.
> There is Constance Leupp, daughter of the former commissioner of Indian Affairs…. When we started from Newark five days ago she was a pretty girl…. Miss Leupp's right knee gave out two days ago. She persists on walking. Pain has carved lines from her nose to the corners of her mouth. Her lips are chapped. Her hair, that floated in soft waves when she started, now straggles.
> And she will tell you "that she is not going to give in if it kills her."
> Ask her: "Why not?," and she will explain that "no one shall [call] her a quitter."
> Explain to her that she may injure her knee for life in persisting in using it, and she will only clinch her teeth the more tightly and hobble on.[40]

Patterson turned her attention next to the indefatigable Martha Klatschken, writing: "She is made of that strange stuff that causes the minds of individuals molded from it to cease to question once they have given themselves to a movement. Her singleness of purpose is great. She says that she fell outside of Trenton and crawled one-half mile on her hands and knees."

Even the warm teas offered by supporters along their path were a mixed blessing for the pilgrims, according to Patterson, who confronted her readers directly with the truth of such rote hospitality. "If you were [a suffrage pilgrim] you would know that there are things pleasanter than to stand with a tea cup in your hand when you have been walking twenty-one miles and answer questions like this one from your hostess: 'Aren't your feet tired? Don't you get cold? Don't you think it makes you thinner to walk? What kind of shoes do you wear?'"

• • •

By the time Rosalie's Army mustered out of Burlington it had good reason to believe its historic crossing of the Delaware River later in the day would be an auspicious one. The veteran marchers had come to speak of a phenomenon known as "Jones Luck," the uncanny ability of the general to snatch victory from the jaws of defeat. Several times they had witnessed it on the On-to-Albany hike—once when she had narrowly escaped a kidnapping by the family doctor acting on the orders of the general's anti-suffragist mother.[41] On another occasion a car the suffragists were riding in on their way home from an evening speaking engagement slipped on a patch of icy road and, but for a tree root, would surely have plunged them to their deaths in an event that generated the *New York Times* headline "Suffrage Hikers Near Death."[42] Shortly thereafter a company calling itself the Weed Chain Tire Grip Company of New York had begun running special notes in the *Times* reminding would-be customers of the pilgrims' misfortune: "If the tires of the car had been equipped with WEED ANTI-SKID CHAINS the accident would not have occurred…. Stop off at your dealer today and fully equip your car with WEED CHAINS." At other times on the march to Albany, Jones had barely missed being badly burned by a pyrotechnic launched in her direction, narrowly missed a massive Christmas Eve snowstorm, and somehow managed to barnstorm her way into a featured role in the inauguration of New York Governor William Sulzer.

Once again, Jones Luck appeared to be in play, as the general had found three pennies on the ground prior to commencing the day's march toward Camden, New Jersey. In addition to the good-luck pennies, Jones had also begun her day with the receipt of a supportive letter from a Civil War veteran that read:

> Dear Rosalie Gardiner Jones—I have seen your pictures in the paper, and I read what you're doing to further a great cause. I lost a leg at Chancellorsville for a great cause, so I sympathize with you…. When this march is over I should like to have the chance

of smoothing the road ... for the rest of our lives. You may say I am an old man, and you are young—but what of that? I may have but one leg, but my heart is bigger than the heart of any two men.[43]

The man concluded his note by admitting that while other men might be afraid of the general because of her nerve, he was comforted by the idea that they were both soldiers.

As potent as Jones Luck may have been, however, it had only served to mitigate a series of otherwise significant setbacks. Once again the On-to-Washington marchers had been thwarted in their attempt to cross the Delaware River—this time from Burlington, New Jersey, to Bristol, Pennsylvania. Had the army been able to follow its original plan they would have notched yet another state on their pilgrims' walking sticks the very next day, but ice dams in the river and the lack of a good bridge prevented what would have been a highly publicized crossing at Bristol. Now the only good alternative seemed to be crossing from Camden, New Jersey, to Philadelphia. The change in plans created dissension among the ranks of marchers, some of whom wanted to spend the following morning, a Sunday, at church or resting up for the march on Philadelphia. But Jones insisted they hike on toward Camden, where the residents of that city were said to be on edge with nervous excitement on learning that the famous women's rights army would be marching through their streets. Camden's Antis, too, were readying themselves for Jones's crossing of the Delaware. For the first time on its march to date, the Army of the Hudson would have no choice but to stop and wait for a ferry—in this case, the boat that would take them across the Delaware River to Philadelphia. The stoppage threatened to turn the army into sitting ducks for Antis who by that time would surely have roosted on the banks of the Delaware.

6

Cheers and Jeers in the
City of Sisterly Love

Haines Pond, New Jersey, made for a delightful stopping point for Rosalie's Army as they marched south in the direction of Philadelphia. The mill
itself dated back to the 1750s when George Washington was still a young man.
Postcards pictured the placid lake in the tiny village of Delran and the rickety
remains of a wooden ice elevator, easily five times the height of the marchers, that once transported ice blocks to a nearby icehouse.[1] The lake along
which the weary suffrage pilgrims now sat for lunch was fed by a narrow,
fast-moving stream, a tributary of the Delaware River known as Swedes Run.
By 1880 the settlement along the little lake had included more than 20 dwell-
ings, a tollhouse, three churches, a store, and a gristmill.

The army had reached something of a gristmill moment itself. After
losing her would-be fiancé, the army's youngest regular, Phoebe Hawn, had
begun grumbling about the food, or lack thereof, on the march and was now
telling any war correspondent who cared to listen of the litany of cravings
she intended to satisfy on reaching Philadelphia.[2] Hawn and the rest of the
marchers were still a long way away from the fine cuisine of that cosmopol-
itan city. The day's hike to Philadelphia would take them along the far western edge of the New Jersey Pine Barrens, a vast region marked by tall pines
and sandy soil. The terrain made an ideal proving ground for the troop of
Boy Scouts that had joined the army at Burlington and were now scamper-
ing around Haines Pond gathering wood for a makeshift campfire. Between
them, the boys found just one match, but it proved sufficient to start the fire
around which Elizabeth Aldrich and Catherine Wend made coffee while the
Scouts shared the sandwiches they had brought with them.

What began as a peaceful if not unlikely picnic—women pilgrims in the
middle of the woods dining with scores of young men in uniform—quickly
turned into a roadside attraction for hundreds of motorists.[3] "They came by
motor," wrote one newspaper columnist, "on foot, on bicycles, and sprang apparently from the very earth, watched and photographed the band of hungry

men and women consuming hard-boiled eggs." Freeman placed a lamp in her gypsy wagon until the little yellow wagon "offered the comforts of home." Traffic on the adjacent road backed up for 100 yards. Visitors stopped to take in the spectacle, either smiling on the scene "commendingly, or adversely, or enviously."[4] The pilgrims shared sandwiches with anyone who stopped, though Hawn, tired of the trail, reportedly wrapped herself in a fur coat to take a nap in the backseat of one of the vehicles parked on the road's shoulder.

The abundance of sandwiches could be attributed in part to the ever-contracting numbers of army regulars, which had now dwindled to eight of the original women hikers in addition to the men serving in support roles. Rosalie Jones, Ida Craft, Martha Klatschken, Mary Boldt, Catherine Wend, Phoebe Hawn, Minerva Crowell, and Elizabeth Aldrich now constituted the only true thru-hikers who had been with the march since the beginning. Elisabeth Freeman still drove the suffrage wagon, while Olive Schultz, Mary Baird, and others rode along in support vehicles and scout cars loaded with rations, supplies, and luggage. Always there were a handful of day-hikers eager to support the march, and their occasional participation caused the army's numbers to ebb and flow. Two of these, Florence Allen, assistant secretary of the National College Equal Suffrage League, and Bertha Miller of Philadelphia Law School, had lately joined the hikers in Burlington, New Jersey, but had only pledged to hike for two days. Meanwhile, Augusta Righter had received an "honorable discharge" from the army and returned home to Newark.[5]

Morale had recently reached a low ebb, with open dissension in the ranks. Hawn's conduct in particular had been a constant source of consternation among the veteran marchers. At Princeton her youthful exuberance had caused her to ride a bicycle for a few blocks on campus, and some of the veteran members of the army wanted her sent home for violating the walking-only policy. Another disagreement had broken out over an unnamed suffragette's decision to hitch a ride on a passing hay wagon. Craft had insisted on walking every mile on the December march to Albany and considered walking requisite for the true pilgrim. Now the colonel had little choice but to soften her hard line. If the two offending members of the regular army were dismissed, its numbers would be reduced to a half dozen.

In Lock Haven, Pennsylvania, editors cheered the Army of the Hudson's dwindling numbers, opining, "Judging from the falling off of the forces of that woman's hike, if it is to be the main feature of the inaugural exercise, the attractions there will be slim. General Rosalie Jones at the start said that the only thing she feared was a thaw. But that prediction, like the marching party, struck a frost."[6] Despite having a suffrage amendment under consideration at the statehouse in Trenton, New Jersey had not proven to be a fruitful recruiting ground for the cause. Freeman's recent attacks on New

Jersian President-elect Woodrow Wilson in Burlington had alienated those who felt the president-elect should be given a chance.[7] Still, the sheer number of passersby stopping to break bread with the pilgrims proved that the On-to-Washington hike still captivated.

The Antis had recently developed a novel strategy to undermine Jones's troops: temptation. As the weary marchers approached their destination each evening, Antis dispatched drivers in luxury cars to offer them rides in an attempt to catch unsuspecting pilgrims in an act of hypocrisy. The strategy had proven mostly unsuccessful, but it had succeeded in planting controversy within the marchers' ranks and in the court of public opinion.[8]

Jones had never pitched the march as an exclusively "all-women" or "women-only" enterprise, but men were expected to be in the minority, and any man who volunteered to accompany the hikers for more than a day would be given close scrutiny. With five more men expected to enlist in Philadelphia, including three from that city's Wanderlust Club, *The Times* was now reporting that there were as many men in the army as women among the day-hikers.[9] Making matters worse, there were serious doubts that the deeply fatigued Minerva Crowell would be able to continue the march. The Smith College graduate, who had been with the marchers since Hudson Terminal in New York City, would require police assistance just to reach Camden.

The idea of a man-less army added novelty to the undertaking, but any such moniker undersold the vital role played by sympathetic men in the march. A large part of the hike's mass appeal lay in its women-only billing, explaining the conspicuous lack of coverage of the "man-hikers"—including the unofficial march historian Ernest Stevens, "pilot" E.S. Lemmon, and bugler Milton Wend.

Perhaps to underscore the female-centric impetus of the march, Jones marched her troops to Palmyra, New Jersey, to visit a man-less farm operated by Anna and Sally Hunter. The women farmers were proud of their independence. Both supported suffrage and described to war correspondents how their experience running their own acres had convinced them that "women could run the country without the help of men and do it more successfully than men." That sentiment had brought cheers from the marchers, many of whom believed that rural women in particular had become overly dependent on their partners for economic wellbeing. In her book *Women and Economics*, suffragist writer Charlotte Perkins Gilman targeted farmers' wives as the most economically and socially deprived of their sex. "The young farmer gets a profitable servant when he marries," Gilman wrote, and elsewhere: "On wide Western prairies, or anywhere in lonely farm houses, the women of today, confined absolutely to this strangling cradle of the race, go mad by scores and hundreds. Our asylums show a greater proportion of insane women among farmers' wives than in any other class."[10]

Economic relations between the sexes in the city were only slightly more enlightened than they were in the hinterlands, according to Gilman, who observed: "The young business man gets ... a pretty girl, a charming girl, ready for 'wifehood and motherhood'—so far as her health holds out—but having no economic value whatever. She is merely a consumer, and he must wait till he can afford to marry." Independent women farmers like Anna and Sally Hunter were helping to turn traditional gender relations on their head, as were woman generals mustering their own marching armies. For her part, General Jones was more of pragmatist than a separatist, arguing that sympathetic men should be allowed to join her march. Still, she was keenly aware of the ideological appeal of a man-less hike and eagerly recruited women hikers to join her ranks.

Buoyed by temperatures nearing 45 degrees and inspired by their visit to the man-less farm, the army entered Camden, New Jersey, marching headlong into a bottleneck of unexpectedly large crowds on Cooper Street. The size of the march had grown almost overnight, swelling to several hundred participants, thanks to pro-suffrage day-hikers who had read about the army's dwindling numbers and rushed to reinforce the brigade between Burlington and Camden, the latter a city that had already been labeled "hostile" to the cause.[11] As the army neared the ferry in Camden that would take them across the Delaware River to Philadelphia, crowds filled the streets, making them all but impassable. "Anti-suffrage sentiment appeared strong in Camden," Emilie Doetsch wrote in the *Baltimore News*. "The crowd, which grew to immense proportions as the army approached the city, often rudely jostled the tired women and taunts and jeers were not infrequent."

"The crossing of General Jones attracted more attention than did the crossing of General Washington," the *New York Times* wrote of Jones's arrival in Philadelphia on the sixth day of her historic march.[12] Another journalist captured the army's larger-than-life quality with an apt sports analogy, writing that the general and her army were received in the city "in much the same manner as the conqueror of Jack Johnson might be" while noting that the suffragettes had been "roughly handled" upon arrival in the city.[13] Johnson, an African American, had been reigning heavyweight boxing champion since 1908 to the consternation of many bigots.

Approximately 2,000 people packed the ferryboat landing on the Philadelphia side of the Delaware River, eager for their first glimpse of the famous general at the prow of the boat holding an American flag while flanked by Colonel Craft and Corporal Klatschken. By the time Jones and her army officially set foot on Pennsylvania soil, many of those assembled had been waiting an entire afternoon. When she and her troops stepped onto the dock they were swallowed "like driftwood on the beach" by "howling, jostling, hooting men and boys." A police force numbered at between six and eight officers

Three cartoons depicting the march. Includes: "The Spirit of '13" by Berryman (top left); "Spirit of 1913" by Satterfield, showing women marching in snow while dreaming of voting for the first time (top right); and "Gen. Jones Crossing the Delaware" by James Donahey, showing Jones standing up in a boat after the fashion of George Washington. Reproductions of drawings by Clifford Berryman, Robert W. Satterfield, and J. H. Donahey originally published in the *Washington Star*, *Central Press Association*, and *Cleveland Plain Dealer*, respectively (Library of Congress, Prints and Photographs Division).

Elisabeth Freeman leads the suffrage horse "Lausanne," also known as "Emmeline" after the militant British suffragette Emmeline Pankhurst. The Library of Congress lists the date published/created as February 17, 1913, which would put the location near Philadelphia (Bain Collection, Library of Congress, Prints and Photographs Division).

attempted to quell the crowd but quickly found themselves overwhelmed and unable to check the onrush sweeping "the little bright-eyed 'general' off her feet." Most in the throng had come to witness history, but others had come to lob hate-speech at the army using language the *Times* called "positively insulting."[14] The jeering only intensified when Wend, the army's 6'2" bugler, picked up the diminutive Craft and carried her through the crowd to safety. Jones, meanwhile, had quite literally been swept off her feet, sending the yellow suffrage banners she and Craft carried "flying through the air like a bit of paper."[15]

Milton Wend's mother, Catherine, later recalled that so many people pushed forward to see the marching suffragettes that the ferry began to tip, and only an attention-diverting diversion by a quick-thinking reporter on the boat stabilized the vessel.[16] For Ethel Lloyd Patterson the riotous scenes at the ferry constituted a turning point. Patterson interrupted her newspaper coverage of the pilgrims' arrival to say, "But just here one bitter word for the Philadelphia police. When we disembarked from the ferry upon which we came from Camden, we were nearly mobbed."[17] She continued, "I shall always remember Philadelphia as the town in which I became militant. I was pulled and hurled and trampled upon by yelling boys and shoving women until my mild spirits turned, and I took to stepping on the toes of anyone who came near me."

Belatedly, reinforcements helped the overwhelmed and insufficient police force clear the way.[18] By the time the army began to move away from the wharf down Market Street toward the Hotel Walton, a robust force of 40 law enforcement officers maintained order in crowds numbering in the thousands.[19] Meanwhile, the city's suffragists had failed to produce the expected show of strength, perhaps anticipating the mob scene on the docks. Others speculated that votes-for-women proponents had stayed away in Philadelphia because, as in New Jersey, a suffrage bill was pending in the Pennsylvania legislature, and votes-for-women advocates wished to avoid any spectacle that might sway public opinion against its passage. In truth, the marchers had encountered signs of opposition not just in Camden but all along their day's march. The innkeeper in Bridgeboro had refused to serve food to Jones and her army earlier that day, claiming that it was a Sunday and that he was understaffed.[20] Klatschken pegged the innkeeper as an Anti, however, telling the press that if she ever got the vote she would make sure such "old fossils" were properly stowed away.

Newspaper accounts of the army's entry into Philadelphia told widely divergent stories. While the *Philadelphia Inquirer* and the *Pittsburgh Post-Gazette* focused on the pilgrims' rough handling, the *News* in nearby Frederick, Maryland, seemed to have witnessed a different march altogether, casting the invasion of Philadelphia in a decidedly sunnier light as a "triumph for the pilgrims" who somehow managed to "throw off their weariness" to receive the attentions of crowds four-deep along the sidewalks.[21] While the *Philadelphia Inquirer* detailed jeering and jostling suffered by the pilgrims, the *News* claimed the crowd, though "pressing against each other like sardines in a box," nevertheless proved "gallant." Every five steps, claimed the newspaper, men removed their hats, uttering a quiet and respectful "General Jones." The *News* described a procession that, by the time it reached Juniper Street, not far from the Liberty Bell and Independence Hall, stood nearly four blocks long. Across the country in San Francisco, however, the *Call*'s coverage tracked more closely with the *Philadelphia Inquirer*'s, detailing a near "riot" characterized by a "jeering, scrambling, pushing mob."[22] Taken together, the day's disparate accounts intimated a tale of two marches: the first a precarious, riotous gauntlet on both the Camden and Philadelphia wharves and, moments later, a triumphant march to the downtown hotel on streets belatedly secured by local law enforcement.

Elsewhere in the East, newspapers boomed with news and views both laudatory and lambasting. The *Morning News* in Wilmington, Delaware, published a poem in place of a traditional editorial of support. The final stanza of "The Hikers" read:

> So here's to the resolute ones
> The hikers, their trials cannot vex,
> The martyrs so willing and firm
> In the cause that is dear, or their sex.
> May good luck attend on their march
> Forgot be occasional moans
> And three cheers for the army resolved
> Of Rosalie Gardiner Jones.[23]

ISN'T IT REMARKABLE WHAT LITTLE THINGS WILL DO?—By DeBeck.

A cartoon by Billy DeBeck titled "Isn't It Remarkable What Little Things Will Do?" appeared in the *Pittsburgh Post* the morning of February 17, 1913, as the suffragettes marched into Philadelphia.

The *Philadelphia Inquirer* led its front-page coverage with several dramatic images, captioned "Photographs of a Revolution," but it was not the same revolution beget by Rosalie's Army in the City of Brotherly Love. The photos showed a charismatic leader acknowledging a crowd of supporters—not Jones but Mexican President Madero riding up the streets toward the national palace half an hour after the slaughter of rebel troops under the command of General Felix Dais. Mexico had descended into civil war, and the sitting president had narrowly escaped an assassin's bullet.[24]

Rosalie's Army made the front page, too, that Monday, February 17 under the headline, "Suffrage Army Limps into City Worn and Weary." The brown-clad army was reported to have "straggled" into Philadelphia "minus the dignity of a well-drilled army." It was true that sometimes half a mile separated Boldt, who often marched out front, from Craft and Klatschken, who tended to bring up the rear, lending the army a distinctly disorganized appearance. Even small differences in gait and speed made for significant gaps by the end of day-hikes that sometimes covered a marathon's distance. Still, the *Inquirer's* lukewarm coverage illustrated an important point; the reporting of the march sometimes boiled down to the political bias of individual newspapers and their readers. In cities like Philadelphia, multiple papers with disparate politics vied for prominence. In nearby Pittsburgh, for example, cartoonist Billy DeBeck preferred more nuanced commentary in a page-one cartoon authored for the *Pittsburgh Post-Gazette*, whose panels showed a horse hitched to a buggy thinking nothing of a car speeding by but spooked at the sight of three diminutive suffragettes carrying pilgrims' staffs. The caption read, "Isn't it remarkable what little things will do?"[25]

DeBeck's comic was purposefully tongue in cheek, suggesting society's overreaction to the cause the hikers represented. And on a day marked by both terror and by triumph, the political cartoonist managed to achieve something few other newspapermen could manage where the suffrage army was concerned: make readers laugh.

In the Footsteps
of America's General

Throngs packed the corridors of the Hotel Walton in anticipation of the day's march from Philadelphia to Chester. The fife and drum corps commissioned by the suffrage-friendly *Evening Times* piped a triumphal tune, though the veterans of the 90-plus mile march stood calm and resolute, taking the pomp in stride, while the new recruits and day-hikers agitated for adventure.[1]

Dressed regally in a blue overcoat, cape, and bright green caps, Harriet May Mills, acting as Jones's local lieutenant, escorted Rosalie's Army out of town down Broad Street to the strains of "Dixie" played by newsboys.[2] The previous day's lack of police protection had been remedied, with the majority of the city's mounted officers now on hand to ensure a safe departure. The army passed proudly under the 37-foot-tall statue of William Penn atop city hall, its outstretched hand looking as if it might be offering benediction.

Philadelphia had changed its tune, and now, less than 24 hours after the mob scene at the docks, jeering had been replaced by cheering. The many good citizens who had felt shame in reading overnight newspaper accounts of violence at the wharf had turned out in such high-spirited numbers that even Emilie Doetsch of the *Baltimore News* found herself at a loss to describe the swift change, opining, "Words fail to describe the march of the suffrage army out of Philadelphia this morning." As a heavy, wet snow fell, the army turned down aristocratic Walnut Street with its plethora of handsome homes to cries of "Goodbye, Honey," and "Don't forget me, Girlie." Strains of sexism could be heard in the earnest farewells, still Jones received each with a dignified bow and smile. Flowers and even a bouquet of orchids, picked up and carried proudly by Mary Boldt, rained down with spontaneous marriage proposals—an estimated 20 in 12 blocks by Doetsch's count. Carrying yellow votes-for-women banners, approximately 500 male students from the University of Pennsylvania turned out to escort the marchers to campus.[3]

By 10 a.m. the army reached the university itself, where they were greeted by "an army of students" sending up a "terrific hullabaloo."[4] Rumors spread of a Princeton-styled plot to kidnap a member of Rosalie's Army, but Mills and the local suffragists she commanded circled tightly around Jones and her officers, creating a human wall that deterred any mischief. Wherever practical, the general included colleges and universities in her itinerary, not just because they could accommodate the large crowds her army attracted but because conventional wisdom held that, among their sex, college-educated men offered the best hope for future equity between the sexes. At times, such wisdom proved false, as it had at Princeton, where otherwise mature, open-minded college men had behaved more like excitable schoolboys or football hooligans.

Police cleared a path through an estimated 1,000 students to allow the army to march into the university law school, where pandemonium ensued.[5] The representatives of the study body had come prepared, flanking each of the most popular suffragettes—Jones, Boldt, and Hawn—with at least two escorts as the army made its way, with great difficulty, to the steps of Price Hall, where the collegiates were so closely packed that student leaders struggled to prevent the overstimulated crowd from "engulfing the brown-clad army."

Jones paused at the top of the steps to shout, "You can all come with us."

"We are with you now," the students answered back.

From behind the lectern, Jones asked for an open-hearted reception, and she was again interrupted by students, this time shouting, "We will open our arms for you" and "our arms are already open." Craft took the podium next, buoyed by the comments of University of Pennsylvania Provost Edgar Fahs Smith, who had recently told the press that Craft and Jones had "done more for suffrage than any other since the day of Susan B. Anthony and Elizabeth Cady Stanton."[6] Craft offered the students a brief history of the movement, concluding with the claim that Brooklyn was "the greatest suffrage town on the map, bar none."

In Price Hall, Craft and Jones spoke to an appreciative crowd estimated at 3,000. Philadelphia was still widely known as a Quaker city, and Quakers had long held what were considered to be enlightened views on gender equity. In his book *Some Fruits of Solitude*, William Penn wrote, "Sexes make no difference, since in souls there is none."[7] War correspondents concluded that the Penn students were "real suffragists,"[8] based on their enthusiastic reception of Rosalie's Army, though once more the zealous crowds blurred the line between high-spirited solidarity and sexist infatuation. A case in point was Hawn, widely regarded as the most attractive suffragette, for whom the reception at the university proved so zealous that she was forced to hide behind a banner designed to shield her from public view. The students repeatedly called for "the prettiest suffragette in the army," though Hawn, likely on the order of the army's commanding officers, refused to show.[9] Next they called for Boldt, who received "extra cheering" before the army concluded its remarks, exiting the building once more to the strains of "Dixie." The members of the army who had reached the City of Brotherly Love would, Emilie Doetsch claimed, "never forget it." Philadelphia had been "the most exciting and eventful of the march," but it had also served to warn of the very real possibility of mob violence to come, of inadequate police protection, and of the marchers themselves being swallowed up by agitated crowds of Antis. With an estimated 1.5 million residents, the city had been by far the largest metropolis the On-to-Washington marchers had yet encountered beyond New York, more than tripling the population of Newark. What would happen when the march of the suffragettes reached Washington, D.C., whose population of approximately 350,000 could double for the national votes-for-women procession on March 3 and Wilson's inauguration on March 4?

Five hundred university students, hundreds of honking automobiles, and a motley crowd of 2,000 Philadelphia men, women, and children now escorted the women from campus to the snow-covered road toward Chester, Pennsylvania.

• • •

While Rosalie's Army needed more marchers for the day's advance on Chester, Pennsylvania, it was not wonting for war correspondents. At times, nearly 50 reporters followed the pilgrims, dwarfing the number of women marchers who had stayed with the march since the beginning. Organizers had hoped Philadelphia would be a public relations triumph, but instead it had turned into an urgent recruiting stop. Beyond the usual liaisoning and planning with local suffrage societies, Jones's priority in the city had been to restock her ranks. Her efforts in Philadelphia had landed her at least four new women recruits for the day's 14-mile hike to Chester, Pennsylvania,[10] bringing the total count to approximately 18, inclusive of the male thru-hikers.[11] Newspapers covering the march cited conflicting numbers of women who had walked the entire way from New York City, with the *Washington Times* reporting that five women hikers had started from the Hudson Terminal in New York City, four had been "picked up along the way," and six had recently been added in greater Philadelphia to augment the three continuing male thru-hikers. The *Press and Sun-Bulletin*, meanwhile, tallied eight women in addition to Jones who had trudged the entire distance, naming them as Klatschken, Craft, Aldrich, Boldt, Hawn, Wend, Leupp, and Crowell.[12] Among the new recruits were Helen Bergmark of Marble, Colorado, Loretta Williams of Philadelphia, and Virginia Patschke of Lebanon, Pennsylvania. More than half of the marchers in line as Rosalie's Army left Philadelphia were men.[13] In addition to the three male members of the Wanderlust Club of Philadelphia, a young man named Roy Trolsen had joined the march in Philadelphia, though the war correspondents had been able to learn precious little about him.[14] The number of new Pennsylvania recruits might have been significantly higher had the army's commanding officers not publicly discouraged unfit or unprepared hikers, whose inevitable desertions stood only to damage the cause. Even among the approximately six new recruits, however, commitment was lacking, with most pledging to hike only as far as their stamina would allow.[15]

Jones fought back her first public tears of the march as the student and police escort turned back at the Philadelphia city limits while the band played the song "Do They Think of Me at Home?"[16] Whether the waterworks had been elicited by the nostalgic tune or the fact that Rosalie's Army would soon trudge its 100th mile, it had dawned on Jones how far she was from New York City. On the bright side, the contingent of 50 local Philadelphia suffragettes had agreed to accompany the army as far as Darby a few miles down the road. The group included 70-year-old Rebecca Linford, who had been the president of the first suffrage society in Pennsylvania. Further down the pike at the crossroads town of Crum Lynne near Ridley Park, four generations of suffragists turned out to shake the general's hand, including a great-grandmother aged 81, a daughter aged 62, a granddaughter, and a great-granddaughter, all of whom had waited hours for the arrival of the army. "You are doing the right thing," the great-grandmother assured the marchers. "We American women must win by persuasion and not by violence." The elder said that she only wished her legs were good enough to take her to Washington, D.C.

In other ways, the hike to Chester disappointed. In Ridley Park the army faced firecrackers shot in its direction by boys bent on mischief. In the tiny village of Leiperville, where the Army of the Hudson arrived just after the school bell rang, 50 rambunctious boys rushed out into the schoolyard armed with snowballs, pelting the suffragettes at will. At their previous stop at the University of Pennsylvania, Freeman had argued that the suffrage movement needed more of a sense of humor, and on this occasion Jones offered just that, smiling bravely through the incoming barrage before, under orders of Colonel Craft, returning fire.[17] "It was mighty glorious fun," wrote the *Brooklyn Daily Eagle* of the spontaneous snowball fight, "and yet it impressed upon the youngsters that they had met women worthy of their steel." A group of young cadets from the nearby Pennsylvania Military College joined the battle on the side of the suffragettes, ending it in a rout.[18] Most of the newspapers made light of the snowball fight, but at least one war correspondent pointed out the painful truth: The snowballs stung, in more ways than one, when they hit their mark.[19]

At Leiperville it had been mere boys aiming snowballs in the hikers' direction, but near Darby, the would-be assailants were grown men, a crowd of 30 of them wielding hardened balls of ice. "It was a moment," wrote Ethel

Lloyd Patterson, "in which the wrong move might have meant much."[20] The general, she noted, didn't flinch or show fear, and the threat passed with little more than a round of derisive laughter from the assembled men. Still, the prospect of violence hung over the day's march as the women passed through factory towns where some working-class men were openly hostile to equal rights for women. Jones had allowed her troops only an abbreviated lunch, determined to get them safely within the city limits of Chester before the factories let out, causing the potential for violence to increase further.

In her February 18 dispatch from Chester, Patterson asked readers back in Washington, D.C., to imagine for themselves the scene that unfolded as the marchers passed through the hard-pressed factory towns of southeast Pennsylvania:

> Picture this to yourself: a narrow uneven street leading into a factory town. The snow is falling. Underfoot, it has been trampled into mud and slush. The houses that line the way are dingy frame dwellings or begrimed hives of industry. In all the windows are faces. No matter where one looks there are faces. Faces that grin derisively or sneer.
>
> The sidewalks are crowded with people—boys, girls, and women—waiting to watch the suffrage pilgrims go by. And down the street they come, walking in single file. "General" Rosalie Jones is first. Her brown pilgrim's cape is almost black because it is very wet. She leans heavily on her pilgrim's staff. She carries a great sheaf of golden jonquils, but even these are spattered with mud…. "General" Jones does not look at the people as she passes them; she plods ahead.
>
> And behind her come the others. There is "Colonel" Craft with her nervous, short steps. Her short skirt and thick leggings are absurdly trouser-like. Her pilgrim's cape, thrown over her knack-sack strapped upon her back, makes her look as though she were bent almost double beneath an awful load.
>
> On they come. Miss [Minerva] Crowell limping painfully. She wears old slippers because her feet are so swollen she cannot get her shoes on them. Her ankles are heavily bandaged.
>
> Miss [Constance] Leupp, hobbling on her injured knee; Miss [Elizabeth] Aldrich, fairly tottering with fatigue. And crowding in upon the ranks of the little army are men and boys. Men who fall into step beside the women to say something like this: "Say—I'd walk to Washington, too, if I could walk alongside of you"; or: "Why don't you go home and make the beds…."
>
> And the women walk on. Sometimes, but pitifully rarely, a woman on the sidewalk breaks into a cheer. She waves her handkerchief. The women who are marching look toward her. Their eyes meet for a moment. Something of warmth and sweetness passes between them. "God bless you," says the woman, on the sidewalk. "God bless you," echoes the marcher in her heart.[21]

Wearing sharp gray uniforms, the cadets on horseback escorted the marchers down Main Street in Chester shortly after 4 p.m. as Milton Wend bugled in celebration and the bells of St. Paul church rang out. The Army of the Hudson had now marched nearly 115 miles from New York City—approaching half of its ultimate goal. Railroad maps tallied the distance between the two cities at 105 miles, with an additional 10 added to allow for detours and winding roads. Washington, D.C., which had once seemed a distant dream, now seemed within reach.[22]

• • •

As Jones and Craft readied themselves for sleep at the Washington House hotel in Chester, Pennsylvania, back home in New York City a battle of equal magnitude reached a fever pitch: the battle to fund the cause.

"Rosalie Jones ... present not in the flesh but in the spirit" had with her contribution "started a money stampede for the cause," reported the *New York Tribune*.[23] NAWSA had booked the city's most iconic venue, Carnegie Hall, and brought in the biggest names in women's rights, including Carrie Chapman Catt, president of the International Woman Suffrage Alliance, NAWSA President Dr. Anna Howard Shaw, and Jane Addams of Hull House. Still, on this night none of the suffrage luminaries exerted a more powerful pull on pocketbooks than the general deployed in the Keystone State. The fundraising had been slow until Jones's pledge, made through an intermediary, opened the floodgates. Gifts of 500 dollars and 100 dollars had come in from anonymous Chicago contributors. On hearing the news, Shaw called out from the front of the room, "How about New York?" and a self-described "aunt of a New York Anti" pledged 10 dollars. "And I hope," Shaw quipped, "that the next time that word 'aunt' will be wiped out and the 'Anti' will give us some cash." The next call from the crowd picked up on the theme. "A converted Anti—converted here tonight—pledges twenty-five dollars." Another dollar came from a "poor Italian girl," while a young girl garment worker in the room offered five dollars.

From that point forward the vows of monetary support had come quickly—almost too quickly for the Wellesley and Barnard college students recording the pledges. Jones's initial gift had been a rainmaker, spurring 6,000 dollars in additional cash donations. Pushing for more, Shaw directed the students to disperse into the crowd to gather as much loose change as possible, leaving attendees with only enough in their pockets to get home by taxi or streetcar. The vigorous pledging lasted long enough that the night's main attraction, a speech by Addams, was delayed until nearly 11 p.m.

Addams was due to set sail for Egypt the following morning on a lengthy sabbatical from her uplift work in Chicago. In her comments that evening she responded to a recent cartoon in which cartoonist John T. McCutcheon had portrayed her standing in front of the sphinx. The legendary social reformer from the Windy City chose the image as an opener for her address to the suffrage faithful gathered in Carnegie Hall, gendering the mighty sphinx as she did so. "I would begin by going back twenty-five centuries to the time when Plato dreamed of an ideal republic in which poverty, disease, and crime would be gradually abolished," Addams declared at an hour when most of the members of the audience would otherwise have been in bed. "Plato taught that an ideal republic could never be established unless women receive equal guardianship in the state with men. And he contended that it remained with those who disagreed with him to prove that women should not have such a share. While women then had no part in government he said that this condition was the result of custom, not of nature, and that until the experiment of giving women an equal share in the guardianship of the state had been tried, the burden of proof remained on those who insisted that women should be excluded.

"And here Plato stopped in his argument," Addams continued, "to request that his fellow citizens would not ridicule him for the position he had taken. He showed that fear of ridicule twenty-five centuries ago which has always been of such power in keeping men from advocating the cause of equal suffrage."

"This experiment proposed by Plato has never been tried until the present century. Whether it is a new compunction seizing the conscience of man, or a gust of moral sentiment which bids him attack the old chimeras of poverty, crime, and disease, or whether it was simply that the time was ripe, all the world suddenly has begun moving toward giving women the vote."

Addams asserted that women, more than men, were the real soldiers fighting on the front lines against society's social ills. Many of the tasks of reform taken on by progressive politicians had been begun by women, and the state must ultimately turn to women for their expertise in solving them. The age-old fear of ridicule men had faced since the days of Plato was, the social reformer reminded, now "dropping from men like a garment which falls from the shoulders of one who is hurrying too fast to care."

The night's fundraiser had been a rousing success. Rent in New York City averaged approximately 480 dollars a year,[24] and in one night NAWSA had raised more than 12 times that amount thanks in large part to Jones. Supporters for the cause had filled Carnegie Hall to the uppermost balcony, while others, waiting outside, had been turned away due to a lack of space.[25]

Had the women of the world who had been waiting 2,500 years for the promise of Plato's republic been too willing to sacrifice, too content to quietly go about the work of municipal housekeeping rather than demand full civic enfranchisement? Suffragists thought so, though they disagreed over how much, and how literally, to adopt the tactics of war. Some, including Elisabeth Freeman, felt that women's armies could and perhaps should demand social change by violence if necessary.

Since the Army of the Hudson had marched out of New York City, British suffragette Sylvia Pankhurst had been arrested a third time for violent unrest. Only days before the Carnegie Hall fundraiser, England's militant suffragists had raided the country's finest championship golf courses, ruining their fabled putting greens with acids. Pankhurst and American Zelle Emerson had been taken into custody for smashing shop windows in London, though they were now free on bail.[26] Emerson, described as the "rich Jackson, Michigan girl" had grown impatient with the peaceful ways of the American protests and traveled to London to join forces with Emmeline Pankhurst and her daughters.[27] Upon her arrest, Emerson had declared that she would show the English that Americans could also be martyrs for the cause.

Was Emerson's violent resistance a model for American women too timid, or too constrained, to defend themselves in a patriarchal system? In near-riot conditions in Philadelphia it had been left to an ill-prepared police force, and to the men in the march, to protect Rosalie's Army from more widespread violence. In Princeton, Mary Boldt had been forcibly kidnapped by students. Two days earlier in Baltimore, where the Army of the Hudson would arrive in less than 10 days, organizer Alice Paul had requested military protection for the grand national suffrage procession scheduled for Washington, D.C., on March 3. The likelihood of violence appeared to be growing by the day, and a projected paucity of policemen promised to further endanger the protestors.[28]

Paul walked a fine line as parade organizer. On one hand, the point of the national suffrage parade, from the women on horseback to the military-style march down Pennsylvania Avenue, was to demonstrate women's strength and independence. On the other hand, Paul would surely be negligent if she did not at least anticipate the need for police protection. Like Emerson, Paul had previously worked with the Pankhursts in their militant campaign in London and knew how quickly street demonstrations could descend into anarchy. Prior to returning to America she had thrice been jailed for civil disobedience on behalf of the cause. Battle lines had already been sharply drawn for the suffrage procession waiting at the end of the On-to-Washington march. Suffragettes led by Paul were working around the clock to anticipate every detail of the coming demonstration. Meanwhile, Antis had mobilized to prepare counter demonstrations and other disruptions for events they considered unwomanly.

One of these Antis was J.B. Sanford, a state senator from California and chairman of the Democratic Caucus. Two years earlier, Sanford had published an "Argument against Women's Suffrage," a screed that read in part:

> The courageous, chivalrous, and manly men and the womanly women, the real mothers and home builders of the country, are opposed to this innovation in American political life. There was a bill (the Sanford bill) before the last legislature which proposed to leave the equal suffrage question to women to decide first before the men should vote on it. This bill was defeated by the suffragettes because they knew that the women would vote down the amendment by a vote of ten to one.[29]

Now Sanford had Rosalie's Army and the planned parade in Washington in his crosshairs, saying, "I am old-fashioned enough to think that woman, instead of rushing headlong into every new fad and 'ism,' should get up a mighty parade and retrace her steps back to her responsibilities—the responsibility of so training the young that less, rather than more, restraining laws will be required."

Paul and the suffragettes likewise hoped to neutralize another legislative enemy, "Cotton Tom" Heflin, by inviting him to the Washington parade and, when he refused, forcing him to publicly defend his refusal. Solutions for Heflin had continued to elude votes-for-women advocates, so much so that often contradictory headlines appeared in newspapers concerning the vexing Alabama congressman. On the same day, a headline reading "Suffragettes Through with Heflin and Will Ignore Him in the Future" appeared on the same page as an announcement that the suffragettes, having grown "peevish" with Heflin and his "wordy war with votes for women advocates," had challenged him to a public debate. No less than the *Washington Post* had published an editorial calling for New York suffragette lawyer Inez Milholland to debate Heflin in a winner-take-all battle royale.[30] Calling Milholland a "fine specimen of young womanhood" and Heflin a "fine specimen of manhood," the editorial offered the following premise: "If Miss Milholland could defeat Mr. Heflin, then women should have the vote…. Or, if Mr. Heflin should win, then the women now seeking the ballot would at once withdraw to their homes, and 'General' Rosalie Gardiner Jones, having marched up the hill, could march right down again." Such a debate would be a far more logical solution to the question, the editorial posited, than "the British method, whereby women seek to prove their right to vote by smashing windows."

Around the nation, the march of Rosalie's Army had galvanized public opinion in comments whose tone ranged from supportive to sardonic to openly sarcastic. Under the heading "Editorial Jottings," the *Baltimore Sun* opined that in hiking more than a hundred miles in boots, the Jones campaign might have singlehandedly ended the trend toward high heels.[31] Meanwhile, as the Army of the Hudson marched out of Chester bound for Wilmington, Delaware, the *New York Times* ran a bit of verse by poet-professor Frank Prentice Rand, whose ambivalent stanzas on the "militant maidens of Rosalie Jones" read:

> Still onward they march through the land of oppression,
> Right onward beneath emblems which so valiantly float
> To wrench from their foes in reluctant concession
> The right to bear arms, chew tobacco, and vote.

Rand's poem, while celebratory of the march, dared to imagine the plight of the men left behind at home, in whose voice he wrote:

> We are waiting in anguish and apprehension
> In whispers we speak of the frightful campaign:
> We pray that The Hague or an armed intervention
> May turn our brave soldier-girls homeward again.[32]

Some 115 miles away from New York City, Rosalie's Army slept soundly in the cradle of American history at the Washington House hotel in Chester, Pennsylvania. General Washington had secured lodging at the same historic inn after the battle of Brandywine in 1777. On September 11 of that year, Washington had written his report of the battle to the Continental Congress from his quarters in the hotel, and it was there on April 20, 1789, that Washington had received the adulation of the people of Chester after his election as the nation's first president.[33] The plain brick hotel may not have been as grand as the Waldorf Astoria or Carnegie Hall, but it proved sufficient for a good night's rest, a place for a general of a dauntless army to lay their weary head and contemplate the vicissitudes of the long march ahead.

In a review of the previous 24 hours, war correspondent Ethel Lloyd Patterson endeavored to put the momentous events happening in Pennsylvania in perspective for readers back in Washington, D.C. "And thus for the second time in American history an American general crossed the Delaware to victory and to triumph," she concluded. "Both generals were fighting against taxing without representation, because they believe it to be tyranny. Washington's name has gone down in history. Who knows but that 'General' Rosalie Jones's may do the same?"[34]

8

A Soldier's Rest
in Wilmington

"Forward, girls… Forward!" Rosalie Jones urged her troops the following morning in Chester. "Come on … it's for the cause. Don't falter, just this one day and then tomorrow you will have a big long rest."[1]

Morning had come too soon for the marchers, some of whom had stayed out late the night before to hear Elisabeth Freeman deliver a ringing suffrage speech in front of the Chester armory. And though they had dutifully donned their pilgrims' uniforms, their readiness belied underlying reluctance. Jones had slept well and appeared "as fresh as she did when she started the journey,"[2] but the same could not be said for a handful of new recruits and day-hikers who had joined up in Philadelphia, many of whom had struggled the previous night to find lodging in the working-class mill town of approximately 40,000. While Jones, Craft, and others among the army's officers had overnighted at the Washington House, others in the growing brigade had been forced to find last-minute lodging in private homes.[3] Most had bunked at the local YMCA, from whence Jones now attempted to muster her footsore troops.

Milton Wend had bugled as usual, but the troops had not responded with their usual resolve. Still, after a night of open-air meetings in Chester, there was little choice but to put one foot in front of the other when the bugle sounded.[4] The morning thus far had challenged the marchers' resolve on several fronts, including the absence of an unlikely elephant escort that had been promised by Leon Washburn, an old friend of Jones's who worked in the circus in New York and overwintered his animals in Chester.[5] Two of Washburn's elephants, Judy and Gypsy, had been fixtures in Jones's visits to the circus at Coney Island as a young woman, and Washburn, ever the showman, had lobbied the general to allow the animals to pull the suffrage wagon for a day or two. Still, by shortly after 9:00 a.m., Washburn and his charges had yet to materialize, and Jones agitated to make a start before her troops lost their will. Tom Hargreaves, owner of the Arcade Hotel and likewise a circus operator, offered as an alternative the six-month-old lion and lioness that served as the star attractions at his lodging. Knowing of Jones's love of animals and sensing a publicity opportunity, a supporter of the army offered to buy one of the cubs from Hargreaves if Jones would volunteer to lead the beast to Washington, but the general refused the stunt, no doubt concerned for the welfare of a wild animal too proud to be led by a leash.

By 9:20 a.m., Washburn's elephant escort still had not appeared, and the army had no choice but to move forward on lightly frozen roads warmed by the sun.[6] As they had in Philadelphia, local residents turned out by the thousands to see the marchers off on their way to Wilmington, where for the first time they would rest for an entire day without marching. Unlike in Philadelphia, where 50 members of the local suffrage societies had trudged alongside the army for the first several miles to Darby, today there was no such large delegation. Still, the suffragettes had enlisted six new recruits to walk with them all or most of the way to the state line.[7] The army was growing once more as it moved toward Delaware. Including men and women, it now numbered nearly 45 marchers.

• • •

The sun shone brightly when Wilmington *Morning News* reporter Eva K. Jones left that city to join the marchers in Chester, Pennsylvania, pledging to play the role of war correspondent for a day. Eva Jones was one of more than 20 dedicated journalists covering the march as it pointed toward Washington, a group that included hiker-reporters Constance Leupp of the *New York Evening Post* and Emilie Doetsch of the *Baltimore News*. By this, the seventh day of their march, a "very cordial camaraderie"[8] had formed between Rosalie's Army and the detachment of war correspondents from nearly all the important metropolitan dailies from New York to Washington, plus some from Chicago newspapers.[9]

The thermometer at Belt Drug Store recorded 26 degrees at 9 a.m., a "cold crisp morning with plenty of frost in the air" that made walking a delight.[10] Still, Eva Jones discovered that keeping up with Rosalie's Army was no easy feat. "The hikers keep up a pace in their march [that] it is hard for a raw recruit to follow," she confessed. "They go at top speed all the time, and the veteran walkers say that is the proper way to march as it keeps the muscles from getting stiff." The hikers, she discovered, were a "companionable lot," which, she admitted, made "the journey from town to town seem less tedious than if one were walking alone."[11]

By shortly after 11 a.m., Rosalie Jones had quite literally tripped across the Pennsylvania state line into the fourth state on the army's long march toward the District of Columbia. Still she landed on her feet, at least so far as the attendant war correspondents were concerned, to whom she quipped, "I have stumbled into Delaware."[12]

The day's hike had begun with a somber reminder of the hardships faced by many of the rural residents the marchers sought to convert to their cause. Often the suffragettes marched past wayside cemeteries. Typically these graveyards were quiet and the mourners few, but today they had encountered an elderly woman carrying a bouquet of flowers. The hikers asked her if she was a supporter of votes-for-women. "My heart is dead," the woman replied, causing Jones to place a comforting hand on the old woman's back.[13] "Years ago," she explained, "I lost my only daughter. She was at the threshold of womanhood. I am sure that had she lived she would have been as good a woman as you, General Jones. She, too, believed in women's rights." The woman turned then and entered the graveyard without a word, leaving Jones speechless and the hardboiled war correspondents standing by as somber witnesses.

At approximately 2:30 p.m., Jones called the march to a second halt at Shellpot Park.[14] In their eagerness to reach Wilmington the army had found itself ahead of schedule. Just beyond the northern outskirts of the city, the wooded land near Shellpot Creek boasted an old mill and an amusement park on a popular trolley line from the city, making it an ideal site for a rendezvous. Legions of supporters had taken the trolley out to meet the army and walk the last couple of miles to the Hotel du Pont. With the influx of day-hikers from the city, the army's numbers surged to more than 200.[15]

Wilmington had been waiting weeks to play host to the Army of the Hudson. On February 17 the *Morning News* had published a page-one story promising that the city at the confluence of the Christina and Brandywine Rivers would not be left behind in the quality of reception given the suffrage pilgrims.[16] Two days earlier on February 15, headlines had trumpeted "Suffrage pilgrims heading this way," with Wilmington mayor Harrison W. Howell promising to offer the visiting delegation the key to his city. There was even talk of sending city firefighters out to sound their horns at first sight of the suffrage pilgrims.

Wilmington's reception did not disappoint. All along the plan had been to send a small delegation to Claymont some seven miles northeast of Wilmington to greet the marchers and escort them into town. Indeed, by the time the army had reached the outskirts of Delaware's largest city, an estimated 200 to 300 enthusiasts had fallen into line behind Jones. At every point along the road, cars lined up to cheer the marchers in what amounted to a "continual ovation."[17]

Jones selected Elizabeth Aldrich to speak to the crowd assembled at Shellpot Park. Lately the general had tapped some of the younger, less publicized members of the army to deliver speeches. At Princeton, for example, 20-year-old Mary Boldt had been given center stage as the leader of a side-march to Woodrow Wilson's residence and had been selected to lead a student rally. Wilmington now appeared as if it would be Aldrich's coming-out party, as the war correspondents scrambled to dig up facts on the upstart marcher. Aldrich, the *News Journal* learned, was kin to the well-known writer-critic Thomas Bailey Aldrich, editor of the *Atlantic Monthly* and the youngest of four generations of Quaker suffragists dating back to Aldrich's great-grandmother, Avis Keen.[18] War correspondent-hiker Emilie Doetsch of the *Baltimore News* had now marched seven days with Aldrich but could convey only the most rudimentary of facts about her, describing the youthful Quaker marcher as "the pretty feminine suffragette who hails from California."[19] Elsewhere in her reportage, Doetsch described Aldrich as a "San Diego girl" who had voted in elections there.[20] Aldrich had previously acted on stage as well, making her theatrical debut in Frederick, Maryland—an event, Doetsch noted, "she remembers with keen pleasure." Still, despite her gift for oratory and her theatrical demeanor, Aldrich, with Quaker modesty, shied away from the autograph signings and schoolboy infatuation on which fellow hiker Phoebe Hawn had capitalized. With the march a week old, now seemed an ideal time for Jones to test a deeper bench. Earlier that morning the general had declared a "Brooklyn Day," allowing Brooklyn's Hawn, Craft, and Crowell to take turns leading the march. "Tomorrow I may have a Bronx Day if I can find any from that borough," Jones joked with the press.[21]

"I suppose you are all anxious to know why we women are walking with bleeding feet," Aldrich told the crowd assembled at Shellpot. "We represent the women who are stumbling on toward a goal. We don't want to antagonize the men; we want to help them, the women, and the children. We want to help the working women. We want to help you." Aldrich paused to regard the curious crowd. "I am a working woman," she continued, "and am interested especially in the laboring class, but we want suffrage for all classes of women. I personally am not a militant…. I am absolutely non-resistant and am just walking on to Washington with that goal in front of me."[22]

Before the marchers could get to Washington, they first had to make it to the Wilmington city center, and that wouldn't be easy. Ahead of them, Olive Schultz had attempted to motor to city hall in her Buick touring car but had suffered a flat tire negotiating the steep hill that led down to the Hotel du Pont. When rumor spread among the estimated 1,200 people gathered at the courthouse steps that at least one member of the party had arrived, they rushed past the fire trucks and practically engulfed Schultz as she worked to repair her vehicle.[23] The sheer number of gawking onlookers caused one reporter from the *Baltimore Sun* to quip: "Evidently the walking suffragette is a new species of bird in this city." The reaction to the brown-clad pilgrims as they strode into town at around 3 p.m. was largely one of "amusement on finding women afoot, tired and footsore, upon the road." Meanwhile, the *Washington Post* described the noisiest welcome the pilgrims had yet received, adding that it seemed as though "all Wilmington was out to meet the marchers."[24] The city had given the protestors their most enthusiastic reception since leaving New York, and Jones beamed on the appreciative crowd, walking "with head erect and soldier-like tread." Rosalie's Army pressed on to the Market Street Bridge in a celebratory scene. Fire engines whistled and car horns blared to mark the occasion, and the streets were so thoroughly overcome with onlookers that police were forced to clear the pilgrims' way into the council chambers where Mayor Howell greeted them with a prepared statement.[25]

"Not for the suffrage cause alone have the people of the city respect for you, but they have profound respect for your grit and your pilgrimage," Howell told onlookers assembled in the historic chambers. "We trust and we hope that Wilmington, Delaware, can be looked back upon as the garden of your pilgrimage." The mayor next moved to do what so many Republican mayors had earlier attempted: praising the pilgrims without necessarily endorsing their cause. "I will not say that I am heartily in accord with your idea," Howell added, "but I do say that an enterprise carried on with such grit as yours should succeed." Often, Rosalie's Army presented host dignitaries and religious officials with a vexing conundrum. On one hand, the mayors and city managers and toastmasters of town-and-gown society wanted to be seen as good and gracious hosts, wishing to promote their fair cities as open-minded and welcoming. But in politically conservative or even politically moderate places, public officials feared praising the pilgrims too enthusiastically lest they alienate conservative constituencies.

Mayor Howell next turned the floor over to Jones, inviting her to make a few brief comments. "Although we come as pilgrims," Jones told the crowd, "we hope to leave you all suffragists. All we ask for is enough soap boxes from which to expound our cause." In her impromptu comments at City Hall, Jones largely demurred, calling herself "only a newspaper general" while redirecting praise toward her stalwart colonel, Ida Craft, who had arrived late to Wilmington after marching "on pure nerve" to overcome a badly injured ankle.[26] Jones also reserved praise for faithful lieutenants like Aldrich, on whom she called to speak once more.

"Believe me, friends," Aldrich said of Jones when it was her turn at the podium, "she's not a straw general. She's the best little general that ever lived, and I swear my allegiance to General Jones."[27] Clenching her fists and tearing up as she declared her loyalty, Aldrich "brought the house down" with an "eloquent address which depicted her former stage career."[28] She praised Wilmington for its warm reception while offering yet another spirited disavowal of militancy in the movement. "I don't approve of militant methods, but I am a thorough suffragist and couldn't be anything else since my great-grandmother was a suffragist, my grandmother was a suffragist, as was my mother, and I come by it honestly," she told them.

Aldrich's views contrasted dramatically with those expressed by the army's chief orator, Elisabeth Freeman, the English militant who organized a massive street meeting later that evening of Tuesday, February 18. Freeman stood in an automobile at 8 p.m. and addressed a throng of nearly 10,000 people crowding into the downtown square[29] for what was said to be the first open-air votes-for-women meeting in the city's long history.[30] She began by reminding those in attendance that American women demanding the vote was not a new or novel request but a plea that dated back to at least the Seneca Falls Convention of 1848. Girls, she pointed out, already outpaced boys in numbers of high school diplomas earned. Women must be allowed and encouraged to seek their own economic salvation independent of men, she asserted. Once fully enfranchised, women would put an end to war while reducing sweatshops and poverty—two causes for which Freeman had worked previously in New York City. Freeman called for the immediate passage of a suffrage amendment in the Delaware statehouse.[31] The Englishwoman's comments met with considerable applause despite their potential paradox, for even as she speculated about women leaders bringing an end to war, she stood before the residents of Wilmington as a self-styled soldier in a woman's army.[32] Her brand of militant activism had caused her to be arrested nine times and imprisoned twice, including one sentence served in the notorious Holloway Prison.

In closing, Freeman returned to her core premise: that votes-for-women was right and just, and that if Colorado, Idaho, Wyoming, Washington, California, and other Western states could make it work, so too could the rest of the nation. Suffrage, claimed the army's orator-in-chief, was everywhere on the rise, as evidenced by the nearly 1,000 American suffrage societies and a growing interest in the movement in the nation's newspapers and periodicals.

• • •

In the lead-up to Wilmington, Jones had increasingly delegated speeches and appearances to the youngest activists in her platoon—Hawn, Aldrich, and Boldt—though the general's youth movement had met with some grumbling from elder members, especially Craft. The strategy had lately yielded dividends of greater press appeal, but it had also exacerbated long-simmering problems within the ranks. Almost from the beginning, Boldt had been walking out in front of the rest of the marching column with the youthful editor of the Brooklyn Boy Scout magazine, Norman Sper. Boldt's speed made sense; she was 20 years old, fit, and without any command responsibilities in the army. She wore a red and white tasseled cap described as "exceedingly becoming" and was "always as fresh at the end of a day's hike as at the beginning." According to reports, Boldt's habit of walking as much as two miles ahead of the main column threatened to upstage Jones, as casual observers sometimes mistook Boldt for the general upon arrival.[33] Headlines accused her of running ahead to steal Jones's glory, while suggesting that the general "could not keep Mrs. Boldt in the ranks of marchers." In Princeton, Boldt's early arrival had likely been a factor in her alleged manhandling. By the time the On-to-Washington marchers reached Wilmington, the press was widely reporting the Boldt controversy, and the usually retiring walker found herself the object of intense media scrutiny.

Boldt had only recently emerged from her room into the lobby of the Hotel du Pont in Wilmington when *Morning News* reporter Eva K. Jones stopped her, hoping to provide readers with insight into the army's most enigmatic regular. Before she would answer any questions from Jones or from any of the other reporters gathered in the ornate, high-ceilinged lobby, the timely hiker took out her wristwatch and set it for exactly the amount she was willing to devote to questions: five minutes.[34]

Eva Jones described her interviewee as "a trim little figure" with a "wealth of golden hair and a pair of brown eyes that the realist would declare a wee bit rolling" and a voice that was "low and entertaining and every inch a suffragette." Boldt was "glowing with the bloom" of youth, Jones reported. A relatively recent convert to the cause, she "spurned the less dynamic term 'suffragist.'" Why, Jones asked Boldt, had she, too, not hobbled into Wilmington like the other pilgrims? Boldt, she learned, had been born and raised in the outdoors of Canada with a love for winter sports. While many of the rest of the pilgrims, especially Klatschken and Craft, trudged with difficulty through the mud and snow, Boldt glided along "with the sprightly step of a schoolgirl out for a bit of natural coloring." Eva Jones's questions implied what other observers had long been thinking—that Boldt made it look almost too easy—that she didn't appear to suffer sufficiently to qualify as a true pilgrim.

In reply, Boldt's brown eyes flashed with a sternness the war correspondents were not accustomed to seeing. No, votes-for-women was far from a fad to her. Yes, she was a society girl who had married a well-to-do Wall Street broker. Yes, she excelled at golf and skiing and snowshoeing. Yes, her husband had plenty of money, but what of it? Boldt had been active in the votes-for-women movement only for a few months, but what mattered was not her past but her present.

"Any of the hikers will tell you that I am young and will learn," Boldt said, apparently aware of the criticisms directed at her from the veteran activists. Asked if she would ever become a militant, she surprised in answering, "if I had to," before adding quickly, "but those five minutes are long since passed." Perhaps, Eva Jones surmised, Boldt had ended the interview sensing the water was getting deep. In any case the allotted time was up, and Boldt was off to the races again, leaving the reporters to give chase.

Like Eva Jones, Ethel Lloyd Patterson was paid to be the ears and eyes of readers who did not have the luxury of accompanying the pilgrims on their quest. Patterson's insightful and often poignant coverage of the march to date had earned praise from readers of the *Evening Star* in Washington, D.C., and from her editors there. Alongside stories announcing a full slate of suffrage meetings and debates in the nation's capital, the *Star* ran an unusual acknowledgment of one of its own, confirming that Patterson's stories of the "joys and trials and tribulations" of Rosalie's Army were being read with "much interest by the suffragists and favorably commented upon."

While other war correspondents retired early from their posts on that first night in Wilmington, content to wait for the bigger headlines to unfold the following day, Patterson stayed attentive, waxing philosophic as she watched the way the trappings of civilization—fine dinners and fancy dresses—transformed individual suffragettes. Her story, datelined Wilmington, opened with the kind of insight readers had come to expect from the talented young journalist:

> So we appeared in our true colors at last. Or, on second thought, were they really…? Perhaps we shall never know. Of course, we each know down in our hearts exactly what we think about the other pilgrims. Some of us even confide our opinions. But about ourselves, are we, beneath everything, more like the dirty, disheveled, tired women who tramped the roads from New York to Wilmington, or are we, beneath everything, the prettily dressed, conventional-looking persons who … came down to dinner? If we knew we should know a lot of other things besides.
>
> For you see it was last night that we emerged. And it was rather amusing to watch.
>
> We found ourselves in a really good hotel since the first time we started…. How our manners changed with our clothes! We became quite formal, even with one another. So the people who thronged the lobby of the hotel and stared at us from doorways found us so nearly human that they had some difficulty in picking us out from the other guests.
>
> But this much I have discovered: It takes a camera's eye to see a person's soul. If you want to know what a woman is really like, watch her have her picture taken. Watch her even when there is a camera in her vicinity. Watch the girl who, when she sees that some person is about to take her picture, keeps as close to that person as she can. Watch her and then steer clear of her. Or watch the girl who in a group picture carefully elbows her way to the front. Watch her and then steer clear of her. Or, as the shutter clicks, watch the elderly woman looking roguish, the young girl looking serious, and the one with the unkind tongue looking chastely exalted. Get a camera and point it at your friends. Then you will know. This much seems quite sure, that which people most ardently try to appear for publication they most certainly are not.

Patterson's deep look into the souls of her sister suffragettes foretold greater dissension within the ranks. But there was one soldier with whom Patterson had no quarrel, and for the general, Patterson reserved praise without reservation, exalting her in the most colorful language:

> I should like to go out and buy a whole lot of hats, maybe fifty or so, and then take them all off, one by one, to "General" Rosalie Gardiner Jones…. For one thing, she does not bustle. It would be very easy to dislike a general who did bustle. Again, one

never hears her give an order. Yet things are done. And I should like to buy fifty more hats and then take them off, one by one, to her unfailing tact and courtesy. Quite as a side issue, General Rosalie Gardiner Jones is really very pretty. And so it goes.[35]

• • •

Rosalie Jones had barely settled into her room at the Hotel du Pont when she found herself answering the door to yet another in a string of visitors, though this one's face proved vaguely familiar. The young man—a student she presumed—who had unexpectedly joined the march near Burlington, New Jersey, now stood before her wearing the kind of sheepish expression that often accompanied a requested favor. The young man confessed that he had lied to his father to come on the march, saying that he was going to Long Island for a long weekend with friends. Now that his "long weekend" had turned into several days, the young marcher was writing a letter to his father to explain that he had joined a women's march. Would General Jones kindly add a postscript to verify that he had behaved like a gentleman thus far?

The young man, Roy Trolsen of Brooklyn, had fooled everyone, including the war correspondents, who had assumed him to be one of the students who would join the march for a few hours or a few days, then quietly drop out to return to class. All the while Trolsen had been secretly courting 21-year-old music student Helen Bergmark, the hiker from Philadelphia by way of Colorado, whom he had met in Brooklyn a year earlier. Now, in an eerie echo of the earlier marriage proposal made by Willie Cator to Phoebe Hawn, Trolsen claimed Bergmark had reportedly promised to marry him once the march was over, generating the page-one headline "Former Brooklyn Boy Joins Hikers to Win a Bride."[36]

Jones agreed to endorse Trolsen's letter home but not without misgivings, and she confided the troubling situation to the *Brooklyn Daily Eagle*, which opened its February 19 coverage with the sentence: "Far be it from us to spoil a perfectly good romance, but news is news, and so here goes, right from the seat of war." The *Daily Eagle* reporter described the good-looking, muscular Trolsen as "belligerent as a bantam rooster" and characterized him as being on "French leave" from his studies in Brooklyn. The *Washington Post* described Trolsen as a "brawny and debonair" athlete with a talent for playing first base and a desire to work as an engineer in Philadelphia.[37] Trolsen's father, the newspaper had learned, superintended a building on Wall Street. Trolsen's greatest worry, outside of the disapproving father he had duped, was that Jones would kick the lovers out of the army, and yet, it reported, "he was assured by the romance-seeking scribes that [Jones] wasn't, after all, devoid of sentiment, and furthermore that, as the paper put it, 'all the world loves a lover.'"[38]

When she learned of the alleged secret engagement, Craft smoldered with indignation, having been one of "the stern-purposed suffragettes" who

HOW THE SCHEME MIGHT FAIL.
A Suffrage Leader Proposes That Women Refuse to Marry Until Granted the Right to Vote.

ARABELLA—"NO, MR. SNIGGSWORTH, MUCH AS I DISLIKE TO SAY IT, I CANNOT BECOME YOUR WIFE UNTIL WOMEN CAN VOTE. IF YOU —"

ALGERNON SNIGGSWORTH—"SAY NO MORE, ARABELLA! SINCE YOU GIVE ME HOPE, ALL THINGS ARE POSSIBLE. I AM OFF TO WASHINGTON AND WILL RETURN WHEN I CAN SAY, 'ARABELLA, YOU ARE A VOTER!'"

ALGERNON (SEVERAL YEARS LATER)—"IT'S NO USE, ARABELLA, SENATOR ALDRICH WILL NOT PERMIT IT."

A cartoon by Ralph Wilder titled "How the Scheme Might Fail: A Suffrage Leader Proposes that Women Refuse to Marry Until Granted the Right to Vote." The cartoon shows a suitor named Algernon Sniggsworth pledging to his love that he has joined the On-to-Washington march. The third cell, time-stamped "several years later," shows the same man, now old, has given up on marrying Arabella, presumably because women still do not have the vote. The cartoon is dated 1909. Miller NAWSA Suffrage Scrapbooks, Library of Congress, Rare Book and Special Collections Division. https://cdn.loc.gov/master/rbc/rbcmil/scrp 5015301/001.jpg had begun "to suspect that Roy and Helen were interested in other things than votes."[39] Seeking out the war correspondents to vent her growing disapproval with the march's youth, Craft sought to inform the press of the promise made by the marchers. "Before leaving New York we all promised General Jones not to get married on the march to Washington," she recalled.[40] "We don't want the march spoiled by romance and we all therefore gave our promise seriously to the general before departure not to contemplate matrimony, at least not until the march is over."

• • •

Trolsen may have kept Jones and Craft up late with his revelation, but for the first time since the march began, the plan for February 19 in Wilmington was that there was no plan—at least nothing definite. Still, the war correspondents, some of whom had stayed in the Hotel du Pont with the marchers, milled about the extravagant lobby waiting for whatever morsels were destined to become news that Wednesday. One by one the weary hikers came down from their fifth-floor rooms with nothing special to do other than chat with the 20 or so reporters awaiting their word.

The night before, Jones had told her troops that they could do as they pleased the following morning, though she had followed that invitation with a wry smile and the caveat "You can make suffrage speeches whenever and wherever you like."[41] She had also issued one other edict: "that there would be no more engagements, elopements, or marriages until the army reaches Washington."

Freeman woke early, making calls to organize the educational campaigns for a day that would include visits to Wilmington factories and businesses.[42] Aldrich and Klatschken would go to the Pusey and Jones Company, a major shipbuilder and industrial equipment manufacturer on the Christina River. Freeman would deliver a solo speech at the town's Pullman works factory. The plan was to address as many workers as they could reach; factories that employed hundreds of laborers proved an especially efficient way to broadcast the message. On this day, the pilgrims would go out in pairs—one to speak and one to sell fundraising postcards and distribute free literature. Tackling sometimes resistant groups in twos or threes allowed for companionship, support, and even, where necessary, a measure of safety.

For the first time in the march to date, Freeman had more than one day in which to canvas a city, and as she readied herself for a day of soapbox speeches and corner meetings she found herself emphatically in her element. "From soapboxes, from garbage pails, from fence corners, from the courthouse and city hall steps, in opera [houses] and schoolhouses—everywhere it's 'Votes for Women' and 'On to Washington!'" reporter Emilie Doetsch enthused of the all-out suffrage invasion carried out by Freeman and Klatschken, the latter of whom had delivered her 19th address by noon, refusing lunch in favor of duty.[43] The buttons and postcards by which the army helped fund its march were sold by the dozens from Freeman's yellow wagon, which was seen everywhere throughout the business districts.[44]

The day's headlines carried the story of the daring exploits of the British suffragettes, who had blown up Chancellor David Lloyd George's residence in London, and now the journalists clamored for the Englishwoman's perspective on the events unfolding across the Atlantic. "They have done right," Freeman told the scrum of reporters following her, adding, "Americans don't understand and have no right to criticize." Hiker May Morgan, a political organizer and occasional newspaperwoman based in New York City, was equally inflammatory, saying she was glad that the home had been destroyed and would not have been sorry if Lloyd George had been damaged along with it.[45] Klatschken concurred, saying, "The Englishwomen are fighting for liberty for women all over the world. And property is of no account compared with liberty." Elizabeth Aldrich, the lone Quaker among the regular army and an avowed pacifist, publicly disagreed with her comrades, interjecting that she "wouldn't break the smallest pane of glass to enfranchise all the women in the world."

Freeman, however, was in a particularly expansive mood and defended the British militants with gusto. "Politicians tell women that they have not sufficiently shown that they are deserving of a vote," she told anyone who cared to listen.[46] She found it less than coincidental that no one had been killed in the burning of David Lloyd George's house. "It was done because the government is forcing the hand of the women," she explained, "and the British political procedure shows how far you have to go in violence before you can get anything. The men have done a great deal of smashing to gain their ends." When men wanted the right of the franchise in 1832 and again in 1867, Freeman pointed out, they caused half a million dollars in damage as well as many lives. No lives had been lost in the latest action by British suffragettes, she pointed out, adding, "But women's lives have been lost by the brutality meted out to them by the employees of the government."

Freeman and Aldrich, representing opposite sides of the militancy question, began to debate the question among themselves, and the argument quickly became heated. Aldrich called the actions of the English suffragettes "unnecessary and outrageous."[47] Freeman countered matter-of-factly, stating, "I am a firm believer in militantism" while adding that she "rejoiced" in violent revolt. "With them, I believe in smashing windows and attacking the mails, and applaud this dynamiting of Lloyd George's house." Voices were raised and accusations leveled until Aldrich broke down weeping in anger and frustration as Freeman disparaged the "pussy-footed element" in the movement. "There is no telling what might have happened," the *Pittsburgh*

Post-Gazette reported, "had not General Jones come along at this juncture and put her arms around the combatants and made them shake hands." The forced reconciliation may have made for a tidy public resolution to the matter, but within the army deep resentments burned.

Earlier that same day, American suffragette Zelle Emerson from Michigan had been arrested in London for the second time in a week for window-breaking and vandalism, and this time the penalties doled out by the British magistrate had been harsh: two months' hard labor.[48] Even Jane Addams had weighed in on the militancy question as she sailed for Europe to attend the International Suffrage Alliance meeting, saying that she "did not believe that the English approve of the methods of the militant."[49] Addams added that she doubted any good could come from the willful violence and took a moment to praise Jones and the On-to-Washington hikers, who, she said, were "doing good for the cause."

• • •

Throughout the day, Ethel Lloyd Patterson took full advantage of what was supposed to have been a day of rest for the pilgrims to conduct interviews with the most important of the thru-hikers who had marched from Newark.[50] In a march in which virtually every minute had been spoken for, Patterson wanted to see what the pilgrims would do with their spare time when given a choice as to how to spend it. Catherine Wend, for example, had risen late, indulging herself in a massage and a manicure. A mother in her early 40s, Wend was the second oldest thru-hiker on the march, though she eschewed the press and never seemed to complain. If the reporters referred to her at all, it was always by her chosen calling card, "Mrs. George Wend," a nod to a husband back in Poughkeepsie who served as her usual travel companion. The march with Rosalie's Army had been Catherine Wend's greatest adventure to date. Though she had recently toured through the U.S., Canada, and Newfoundland with a beloved husband who had made his fortune in the New York lumber industry, the march of Rosalie's Army had been the highlight of her life.[51]

Minerva Crowell, meanwhile, had stayed in to mend her fraying clothes, prevented from exploring the town by two bad ankles. Phoebe Hawn and Constance Leupp had gone out shopping for shoes and other supplies needed for the hike while also making speeches and factory visits along with Klatschken and Aldrich. Freeman delivered addresses around the city without cessation, while Mary Boldt spent her free time writing to fans she had made at the rally she had given at Princeton.

Patterson's interview with Jones revealed a general intent on getting to the bottom of the pile of mail awaiting her in Wilmington.

"I cannot tell you how the letters have accumulated," Jones lamented.

"People who ask me to marry them, or who tell me I ought to be ashamed of myself for my unwomanly behavior, or who want me to advertise something. One woman wrote me and asked if she could name a brand of corsets after me. I told her I felt unworthy of the honor." Jones had set out to open a pile of letters as tall as her bed and had been interrupted so often that she had finally been left with no choice but to disconnect the phone.

Craft had been writing letters as well, Patterson discovered, principally to correct the record in the many newspapers where she felt she had been misquoted or misrepresented. Several publications had reported that Craft had fainted, a rumor she denied in the strongest possible terms. For Craft, insinuations about her failing health called into question her ability to continue the mission, something she had vowed to do at any cost, and therefore must be responded to aggressively. By the time Patterson caught up with the second-in-command she described as "a busy little person," the colonel had written 50 such disavowals while preparing an additional 50 suffrage hat bands for sale. For good measure, she had then sorted 500 suffrage flags and ordered 1,000 additional suffrage buttons to be sent to the marchers en route. "She is like a sparrow," Patterson observed. "I knew before I asked her that probably her idea of a day of rest would be to turn out the work of three ordinary boilermakers."

After a dance and ice cream social sponsored by the Patternmakers of North America, the pilgrims gathered later that evening at the Garrick Theatre on Market Street, where the crowd had been promised an appearance by famous marching suffragettes. A handsome brick building with a dramatic archway supported by Corinthian columns, the Garrick was a fitting backdrop for a celebrity appearance.

"It is probable," declared Wilmington's *Morning News*, "that a performance at the Garrick was never more largely attended."[52] By the middle of the night's scheduled vaudeville, the audience had begun to agitate, having been promised that the suffragettes would speak between acts. Thus far, however, the members of Rosalie's Army had not budged from their box seats on the right side of the theater. At the end of the third act, however, the orchestra began playing a familiar tune, the marching song of the suffragettes that went "Tramp, Tramp, Tramp, the girls are marching." The audience erupted in applause at the sight of Jones as she marched on stage with her pilgrim's staff decorated with suffrage pennants and ribbons. On her brown cloak she had pinned pink flowers. "We have been traveling for something like one hundred and twenty-five miles," Jones told the audience as the applause died down, "and this is the best reception we have received on our trip. We come to bring you a message of equality and we go on to Maryland tomorrow to carry the same message." Once the rest of the pilgrims had arrived on stage, they assembled in a semi-circle around General Jones, Colonel Craft, and

Corporal Klatschken. The pilgrims wore their regulation cloaks and hoods with evening dresses underneath. Corporal Klatschken spoke next, choosing to address the women whom she viewed as the future of Delaware. "We are working," she said, "to bring about freedom for the human race, and we come here to bring you a message of common sense." Women needed the ballot to solve societal problems such as child labor and human trafficking, she maintained, adding, "We ask you to bring to this question an open mind." Once the individual pilgrims had said their piece, Jones stepped forward to tell the theater-goers that she and her sister soldiers were "marching for the ballot as the crusaders of old marched for the cross."

Once more, however, it was Freeman, rather than the thespian Aldrich, who had taken center stage at the Garrick. Among the marchers, Freeman had been the only one to remove her pilgrim's cloak to reveal her gypsy dress underneath. "Miss Freeman," noted the *Morning News*, "won the title of Gypsy Freeman for her picturesque dress and her manner of forecasting the future of the suffrage cause." On this night, Freeman found herself in a soothsaying mood, focusing on boys and girls as the future of the movement. Between speakers, the Englishwoman recounted the street meeting she had organized on the courthouse plaza the night before, describing a conversation overheard between two girls waiting to hear her speak. One had complained that she was tired of standing and was ready to go home. The other resisted, saying that she wanted to stay and see "the window smashing began." The suffrage-friendly crowd laughed at the humorous recounting, but some laughed more uneasily than others. It was true that the suffragettes had become role models for young activists; in fact, Charlotte Quigley, said to be the youngest suffragist in Delaware, had been inspired to join the following day's march to Newark, Delaware. With impressionable young women like Quigley among the protest marchers, Freeman's history of militancy was anything but a joke, and with a suffrage bill pending in the Delaware legislature, any perceived condoning of violence could endanger future legislative gains.

By the time Freeman and the rest of the marching suffragettes returned from the Garrick that night, it was late, and the buzz in the busy hive that was the Hotel du Pont had begun to die down. After the women had gone to bed, one of the few male thru-hikers on the march, Dr. Ernest Stevens, seized the opportunity to sit down with reporters. Thus far, the war correspondents had written very little about Stevens and Milton Wend and E.S. Lemmon. Both Stevens and Wend had been given quasi-official supporting roles that allowed them to disappear into the background. Stevens served as the unofficial poet and historian of the march, Wend the bugler and standard-bearer.

Both men were more than their ceremonial titles suggested, a fact becoming increasingly clear as Rosalie's Army neared the midway point of its journey. In addition to serving as the march's whimsical poet-historian, the well-to-do Stevens was a former member of the Board of Trade of Philadelphia and a three-term president of the Literary and Debating Society of the Men's High School of Philadelphia.[53]

"People are very curious about us," Stevens confided to reporters in the hotel lobby long after the suffragettes had gone to bed, "and now they have discovered at least that we are not a set of bums. We are all educated people, and many of us are also wealthy. We pilgrims are an independent suffrage party. We all pay our own expenses on the march, and have undertaken it to advertise our cause." The doctor wished to make certain things known while he had the ear of the war correspondents. First, he pointed out that he had not heard a single complaint for the duration of the march, a point which strained credulity but which he nevertheless spoke in earnest. "The women have by their endurance shown themselves qualified to be soldiers," the doctor insisted, "in all ways but spilling blood." Asked about the overall objective of the march, the doctor opined, "It has been discovered that man has been using but half of the force and power available in the world for achieving the onward and upward march of progress in civilization." Young women, he maintained, lacked nothing but experience in politics. "This will not take them from the home," Stevens assured the press. "They will still control the home, and as the city is only a great community of homes they should have some control of the city of homes."

While Stevens was more than happy to share his views on gender equality, the reporters gathered around him were more interested in hearing the overlooked details of the journey thus far, and the doctor was happy to oblige. He dished that a Pennsylvania legislator and former Army major had carried a large box of provisions all the way from Lebanon, Pennsylvania. When opened, the larger box gave way to smaller boxes, yielding one for each hiker that, when opened, contained an individual supply of pretzels. Stevens also maintained that Rosalie's Army had had "absolutely no unpleasant experiences with people in spite of the contrary reports."

The perceived difference between the accounts of the women (and men) participating in the march and the war correspondents following them proved an enduring theme on the hikers' first night in Wilmington. The Army of the Hudson wanted to downplay the resistance it met along the route, preferring a sunnier, more positive narrative of human nature and its capacity to embrace change. The journalists, on the other hand, attempted to see past this façade to the roiling ideological undercurrents underneath. Lately, for example, the war correspondents had described the hikers' bleeding feet and broken shoes, while the marchers themselves, including marcher-journalist Constance Leupp, countered that many of the press reports had been exaggerated.[54] Indeed, a case in point may have been the *Brooklyn Daily Eagle*'s recounting of the alleged secret engagement between Trolsen and hiker Helen Bergmark. Twenty-four hours after Trolsen reportedly revealed his intentions to Jones, Bergmark was denying knowing the young man in question. "Whoever started such a report is cruel. It's a hoax," she insisted during the army's Wilmington stayover.[55]

In Washington, D.C., Leupp had likewise hoped to correct the record on a number of facts, starting with the notion that the march had merely become a joyless slog for social justice. Leupp told the *Washington Times* that she was "having the time of her life" on the journey despite its physical and emotional demands. In fact, Leupp had told the newspaper that the unbearable hardships described in the newspaper accounts were mostly "suffered only by the correspondents."[56]

Now, as the hour grew late at the Hotel du Pont, Dr. Ernest Stevens attempted to convince skeptical journalists of these same, sunnier accounts, and before they retired to their respective hotel rooms, they had achieved something of a truce on matters of the truth—one they hoped would last until morning.

9

Marching on Maryland

If New York City had served as a launch pad, and Princeton and Philadelphia a test of mettle, Wilmington had served to underscore the disparate personalities within Rosalie's Army.

As the pilgrims mustered the following morning to begin their long march to Elkton, Maryland, everyone seemed to have an opinion on the day and a half the marchers had spent in Wilmington. For the most part, the army's time there had been a triumph. Indeed, inspired by their visit, John S. Hamilton had been moved to pen "Hike On, Hike On," a poem sent to the *Morning News* that read in part:

> Here's welcome to you, suffragists;
> Here's speed to all who hike.
> The town is yours, you have the key
> You own this side the pike.
>
> Go on! Go on! Let scoffers sneer
> And hoodwinked remain blind
> Tis yours to claim the right of peer
> Yours the freedom of the mind.[1]

Others were sufficiently enamored with the On-to-Washington army that they wished for bigger and better, a view expressed by the editors at the *News*, who maintained that Delaware's military generals should have turned out to meet the suffrage general, lamenting, "We cannot understand the lack of gallantry on the part of Delaware general and colonels."[2] Others, however, resented the inroads made by the women's rights crusaders in Delaware. In a letter addressed to the editor of the *Washington Post*, a writer identifying himself only as "J.M." characterized the British suffragettes as a band of women involved in "lawless anarchism" that made them a "menace to ... civilization."[3] Rosalie's Army, contended J.M., amounted to "another instance of misspent energy and enthusiasm." Addressing the women of the cause, the letter-writer insisted: "We lean for our justice among men, upon the lawyers, the judges, who sit in their offices and hold the reins of government. If you wish to gain a vantage point that will dedicate you to the highest service of humanity, do not join the noisy, the ineffectual proletariat, but emulate such as these." J.M.'s letter smacked of classism if not elitism, but in a roundabout way he had made the point of the suffragettes as well as they might have made it themselves: Women had indeed leaned on men's jurisprudence for millennia, and that dependency had deprived them of a voice in their own government.

J.M.'s letter acknowledged the rising power of the suffragettes to influence public opinion, and recent events on the ground corroborated that influence. In the army's wake, the women of New Jersey and Pennsylvania had taken direct action to better their circumstance. In Harrisburg, the women of Pennsylvania had stormed the capitol building to advocate for votes-for-women, and the judiciary committee had relented, agreeing to give a public hearing to the resolution in March.[4] In Trenton, 1,500 women led by Dr. Anna Shaw, president of NAWSA, crowded the New Jersey statehouse galleries to attend a hearing by the judiciary committee on a proposed suffrage amendment to the state constitution. Called a "suffrage army" in a nod to Jones and her troops, the "army of 1000 women" was reported to have "invaded the statehouse," causing New Jersey Governor and President-elect Woodrow Wilson to lament, "I am surrounded," and engendering the headline, "Gov. Wilson Hides from Army of Suffragettes."[5] Crowds made up of suffragettes and Antis grew so large and vociferous that the president-elect reportedly "stole away" to offices on the top floor of the statehouse to avoid them.[6] Suffrage protests made news in Australia, too, where a single determined woman stood up in a citizen's association meeting to say that the passage of votes-for-women in England should be a greater priority to Australian men and women than Home Rule.[7]

Others in the press attempted to squelch the rising enthusiasm for the cause with quips and jibes. The editors at the *Philadelphia Inquirer* printed a sardonic item that read:

"Why don't you stay at home and mend your husband's socks?" asked an eighty-year-old cynic of the feminine gender of General Rosalie Jones's band of ground-burners. Apparently there is no one more opposed to woman suffrage than a woman who doesn't want it.[8]

Meanwhile, the *Dover Index* dared to raise the race question. Put simply, if suffrage was truly the cause of all humanity, as Klatschken had claimed in Wilmington, then the movement must address African American women. The *Index* began its editorial by announcing its support for the movement overall before clarifying that the paper would prefer "qualified suffrage."[9] "Partisanship aside," the editorialists conceded, "we should dislike to see about 10,000 negro women added to our voters. At the same time, we should like to see the intelligent women of the state accorded every privilege and right that the men enjoy."

In Wilmington, Rosalie's Army could avoid the race question no longer.

While the incident had not been widely reported, the *Pittsburgh Post-Gazette* had filed a story detailing "threats of bodily harm and mental anguish" made to Jones in particular.[10] The newspaper described two businessmen from Baltimore who called on the general early on the morning of the army's first full day in Wilmington to ask her where she stood on the question of "votes for negro women." Their understanding, the businessmen said, was that Jones backed suffrage for all women, even Black women south of the Mason-Dixon line. The men strongly suggested Jones clarify her position against universal suffrage and "set the public straight" on the matter. "If you declare that you would give the vote to colored women," one of the men predicted, Rosalie's Army would be "mobbed" when it reached Baltimore.

In the past, Jones had followed the company line of the national suffrage associations on the question of enfranchisement for women of color—falling back on the constitutional right of the states to decide for themselves. But as the hopes and fears of enfranchisement began to crystalize coincident with her march, Jones's evasions were becoming problematic. In Wilmington she had equivocated badly, saying that she was "not prepared to enter into details on this question." Jones understood intuitively that NAWSA leadership would tolerate little in the way of negative publicity that might risk the success of the Washington, D.C., suffrage procession ahead. In January, Paul had written to *Woman's Journal* editor Alice Blackwell, remarking, "As far as I can see we must have a white procession, or a negro procession or no procession at all."[11] Like Ida Craft, Paul worried that the sight of African American women marching for the vote alongside their white counterparts would turn Southern women away from the greater cause of enfranchisement.

· · ·

The march was once more afoot. To be moving again—away from shady businessmen, prying reporters, and angry Antis—came as a relief, and more so given the warm-spirited send-off the city of Wilmington had arranged for the pilgrims. The army's morale had improved dramatically as that morning's march to Elkton, Maryland, got underway shortly after 9 a.m. with Mayor Howell, at the front of a column of 29 policemen, escorting the army to the outskirts of his city.[12]

"Unity, Peace, and Concord Is Restored," trumpeted a page-one headline from the *Democrat and Chronicle* in Rochester, New York, adding "race discussion and militantism left behind by suffragists."[13] "There is an unmistakable air of jauntiness about the army today," Emilie Doetsch wrote as she marched. "Refreshed and reinvigorated by the day's rest in Wilmington; Baltimore and Washington seem just around the corner."[14] Minerva Crowell showed perhaps the most dramatic improvement, as the hiker described as "one of the pluckiest of all the pilgrims" had received a massage for her aching muscles. Crowell now appeared "to be able to walk to the bitter end without the least trouble." Even Lausanne, the bargain horse purchased for 60 dollars that pulled Freeman's votes-for-women wagon, had been examined by a veterinarian and declared fit for further service after receiving an afternoon rub in the stables.[15] General Jones, Doetsch declared, looked "fresh as a rose" after the extra day in Wilmington. Her famously battered army cap had been brushed clean, her pilgrim cloak had been mended.[16] Indeed, the platoon appeared rejuvenated even to Jones, who could be overheard saying, "The army really looks civilized again." The little general with the weight of the suffrage world on her shoulders and a big message for Woodrow Wilson from the NAWSA executive committee in her luggage seemed more at ease. When asked about her plan to deliver the message to the president-elect if, as expected, he refused to see the marchers, Jones replied, "No matter. If he refuses before the inauguration we shall see him the first thing afterward."[17]

Wilmington turned out in force to say a proper goodbye. Clerks and saleswomen emptied out of shops on Market Street to watch the hikers as they waved farewell.[18] Hundreds of young women who worked in the downtown department stores lined the curb to cheer Rosalie's Army onward. On Maryland Avenue, near the city limits, the Betts Machine Company shut down its operations so its employees could witness history in the making. In Doetsch's view, Wilmington had been an oasis to the hikers, a place with a "kind-hearted mayor" and "hospitable citizens."[19] It is a place, she wrote, "where swollen feet can be reduced and blisters made to disappear."

And yet in a little-covered story, the *Washington Post* reported the delivery of several suspicious packages by young men, labeled "handle with care."[20] This in itself was not unusual, as the army relied on general delivery mail for much-anticipated care packages and letters from home. However, instead of notes from loved ones or provisions for the trail, Jones had found two black sticks labeled dynamite. A small tag attached to each said, "use judiciously." On further examination, the sticks turned out to be carbon, but the initial effect had been chilling. Had the package been a tribute to the explosive power of Rosalie's Army to blow up opposition to votes-for-women, a veiled reference to the recent bombings in London, or an implied threat of bodily harm? From New York arrived another large envelope addressed to Jones bearing a picture of a skull and crossbones. The note inside turned out to be a protest letter from an organization calling itself the Association of Husbands. Husbands, the letter warned, were growing tired of the army's insolent "cross-country running."[21]

The pressure for the suffragettes to embrace quiet domesticity proved intense. In Wilmington they had made a concerted effort to darn their own socks to counter rumors that they did not know how to mend their own clothes. At the same time that Rosalie's Army was accused of being overly masculine, it found itself deluged with product samples from across the nation. Tellingly, the products sent for consideration—cold creams, soaps, warm and comfortable socks—were stereotypically feminine; more practical items such as marching boots or knickerbockers were rarely if ever sent for potential endorsement.

Even the progressive press often printed stories that nudged women closer to gender orthodoxies. Two months earlier, as Rosalie's Army marched on Poughkeepsie, New York, an article had appeared in the national newspapers whose headline read, "Wellesleyites Welcome Stork."[22] Apparently, the alumnae of the renowned Massachusetts women's college had produced more babies since its inception than rival Holyoke, as if baby-making and baby-birthing were contests won by volume. Wellesley women, the news reporters glowed, were especially fertile; the school's approximately 1,500 alums had produced more than 4,000 babies among them. Newspaper editors across middle America often included such stories on the same page as their suffrage coverage in an attempt to assuage traditional women readers as well as to offer ironic comment on progressive agendas.

The suffragettes' respect for children as thinking beings rather than products of mere procreation made political sense. With luminaries like Jane Addams predicting American women would have the vote en masse in less than two years, the suffragists sought to court youth sympathies that might help sway conservative parents. Others more sanguine than Addams had examined individual states' laws and projected that the hoped-for constitutional amendment might yet be five or six years away.[23] In any case, the young adults Rosalie's Army encountered on its historic march might well be difference-makers in future votes. With the grand procession parade in Washington, D.C., now little more than 10 days away, suffragists in that city had successfully lobbied the Board of Education for a district-wide school dismissal so that children and their teachers might participate.[24]

South of Wilmington in Newark, Delaware, men again attempted to undermine Jones's equal rights message in a sleepy little town where, observed the *New York Post*, locals "thought suffrage was a joke and the pilgrims a scream."[25] Shortly after the army's arrival, a group of young men bent on mischief released mice into its ranks, and at least a few of the reporters covering the march appeared gleeful at the resulting "stampede."[26] Belittling headlines such as the *Post*'s "Mice Scatter Army: Small Boys' Tricks Make Hikers Stampede and Faint" suggested more amusement on the part of journalists than righteous indignation.

Boys and young men playing pranks had been a constant theme in the march thus far, and Newark, Delaware, proved no different. As the army neared town, Phoebe Hawn, the "army belle" who had been forcibly kidnapped by a group of young men at the academy in Lawrenceville, New Jersey, worried that the college students in Newark would attempt a similar heist. Hawn tied a large towel around her head so that she would not be recognized. The attempt at improvised disguise failed, though it turned out not to matter, as student leaders presented Jones with a formal resolution declaring that they had no intention of kidnapping Hawn or any other member of the women's army.

The pressure on the youngest and most conventionally attractive of the suffragettes proved intense. At all-male colleges, universities, and military academies boys would often either attempt to kidnap Mary Boldt or Phoebe Hawn, or loudly call for them until they were forced to appear. Meanwhile, older marchers felt compelled to convince a dubious press of their femininity. After marching 20 or more miles per day in wintry conditions, the women hikers were nevertheless expected to attend dances, balls, and galas, where they would be criticized if they did not dance or wear evening gowns. The night before in Wilmington, a dance in honor of the hikers had been given by the Pattern Makers of America, with the *Baltimore Sun* remarking that "at least half of the army attended—and danced."[27] The sexist preoccupation with youthful good looks extended to the Antis as well, who had publicly announced their intentions to give "the prettiest girls" in their movement complete run of their new national headquarters in Washington, D.C.[28] At least two beauty competitions would be staged to determine the right candidates in the lead-up to the national suffrage parade scheduled for March 3.

If the marchers stopped to confront the pranksters, as they had the snowball-throwing boys of Leiperville, Pennsylvania, many in the media would portray them as humorless matrons or killjoys. The suffragist strategy, therefore, had mostly been to turn a collective cheek to adolescent mischief, though it wounded the pride to be pelted with ice, grazed by fireworks, or frightened by mice. For her part, Jones merely sighed at the vermin, muttering to a war correspondent walking nearby, "I'd like to be the mother of those imps for just one day."[29]

Anti-suffragist parents also used children as weapons in the war against enfranchisement. The majority of the women thru-hikers in Rosalie's Army were young and childless—a demographic status resented by many Antis who believed suffrage to be anti-family. The idea that selfish suffragettes were somehow neglecting their womanly duties to marry, settle down, and raise families proved a persistent if not pernicious myth. Instead, many Antis found fault in the suffragettes' choice to pursue education, cause, and career. Two days earlier, Dr. Frederick Stykes of the Teachers College of New York had made national news with his claim that women's colleges failed by preparing students for careers at the expense of domestic duties.[30] Stykes had recently accepted the presidency of the yet-to-be-built Connecticut College of Women, a college bankrolled by the philanthropic giving of steamship tycoon Morton F. Plant. Stykes himself claimed to be a suffragist, and yet the *New York Tribune*, reporting on his most recent speech, suggested that the professor's comments "appeared to indicate that babies and homemaking will be star subjects in the curriculum of the projected Connecticut College for Women."

Newark, Delaware, may have been a sleepy college town, but it was a town where suffrage sentiments were on the rise, as the marchers found themselves greeted by signs reading, "For president, General Jones," "Let Women Vote," "Jonesy, You're All Right," and "Votes for Women; Kisses for Boys."[31] A week earlier the president of Delaware College had been reluctant to invite Rosalie's Army to speak on campus because he feared he could not trust his cadets to behave,[32] but after a group of faculty and staff traveled to Wilmington the night before to hear the army's speeches at the Garrick Theatre, at least some of them had returned converted. A vote had been taken as to whether or not the college's cadets should be allowed to meet the women warriors, and the answer had been "no" on the first ballot until one of the converts made a speech and changed minds. Less than 24 hours later, the college had offered Rosalie's Army a military escort through town. One hundred and seventy-five uniformed cadets skipped class so that they might present arms.

Marching south out of Newark after a brief lunch at the Deer Park Inn, the suffragettes reached their first profoundly rural landscape of the journey, so rural, in fact, that many of the citified war correspondents preferred to take alternate routes, leaving "cloaked and hooded pilgrims … on the open road without escort or observers." "With gypsy Freeman and her yellow cart in the center and a moderate-sized following of boys, the party gave a very plausible imitation of a medieval band of wanderers," noted the *New York Post*. Pigs wandered freely across the road before the pilgrims, and a "fresh-faced young German girl" with a "very small, very fuzzy donkey" joined the ranks of the hikers with a pledge to march all the way to Washington. Her name was Margaret Geist, and she had been in America exactly four months.

By the time the army had reached the bridge outside of the village of Elkton, anticipation for Maryland had turned into outright revelry. One of the boy hikers blew his harmonica, and sexagenarian day-hiker G.H. Lehman danced an Irish jig in her hiking boots, as "something the boy played touched a vibration in her memory." The music in turn stirred the muse of Dr. Stevens, who composed extemporaneous verse as the army approached the Maryland border:

> The Suffragette is at the door
> Maryland, My Maryland.
> On foot she hikes to Baltimore,
> Maryland, My Maryland
> Come, join the Hudson's Hiking Throng
> Stalking with Rosalie Along
> And chant the dauntless Suffrage Song,
> Maryland, my Maryland.

When the state line was reached just outside Elkton, Jones bent down and grabbed a ceremonial handful of dirt to offer benediction: "Maryland soil, we bless thee in the name of equal suffrage. May our journey be pleasant and our cause prosper within your borders."[33]

The pilgrims followed Jones's benediction with a makeshift ceremony of their own, drawing a line across the road that they would bend over and touch as they crossed the threshold into the final state on their journey. "It proved an ungraceful ceremony," writer-hiker Ethel Lloyd Patterson confided to her readers. "Most of us were too stiff to do the thing with charm. [Mary] Baird balked altogether. She feared if she leaned over she would not be able to rise again."

The general's prayers were in many ways apropos, as Maryland threatened to make or break the ultimate success of the On-to-Washington crusade. Supporters in Baltimore had been readying themselves for weeks for the arrival of the Army of the Hudson and would march from that city to reinforce it. Still, racial tensions threatened to undermine fragile unity. The *Baltimore Sun* issued an 11th-hour editorial speaking to the ambivalent reception Rosalie's Army appeared likely to receive, especially from the city's men. The editorial praised the suffragettes' plucky persistence and promised a city whose gates would be "wide open for them." It offered a benediction of sorts—"may no blizzard obstruct their path and no corns develop on their feet"[34]—while simultaneously sounding a lengthy cautionary note:

> To us poor, affrighted men, who feel dominion slipping from our grasp, and who fear the approach of the time when we shall be reduced to a condition of complete vassalage, it is a consolation to recur in thought to that period when ... man was woman's absolute overlord, and when she approached him with proper deference and respect.

The play *Kismet* by American-born British playwright Edward Knoblock, then being staged at the city's Academy of Music, had occasioned the newspaper's nostalgic comments about a drama "no self-respecting suffragette could see ... without indignation, and no downtrodden husband without a sigh of regret." The *Sun* added that the "deposed kings of the present can, however, derive a melancholy satisfaction from the portrayal of those halcyon days when the reign of man was undisputed, when the battle cries of no hiking suffragettes disturbed."

By the time the marchers neared the outskirts of Elkton, Maryland, after the day's 21-mile hike, Baltimore waited just 60 miles away. Washington, D.C., where battle lines were already sharply drawn, lay little more than 100 miles distant. In the anxious national capital, suffragists and Antis, whose national headquarters stood within a block of one another, had hired guards for protection.[35] With the recent opening of the Antis' national headquarters, tensions between the competing organizations had reached "a boiling point."[36]

Jones had intimated the marchers' uneasiness about the campaign in Maryland only the day before while speaking to the press in anticipation of notching the army's first state south of the Mason-Dixon line. The general relayed that her lieutenant on the ground in Baltimore, Mrs. Charles Keller, had written to say that they were "awake at night in Baltimore" waiting for the army's coming. "General Washington and his army were liked and always welcomed in Maryland," Jones told the war correspondents. "Though I would hesitate to compare myself to Washington, or this army to that of the Revolution: yet both armies marched and fought in the name of freedom and equal rights."

It was after dark by the time the main marching column reached Elkton at 7 p.m. a badly scattered band rather than a well-disciplined army. "The pilgrimage has become a sort of free-for-all," Patterson remarked. "Each woman is so absorbed in her own weariness that she plods ahead at her own gait, unmindful of the others."[37] The young reporter enjoined her readers back in the relative comfort of the nation's capital to put themselves in the weary suffragettes' shoes as they approached Elkton:

> Imagine us drawing near.... First we see a light somewhere ahead of us between the trees. It is star; no thank God, it is a street lamp. Courage now, another half mile and we can sit down for a while. Blessed thought.
>
> On down the center of the road, then, splash into a puddle. Who cares? It would take three more weary steps to walk around it. On then, keep on. There is a little clump of citizens watching for the pilgrims to arrive, though it is past dinner time and usually nothing could drag them out of doors then. Are they going to laugh because you are so stiff you can scarcely move? Deep down inside, you almost pray they will not. It is barely possible you would cry if they did. That would be bad. Not a pilgrim has cried yet.
>
> This must be Main Street, or is it that one? Funny, how your head gets queer when your feet do. Ah, there is a big crowd. That must be the hotel. Brace up; hold your chin up; bite your lips; wink hard; don't you dare let the tears come in your eyes....
>
> Now for a room. What is that? The rooms are short, so you have to sleep with some of the other pilgrims? Well, no matter. Is there a bath? One bath on each floor with no hot water. The last you remember is a ... hopeless, distorted-looking caricature of yourself gazing back at you from a looking glass.

"It was a very tired 'General' Jones indeed who climbed gallantly into the seat of the scout car ... and made a little speech to the crowds that had been waiting for an hour," observed the *New York Post*. The long day's hike to Elkton had delivered many surprises, not the least of which was a marriage proposal sent by postcard to Jones that read: "Stick it out and I'll meet you in Washington and the happy event will take place on the Capitol steps. I'll be famous, too, by that time, and we'll take to the vaudeville stage after the ceremony."[38] As heartfelt as the marriage proposal may have been, the weary general preferred the comforts of her own bed that evening to all the fame and notoriety vaudeville might bring.

• • •

Maryland continued to dominate the conversation around the breakfast table the following morning in Elkton. "Hogs and Hominy Put New Life in Hikers," declared Emilie Doetsch's cheeky headline in the *Baltimore News*, adding, "Maryland corn pone, Maryland country sausage, hog and hominy and Maryland hospitality gave the hikers the necessary moral and spiritual support to press on to Havre de Grace today."[39]

After marching with the pilgrims from New York City, Doetsch had finally returned to her home state. A city girl from Baltimore, she couldn't resist asking Jones, over a breakfast of sausage and buckwheat pancakes, what the suffrage general thought of Maryland. "I think it's the most friendly state we have been in so far," the general told her. "In other places people have come out to see us and have been very kind, but I have always felt their kindness was due in great measure to the fact that they were curious. In Maryland all seem to think they must be hospitable because we are strangers within their gates."

Maryland's roads, meanwhile, were considerably less welcoming and had a reputation up and down the Eastern Seaboard for their impassability. In January, well before the march had begun, the *Morning News* in Wilmington, quoting the *Baltimore American*, opined at great length about the very quagmire that now stood between Rosalie's Army and Washington:

> In a statement given out at Quakertown [Philadelphia] General Jones declares she expects little trouble, except, possibly at Elkton, Maryland. Why trouble at Elkton.... Very likely General Jones has in mind the stretch of mud pike that begins somewhere north of Elkton and constitutes a slough of despond for automobiles and hikers. Let us hope that there will be a benevolent freeze up about the time the hike strikes this bit of Maryland bad road.[40]

Deluged by heavy overnight rains, this "slough of despond" had only worsened. "No one denies the Maryland mud is the deepest and the most adhesive,"[41] the *Baltimore Sun* remarked, while the *New York Times* officially declared the stretch of road from Elkton to Havre de Grace to be the "worst stretch … between Boston and Atlanta."[42] The *Washington Herald*, citing the opinion of locals, declared them to be "roads that totally defy description" and "the worst roads in the United States."[43] The *Morning News* in Wilmington reported that county commissioners in Wilmco County, Maryland, had ordered 5,000 bushels of shells to be spread onto the roads. Farmers, desperate for better roads themselves, had volunteered to haul and spread the shells for free.[44]

By noon, when the suffragettes reached the town of North East, more than 45 minutes separated Minerva Crowell and Mary Boldt from General Jones. "At no point was the mud less than three inches deep," the *Washington Herald* reported, "and often it surged over the shoe tops of the suffragettes."[45] So awful were the roads that Boldt had opted to walk the nearby train tracks, and Colonel Craft and Dr. Stevens had been forced to rest at a mudhole where they worried aloud that they might not reach Havre de Grace until midnight if their sluggish pace continued. Even the baggage car driven by Alphonse Major had temporarily bogged down.

By the time the Army of the Hudson reached Havre de Grace, the full extent of the hardship became clear. Headlines in the *Morning Herald* in Uniontown, Pennsylvania, declared, "Suffragette Army near extinction" from the extreme hardships of the day's march.[46] "Another mile and General Rosalie Jones's suffragette army would have been no more," read the story delivered by special telegram and datelined Havre de Grace. Craft had collapsed in six inches of seeping mud at a place called Hog Wallow, a mile east of Charlestown, Maryland, and had to be carried to a farmhouse to be consulted by a physician. A generation younger than Craft, but likewise plagued by poor feet, Crowell had collapsed on the road outside Perryville.[47] By all accounts the day's march had been the most difficult since the army left New York.[48] The equal rights marchers had "plunged and floundered all the way from Elkton" and arrived in Havre de Grace utterly exhausted. In an attempt to detour around the quicksand-like soil, some marchers had opted for the grassy pastures alongside the road, hoping to find firmer footing there, only to become lost in the "mazes of farm roads and forests."[49] The headlines in that day's *New Castle News* told a dire tale of "women ... crazed by pain" and predicted that "General Jones may not finish [the] trip."

Craft's grim predictions of a late arrival in Havre de Grace proved true, as it was 9 p.m. by the time she arrived, separated from the rest of the army, bathed in mud and nearly frozen, having declared that she would make it to Washington if it killed her.[50] Craft had limped into camp in a "sadly bedraggled condition."[51] Observers noted that the march into Maryland was the least orderly of any stage of the journey and that the day's hike had devolved into a survival of the fittest of every-woman-for-herself. At least one of the marchers who had joined in Pennsylvania was alleged to have "turned traitor," agreeing to a one-mile lift in a car. Newspapers buzzed with the salacious rumors that others in the party had sneaked rides on the lonely roads, though most such reports were declared "canards."[52]

Critics of the march seized on the army's difficulties in Maryland as an instance of I-told-you-so, demonstrating the inevitable humbling of ambitious women. Typifying the down-in-the-mouth reportage was the front-page coverage in the *Akron Beacon Journal*, which declared that the once-proud march was "assuming the aspects of a tragedy" and a "pitiless, terrible struggle of women, almost frenzied by pain and suffering, who have grown almost fanatical in their consuming ambition to reach Washington on foot."[53] Referring obliquely to Craft, who in her early 50s was the eldest thru-hiker, the newspaper warned that some of the women might "suffer fatally" and that it would be a "suicide to proceed farther." The *New Castle News* reported that the Army of the Hudson was "near collapse"[54] and likewise suggested that if Craft continued the march it might prove fatal. The diminutive Corporal Klatschken, who weighed less than 100 pounds when the hike began, had also collapsed en route and been reduced to crawling on her hands and knees through the mud.[55]

Since entering Maryland, Craft had been a source of inspiration and concern for reporter Ethel Lloyd Patterson. "Ask yourself whether you would have the courage to do what she is doing," the reporter demanded of readers who wondered if coverage of the second-in-command's chutzpah wasn't a bit exaggerated. "Would you dare walk five miles of a strange country road at night far behind your companions, when you had already walked sixteen miles earlier in the day? Let the person who cares to make light of it try it before he laughs."[56] On the road to Elkton the younger marchers had fared scarcely better. Elizabeth Aldrich was said to be in an "almost hysterical condition." Phoebe Hawn marched on badly blistered feet, and her mental health appeared to be faltering. She was reported to have "retired early and forlorn," only to be woken up with a nightmare that caused her to scream "Votes for women!" repeatedly from her hotel room around midnight.[57] Even Minerva Crowell, the Smith College graduate known for her persistence in the face of injury, now neared the end of her endurance.[58] Helen Bergmark, the "pretty Philadelphia girl" who had told the press only the day before that she had no intentions of marrying suitor Roy Trolsen, had been "hardly able to leave her bed" that morning.

Newspapers reported with morbid fascination the declining condition of General Jones in particular. Dark rings encircled her eyes. The *Akron Beacon Journal* observed that she had lost at least five pounds from her already delicate frame. "The hikers are generally concerned over the condition of 'General' Jones," reported the *Press and Sun-Bulletin*, adding that "her face appeared drawn."[59] The *Baltimore Sun* headlined its coverage of the mud-slowed day with its sobering math: "16½ Miles in 13 Hours."[60] On their best days the suffragettes had easily managed a walking speed of three to four miles an hour, but now, ankle-deep in Maryland mud, they could barely muster one. Meanwhile, the *New Castle News* reported renewed fear that Jones might collapse. "The way this delicate little woman has withstood the terrible grind has been marvelous," the news service wrote, "but it seems that only her wonderful willpower and determination have carried her through, while other women with stronger constitutions have broken down."[61] Jones had begun to shake, the organization reported, "as if with palsy," and had seemed to "reach the end of her marvelous endurance."

Despite her fatigue Jones and the bulk of her platoon nevertheless managed to march across the Susquehanna River into Havre de Grace by dusk and into a reception both "whole-souled and inspiring" given by the city's mayor and townspeople.[62] Half of the small city turned out to welcome the On-to-Washington hikers, and many stayed to listen to the general's impromptu comments at City Hall. "I know nothing of Maryland today, but mud," she told them. "I see and feel nothing but mud; I hear nothing but the suction-pump action of shoes being withdrawn from mud. I expect to dream tonight that I am a mud turtle and have to waddle to Washington." Once again, Jones was received by a sympathetic mayor who was nevertheless not wholly convinced by her cause. "I am already a halfway suffragette," he told Jones. "I think women should vote on school questions and on taxation. They should be given the ballot to protect their homes and their children. I have gone so far but not further."

The day's many trials would surely have proven unbearable for anyone without a pilgrim's faith. The six miles between Elkton and the town of North East had been covered in two hours and twenty minutes by younger hikers, such as Hawn and Boldt, and in four hours by slower hikers, such as Craft and Klatschken. The baggage car driven by Alphonse Major had become stuck in the mud on two occasions and caught fire three times until finally Major had no choice but to empty the pilgrims' baggage onto the roadside near Principio, Maryland, so the car could be towed.[63] The scout car driven by Olive Schultz had likewise bogged down near the small town of Charlestown and also required towing. Meanwhile, Elisabeth Freeman had been forced to temporarily abandon the suffrage wagon in the mud. To make matters worse, upon arriving in Havre de Grace, the suffragettes were met by the chief of police, who informed them that pickpockets had infiltrated the army. Recently, several items had disappeared en route,[64] and now at least some of the marchers would have to do without their luggage altogether.[65]

The cause was not lost, however. Jones made a short soapbox speech at city hall, and Freeman rallied enthusiasts at a street meeting in Fountain Square. Along the way there had been history aplenty as the marchers followed the old New York to Washington, D.C., stagecoach route. The hikers had passed Beacon Hill between Elkton and Charlestown, the place where signal fires had been lit during the American Revolution to warn George Washington that British troops lay in wait for him at Elkton, and had come very near Cooch's Bridge, where the American flag had first flown in battle.[66]

One good revolution, the On-to-Washington army felt as a difficult day ended in Havre de Grace, surely deserved another.

10

Militancy and Mud-slinging

"Tell my Brooklyn friends and sister suffragettes that I have absolutely no intention of giving up," Ida Craft told her hometown war correspondent from the *Brooklyn Daily Eagle*.[1] On the way to their next stop in Bel Air, Maryland, the undersized colonel with the heart of a lion had once again fallen hours behind. Physicians had repeatedly advised Craft to quit the march, and yet she refused. Instead, Jones had assigned the lone Scout who had marched the length of the journey, 17-year-old Brooklyn Boy Scout magazine editor Norman Sper, to walk alongside her as an attendant.

"No amount of persuasion can get me to quit. I am doing this for a noble, worthy cause and there are other women besides myself who are not only willing, but happy, to make sacrifices for womankind," the colonel told the press. Craft's rhetoric tended toward the grandiose, but on yet another 18-mile march through rain and mud, her assessment of the situation now struck many of the war correspondents as clear-eyed. "True," she confessed, "I am suffering … but nevertheless I am determined to walk every foot of the way to Washington, even if I have to crawl on hands and knees." After a moment's pause she added, "I don't mean to pose as a martyr—I am only doing a duty—a duty to my fellow woman who is disenfranchised."

What to do about the rapidly declining condition of its second-in-command had become a major preoccupation of Rosalie's Army. Since entering Maryland, Craft had begun leaving up to two hours earlier than the rest of the troops in an attempt to make up for her painstaking pace, but by late morning the main column typically passed her. Jones had offered to slow the march to accommodate, and Hawn, Crowell, and several of the younger hikers had volunteered to stay behind with the colonel, but all had been rebuffed. Craft insisted she would walk alone if necessary and wanted no special treatment.

Earlier that day on the march to Bel Air, Maryland, the obstacles confronting Jones had continued to mount. The roads led through Dogtown and Howling Run, place names that hinted at a bare-bones existence. The rain had continued to fall in torrents, turning the pocked roads leading to Bel Air into small lakes. From Washington, D.C., had come a special weather bulletin advising local weather bureaus to hoist storm warnings for torrential rain and high winds from the Delaware breakwaters to Eastport, Maryland.[2] In Chicago, the trailing edge of the same massive storm system had punished the Windy City for over 20 hours, causing more than a million dollars in damage.

On the warmer, southern side of the front, temperatures in central Maryland had topped the 50-degree mark, and the extreme rain and wind had rendered conditions virtually unbearable for at least two of the hikers, Loretta Williams and Virginia Patschke. Citing deteriorating weather conditions, both deserters quit the march in order to ride ahead to Baltimore.[3] Beyond the worsening weather, bad roads, and dangerously poor condition of Craft, Jones was forced to confront the growing estrangement of Elizabeth Aldrich, the Quaker pacifist who had been brought to tears of anger in Wilmington over her clash with Freeman over the question of militancy. In Baltimore, the next major stop on the march, newspapers enthusiastically reported the growing rift, with the *Sun* insisting, "The only real martyr among the pilgrims to Washington is a suffragist on whom the muzzle of silence has been placed."[4] Aldrich had been a rising star prior to her confrontation with Freeman in Wilmington and had been called on with increasing frequency to deliver soapbox speeches. But Aldrich's last such speech had come days earlier in Wilmington, prior to her confrontation with Freeman, whom the press now referred to as her "antithesis." While Freeman celebrated violence in the streets of London, Aldrich insisted she would not break a single pane of glass for the cause. While Freeman habitually confronted her mostly male audiences with difficult truths, Aldrich befriended rather than antagonized, empathizing with male fears while nevertheless advocating passionately for her sex. Aldrich insisted that American women did not approve of the campaign of destruction and property damage mounted by British suffragettes like Freeman.

"The American women want the ballot to bring happiness, best living conditions, clean cities, and better government," Aldrich said, advocating a philosophy very much in line with municipal housekeeping. "She must prove her purpose to the men before they think her sincere. Every violent word and deed puts just that many more women and men against us. This especially applies to Southern women." The *Sun* largely agreed with Aldrich's moderate stance, praising her as a woman who "subordinates all for the good of the cause and [is] a prince among pilgrims."

Now Aldrich herself was threatening to quit the march over the alleged vow of silence to which she had been sentenced. Her human failing, as the war correspondents had come to understand it, was her longing for public speaking.[5] Since joining Rosalie's Army she had yearned to stand at the lectern and "sway the great American populace with her ringing voice." Aldrich had been trained as an actress, and yet Freeman, from the march's beginning, had been the official orator. Aldrich, perhaps looking for a graceful way out of a personal and ideological conflict with a sister suffragette, was now intimating that she had developed a case of tonsillitis and would need to quit.

When Jones visited Aldrich in her room, the war correspondents pressed their ears to the keyhole as the two talked privately for half an hour before emerging to deliver the good news that Aldrich had agreed to continue to Baltimore. However, Aldrich's warning of the dangers of militant suffrage in the South proved prophetic. Baltimore was restive, and church leaders and parishioners there had sent word ahead to Jones that they would not tolerate the marching of a woman's army into their city on a Sunday. The army's position on enfranchisement was seen as inconsistent with Catholic doctrine, and nowhere more so than in Baltimore with its numerous churches and its powerful and influential cardinal. While church leaders drew red lines on the idea of a Sunday arrival, friends of the army in the city on the Chesapeake Bay insisted their heroines would receive a royal welcome and would be properly feted by civic and suffrage organizations with a full slate of luncheons and dinners.[6] Jones found herself in a logistical quandary. If she marched on the city on its sabbath day there were sure to be repercussions. If she slowed her pace and overnighted in Overlea on the outskirts of Baltimore as originally planned, the march would lose an extra day in a city in which they stood to gain valuable new recruits for the final push into the District of Columbia.

"Sunday is an excellent day for propaganda work," Jones told the *Baltimore News*, defending her choice of arrival day.[7] The general pointed out that more people would be in the streets on Sunday, allowing the activist army to reach the masses with its message, as had been the case with their Sunday arrival in Philadelphia. Jones conceded, "We have marched on Sundays, but we have also observed the Biblical injunction of resting every seventh day." Indeed, a Sunday arrival in Baltimore would allow the marchers an extra day of richly deserved rest of the sort they had benefited from in Wilmington, where Jones had been somewhat cavalier in comments made to reporter Emilie Doetsch about the city's Antis. "They are very estimable people, the Baltimore Antis, but different from us. Constitutionally different, I mean," Jones had said. "You know the Antis are much braver than we are. They are working for a lost cause and that makes it a lot more difficult."[8]

As Rosalie's Army battled rain-swollen roads on the way to Bel Air, Cristobel Pankhurst, daughter of Emmeline Pankhurst, declared outright war in England. She called on the women of England to rise in civil war "just as the people of Mexico did" in the Mexican Civil War.[9] Pankhurst had lately expressed public delight at the bombing of chancellor Lloyd George's country home outside London. "Look at Mexico," she declared to reporters. "Never let it be written in history that the blowing up of a house with dynamite was the worst crime committed by the people of England. Let the Englishwoman take a message from Mexico." According to reports from the *London Standard*, the latest plan of the militant suffragettes aligned with the Pankhursts was to kidnap the cabinet minister as part of a larger coup d'état.[10] Pankhurst herself had appeared at the Chelsea Town Hall under the auspices of the Women's Social and Political Union to declare responsibility for the bombing of Lloyd George's home, the news of which was received with a mixture of hissing, groans, jeering, and cheering in an environment where only a large police presence had prevented hostile parties in the audience from attacking her. In London, forces loyal to the Pankhursts were reported to have destroyed thousands of letters and packages with acid. Postmen in that country had effectively been deputized and given the power to investigate and make arrests, though thus far the offending militants had proven elusive.

The Mexican Civil War that Pankhurst had conjured as a model of resistance had, days earlier, elicited the headlines "City of Corpses" and "Bodies Burned on Pyres," with the number of fatalities estimated at not less than 2,000.[11] Marines had been called up from nearby Annapolis, Maryland, to respond to the Mexican crisis that found General Victoriano Huerta installing himself as the new provisional president in a bloody coup.

Was the bloodbath in Mexico truly what the Pankhursts wanted? Officially, the British suffragettes had embraced any and all methods to win the vote short of willful loss of life. By contrast, the march of Rosalie's Army had been a peaceful, law-abiding enterprise thus far, though there was little arguing the revolutionary impact the marchers had on the states through which they passed. Behind them in Pennsylvania, equal rights now dominated the headlines. Two hundred women from that state would be joining the grand suffrage protest procession in Washington at the terminus of the army's march.[12] Mrs. Lawrence Lewis, the organizer of the Pennsylvania contingent, had hiked with the army from Philadelphia to Chester, Pennsylvania, and was now headed to Washington, D.C., to organize a banquet reception for the army on March 1. Meanwhile, in Chester, another of the cities where sentiments had been stirred by the army's street meetings, the president of the county branch of the Pennsylvania Association, Mrs. Arthur M. Comey, had denounced the On-to-Washington hike as a public relations stunt, calling it "dreadful" that women could be found to take part in "glaring displays of this kind."[13] In Philadelphia the debate between votes-for-women supporters and Antis had reached a fevered pitch. A man-versus-woman debate had been arranged in Witherspoon Hall between Philadelphia literary critic Francis Howard Williams and New York suffragette lawyer Inez Milholland. Williams was a well-known critic, author, and friend to several literary greats, including Walt Whitman and Louisa May Alcott. He was also young, sophisticated, and well-versed—the opposite in many ways of the boorish, bullying men the suffragists were more than happy to antagonize. Williams predicted that the enfranchisement of women would lead inexorably to the disintegration of marriage and family, while Milholland countered that none of the established suffrage organizations had called for the abolition of marriage. A deeply divided crowd had hissed at the anti-suffrage Williams, and tensions had quickly escalated.

As the army's information campaign brought new attention to the issue of equal rights, it also coincided with rising separatist sentiments around the country. In Illinois, suffragists commissioned man-less "suffrage special" trains to take them to the procession scheduled for the day before Wilson's inauguration. Women porters would replace male attendants on the suffrage special, and only one man, a shoe-shiner, would be allowed to be present, utilized only to "shine shoes and perform all the menial tasks necessary."[14] Meanwhile, the women of New York City had opened a votes-for-women suffragette grocery store advertising a full line of groceries and making a specialty of fresh eggs and butter. The store, it was reported, was handling "an unusually heavy trade" and had recently opened a delivery department to meet increased demand.[15]

The peace between the genders that Aldrich had called for, and that had led to the Quaker hiker's silencing, appeared to be little more than a distant pipedream as the army reached Bel Air on February 22, Washington's birthday. Both President Taft and President-elect Wilson had announced that they would not be attending the national protest parade planned for March 3. Taft had hinted at the potential need to call out a cavalry to protect the women protestors, though the president may well have needed his own additional security. Isaiah Clark of Denton, Maryland, declared on the street that Taft would be killed on Washington's birthday and that President-elect Wilson would die shortly after his inauguration on March 4.[16] Whether the prophesy qualified as a macabre premonition or an actionable threat against the nation's chief executives, the state's attorney had locked Clark up and initiated his commitment, citing derangement.

The intended recipient of the suffrage message carried by Rosalie's Army, Woodrow Wilson, would also not be attending the historic procession in Washington.[17] His arrival had been strategically scheduled for just after the hour when the March 3 national suffrage procession would conclude. Both Vice President-elect Thomas R. Marshall and his wife, Lois, had publicly declared that they did not consider themselves suffragists.[18] Of the incoming and outgoing vice presidents, presidents, and their wives, only Helen Taft had formally accepted an invitation to view the votes-for-women procession from a special VIP box set up in a grandstand opposite the south plaza and the steps of the U.S. Treasury Building.[19]

In New York, the suffragists' most cerebral speechmaker, NAWSA President Dr. Anna Howard Shaw, tackled the suffrage-and-family question head-on in a speech to the all-male student body of New York University. "People are always saying that there will be no one to take care of the children when the women

vote," she said, adding, "Why, there isn't a politician living who wouldn't be delighted to handle a baby carriage for anyone who might possibly vote for him."[20]
Still, the reality among the congressmen in Washington was not so simple, with
the *Washington Post* reporting that the majority of senators and representatives
were "showing signs of nervousness over the prospect of being caught between
two fires on the universal suffrage question."[21] At least two of the congressmen
had pledged to march in the suffrage parade, but many, caught between rival
lobbies, had opted to lay low or leave town, and there were new doubts that a
quorum could be achieved on the day of the procession through the capital.

In Washington, tensions peaked between the suffragist and anti-suffragist
headquarters, located just one block away from one another, as Antis accused
votes-for-women activists of complicity in the obstruction of mail delivery
and with the literal slinging of mud at their windows.[22] Alice Paul, chair of the
committee in charge of the procession, had thus far taken the high road in the
controversy between rival camps. "This is a woman's movement and we will not
attack any woman even with words," she had said, adding, "If the women opposed to suffrage choose to attack us, that is their business."[23] Other more visible signs of friction between the camps abounded. Muscle-bound body guards
posted at the doors of the respective headquarters had, as a consequence of
the literal mud-slinging campaign, recently stepped up security patrols. The
anti-suffrage headquarters buzzed with indignation over what they alleged
were the militant tactics of the suffragists down the street who, they claimed,
had hurled mud at their front wall and windows. The two warring parties had
lately engaged in a period of reconciliatory détente, however, with leaders of the
respective organizations agreeing to meet in the hopes of deescalating tensions.

Despite attempts at peacemaking, enmity existed on both sides of the fight.
With Washington's and Lincoln's birthday observances imminent, anti-suffrage
forces had sought to refute suffragist affiliations with both liberator-presidents,
especially Lincoln. Antis had searched the archives of the Library of Congress
for quotes showing Lincoln's opposition to, or at least neutrality in, the question of votes-for-women, and they had found at least one: an excerpt from his
Sangamon Address of June 13, 1836, delivered when the future president was
just 27 years old.[24] In it Lincoln wrote, "I go for all the sharing the privileges
of the government who assist in bearing its burdens. Consequently, I go for
admitting all whites to the rights of suffrage who pay taxes or bear arms." Antis,
led by the general secretary of the national anti-suffrage association, Minnie
Bronson, pointed out that suffragists too conveniently ignored the "white" and
"bear arms" caveats in Lincoln's speech. If votes-for-women advocates could
twist the rhetoric of one of the nation's most revered martyr-presidents, implied
Bronson, what other historical facts might they be manipulating to drum up
support for their cause?

Threatened by the prospect of a votes-for-women triumph in the March

3 parade, Bronson and her allies answered aggressively in the press, offering the "Antis' Arguments Against Suffrage" for publication in the *Washington Post*, a list that read in part:

- For the minority to force the ballot on a majority is injustice.
- Women's suffrage today means the Socialist party in power.
- Women have not begun to grasp their opportunities. Why give them the extra burden?
- The way women are pitching into suffrage means a hold-up of educational and philanthropic work all over the world. Some suffragists even pledge themselves to refuse to do good in other ways until suffrage is won.

In countering the better-publicized arguments of Rosalie's Army, Bronson and the Antis hoped to make a logical appeal to common-sense readers, and yet for many Antis such appeals to rationality fell short of fighting fire with fire. Increasingly, anti-suffragists received letters at their 1307 F. Street headquarters calling for an anti-suffrage parade full of dramatic displays satirizing the social agenda of the suffragettes.[25] One letter-writer called for a three-part display as follows: "First group, have the father carrying a flag, an ax, and a gun, the wife carrying a babe and a banner, 'John works and votes for me and the children.'" The second display would flip the traditional scenario, featuring the wife carrying the flag, ax, and gun while the father carried the baby and a nursing bottle, his placard reading, "Jane works and votes for me and the children." One letter-writer, Amos Reeves, from Rock Falls, Illinois, concluded his missive with this parting shot: "Excuse an old veteran who does not like to see women pulled down into the slums of politics."

Perhaps the most artful parody of the ambitions of the marching suffragettes came from an anonymous Shakespeare scholar who had posted an anti-suffrage parody of Hamlet's soliloquy on the front door of headquarters whose lines read:

> To vote or not to vote, that is the question. Whether 'tis nobler in the mind to suffer the slings and arrows of "man-made" laws, or to take the ballot and by opposing, end them. To vote, to reform, and by our reforms to end the strifes of government 'tis a consummation devoutly to be wished for. But to vote, to reform, to make men better than they wish to be, ay, there's the rub, for in those reforms the trouble we'd get into must give us pause and make us rather bear those ills we have than fly to others that we know not of.

• • •

A day that had begun with a brass band send-off by the good people of Havre de Grace, Maryland, and a breakfast of hotcakes and honey that had left Ida Craft "chipper as an English Sparrow" had ended with yet another change in itinerary.[26] In an attempt to mollify the protests of parishioners objecting to a Sunday march on Baltimore, General Jones had apparently returned to her original plan of overnighting in Overlea, Maryland, on Sunday night before plunging into Baltimore early on Monday.

When the army arrived in Bel Air, Maryland, later that afternoon they found to their delight that the town of scarcely over 1,000 had turned out in full patriotic fervor. It was Saturday, February 22, Washington's birthday, and Bel Air's proud citizens were in a flag-waving mood. The majority waved the stars and bars, but at least six women on the outskirts of town displayed white flags bearing the words "anti-suffragist," shouting after the marchers that they "ought to be ashamed of themselves."[27] Rosalie's Army was still 26 miles from Baltimore, but it could feel anti-suffragist sentiments rising. On Washington's birthday, the question of whether or not ardent support of women's rights could coexist with proper *amor patriae* had come to a head that day 60 miles south in Washington, D.C., where the grand marshal of the monster suffrage parade had objected to Alice Paul's plan to have the suffrage flag appear before the American flag in the March 3 parade. "No one with a spark of Americanism or patriotism would think of marching … if the American flag were slighted," Mrs. R.C. Burleson, an ardent suffragist, had said, providing further ammunition to those who believed the votes-for-women movement to be inherently anti-American.[28]

Helping to provide an antidote to anti-suffragist venom in Bel Air, a local Boy Scout troop known as the Owl Patrol proudly escorted the army into town while bearing the American flag. Suffering badly from bloodied feet, Craft, however, did not arrive until dusk when a driving rainstorm drenched the small city. The swelling in her feet prevented the colonel from so much as fastening her shoes. Jones had implored her second-in-command to give up the hike for her own health but to no avail. While Jones had marched that day with "a lively stride," others in the marching platoon took up the task with "no enthusiasm." Some walked with shoes unbuttoned or unlaced, while others, including Phoebe Hawn, walked completely barefoot. They marched, some observers said, like the living dead. As if to add to the macabre tenor of the procession, the army had marched past the Maryland farm of Lincoln assassin John Wilkes Booth.

As Craft and her companions rested ailing feet at the inn that night, the headlines of the day spoke to the larger battles for gender equity erupting all around them. In Chicago, former South Dakota governor Robert Vessey had predicted that the entire West would grant the vote to women within the space of a few years. "The women know as much about how to legislate for the good of humanity as the men do," Vessey told a gathering of church members, "and if given the vote would bring better conditions to schools, the prisons, and political life in general. Forty percent of the men in our penitentiaries are there by accident. I think if women had the ballot they would find a way of redeeming a large number of these and sending them back into society with a chance to become good and useful men."[29]

On the other side of the suffrage divide New York senator Elihu Root, Theodore Roosevelt's former secretary of state, made news with a lengthy speech explaining why, unlike his former boss, he would oppose enfranchisement:

> I have said that I thought suffrage would be a loss for women. I think so, because suffrage implies not merely the casting of the ballot, the gentle and peaceful fall of the snowflake, but suffrage, if it means anything, means entering upon the field of political life, and politics is modified war. In politics there is struggle, strife, contention, bitterness, heartbursting, excitement, agitation, every which is adverse to the character of women.[30]

One thing was certain: The marching suffragettes knew something about struggle, strife, and contention. And yet, to a woman, they felt their character growing rather than shrinking as they faced obstacles that would make many men tremble.

The women of Rosalie's Army were anything but snowflakes.

11

Rebels Reach Baltimore

"If General Jones doesn't come here in the morning and lead the army into the city.... I, as colonel and second-in-command, will lead the remainder of the army that is coming here in the morning," crowed Ida Craft to her hometown newspaper, the *Brooklyn Daily Eagle*.[1]

Craft's stern words referred to a split of the army into two camps, a main body that had marched with Jones into Baltimore Sunday evening and a "lost tribe,"[2] "lost vanguard," or "broken remnant"[3] led by Craft that had mistakenly—or so it was said—splintered form the main column and marched into the small city of Overlea, Maryland, five miles from Baltimore. Of all the headlines the march had generated to date, the lost tribe was perhaps the most sensational, for it implied a Judas-like betrayal of a leader by her closest and most trusted advisor. "A mutiny was hatched there [in Overlea]," the *Baltimore Sun* declared, "alleged to have been led by 'Colonel' Ida Craft."

The seeds of the so-called splinter group had been planted days in advance of Jones's indecision regarding whether or not to march into Baltimore on a Sunday and risk alienating religious conservatives, many of whom were already vehemently anti-suffrage, or to overnight in Overlea, with a Baltimore arrival to follow on Monday. In fact, the indecision could be traced all the way back to early January when Jones, in a candid interview with the *Washington Herald*, had worried aloud over the final leg of the journey. "We will limp into Washington March 1 if all goes well," she had told D.C. reporters. "I know we will literally limp in, too.... We are to cover the distance between here [Washington] and Baltimore in two days, and it's 40 miles."[4]

As of the previous night, the plan agreed to by Jones and her officers, the "war counsel" as they called themselves, had been to march to Overlea, though Jones, "exercising the eternal feminine prerogative,"[5] had changed her mind once again.[6] The general took a second vote at 1 p.m. as the Army of the Hudson reached Mount Vista, Maryland, and those present for the impromptu roadside straw poll had voted to march on to the Stafford Hotel in Baltimore to arrive later that very evening, Sunday, February 23. The message, however, had failed to reach those at the front of the marching column, including

Craft, who had recently been leaving one to two hours earlier than the rest of the marchers. Consequently, nearly half of the army had been left in the lurch.[7] Craft had stepped up to lead the lost tribe consisting of Dr. Ernest Stevens, Norman Sper—the Boy Scout magazine editor who had marched every step of the way from New York and was now charged with watching over the ailing Craft—Elisabeth Freeman, Mary Boldt, Mary Baird, and Margaret Geist, a recent recruit traveling with a donkey.

The *Daily Eagle* correspondent described Craft as "angry" at the change of plans that had caused "serious trouble in the ranks of the hikers." The colonel had always been in favor of marching both to Towson and Overlea, as originally planned, citing the disappointment in those communities if Rosalie's Army failed to make the promised appearance. Had Craft purposefully disobeyed Jones's order to march on Baltimore, gathering around her a series of followers in what amounted to a coup or a mutiny?[8] Had Jones made the sudden change en route to humble Boldt, who had been in the habit of arriving first to every town, thereby stealing some of the general's glory? The previous night, a majority of the army had voted to overnight in Overlea, where a gala reception had been planned in addition to a rendezvous with Baltimore activists who had traveled to Overlea to greet the army. Indeed, hundreds of Baltimoreans had taken the trolley to the village to greet the On-to-Washington marchers and to hear Craft deliver a rousing votes-for-women address despite her frail condition.[9] Another grueling day's march had left the colonel with "bleeding feet and profound exhaustion."[10]

From rival newspapers came conflicting accounts of the monumental mix-up. Wilmington's *Morning News* explained that there had been a roadside discussion among the hikers and that the decision had been made to advance on Baltimore given improving weather and road conditions.[11] Jones and the main army had thus arrived in Baltimore at 6 p.m. local time to a police escort and crowds estimated at 5,000 strong. A thousand gathered in the historic Mount Vernon Place alone, the park-like plaza opposite the hotel where stood the original Washington Monument, a 178-foot-and-8-inch Doric column made of white marble. Baltimore had turned out in force to commemorate the arrival of the equal rights army, though the raucous celebration, insisted the *Daily Eagle*, was "mild" compared with what it might have been had the platoon marched into the city at full strength.[12]

The arrival of the army at the monument one day after Washington's birthday made for significant symbolism, as only the day before government business in Washington, D.C., had reached a standstill to commemorate the 150th anniversary of General Washington's birthday.[13] Washington's farewell address had been read in full in both chambers of Congress. Speaking to the Sons of the American Revolution, Senator Theodore Burton of Ohio imagined Washington's politics as they might be in the present. Were he alive,

Washington would be a progressive, Burton declared, a man with an eye toward the future and an aversion to hasty or inconsiderate judgment. Would Washington, were he alive on his 150th birthday, be a votes-for-women advocate, too? Certainly, the suffragists celebrating Washington's and Lincoln's birthdays liked to think so. As strains of "America" and "The Star-Spangled Banner" played behind him, Burton asserted that Washington would be a man for reform. "This country needs to call back to its memory the thoughts and ideals of Washington not only on February 22," declared the congressman, "but every day of the year." His spirit, activists maintained, was alive and marching in the figure of General Rosalie Jones.

The following morning, Monday, February 24, Craft followed through on her pledge to lead her own lost tribe into Baltimore while adding a controversial new wrinkle—her detachment would circle back to visit the village of Towson, Maryland, which had also lost out on its chance to host Rosalie's Army as a result of Jones's 11th-hour change in route. Margaret Geist, the German immigrant who had recently joined the march driving a donkey named Jerry, led the march out of Overlea with the help of a Baltimore man named Henry Harvey, who had offered to help the lost tribe find its way.[14] With Harvey's help, clearing skies, and a firmer road, the lost tribe left Overlea for Baltimore to an ovation offered by 100 cheering supporters. The marchers were in especially high spirits, buoyed by animal companionship. In addition to Jerry the Democratic Donkey, Elizabeth Aldrich had adopted a yellow dog she dubbed "Lord Baltimore" and pledged to lead the animal into Washington as a mascot if it was willing. Aldrich and her new companion had been presented with a bouquet of flowers by two girls in the tiny village of Raspeburg, one of whom, six-year-old Julia Raspe, proudly counted herself as a member of the town's namesake family.

In Govans, Maryland, Craft and her followers were given a luncheon at the home of the president of the Baltimore Just Government League, Mrs. Donald Hooker, who, tellingly, had not gone to Baltimore to greet the contingent led by Jones.[15] The fact that Craft, rather than Jones, had met with someone as important as Hooker, the *Daily Eagle* maintained, presaged a "serious breach in the ranks of the local suffragettes and … is certain to cause no little ill-feeling in among the now divided army."[16] Post-luncheon, the leaders of the Baltimore movement appeared to side with Craft in the civil war, forming a committee that pledged to present the colonel with a gold medal for valor. The medal would be inscribed, "Presented by the suffragettes of Overlea to Miss Ida Craft for her courage and devotion to the cause."[17]

Adding to the troubling headlines of a breach in the army was a smaller story first reported when the army reached Bel Air, Maryland. Two of the Lebanon, Pennsylvania, hikers, Virginia Patschke and Loretta Williams, were said to have deserted in Bel Air. Indeed, the women had caught a train to Baltimore, they confessed, with the intention of rejoining the army there in time for its advance on Washington. "The report in the metropolitan newspapers that the Lebanon members of the party were seriously discontented, and had left the army to make the rest of the journey by train, occasioned much genuine apprehension," the Lebanon newspaper admitted, explaining that both women were now "recuperating" in Baltimore and intended to march into Washington.[18] Williams, the *New York Times* had learned, had been called back to New York by her husband after one of the Williams's twins had contracted the measles.[19]

Unlike Patshcke and Williams, Craft had endured the rugged road thus far in its entirety. Arriving in Baltimore nearly 24 hours after her commanding officer, she, too, won the "plaudits of the multitudes" that turned out to greet the lost tribe led by the badly limping colonel. Craft's hometown *Daily Eagle* reported that the tribe basked in an ovation that "outdid in every respect the welcome given General Jones."[20] Crowds turned out to see the second brigade in such impressive numbers that the police escort had difficulty finding the marchers in a sea of onlookers, as did the women of Goucher College, who turned out to march in solidarity with the cause.[21]

Jones, meanwhile, decamped in the hotel, sending troops individually and in small groups to street meetings and soapboxes. She sent hiker-war correspondent Constance Leupp ahead to meet with suffrage parade organizer Alice Paul in Washington, D.C., to finalize plans for the army's arrival there in just three days' time, though rumors of the army's disintegration followed Leupp on her mission. Responding to reporter queries in what amounted to an emphatic denial of the army's decline, Leupp maintained that recent days on the march had been "glorious" and that "everybody in the party" was "looking forward with great enthusiasm" to the army's imminent arrival in the capital.[22]

When finally Craft marched her splinter brigade into the lobby of the Stafford Hotel in Baltimore, she was willing to share with anyone who would listen the depths of her discontentment. "I don't think General Jones did right," she declared to a circle of reporters. "I don't believe in this rushing about the country. We are now engaged in going at a ... bicycle race speed, and I am frank to say that I don't like it. There must be consideration shown to both pilgrims and to those who offer us their hospitality. I will obey the reasonable commands of General Jones, but when General Jones wants to cut out all social functions, which I think are necessary to the cause, she is going too far. We cannot slight Southern hospitality. I am going on to Washington, and if General Jones cares to push on in this ... manner I will not. I started to Washington and I intend to get there."[23] Craft could be a stubborn, indignant, and self-righteous second-in-command, but always before she had been loyal; now for the first time, Jones risked outright insubordination.

The *Pittsburgh Post-Gazette* described the marchers as "torn by dissension, jealously, and incipient mutiny."[24] The insurgent camp led by the colonel had effectively split the ranks into two parties. Craft, fresh from commanding the lost tribe on its rogue journey, had asserted herself anew, announcing that she would be leading her own future suffrage marches in Pennsylvania, Maryland, and Ohio and that she would be doing so under her own command. In a break with the more tolerant Jones, Craft would bar any "pleasure-seeking girls bent on having a lark" from her future marches, insisting that the ranks be made up exclusively of suffragists with a mature commitment to the cause. She would not, she declared, tolerate a "circus affair."[25] Young women of the sort that had made the trip to Washington for what Craft considered superficial reasons—improved health or an improved figure—would be barred. Daily marches would be shortened to accommodate more seasoned hikers. "There is absolutely no sense in these twenty- and twenty-seven mile marchers," Craft insisted. The pilgrimage had opened [her] eyes to the foolishness of "forced heartrending hikes which tax your strength and leave you a weak and nervous wreck by nightfall." Many of the hikers, she avowed, had needlessly suffered. As a result she would limit a single day's hike to 10 miles when she took command of her own regiment.

Jones did not immediately emerge from her hotel room to greet Craft's lost detachment, waiting instead until the hubbub had died down to make a more cautious approach. As Craft vented to the war correspondents, Jones put a gentle hand on her second-in-command's shoulder and asked how she was feeling, only to be given a cold shoulder in return.[26] Over dinner later that evening, Elisabeth Freeman attempted to broker a truce between the long-time friends, an attempt that appeared to meet with modest success. Craft maintained that her actions intended no disrespect to the general, at whose side she had marched not just on the way to Washington but to Albany, New York, several months earlier.

Jones, meanwhile, sought to downplay growing rifts attributed to jealousy and in-fighting, saying she was delighted at the warm reception given the splinter army in the city. "Colonel Craft deserves more honors than could possibly be bestowed upon her," Jones told reporters.[27] "She is deserving of all the plaudits and glory that those who admire a brave woman can give. After what she has gone through, the sufferings, hardships, and privations she has endured, she cannot be honored enough; this is her day." To be fair, Jones's Sunday march to Baltimore had entailed its share of privations as well; at approximately 27 miles, the hike from Bel Air to Baltimore had been the longest stretch of the march to date.

Extreme fatigue and poor health had no doubt contributed to the dramatic fraying of the army. Several days into the historic march, Craft had been advised by physicians to quit the hike, and she had clearly endangered herself and the mission itself in her stubborn refusal to comply. In arguing for time-consuming visits to smaller cities such as Overlea, Rapseburg, and Towson, the colonel had given the impression of great magnanimity. Others perceived Craft's actions as self-interested grandstanding, implying that she had merely slowed the march's pace to a speed she could sustain in her compromised condition. For nearly a week, Craft's personal struggle to continue had been coopting what might have been more optimistic headlines. To date the army had averaged nearly 20 miles a day,[28] a feat of endurance for the youthful General Jones and a small miracle for the older colonel. To address the growing fatigue in the ranks, Jones had ordered longer marches with fewer social calls so that she and her troops could spend an extra day resting (and rallying) in major cities like Baltimore. She had pushed hard to make it to Baltimore a day ahead of schedule, in part to bolster her troops' failing health. Six of the members of Rosalie's Army had caught cold, and another, the *New York Post* reported, suffered from "a plain grouch."[29]

Craft had been bitterly disappointed at Jones's decision to skip Overlea and Towson, but she refused to be baited by the press into comments intimating outright rebellion. By the time the members of her lost tribe had settled into their respective rooms at the Stafford Hotel, Rosalie's Army had taken great pains to close the growing rift, at least in the pages of the *Baltimore News*, which offered cover for the breach in its subheadline of February 24: "Resent the Insinuation That they intended to Desert. Trusted a Man, Regret It of Course."[30]

The story of the army's split had now been revised in some of the more suffrage-friendly dailies to include an alternate account of the divorce. The *Baltimore News* reported that Craft had been given erroneous directions by a man that sent her down the Overlea and Bel Air road rather than down the Hamilton and Hartford road shortcut Jones had taken. Members of Craft's "delayed detachment" had reached a consensus opinion that they would "never again trust a man." The decision of the second army to march to Overlea was now being spun as an honest mistake; they were not insurgents threatening the command of their superior officer; there had been no intention to "overstep the authority of 'General' Jones." The day's new crop of revisionist accounts claimed that Jones was "not at all perturbed by the temporary break in the ranks" and would endeavor to keep the army marching in lock-step to avoid such confusion in the future.

While the revisionist accounts were accepted by many, some, including the editors of the *Philadelphia Record*, found the explanations less than plausible. "A big corn crop appears to be growing on the 'hike' to Washington," it observed, the analogy reminding readers that the suffragette spin on events should be taken with a grain of salt. The published schedule for the army's time in Baltimore likewise hinted at deeper disunity. On February 20, the *Bal-*

timore Sun published articles worrying over the pilgrims' inability to accept the surfeit of invitations given them in the city while preparing Baltimoreans for disappointment in noting: "So many invitations have come in, and the stay of the visitors will be so short that a selection of entertainments will be hard to make."[31] Now the guest list for the first scheduled event on Monday, February 24, an important luncheon with one of Baltimore's most important suffragists, Mrs. Donald Hooker, at her home in Govans on the far north side of Baltimore had been reduced to "all pilgrims able to be there"; Craft's lost tribe had met with Hooker en route to its belated advance on downtown Baltimore; Jones, already headquartered at the Stafford Hotel, had not.[32] Nor would Jones likely attend the mental health congress scheduled for later that evening, the likelihood of her attendance having been downgraded to "not certain." On Tuesday, February 25, a luncheon scheduled in honor of General Jones put on by the fraternal organization Sons of Jove was firmly fixed, but the published itinerary noted that, where the "many invitations to teas and luncheons" were concerned, "the army as a whole [would] accept none."

In laying out its counternarrative, the *Baltimore News* couldn't resist sharing the story of its own reporter, Emilie Doetsch, who, it revealed, had traveled to New York two days before the march began to obtain her pilgrim's hiking uniform and had "reported the story of the hike for this paper from the start."[33] She had, the newspaper proudly proclaimed, "marched the entire distance" to Baltimore. "Miss Doetsch," the paper proudly confessed in the concluding paragraph, "is an ardent advocate of woman suffrage."

As the army rested in Baltimore on Monday, February 24, it now stood little more than 30 miles from its ultimate goal, and preparations had begun in earnest for its triumphant arrival. Thanks to careful time management, the shortcut to Baltimore, and the hours saved by other strategic changes en route, Rosalie's Army would now arrive in the nation's capital on Friday, February 28, two days ahead of the originally scheduled March 2 arrival and a mere 16 days after leaving New York City.[34] A brass band, a column of marching suffragists numbering in the hundreds, and a company of women on horseback, a so-called "petticoat cavalry," would escort the On-to-Washington marchers into the District of Columbia with automobiles forming a guard of honor. Additionally, plans were being finalized for a banquet at which the members of Rosalie's Army would be guests of honor.[35]

The army's arrival in Baltimore occasioned a torrent of news regarding the upcoming votes-for-women procession in Washington. Now, even cynics and skeptics granted that the arrival of Rosalie's Army was inevitable. A picture of a smiling Jones and three other women, headlined "women who will play a prominent part in the suffrage parade March 3," appeared in the *Washington Herald* of February 23—a full five days in advance of the army's projected arrival and eight days before the grand procession.[36] Likewise, the

Oakland Tribune could now report with certainty that Jones and her army would play a "prominent role" in the historic parade of March 3, in anticipation of Jones "marching at the head of her hikers with the same martial stride that carried her through the 250-mile journey from New York."[37] The procession-cum-protest demonstration would be "impressive to the extreme of impressiveness" with "enough novelties to furnish talk in suffrage circles for many moons to come." Ten thousand strong would march, according to organizer Alice Paul, led by Inez Milholland, the official trumpeter and herald, on horseback dressed in white classical robes, followed by a mounted women's brigade and countless floats attended by loyal foot soldiers spread over seven divisions of marchers. The mere thought of Rosalie's Army on the triumphant final leg of its march led the *Washington Post* to publish a kind of Homeric ode to the troops. Penned by feminist poet Mary Nimmo Balentine, its first stanza read:

> Sing, sing, sing, the girls are coming.
> Let the land rejoice as they pass
> To the sunshine girls, the day,
> As they tread the common way,
> On a mission that will elevate each class.[38]

As tempting as it may have been to think ahead to Washington, Baltimore now demanded the full attention of Rosalie's Army. To Craft's frustration, Jones had scaled back on many of the army's social engagements in the city, arguing that the troops needed rest. But there were still street meetings to be conducted, speeches to give, and banquets thrown by loyal supporters to attend. As always, the hikers hoped to convert citizens to the votes-for-women cause and gain fresh recruits for the final leg to Washington and the great suffrage procession awaiting them there. But with the number of public appearances being steadily reduced to allow time for recuperation, the question of just how to undertake the necessary public relations campaign in Baltimore and Washington, D.C., eluded Rosalie's Army. In interviews with war correspondents, Jones had confided her disappointment that the army had not held as many street meetings, nor given as many soapbox speeches, as they would have liked since crossing into the state. The distances needing to be covered each day had made such meetings nearly impossible, and thus public outreach had suffered where it was needed most.

Many in Baltimore and Washington had heard of General Jones and Colonel Craft, but far fewer understood the personalities of the less prominent thru-hikers. For the casual observer, the pilgrims, beyond Jones and Craft, were a collective better known for their shared cause than for their individual personalities. Hiker-war correspondent Ethel Lloyd Patterson believed her readers in Washington, D.C., and beyond must become better acquainted with the lesser-known soldiers if Rosalie's Army hoped to win new converts. Capturing the questions of many about the marching suffragettes, she asked:

> What kind of woman would undertake a suffrage pilgrimage? Have you ever asked yourself that? Have you wondered, as you read of the women on their way to Washington, a distance of 259 miles by marching route, who these individuals are when they are not pilgrims...; are they workers, do they earn their own livelihood?...When the pilgrimage is over to what sort of life do they return?[39]

Patterson hoped to satisfy her readers' innate curiosity in writing a "Who's Who in Ranks" that purported to offer a "glimpse of suffrage soldiers in private lives." She began her series of short profiles of lesser-known marchers with "Corporal" Martha Klatschken:

> Certainly she places the advancement of the cause before her own wellbeing. She has worked all her life. She has earned every mouthful of bread she has eaten. She had had to dig her education as a stenographer from the none too generous economic soil as a miner digs for his gold. From her labor she has saved enough money to support herself for one year.... She proposes to give that year to suffrage work. At the end of that time she goes back to her stenography. A peculiarly single-minded, beautiful, and unrewarded sacrifice, that of Martha Klatschken....
>
> Miss Elizabeth Aldrich is a worker. Miss Aldrich supports herself and her mother. She has been on the stage for some years but more recently she has been writing. She has written a novel and a play, which she hopes soon to see produced. Miss Aldrich is interested in suffrage on broad and rather sentimental grounds. Being a worker herself, and having always had to work, she has an overflowing sympathy for other women placed in a similar position. She believes the ballot to be the lever that will raise labor conditions for women to a higher plane....
>
> Miss [Minerva] Crowell is a Smith College graduate. She lives at home with her mother.... She is a quiet, rather fine-looking girl of perhaps twenty-eight years, given rather more to doing things than to talking about them. She does not make friends very quickly, but the people who learn to know and love her never lose their affection for her.
>
> Miss Phoebe Hawn is not more than twenty years of age. She is very pretty. This has been deadly to the hearts of those youths who live in that part of Brooklyn which Phoebe graces with her presence. Consequently, Miss Phoebe is a bit of a queen in her own way, and has at times a bit of the royal manner with her own and other people's vassals. But she is a very sweet and wholesome girl for all that, and some day she will leave her father, who is an instructor in a school of dramatic expression, and go to the home of some particular vassal to bring his home particular joy all the rest of his days.
>
> Miss Constance Leupp is a sturdy young woman, who some years ago graduated from Bryn Mawr. At present she divides her time between the Consumers' League and literary effort.
>
> Mrs. [Mary] Boldt is a young married woman. Her husband is a broker and she eloped with him when she was sixteen. A calm of three years ensued. Now she has eloped with the suffrage pilgrims.
>
> Miss [Emilie] Doetsch is a tall classic goddess who writes for newspapers. She lives at home with her mother and some sisters who are each prettier than the other and the whole lot just as pretty as she is....

Mrs. [Catherine] Wend is a middle-aged woman who has good modern ideals. She has brought up her son [Milton] to revere women and to walk in equal suffrage parades with them. A combination that is hard to beat. Mrs. Wend has money of her own....

So—there's most of the army for you. Divest them of their pilgrims' capes and that which I have written is what you have.

Shoulder to shoulder, after their two-day rest in Baltimore, they set forth on the last lap of their walk to Washington.

• • •

The Sunday of Jones's arrival in Baltimore, Archbishop Owen Corrigan stood at the pulpit at St. Gregory's Catholic Church on Gilmore Street and addressed his flock on the dangers of militant suffrage, which, he claimed, would result in "lowering womanhood."[40] Quoting the Lenten pastoral of Cardinal Bourne in Westminster, England, Corrigan reminded his parishioners that, from a perspective of the church, they were free to choose either for or against women's suffrage but not without all due caution. "It is one of the duties belonging to our pastoral office to warn our flocks against ... possible moral faults which may easily be committed in the pursuit of an object in itself legitimate," Corrigan opined in recitation of Bourne's letter. "We refer especially to those acts of violence to persons and property which have disgraced this movement and which are manifestly contrary to justice and charity."

In citing a cardinal virtue (justice) and a heavenly grace (charity), Bourne, channeling Corrigan, suggested that militant suffrage should be considered sinful. While Rosalie's Army believed itself to be marching for social justice, many in the church believed that its military stylings and nom de guerres paid at least ostensible homage to violent votes-for-women activists in Britain. Here Corrigan deviated from Cardinal Bourne's letter and addressed his church members directly. "We are glad, indeed, that this country has not yet witnessed such scenes as have disgraced England, and yet such spectacles as this so-called 'hike' now at our doors are by no means edifying. Long ago Christian manhood elevated womanhood and place it on a high pedestal; woman will remain there until she takes herself down."

Did the women of Rosalie's Army wish to be removed from the pedestal on which they had been placed? In refusing car rides and other chivalric forms of help offered by men, in mustering an independent army led by a woman general with woman officers attempting to do by and for themselves, the army certainly seemed to reject such veneration. Indeed, could a woman remove herself from a pedestal society had placed her on, and, if so, how should she enact such a removal? The English militants had chosen "unwomanly" acts of violence, terror, anarchy—in short the revolutionary tactics of men—to unshackle themselves from repressive societal expectations, while the Army of the Hudson had attempted similar ends through soapbox speeches and street meetings coupled with demonstrations of physical endurance in adverse hiking conditions.

Tuesday morning in Baltimore offered Jones a chance to publicly comment on the militancy. The day's headlines from London, where suffragette Emmeline Pankhurst had been arrested for "incitement to commit damage" in conjunction with the bombing of the country residence of Chancellor David Lloyd George, had brought the question to a head.[41] When a gathering of suffrage faithful in London heard news of Pankhurst's arrest, they were reported to have cheered at their leader's act of civil disobedience. Under the Malicious Damage Act, Pankhurst's crime carried a maximum sentence of 14 years in a prison work camp, though few expected her to receive even a fraction of that time. Meanwhile, the president of the local government board in London had declared an all-out war against the suffragettes, calling the militant side of the movement a "tyranny of organized blackguardism" before adding, "It is in the interest of the people and democracy that this despotism that has desecrated the cause of women and put back their movement many years, be terminated at once."

Bishop Corrigan's cautionary note certainly didn't help the cause in Baltimore, though it wasn't Corrigan with whom Jones had been for several days seeking audience but Cardinal Gibbons, leader of the city's powerful archdiocese and Bishop Corrigan's superior. And yet for her declaration in the press days earlier of her intention to see the prelate, Jones had not yet succeeded in securing an audience with him. Instead, she left the Stafford Hotel on Tuesday morning stating only that she would at least like to march by his palace.[42] When the marchers reached the cardinal's residence on Mulberry Street, Jones declared she could not resist and led her troops, journalists and photographers in tow, to Gibbons's home, where with some consternation the entourage was ushered into the red room to wait. Several minutes later Gibbons entered and invited the pilgrims to be seated.[43]

The rail-thin cardinal struck an imposing figure. White-haired and solemn, he sat alone in his crimson robes and biretta cap. Gibbons, the first chancellor of the Catholic University of America and head of the oldest archdiocese in the country, was now nearly 80. He had served as the city's archbishop for more than 35 years, a tenure during which time he frequently called upon Presidents Cleveland, Roosevelt, and Taft, the latter of whom had honored the cardinal for his contributions at the golden jubilee celebration of Gibbons's ordination.[44] An advocate for workers' rights, Gibbons had likewise been lauded by Roosevelt as the most venerated, respected, and useful citizen in America.

General Jones presented Gibbons with a small votes-for-women flag of the kind the Army of the Hudson had distributed to onlookers throughout their journey. "We have come to call on you, Cardinal," she announced, "to present you with this flag and hope you will join us in our fight for women's rights."[45]

"This does not necessarily involve a conversation to your cause?"

"Not at all," Jones replied. "It is merely that we women marching through your city want to pay our respects to one of the great heads of the church."

"This is quite an honor, ladies, I assure you. I admire your persistence and hope the legislature's hearts will be soft and not as hard as the earth you have tread over nor the stones you have stumbled over in your long journey."

Gibbons's comments translated the army's pilgrim journey into a metaphor with expressly religious overtones—hard earth underfoot on a pilgrim journey toward epiphany—but the prelate stopped short of endorsing their cause as just. Instead, he asked a series of questions. Was the army fatigued? How was it organized? How were the feet of the famous pilgrims holding up under the rigors of march? Who was the army's "Secretary of War?" Given Bishop Corrigan's recent comments on violent suffrage in Britain, the army might reasonably have interpreted the cardinal's query as an attempt to single out Freeman for her support of militancy. In the prelate's presence, Freeman modified the hard line of some of her recent soapbox speeches, emphasizing instead the religious qualities of the march. The penitents of the church, Freeman told the archbishop, had for centuries made pilgrimage for the causes they loved; the suffrage pilgrims were kindred spirits to those faithful marchers.

Calling the marchers modern Joans of Arc, Gibbons nevertheless refused when asked by war correspondents to expressly condone their cause. Still, the army left for its next stop at the Baltimore mayor's office relieved that they had been able to barnstorm an audience with him. Once again, however, they discovered yet another mayor absent when called upon, finding instead the mayor's proxy, John Hubert, who had agreed to serve as acting mayor for the day. Like Cardinal Gibbons, Hubert was careful not to be seen as endorsing the cause of the marchers, though he did offer a letter of introduction for the army to be given to the mayor at their next stop: Laurel, Maryland.

After their brief ceremonial stop at city hall, where once again Jones pinned local dignitaries with miniature suffrage flags, the army marched to its pre-arranged luncheon with the Sons of Jove, a fraternal organization with national membership rolls numbering in the thousands. The luncheon itself was not unique—the On-to-Washington marchers had accepted many such invitations offered by the well-networked fraternal organizations that served as influencers and connectors within their respective communities. If the members of such male-only social societies could be converted, the theory went, other prominent men in society might be convinced of the merits of equal rights for women.

In charge of organizing the gathering, Freeman opted for a gala-like atmosphere. She had arranged in advance for the issuance of special badges showing the suffrage colors mingled with the colors of the fraternal order. Members of the Sons of Jove would escort individual members of the army according to a list supplied by Freeman, which included not just the regulars—Jones, Craft, Aldrich, Hawn, Crowell, Klatschken, and Boldt—but also more recent recruits like Virginia Patschke and Helen Bergmark, hiker and mule-driver Margaret Geist, and Jones's Baltimore "lieutenant" Mrs. Charles J. Keller. Two women war correspondents who had marched with the pilgrims, Emilie Doetsch and Constance Leupp, also attended.

Increasingly, who marched with the army mattered greatly, as supporters and sycophants sought to associate themselves with the crusaders. The *Baltimore News* ran a half-page spread under the banner headline, "Baltimore Suffragists Who Will Accompany Hikers to Capital," featuring "Lieutenant Mrs. Charles J. Keller" and "Mrs. Donald R. Hooker," among seven others, listed not by their own names but by the names of their Baltimore husbands, who were both prominent physicians. In fact, in the many times that Keller's name had appeared in local newspapers in the army's advance on Baltimore, it appeared only as "Mrs. Charles J. Keller."

The formal list given the press in advance of the Sons of Jove luncheon illustrated an important difference among the hikers, at least in the eyes of the public. While the unmarried General Jones and Colonel Craft could obscure their marital status behind their respective nom de guerres, Miss Elizabeth Aldrich, Miss Phoebe Hawn, Miss Emilie Doetsch, and Miss Elisabeth Freeman, for example, could not. The "Miss" versus "Mrs." controversy came to a head that very day, in fact, with Freeman speaking out about what she perceived to be yet another sexist slight. "I am not Miss Freeman," the hikers' official speech-maker told the press, "I am plain Elisabeth Freeman. If I get married I shall be Elisabeth Freeman to the end of the chapter. Why should I have to announce my name by answering such a strictly private matter as to whether I am married or not."[46] Craft embraced her quasi-military title and would "hold on to 'Colonel' until it had been raised to 'General.'" Miss Margaret Geist, meanwhile, was content, she said, to become a "Mrs." only upon marriage.

The pilgrims' public comments on the matter had been prompted in part by the previous day's page-one story in the *Baltimore Sun*, headlined "'Mrs.' Title for All Women," which relayed the case of Chicago suffragist Belle Squire, who, while unmarried, had assumed the title "Mrs." and advocated all women do likewise, whether married or not. Squire was a member of that city's "No Vote No Tax League," a group that endorsed the militant tactics of the British suffragettes.[47] "'Miss' Belle Squire of Chicago has become 'Mrs.' with less trouble than most women—no minister, no wedding, and no trousseau," led the story in the *New York Times*. As part of her plan to remake her identity on her own terms, Squire had begun with the radical act of changing "Miss" to "Mrs." on her personal calling cards.[48]

"I do not like Miss Squire's plan of calling herself 'Mrs.' She should just be plain Belle Squire," Freeman said, commenting on the day's headlines.[49] By contrast, marcher Phoebe Hawn demurred on the question, asserting that the battle over suffrage itself was the bigger battle to fight. Hawn's stance closely aligned with the company line at suffrage headquarters in New York City, where the women were reported to have groaned when the same question was posed them, viewing it as a distraction from more pressing issues in a world hampered by "so much real trouble."[50]

After two weeks on the march, the Army of the Hudson had become opinion leaders on many pressing gender equity questions, spawning imitation and homage not just across the United States but around the world. On the day of Jones's ballyhooed Sunday arrival in Baltimore, the *San Francisco Call* trumpeted the headline, "Austrian Feminist 'Hikers'…Cue Taken from Rosalie Jones." Datelined Vienna, Austria, the special cable to the *Call* told the story of a group of "300 charming young women of good families" organizing a march to Budapest "in the interest of the feminist movement."[51] Sixteen young women between the ages of 17 and 25 had already enlisted in the Austrian version of Rosalie's Army. Meanwhile, the Army of the Hudson had apparently inspired a single man to make his own cross-country, General Jones–styled hike. "A pedestrian who as a 'hiker' has greater pretensions than Rosalie Jones's footsore suffragettes," reported the *Lock Haven Express*, had overnighted in that Pennsylvania city on a 5,000-mile hike from Elmira, New York, to San Francisco.[52] S.F. Albee's stated goal was to reach the Golden Gate Bridge by the following August, though already he had lost two weeks recovering from a twisted ankle suffered on one of the earliest legs of his journey. Like Jones, Albee impressed with his poise and confidence, causing the *Express* to conclude that "he has none of the characteristics of the average 'bug' or 'crank' and appears to be sincere in his undertaking."

Americans were on the move and on to march, as writer Elbert Hubbard noted in his *Hearst's Magazine* tribute to the suffrage pilgrims. The heroics of the Army of the Hudson would be talked about for "many moons to come," Hubbard claimed. "Anything that gets us out in the storm, out on the open road, and makes us bigger than the elements, is good," he wrote of the army and its mission, adding, "Life is a fight—a fight against inertia, against the love of ease, against 'well enough.' And these suffragettes are certainly doing the world good in their invitation to 'fall in, everybody!' Not only will we fall in line and hike with them for a few miles, but we will, in sympathy, fall in love with their cause."[53]

• • •

In the past, reporters had pressed Jones for specifics on her feelings on militant suffrage. Mostly she left the pontificating to Freeman and others while choosing to focus instead on the exigencies of the march. By the time Jones reached Baltimore, however, the general could no longer avoid the militancy question.

"We hope, and you can put the 'hope' in capitals, that women in the United States will never have to break a window," Jones told reporters.[54] "We hikers are assured of one thing. We will have the coming generation with us. At every schoolhouse we have passed since leaving New York the pupils have left their seats and turned out to welcome us." Unusually expansive in her comments, Jones continued, "We are having a bloodless revolution in this country. Slowly but surely women are getting into the fight…. We pilgrims are shedding blood…. Their shoes, after the mud the other day, were hard enough yesterday to tear their feet. When they arrived they reported to me that blood had at last been spilled for the cause. And I think this will be about all the bloodshed this nation will see. At least, I hope so."

As Rosalie's Army prepared to leave Baltimore, the terminus of its long march—the great suffrage procession in Washington—drew into sharper focus. Plans for the parade-to-end-all-parades seemed only to grow grander and, in some cases, more novel. Margaret Gast, the national champion endurance bicycle racer, had recently announced that she would attempt to ride her bicycle from New York to Washington, D.C., and had reached out to the Army of the Hudson for a field report on the navigability, or lack thereof, of the infamous Maryland mud roads. Gast had once covered 2,000 miles in 222 hours on her bicycle, leaving her plenty of time to make it to the nation's capital, assuming passable roads. She promised to carry a votes-for-women banner on her handlebars in honor of Rosalie's Army.

From points south came avowals of just how heartily Rosalie's Army would be received by the grateful activists awaiting its arrival in the northern D.C. suburbs. At least 200 suffragists would meet the platoon in Hyattsville, Maryland, accompanied by a brass band playing "stirring strains of martial and religious music,"[55] including "Onward Christian Soldiers" and "The Star-Spangled Banner."[56] Automobiles would parade in honor of the Army of the Hudson. Headed by "Colonel" Genevieve Wimsatt, a detachment of horsewomen would accompany the marchers on their triumphal entry to the city.[57] A nearly continuous line of escort would be formed that would take the pilgrims down Pennsylvania Avenue to the Treasury Building, where they would be officially welcomed by Alice Paul before marching to the national suffrage headquarters on F. Street.[58] A rostrum would be erected from which Craft, Freeman, Jones, and others would address eager Washingtonians. In sum, the pilgrims would be feted like "conquering heroes" on a march to "final victory."[59] Lucy Burns of Brooklyn, second in command behind Paul of the March 3 national suffrage parade, vowed that the celebration would be sufficient to "make the tired pilgrims forget their long days of hardship." Jones and her troops would be the guests of honor at a banquet dinner attended by NAWSA President Dr. Anna Howard Shaw.

For all the excitement awaiting the pilgrims in Washington, behind them the marching suffragettes had left a trail of agitation. Already their visit to Cardinal Gibbons in Baltimore was being cast by the faithful as a public affront. Instead of kneeling before the archbishop, Jones had reportedly reached to shake Gibbons's hand, a break with tradition that had the city's Catholics crying foul. "No one told us what we should do," Jones explained of the gaffe, "and of course we could not know. I would have been only too glad to kneel and kiss his hand, as I have great reverence for the venerable prelate. As soon as I heard of the frightful manner in which we had failed to observe the proper forms I wrote to Cardinal Gibbons assuring him that no disrespect was meant. As he is a man of broad mind, I feel sure that he will understand."[60] Complicating matters had been the behavior of the pilgrims' orator-in-chief, Elisabeth Freeman, who had later that same day dared to smoke a cigarette in front of the 150 male members of the Jovian Order.

Maryland had galvanized opinions on the march, not just because of the pilgrims' controversial encounter with Cardinal Gibbons in Baltimore but because the suffragettes had thus far refused to call unequivocally for universal suffrage for African American women. Some editorial writers, including those at the *Lock Haven Express*, scolded Jones for her equivocation on the race question. "If the ballot is a 'right belonging to every human being,' as General Jones claims it is," wrote one such editorialist, "how could she sanction the denial of it to colored women. Aren't they human beings?"[61]

Others, including Elmer Halle, writing for the *Jeffersonian* in Towson, Maryland, drew a cynical message from the public relations successes of the On-to-Washington hike, observing:

> Whatever may be said derogatory of "General" Jones and her "army," they have learned the fine art of advertising. Who in the broad land has not by this point heard the name of "General" Rosalie Jones and her army of suffragettes? If mere man were engaged in battle of this sort he would have to spend thousands of dollars to get his cause before the public. But not so with "General" Rosalie Jones. She musters a little army of 13 and goes on a hike. "War Correspondents" follow in her wake and every move she makes is heralded by the press far and wide.[62]

But Maryland had offered just as many blessings to the troops, including many sincere conversions recorded in the towns through which the suffragettes had passed. While some registered indignation at what they considered the suffragettes' boorish behavior, others, including George Garey of the *Cecil Star* in Maryland, had had their minds changed in favor of votes-for-women. Garey, who had traveled to North East, Maryland, to see the marchers in person, concluded, "This hike is just an incident in a movement that is founded on right and is winning its way by reason. The ennobling influence of women is just as much needed in civic affairs as it is in the home circle, and, like charity, it should not be kept at home. A good mother can be as good a citizen as a good father. Perhaps a better one."[63]

The question of a mother's duties had once again come to a head in the march, this time with a headline from the United Press syndicate titled "Measles Halt Mother." For at least the second time on the On-to-Washington march, a serious illness suffered by a child back home had left one of the marching mothers in a public relations quandary. This time it was Mrs. Loretta Williams of Lebanon, Pennsylvania, leaving the march to take care of her ailing children back home, and her defection had put the general in a public relations bind from which there was no easy exit. "Never shall it be said that we suffragists are callous to the call of home," Jones declared to the press in the wake of Williams's leaving, though she also confessed that the defection of yet another mother in the march would "not be lost on the enemies of our cause."[64] That very same day, Dr. Shaw had taken to the op-ed pages of the *Washington Post* to clarify the movement's view on domestic duties. "We are forever being told that the place for women is in the home…. But what do we expect of her in the home?" Shaw asked the *Post*'s readers.[65] "Merely to stay in the home is not enough. She is a failure unless she attends to health and welfare, moral as well as physical, of her family, and especially of her children. She, more than anyone else, is responsible for what they become."

As the march passed its two-week anniversary the question of whether the mothers on the march had been derelict in their domestic duties continued to vex. Some working women encountered by the army on its hike to Washington marveled at the freedom of such well-to-do women to leave husbands and domestic responsibilities behind for weeks of sisterhood and activism. To them, the luxury of a two-week march seemed as unattainable as the right to vote itself. Were such women existential cowards for not joining up, as some of the marching suffragettes had implied in recent comments to the press, or legitimately hampered by real-life exigencies the marchers were privileged enough to overlook?

Who marched, and who didn't, persisted as an issue with which Jones and her band of followers would have to reckon. Baltimore had proved every bit as much of an enigma as predicted. While there had been enthusiastic crowds and full slates of street meetings, the city itself had not embraced the cause with a passion equal to the other metropolises through which Rosalie's Army had passed. That much could be readily discerned by the relatively small handful of local supporters that accompanied the marchers on their departure from the Oriole City.

Elisabeth Freeman pulled no punches in stating her reaction to the lukewarm sentiments of the Baltimore suffragists. "They're merely seeking cheap advertisement," Freeman said of local activists who talked a good game but who had been unwilling to go the distance, "and are not even willing to pay for it with a little footwork.... The Baltimore women are so busy fighting around with their various societies that they haven't time for the hike."[66] Jones, too, confided her disappointment to the war correspondent from the *New York Times*[67] as she led the pilgrims out of the city, determined to look forward rather than behind, with her eyes, like those of any good general, fixed on a distant horizon.

12

Marching to Their
Own Drummer

Upon leaving Baltimore the morning of Wednesday, February 26, Rosalie's Army faced a daunting 22-mile hike to Laurel, Maryland, and growing rumors that a small group of African American women in a Maryland enclave called Buzzards Glory would bring the race question to a boil in what the *Washington Herald* now drummed up as "an incipient race war."[1]

The women in question had reportedly pledged to hike with the Army of the Hudson the rest of the way to Washington to publicize the need for truly universal suffrage. Meanwhile, some local whites had threatened to take matters into their own hands if Jones allowed the black women to join the march.[2] Jones neither endorsed nor refused the idea, her comments stopping short of inviting the women on the march while intimating that she would not prevent them from joining if they insisted. Craft promised that she would shut the march down if the African American marchers were allowed to join because she and others suspected the Antis of hiring them as counteragents to sow disunion in the ranks.[3] The rift between the general and the colonel begun on the road to Overlea continued, though a "temporary truce" had been made by the two warring parties—the original Jones guard and the "rebels."[4] While Jones, uneasy with the intense public scrutiny directed her way, had intimated that the hike to Washington would be her last, Craft had announced plans to lead a women's army into Maryland, Pennsylvania, and Ohio. The declaration appeared to have energized the colonel, as she enthused to the war correspondents, "I've got my walking feet back again!" Jones and Craft may have marched under a truce, but for the embedded journalists who observed their every move, the "battle ax was still evident." The two leaders kept a mile of distance between them on the macadam road to Laurel, and Jones was observed to be "in a bad humor as a result of the weak spirits shown by the Baltimore suffragists and the criticism ... of the army for its violation of all rules of conduct in its audience with Cardinal Gibbons."

By the time the army reached Elk Ridge, Maryland, nine miles south of Baltimore, Jones and Craft had almost completely swapped roles, if not personalities. Now it was Craft playing the role of sunny optimist, reminding a group of about 100 schoolchildren of the goodness and inherent virtue of the movement. Jones, by contrast, surprised many of the war correspondents by deviating from her usually upbeat message to a darker critique of Baltimore suffragists she characterized as "chicken-hearted." The Baltimore brand of suffrage, she said, "furnishes good ground for the masculine cynicism that women seek the ballot for a fad. I suppose our ranks won't miss them."[5]

Criticisms like these left Jones's Baltimore "lieutenant," Mrs. Charles Keller, in a decidedly difficult position back in the Oriole City. Keller was obliged to thank Jones for her visit while endeavoring to explain the city's particular attitude toward the hike in saying:

> Just because Miss Jones has called us chicken-hearted it is not proved that we are so. Personally, I would have liked to hike to Washington, but gave up on the idea, although I had expected to for some time. But the way we looked at it is this: the army of "General" Jones has hiked all the way from New York and every member is in condition. Consequently, they will not be stiff and worn when they reach Washington. But we Baltimore women are not in practice.[6]

As the army left Elk Ridge it appeared as if General Jones might lose control of her platoon. Mrs. R.W. Roulon, who had joined the hikers in Philadelphia, had flagrantly broken the "no-ride" rule, causing a sensation by riding into Laurel in an automobile after claiming she had pulled a muscle. Her claim met with immediate skepticism from the other marchers, who quipped that the latest muscle pull "must have been an auxiliary set of muscles," since Roulon had used the same excuse in soliciting a previous lift.[7] Another recent recruit, a day-hiker from Baltimore named Emma Shuey, hitched a two-mile ride with a farmer. And to make matter worse, Jones was now facing a possible defection from male thru-hiker E.S. Lemmon, who in marching all the way from New York City had clung zealously to his role as march pilot and who had chosen the road to Laurel as the occasion for a strike over a missing flag. Without the flag, Lemmon insisted, he could not be seen at the front of the marching column and therefore could not dispatch his duties as pilot. He had selected what he believed to be an ideal route for the army to follow and had set off, flagless, to mark the path, only to have Jones disregard his advice and choose an alternate route instead.

Lemmon figured at the center of another growing anxiety over the army's entry into Washington. Rumors circulated that "the whole army would be locked up and arrested" if it tried to march through the streets of Washington without a permit from Superintendent of the District of Columbia Richard Sylvester. Worried over the possible arrests and eager to find a more satisfying role for Lemmon in the march, Jones sent him by train to Washington, D.C., to obtain the necessary license.

Meanwhile, another budding controversy over the march's inclusivity threatened, as Jones received word from Alice Paul's Committee of Arrangements in Washington that only the women who had hiked every step of the way would be allowed to march with Jones and her pilgrims in the Washington, D.C., national suffrage procession on March 3. Paul wrote Jones to advise that if men marched alongside the pilgrims through the streets of the nation's capital, the suffrage parade would take on "the character of a lark rather than of a serious crusade."[8] Jones vehemently objected to Paul's directive, pointing out that the men who had served in invaluable support roles deserved to march as well, as did women like Elisabeth Freeman, the army's official orator who had piloted the horse-drawn suffrage wagon, and Olive Schultz, who had expertly driven the scout car throughout. How could Jones look bugler Milton Wend in the eye, for example, and tell him that after 250 miles spent uncomplainingly at her side he could not take part? Barring Wend from the procession would be doubly unfortunate, as it would separate him from his mother, Catherine Wend, a thru-hiker.

Before leaving Baltimore Jones had wired to Washington with a message saying, "either the war correspondents march with me or I do not march." As she handed her defiant communiqué to the local telegraph operator, she could be heard saying, "Miss Alice Paul should worry." That her army would deliver the suffrage message they had carried with them since leaving New York City, Jones declared, was "emphatic and final."[9] For more than two weeks the general had made decisions with little interference from New York or from the national committee in Washington, D.C., but as her army neared the finish line, the tug-of-war over who controlled the march and its growing celebrity threatened to bring its historic progress to a grinding halt. Many of the war correspondents who had helped publicize the hike had come to love Jones since its start, and the general felt a fierce and reciprocal loyalty to them, especially to those writers who had logged every mile with her. Jones viewed the war correspondents' fealty as a special kind of loyalty. They, after all, owed no particular allegiance to Jones, to her march, or even to the cause of votes-for-women, and yet they had fought for the general and her troops on multiple occasions and would no doubt do so again if called upon. Now, Jones's fidelity to them had become a major impediment to the viability of the march itself. After two weeks of near-continuous headlines in the nation's newspapers, the general's popular appeal now easily eclipsed that of the movement's duly elected leaders.

Ethel Lloyd Patterson was among the many war correspondents whose personal admiration for Jones had caused her to abandon all notions of journalistic objectivity. She badly wanted her readers to understand what a remarkable American character the general really was, though as she put pen to paper she reminded herself that she must keep exactly those overflowing sympathies in check:

Before I write I shall have to clear my eyes from their love of her. A suffrage pilgrimage is a forcing house of hate or affection. Beneath discomfort emotions blossom quickly. With the first weariness a woman loses her mannerisms. With the second weariness she loses the qualities she has tried to cultivate.... With the third weariness one gets her morally in the raw. She ceases to be either what she thinks she is or what she hopes other people believe her to be and becomes herself.

General Jones, as much as any woman I have ever met, is like a flower. The nearer the heart, the more perfect the fragrance. She is all the best of what we mean when we say a woman is essentially feminine.... She delights in chiffons and fringe and trailing things. She likes high-heeled slippers with beads on their toes. A pair of these were the first things she fished out of her dress suit case when she reached Baltimore....

Now, ask me how such a woman has managed to persevere through the real hardships of a suffrage pilgrimage. I will answer you that the quality of Rosalie Jones which has kept her going is essentially feminine. It is the same quality ... that drives a woman on through the marshes in the endless pursuit of will-o'-the-wisp called ideals.[10]

Now the act of putting one foot in front of the other through the Maryland mud seemed the only reasonable remedy for the pilgrims' anxieties about the future. The view of farmers and their families standing by the roadside to witness history had become a familiar sight for the marchers and one that reminded them of their core mission: to bring the equal rights cause to forgotten rural people and the neglected places where they lived. The pilgrims' familiar cries of "Votes for Women!" and "On to Washington!" were met with subtle yet respectful gestures of acknowledgment—quiet hellos and tips of the cap—that typified rural stoicism. Even the names of the Maryland country towns through which the army now passed on its way from Elk Ridge to Laurel, Maryland, seemed to connote an almost biblical struggle. In villages named Long Green, Waterloo, Glory, and Jerusalem, Rosalie's Army met hundreds of enthusiastic schoolchildren and thoughtful tillers of the Maryland soil.[11] Still, not every encounter on the long road to Laurel, Maryland proved redemptive. Some onlookers turned to "rustic humor" to register their discomfort in seeing a women's army marching through their streets.[12] Outside of the tiny hamlet of Halethorpe, Maryland, boys raised a rebel yell and threw rocks at the marchers. In another nameless crossroads village a small group of four to five African American women had indeed trailed behind the army with a homemade suffrage flag but had dropped out of the march without disclosing whether or not the Antis had hired them.

Afternoon temperatures along the route warmed to the mid- to upper 40s, further drying and firming the road. By the time the troops reached the outskirts of Laurel, "footsore, hungry, and peeved," as one war correspondent put it, they found waiting an escort of four uniformed postmen eager to walk them into the city.[13] Still, the reception was something less than hoped for—"not cordial but cold."[14] The keepers of the town's only working hotel claimed to have space for only 10 marchers and insisted on picking exactly which 10 they would lodge; the others would be left to find private lodging and makeshift beds on sofas.

Joined by the town's mayor, Rosalie's Army addressed a crowd of nearly 1,000, but those gathered proved less than sympathetic to Freeman in particular, who arrived smoking her trademark gold-initialed cigarette before a group of the town's "astonished natives."[15] "Well," Freeman said in answer to the gaping looks, "lots of us smoke, only I have the nerve to do what I want in public." Still, the mayor proudly offered Jones the key to his city, and all stood in wonderment at the achievements of sexagenarian day-hiker Georgianna Lehman, nicknamed "Ginny Bull," who had been the first hiker to arrive in Laurel, despite her age. The stoppage for the evening offered the most road-weary pilgrims the chance to gather themselves for the journey ahead, and for Jones in particular, the stayover at the Clover Leaf Hotel offered a chance to post a short missive to President-elect Woodrow Wilson, a note whose contents read: "We send and beg of you to accept this votes for women flag as a memento of our pilgrimage through New York, New Jersey, Delaware, and Maryland." With Washington, D.C., now on the horizon, Jones had grown more vocal about her plans to barnstorm an audience with Wilson as she had with New York Governor William Sulzer two months earlier in Albany. Wilson, Jones vowed to reporters, would not "escape her."[16]

Two plots had been hatched for the delivery of the suffrage message Rosalie's Army had now carried well over 200 miles. The first such plan directed Jones to deliver the message to suffrage leaders in Washington who would, in turn, mail it to Wilson. "Nix," Jones replied to the war correspondents when asked for her reaction to that particular scheme. "We'll be the little deliverers ourselves."[17] Still, for all the general's bravado, Wilson's representatives claimed the On-to-Washington marchers would not be given an audience at all. "We'll deliver the letter to Mr. Wilson if we have to stay in Washington until 1917," Jones vowed. "We will try to deliver the message the very minute Mr. Wilson arrives in Washington. And we will keep after him until we are successful."

The "we" in Jones's formulation seemed more tenuous than ever as the suffragettes retired to their respective beds in Laurel. The pilgrims, observed the *Pittsburgh Post-Gazette*, were "torn by dissension, jealousy, and incipient mutiny," adding that "only common cause holds the pilgrims together."[18] Colonel Craft, the paper noted, led the "insurgents, including Elisabeth Freeman and Elizabeth Aldrich who do not love each other." General Jones, the *Post-Gazette* added, "wearily protests when the insurrection is mentioned" while intimating to the press that she would retire from hiking after the inauguration and devote herself to "other forms of militancy."

• • •

Precipitation came in buckets as Jones and her army trudged south out of Laurel on the road to the District of Columbia. Morale had reached a new low, not just for the poorly slept marchers but also for the war correspondents who marched alongside them in a downpour. Reporter Ethel Lloyd Patterson captured the gray tenor of the day in her dispatch to the Washington, D.C., *Evening Star*:

> Nobody could get up much enthusiasm after a sleepless, uncomfortable night. And how it did rain. We all made a dive for our dress suit cases for rubber caps and raincoats. Nobody cheered us on our way. Milton Wend tried to blow the bugle and a dismal, bubbly sound came from the brass.
>
> [Elizabeth] Aldrich draped a piece of white oilcloth around her shoulders and somebody said she looked like a pantry shelf. We all smiled wearily. The townspeople stood beneath dripping umbrellas and stared.
>
> Only General Jones looked nice. She temporarily discarded her pilgrim cape. Her trim little figure was outlined in a black suit. She wore a black rubber cap. The rain made her cheeks a deep red. Her hair curls naturally. But she walked ahead of us preoccupied. Something was bothering her. We thought it was the day.[19]

Near Hyattsville, Patterson's prescient hunch proved true, as the general called an unexpected halt, motioning her drenched infantrywomen to the shelter of an old brick kiln along the road for the sort of serious meeting the army had taken to calling a counsel of war.[20] Jones had difficult news to deliver, news that could not wait until evening. The Army of the Hudson, she revealed to the marchers with a heavy heart, would not be allowed to deliver the suffrage message to President-elect Wilson after all.

"The message directed to President-elect Wilson was given to me by Mrs. Mary Ware Dennett, executive secretary of the national association, and it certainly was autographed by Mrs. Jane Addams, Dr. Anna Howard Shaw, Mrs. James Lees Laidlaw, and other members of the board," Jones explained to a rain-soaked and moribund group.[21] "I remember that when I first went to see Dr. Shaw, to ask her if she would like to entrust us with a message to the President-elect, she told me she was a bit doubtful whether it wouldn't be intruding on the rights of the association's Congress Committee. That was ten days before we started. I thought, 'Well, if Dr. Shaw feels so, that is all right; we'll find something else to do.' But when I went to the national headquarters just before we left, Mrs. Dennett told me we were to be the bearers of the message, and the next day it was sent on to me in New Jersey—the autographs hadn't all been secured when we left. A week ago I was surprised to receive a letter from Mrs. Dennett saying that she thought Dr. Shaw wished to head the delegation presenting the letter to Mr. Wilson. Miss Florence Allen, and Miss Florence Miller, of the national headquarters, had come from New York to march into Baltimore, and I talked the matter over with them. They were very angry with the association for wanting to take the message from the army. However, this morning I got the telegraph: 'The board voted to present the message themselves with the Congress Committee.'"

"I know," Jones confessed, "that Dr. Shaw disapproved of this pilgrimage and Miss Addams, too, but Mrs. Dennett thought it was fine." The pilgrims responded to Jones's news with both anger and indignation, charging that the "high-brow suffragettes in Washington" were jealous of the publicity the march had received and were now eager to coopt it for themselves.[22]

"Do you mean to say," Constance Leupp demanded, "that after we have walked two hundred miles you are going to let them take the honor of presenting the message away from us?"[23]

"You owe it to yourself, General," Milton Wend said firmly.

"You owe it to all of us," Craft added, "to deliver that message to Wilson in person. How the general can take that slap so quietly I don't know," she said, her anger palpable.[24] Other marchers called the national committee's decision a "mean trick." Corporal Klatschken received the news in utter disbelief, her hiking boots so caked with heavy mud she could hardly raise her feet onto the brick kiln to rest them. "After we plodded through all that mud last week," she said, "and then to have Dr. Shaw and those women roll into Washington in their Pullman cars and take that message from us! They don't know what it means to walk as we have walked."

Jones, the war correspondents noted euphemistically, "had a few things to say about Washington and New York suffragettes" but counseled her troops against outright rebellion. "The most dignified and soldierly thing to do is to obey our superior officers. We will turn the message over to the committee," Jones said.[25] Jones called a vote on the matter as the war correspondents looked on. To their shock, Craft, who until that very morning had "been in a state of rebellion against General Jones" for several days, helped sway the army's sentiments in the general's favor. Earlier that same morning, reporters had noticed Craft quiet literally breaking bread with Jones on the side of the road, and now, true to that peace accord, Craft stood by Jones during a crucial test of the general's leadership.

While the majority had voted with Jones and Craft, the marchers further up the road, including Freeman, had not had a chance to cast their ballot, and when word of the decision reached them, they were livid. Led by Freeman, they vowed they would quit the march immediately if Jones surrendered the honor of the suffrage message delivery. Freeman and her supporters vowed they would write a message of their own if Jones deferred and walk to Washington to present it themselves.[26]

For the main marching column that stayed behind with Jones, the grim news slowly sank in, further darkening the day. Jones walked alone ahead of her contingent after the announcement, maintaining a weighty silence. Mary Baird, who had once more begun marching after her early collapse at Princeton, collapsed again and had to be supported by two newspapermen, one on each side. "The day," summarized Patterson, "seemed heavy with small unhappinesses." Desertions would surely have followed had the army not agreed to attend a luncheon in their honor at Hyattsville at around 2 p.m. First, though, they would have to make it through College Park, Maryland, home to the Maryland Agricultural College, another male-dominated institution of higher learning where the hikers expected trouble.

A mob of 200 young men greeted the marchers as they reached campus, with some hurling insults. Two members of Rosalie's Army were jostled; another was knocked to the ground.[27] In their zealotry, students pushed against the army's support vehicles, ripping the iconic votes-for-women pennant from the baggage car while attempting to steal the marchers' luggage. At one point the jeering from the crowd grew so intense that the male war correspondents engaged in fisticuffs with the students, "with the students getting the worst of the argument."[28] The mob "captured" Jones and forced her to deliver a brief speech before allowing the army to march on to Hyattsville. The episode unsettled the war correspondents, whose subsequent reports described correspondents "engaged in battle with students"[29] and "fistfights with students."[30]

Hyattsville had worried that the pilgrims would arrive early and that they would not be ready to properly fete them, but the events that afternoon in College Park had since rendered those anxieties moot. The local businessmen's association in Hyattsville, fearing an early arrival, had posted scouts all along the road back to Laurel to alert them by telephone as to the pilgrims' progress.[31] By the time the army arrived there, shaken from the disorderly scene at the agricultural college, the businessmen had laid out two long tables of food and drink with their hosts practically "falling over each other in their anxiety to do the pilgrims honor."

At least one reporter compared the feast awaiting the pilgrims to Thanksgiving. The town had outdone itself with the strength of its enthusiasm. That very morning it had woken up to a surprise votes-for-women message printed atop the water tower by an anonymous hand. Under the cover of darkness a brave soul had scaled the shaky ladder leading to the 150-foot water tank.

Local Antis regarded the episode with chagrin, issuing a statement that read:

> Hyattsville has the highest respect for women, and will greet the hikers as such, but it does not encourage their propaganda. If the town officials 'winked' at the painting of this huge sign on the water tank it will become a political issue. They are elected to serve all the people, and if the Antis find that the officials promote favoritism to the suffrage cause, there will be a sharp reply at the polls.[32]

Celebratory though it may have been, the Hyattsville luncheon occasioned new and troubling subplots. Three of the hikers had been unable to attend due to physical exhaustion brought on by the day's inclement conditions.[33] To make matters worse Jones had learned that her anti-suffragist mother and sister were reportedly headed to Washington in an attempt, presumably, to dissuade her from completing the march. Her mother had made a similar attempt to discourage her daughter on the December march on Albany, and Mary Jones's public protestations only gave further ammunition to the Antis, who pointed to the Jones family discord as indicative of just what damage suffrage support could do within an otherwise tight-knit clan. Under the headline "Suffrage Divides Family," the longstanding mother-daughter feud had received top billing in that day's news, wherein the president of the National Association Opposed to Woman Suffrage, Josephine Jewell Dodge, had told the *Washington Post*, "You know I am a great friend of 'General' Jones's mother ... who is a member of our organization and who is strongly opposed to women's suffrage. In fact, Mrs. Jones and the 'General's' sister will be with us at our mass meeting…. Both are coming from New York with the two hundred women from that city."[34]

Less than 10 miles away, Washington, D.C., thrilled and roiled while the army thanked their gracious hosts and pushed on toward Hyattsville's sister city of Bladensburg, located less than two miles away. The unannounced advance arrival in the District of Columbia by the army's scout car driver Olive Schultz had itself caused a stir. Arriving on February 26, Schultz received a "continued ovation" from people gathered on every street corner.[35] Small boys ran alongside the automobile as Schultz struggled to make her way through the throngs to national headquarters at F. Street. There she spoke briefly with the press, assuring them that the marchers had had a "grand time" and recommending cross-country hikes to "all people who want perfect health." Schultz had logged 300 miles in the scout car rather than on foot with the rest of the marchers, but she had kept in close touch with the marchers plodding the difficult road behind her. "You can call my sisters mud hens if you want to," Schultz commented, "but they'll deliver the goods and reach Washington Friday morning ready for any calls made upon them."[36]

Meanwhile, Massachusetts suffragist Margaret Foley, known as the "suffrage cyclone" for her uniquely powerful voice said to carry three city blocks, had arrived in Washington from Boston to whip the crowds into a frenzy in advance of the Army of the Hudson's arrival. Foley had organized her own street meeting outside the State, War, and Navy Building, drawing an audience of more than 500[37] while rousing a crowd of government clerks to "wild enthusiasm."[38] Foley's was just one of 11 suffrage meetings held throughout the capital on the day before the scheduled arrival of Rosalie's Army.

As the suffragettes pushed southward to Bladensburg under General Jones's command, it was Craft who spoke to the press. The colonel used the opportunity to revise the critical comments Jones had made about Baltimore activists. "The people with whom we came into direct contact were most gracious," she explained. "The suffragists of Baltimore are not chicken-hearted or feeble in their patriotism for the cause. They are just as loyal as any suffragettes in the world and the fact that they could not all stand the rigors of walking does not signify that they are chicken-hearted. They were only physically weak. Their hearts are strong and their enthusiasm for the votes-for-women-crusade is just as keen as anybody's." In a reversal of her earlier statements on African American marchers, Craft used her newfound platform to declare that there would be no discrimination against "respectable women" who wished to march with the pilgrims into Washington, saying, "We welcome as many recruits as we can get. It is a great cause and needs the support of as many respectable women as is possible to get."[39]

As the army settled into Bladensburg for the evening, Jones received yet another blow to morale, this time from Alice Paul, who had left Washington on a mission to personally retrieve the paper copy of the suffrage message from Jones's command. Though the general acquiesced, saying that she was a "soldier who obeyed orders," Paul's intervention meant, in effect, that Rosalie's Army had become, in the 11th-hour, an independent organization lacking a clear mandate from NAWSA.[40] In taking the message with her back to Washington, Paul offered that Rosalie's Army could still attend the banquet to be held in their honor the following day but that the male marchers and war correspondents were to be excluded from any such celebration. Jones said nothing to Paul's decree, but the rest of her indignant army vowed that they would take part in the grand suffrage parade scheduled for March 3 with the male marchers and war correspondents at their side. "I turned over the letter to Miss Paul without comment," a solemn Jones told the press corps. "If the New York suffragettes feel it is better for the [NAWSA] Congressional Committee to deliver the letter it seems little else for me to do than to bow to its wishes."

"The army of tonight," observed a somber *Washington Herald*, "is an army without a purpose. With one fell swoop ... the National American Woman Suffrage Association snatched from the pilgrims all the laurels of the long hike by the action of the executive board."[41] The meeting with Paul served as a devastating denouement to the marchers' most challenging day on the road yet. They had arrived in Bladensburg in a driving rainstorm wearing makeshift rain slickers. They had encountered as much "insults and rowdyism" in one day as they had on the entire 240-mile hike from New York.[42] Mary Baird collapsed on the road and had to be assisted into the village, and Mary Boldt, already battling a case of tonsillitis, had been insulted by men passing her on the road.

A little more than a mile away, the good people of Hyattsville had left their Main Street town hall open and well-lit in the event the marching suffragettes desired to make an evening speech there. "We had no heart for it," Ethel Lloyd Patterson wrote, adding:

> The people went to the door and looked in. No pilgrims were there. Presently, they put the lights out again. And presently, one by one the lights in our rooms went out. Each pilgrim crept into bed, and each pilgrim thought, as she lay and stared wide-eyed into the dark that she would have given a great many things rather than have had unpleasantness come to Gen. Rosalie Gardiner Jones.
>
> The last night of the pilgrimage was not happy.[43]

That evening, Jones attempted to buoy the spirits of her weary army with an inspirational poem, whose opening verse read:

> Oh sisters, my sisters!
> The trip is nearly done;
>
> The hikers slowly plod along,
> The towns pass one by one.
>
> The weary miles are left behind,
> The Capitol draws near;
>
> And soon our lengthy march will end,
> Amid a deafening cheer.[44]

And while it was certain their arrival would bring the plaudits of thousands, February 28 was to have been devoted to their triumphant march into the capital carrying the suffrage message for Wilson. Now Paul had taken even that laurel from them, ordering Rosalie's Army to march to national headquarters by way of the backstreets. After nearly 250 miles of flying the suffrage banner, they were now an army relieved of any obligation to their sponsoring organizations and therefore free, at long last, to march to their own drummer.

13

General Jones Goes
to Washington

Elisabeth Freeman's threat to desert on the brink of the army's historic march into the capital kept the war correspondents up late in Bladensburg. On the eve of what was expected to be its finest hour, the fate of the march now seemed uncertain. A steady influx of marchers arriving to Bladensburg from nearby Washington quickly filled the town's two hotels, leaving many of the war correspondents without lodging.[1] Reporters paced the lobbies with worry written plainly on their faces. At the beginning of the march many of the hardboiled journalists had been skeptical, but now, hundreds of miles later, a majority had been converted. "We'd do anything to aid this cause," the war correspondents were quoted as saying. "And especially would do anything for 'General Jones.'"

Meanwhile, national headquarters found itself deluged by angry telegrams and mail addressed to Mary Ware Dennett, the secretary who had been the bearer of the bad news that Jones and her army would not be allowed to deliver the suffrage message to Wilson. The populist groundswell of support for Jones and against the party dignitaries had surprised Dennett, who was now on full-time damage control in an effort to reassure an indignant public that her organization had not gone back on their promise to Jones.[2] "Everything is just as it always was," she told the press. "Rosalie is a darling, and I'm sure she realized we are all friends. There has been some misunderstanding." In her interview with reporters Dennett spoke at length in an attempt to set the record straight. "When [General Jones] came to us offering to take a message to Wilson, of course, we were very glad to let her do it. The cause needs just such advertising. There was so little possibility of anyone's disapproving that Dr. Shaw let her start before we had heard from all the members of the national board who, of course, must vote on all questions of national work. After the pilgrims had started with the message, we heard from Miss Jane Addams and the other out-of-town members."

Addams and the others had apparently given their approval with one proviso—that the message be delivered to Wilson by members of the national delegation in addition to the pilgrims, because it was "felt that it would be more dignified to have the national officers represented." Dennett had since sent a second, follow-up telegram to Jones hoping to clarify the alleged miscommunication, this one reading, "Regret misunderstanding. Board with you from the beginning. Delegation to present message to consist of national officers, Congressional Committee, and pilgrims if interview with Wilson is secured." The key, it now seemed, lay in the fine print, as it appeared unlikely that Wilson would grant an interview, and thus Jones's plan of barnstorming the president-elect would be nixed. "Miss Addams thought it wouldn't be dignified to trail him about the city or thrust it at him in the railroad station," Dennett said of the incoming Wilson. Dennett's comments did little to stem the national outcry and, in other ways, only increased it, as Addams, the rumored obstacle to the front-and-center role owed the On-to-Washington hikers, had weeks ago left for an extended stay overseas.

The army's shared desire to deliver the message had lately galvanized their fraying unity, uniting them against a common enemy, but already that accord had begun to erode over what the Army of the Hudson widely regarded as a betrayal of their core mandate. Little more than a month earlier, newspapers had pitched Rosalie's Army as the single greatest attraction of Paul's momentous March 3 parade in Washington, trumpeting that "foremost among the ranks of marching suffragettes would be the little band of hikers led by General Rosalie Jones."[3] Now their participation in the history-making event appeared to be in jeopardy.

Among the visiting dignitaries arriving in Bladensburg for the final seven-mile advance on Washington was Genevieve Clark, daughter of U.S. Speaker of the House Champ Clark. "Bladensburg," Clark wrote, "woke up from its years of sleep" at the coming of the suffragette army. "The old town whose beginnings date back to the time of Washington has not seen as much excitement since the British captured Bladensburg bridge."[4] Clark had eagerly agreed to cover the last leg of the march for the *Washington Times*, walking along for the day as a reporter-embed. Jones mustered her troops out of Bladensburg at 9 a.m. The mud still reached the marchers' ankles as forecasters called for temperatures to soar into the mid– and upper 60s on this, the final day of February. Newspapers reported scores of 11th-hour marchers streaming into Hyattsville and Bladensburg in the pre-dawn hours "in hopes of deceiving people into the belief that they had hiked the entire 250 miles from New York."

By noon the burgeoning army crossed into the District of Columbia via the old toll gate at 15th Street Northeast and Maryland Avenue. As she had throughout, Jones wore her pilgrim's cloak and carried her birchbark walking stick. At her side walked Milton Wend, the bugler, and behind him Catherine

The Suffragette "Hikers" Are on Their Way to the Capital

An editorial cartoon appearing in the February 24, 1913, *Washington Times* showing the public anticipation of the marchers' expected arrival in Washington, D.C., on February 28, while also making light of Jones's "incidental walking-only" policy. The cartoon shows suffragettes bending the rules to receive rides in cars, on roller skates, and via Lausanne, the suffrage mare.

Wend accompanied Ida Craft. To Jones's left, Dr. Ernest Stevens of Philadelphia carried an oversized American flag, and behind Stevens the rest of the army marched without regard to rank. Elisabeth Freeman brought up the rear, driving her horse-drawn gypsy wagon, with Margaret Geist leading the donkey she hoped to present as a gift to President-elect Wilson. At the beginning of Maryland Avenue the army caught sight of the distant Capitol building, and Jones called a halt to savor the moment. The white dome glistened in the bright, late-winter sunlight, causing the army to issue a resounding cheer.

Paul had ordered Jones to enter the city by way of a side street, Rhode Island Avenue, where a "petticoat cavalry" and Paul herself would be waiting to escort the marchers into headquarters. But Jones, acting on her own authority, defied those orders. "We will enter the city by our own way," the general told the war correspondents.[5] Shortly thereafter the promised escort arrived—two women on horseback dressed in white riding habits and plumed hats. Following behind them were Paul and the suffrage cyclone, Margaret Foley of Boston. Paul spoke briefly with Jones at the corner of 10th and Maryland, asking

for an explanation for her deviation from the prescribed route. The brief meeting was not cordial, and Jones sent Paul away without a satisfactory explanation.[6]

Fully 10,000 spectators massed in the blocks between Seventh Street and Ninth Street alone. Thousands more waited along 14th Street.[7] At North Capitol Street, crowds screamed "Three Cheers for Rosalie Jones!" and the general halted her troops for a second time. The war correspondents that Paul had barred from participation in the March 3 suffrage procession now served as Jones's personal escort into the city.

By the time the army turned down Pennsylvania Avenue, the crowd, numbered at an estimated 100,000, had grown beyond the capacity of Richard Sylvester's 400 District policemen to control in

Alice Paul works at her desk, 1913 (Harris and Ewing Collection, Library of Congress, Prints and Photographs Division).

a reception the *Baltimore Sun* described as "almost barbaric in its splendor."[8] Street peddlers sold pennants, balloons, flags and confetti. "All Washington was out in force," reported *The Sun*, "and every sort of automobile….had been commandeered for the occasion." For Ethel Lloyd Patterson the route ahead promised real danger, as District police struggled to clear a path for the pilgrims: "When [we] turned into Pennsylvania Avenue, it was easily seen that the march … would be fraught with difficulties."[9]

There Jones stopped and ordered the marchers who had hiked the entire distance to form a line across the street. At one end of the line was Dr. Stevens with the flag and at the other end Milton Wend the bugler. As promised, Jones insisted that the war correspondents march at either side of the line of pilgrims and out in front of them. Behind the first line came the women

The suffragettes march into Washington, D.C., on February 28, 1913, linking their walking sticks to stay together amid crowds estimated at 100,000. Jones walks out front in her pilgrim's cloak and hood. In the front, from left to right are Milton Wend, Norman Sper, Mary Boldt (in tasseled cap), Elizabeth Aldrich, Minerva Crowell (holding the flag aloft) and Phoebe Hawn, whose face is partially obscured by Jones. At Jones' left side (left to right) are Catherine Wend, Ida Craft, and Martha Klatschken. Just visible in the gap between Wendt and Craft is Margaret Geist, in the second row (Harris and Ewing Collection, Library of Congress, Prints and Photographs Division).

who had marched most of the way, and behind them the day-hikers who had walked individual legs of the journey to Washington. Rosalie and her thru-hikers locked arms, walking sticks arrayed horizontally, binding them together, and marched forward into the small space cleared for them by mounted police increasingly powerless to restrain the crowds.[10] The police led the way, followed by the automobiles carrying NAWSA leadership.[11] Next came the petticoat cavalry on horseback.

"It was evident that the police had expected no such turnout of Washingtonians as greeted the army," wrote Patterson.[12] "Numerous gibes were shouted at the pilgrims, but if they were heard they were unnoticed. In many places, especially at the foot of the Capitol grounds, large parties of women waving suffragist banners cheered. Several men cheered, too. In many instances woman enthusiasts tried to break through the guard of the war correspondents to speak to 'Gen.' Jones, but they were quickly turned away."

Spectators hoisted children above their heads to catch a glimpse of the historic moment. "Men and women alike," wrote the *Washington Post*, "braved horses' hoofs and chugging automobiles of the suffrage army escort to grasp the hands of the suffrage pilgrims."[13] The reception was said to rival that given many presidents at their inauguration. Helen Keller, arrived from New York to experience the moment in person, praised Jones and her army as the bravest women in the world. "I think they are magnificent," Keller told reporters. "Their courage is wonderful. No one knows what they suffered who has not seen the poor blistered feet which they brought to Washington."[14]

Upon reaching the F. Street headquarters Jones was hoisted into an automobile and handed a megaphone, and newspapermen spotted Mary Jones, Rosalie's anti-suffrage mother, watching from an automobile parked at the edge of the throng. The elder Jones had come to town for the Anti rally

The marching suffragettes arrive from New York in Washington, D.C., February 28, 1913, escorted by a "petticoat cavalry" on horseback. The Capitol building looms in the background (Harris and Ewing Collection, Library of Congress, Prints and Photographs Division).

scheduled for later that afternoon but had detoured to see her daughter in her crowning moment, prompting reports that Rosalie's heroics had in some small way opened even her disapproving mother's mind. "It has been worth all it has cost, the hardships, and privations, the disappointments, footaches, and maybe at times a little heartache," Jones told the crowd straining for a glimpse of the diminutive general.[15] "We have reached the country.... We have set people thinking, and ... we will win," she declared.

Craft spoke next, amplifying the general's claims regarding the historic nature of their march. "It is the most tremendous thing that has been done for suffrage since 1864," she declared, adding, "I am convinced that we have converted thousands. We have penetrated the conservative states and given them an object lesson in the earnestness of those who fight for the cause." Jones's and Craft's sentiments so enthused onlookers that it took fully 20 minutes for District police to disperse the crowd after their speeches were completed.[16]

"Tonight, everyone is talking about suffrage," observed the *Baltimore Sun*, "and there is not the slightest doubt that the cause won hundreds when the valiant Army of the Hudson, foot-sore, dead-tired, but game ... plodded slowly along past the Capitol and up Pennsylvania Avenue." Headlines in the *New York Post* described marchers left to push their way through "mile-long walls of shouting humanity" and observed a police force "powerless to control the crowd."[17] Chief of Washington, D.C., police Richard Sylvester reported that crowds numbering 100,000 greeted the marchers. The *Baltimore News* described Rosalie's Army's march through the city as "one of the most remarkable demonstrations Washington has seen in years."[18] Tens of thousands crowded Pennsylvania Avenue alone, causing the *Baltimore News* to opine that "a Presidential inauguration could hardly have presented a more enthusiastic spectacle than Pennsylvania Avenue from the Capitol to the Treasury building." Writing for the *Washington Times*, Genevieve Clark agreed, calling the march of Rosalie's Army "the greatest and most enthusiastic demonstration here in years."[19] Clark came away convinced, more than ever, of the pilgrims' greatness. "The English suffragist martyr has nothing on her American sister when it comes to capacity for suffering in a good and righteous cause or when it comes to downright never, pluck, perseverance, and a convincing power of deeds that should convert the most stubborn-hearted," Clark wrote. "If ever women have suffered for the sake of their convictions I think it is [the] little band of pilgrims who today reached the mecca of their hopes and with flying banners and happy hearts entered the national capital. The outside world will in all probability never know what they endured because they have suffered in silence."

Clark continued, "Before I came upon those heroic women on the outskirts of Hyattsville yesterday, plunging knee-deep in mud and in heavy rain, I had regarded the hike as a sort of lark. Honest confession is good for the soul, and I felt ashamed of myself for the thought as soon as I looked into their earnest, lovely faces, aglow with enthusiasm and high resolve. After that I saw it as a very serious thing and could not but regard these women as martyrs." All of the approximately 16 war correspondents from major metropolitan dailies who had traveled along with the hikers, Clark reported, spoke in the highest terms of Jones and her fellow hikers. This, she concluded, was the "real tribute" because "newspapermen look with critical eyes upon the subjects of their stories and are not slow to recognize human weakness." One of the journalists had observed to her that "American history does not contain a more heroic scene than that of diminutive Martha Klatschken [crawling] for three miles along a lonely country road on a freezing day into Burlington, New Jersey, rather than be carried or abandon the enterprise."

The *Chicago Tribune* agreed wholeheartedly, noting:

> If General Jones and her pilgrims had come by car at the expense of no aches, no one but the hotel clerk would have known they were in Washington, and what the general did in legitimate advertising of the suffrage cause may be measured by the crowds in Pennsylvania Avenue.
>
> Gen. Jones is a good soldier as well as a good general. When the orders came to her near the finish of the tramp to surrender the letter she carried to Wilson to ladies who had been at no pains to reach Washington and to permit them to present it to Mr. Wilson she gave it up and marched on. She has earned a garlanded ride in a chariot.[20]

• • •

The morning after their triumphant arrival in Washington the pilgrims woke early to take in the sights and sounds of the capital on the first of March. "Early rising is our forte," Jones told reporters. The army was said to have "captured the city," and less than 24 hours after they had crossed into the District of Columbia, the capital's largest newspapers had declared "even the inauguration is forgotten today."[21] Rosalie's Army had acted quickly to set up their own headquarters at 422 Fourth Street Northeast, free of the overwatching influence of the national suffrage society, which feted them even as it feared their growing fame.

The day offered the marchers a chance to take stock of the momentous events of the last two weeks. For Ethel Lloyd Patterson, the grueling hike had offered perspective, humility, and self-discipline, takeaways she attempted to articulate for her readers in Washington, writing: "Some of us really suffered. And we had our tempers and our spirits tried. It may be that one of the real victories of the army is the way each pilgrim conquered herself, learned to remember that others were weary while she was weary, too."[22]

In an interview granted Patterson shortly before the march into Washington, Jones had offered a realistic appraisal of the march not as the defining moment in the votes-for-women crusade but as paving the way to something

Mother-son marchers Catherine and Milton Wend marched 250 miles together for the cause. Milton, a Union College student, accompanied Jones on all three of her long-distance suffrage marches, serving as bugler and flag-bearer. While the Library of Congress does not identify the suffrage hikers in this photograph, other newspaper photographs of the Wends individually make identification possible (Harris and Ewing Collection, Library of Congress, Prints and Photographs Division).

more lasting. "We feel we have ... tilled the ground; it remains for the people interested in suffrage in the states through which we have passed to plant and reap, if they can," Jones said. "Now the people are curious about suffrage. If nothing more is done their curiosity will soon lapse into lassitude. Unless the work is carried on, for all practical purposes the pilgrimages might never had been made.... Everything has to be started, and to have accomplished half of one's purpose is, after all, not such a little thing."[23]

Jones was characteristically self-effacing in reflection, though Washington hailed the pilgrims as heroes. Later that evening, the soldiers of Rosalie's Army were the guests of honor at a banquet attended by 200 supporters, including congressmen from Alabama to Colorado. Journalists flocked to the event, in which it was expected that members of Alice Paul's Congressional Committee would be "eating crow" for their poor treatment of the Army of the Hudson.[24] The marchers surprised and delighted observers by wearing evening gowns underneath their tattered brown pilgrims' cloaks. "None who took the long march with the hikers and saw them enter country towns tired, bedraggled, and bespattered with mud would have recognized them," observed the *Washington Herald*. Jones wore a short-sleeved dress of brown satin trimmed with coffee-colored lace and a long train. Harmony was to have been the theme of the evening's tribute, and while a partial peace was made between the pilgrims and NAWSA's Dr. Anna Howard Shaw, any reconciliation with Paul would have to wait. Whether by accident or by design, Paul arrived at the event too late to greet Rosalie's Army.

Attendees of the banquet had other happy news to celebrate, including the recent announcement that Congress would take up the question of women's suffrage by the designation of a subcommittee headed by representative Richmond Hobson. The committee would report to the House whether it would be best to leave the question of votes-for-women to the individual states or seek a constitutional amendment. Hobson, who attended the banquet in honor of Jones and her army, pledged that he was willing to risk his entire political career to secure the passage of the proposed amendment for which Jones and her troops had bravely marched. Already Hobson had been weakened by a vicious floor debate pitting two Alabama congressmen against one another—Hobson in favor, and the old suffrage nemesis, representative "Cotton Tom" Heflin, against. In the debate Heflin satirized the marchers while making frequent derogatory reference to "women who wanted to wear pants."[25] He suggested that the House furnish representative Hobson, a decorated veteran of the Spanish-American War, with a "frock and a bonnet" so that he might better enjoy the national suffrage parade planned for March 3. Hobson fired back that any truly enlightened society would want to educate mothers in governmental affairs.

The announcement that Congress would take up the question of women's enfranchisement was met with rejoicing in suffrage circles and no small amount of cynicism elsewhere, as editorials debated whether the sheer magnitude of the question—states' rights versus amendments to the Constitution—might itself delay votes for women. "General Rosalie Jones and her cohort of suffragists have finished their hike from New York to Washington," read an editorial in the *Oakland Tribune*.[26] "Surely this ought to convince Congress that women are qualified to use the ballot. But Congress is likely to say let them keep walking." From San Francisco came a more hopeful assessment of the legislative breakthrough occasioned by the On-to-Washington army, a retrospective tribute reading:

> "General" Rosalie Jones and her little "army" marched from New York to Washington. They carried the banner of suffrage farther than that, won more than a triumph over storm and mud. Theirs is a victory over the storm of opposition and the mud of rancor which has assailed the cause of votes for women since its inception. At no time has suffrage been considered nationally so seriously or with so friendly an attitude as now.[27]

Of all the country's major metropolitan newspapers, however, the *Washington Post* landed the biggest scoop on that celebratory Saturday, March 1st, an exclusive look back at the arduous trip recently completed penned by Jones herself. The *Post* proudly ran the piece in full:

> It is difficult to realize that our pilgrimage is over; that the brave little band of pilgrims that started from New York are almost all here. It is strange to feel that now, after fourteen days of marching, in which we have banded closely together, we must now separate. For no matter how rough the walking, how sore the feet, there has always been a touch of understanding and quick sympathy that held the marchers together in a beloved circle. And now it is all over.
>
> The remembrance of the march into the national capital is one that will remain forever fresh in the minds of our little army. Between densely packed streets of people who cheered or even silently expressed their interest in our cause we marched with happy hearts to the end of a journey that has been harder than most people realize.
>
> The very fact that the crowd was so curious and so large that the police had difficulty in its management, showed how wide awake the people of the national capital are. And suffrage is one of the greatest questions of the day. It is the one question whose answer is already seen. Women will vote.
>
> And what have we gained? We have gained that for which we left New York, and have trudged the weary miles here, and we have learned even more arguments in favor of women's suffrage. We have learned what loyalty to a cause is and what hardships women can endure for that which they love. We have learned that "mere man" as represented by the "war correspondents" who have trudged by our sides through rain and shine, are far better, kinder, and more thoughtful than we had imagined. We have found that the great things in life are not those that come most easily, but those for which we suffer.
>
> When we left New York we were a carefree, happy, enthusiastic group of suffrage advocates, most of us knowing nothing about what was ahead. At first there was a novelty that made the miles seem short and the hills small, but when this wore off, the real work began. For then it seemed that the road wound unendingly between barren fields.
>
> You see, we all walked at a different pace, and each wished to walk at her own pace, because it was easiest for her. So after a half mile or so of keeping together at the start

we soon spread out, and the end of the day usually found us from two to five miles apart.

In conclusion, I cannot say enough in praise of the bravery and heroism shown by my small "army," and as I have often heard the "war correspondents" say, "Many a man would have dropped out long before some of the women really admitted to themselves that they were suffering."

On March 3 the advocates of a real democracy, a government of the people, by the people, and for the people (and women are people) intend giving a mammoth pageant. Join in it if you believe that a woman should not be disenfranchised owing to an accident of birth.[28]

•　•　•

In the 24 hours after the Army of the Hudson's arrival in Washington, newswires hummed with word of the special edition suffrage trains departing depots across the nation to join Rosalie's Army and hundreds of other VIPs for the great national suffrage procession scheduled for March 3. On March 1 a special train bearing 150 Illinois suffragists left Chicago while a crowd of men and women sang "America" to mark the historic occasion. From New York, Mary Ware Dennett and Harriet Burton Laidlaw embarked to join Carrie Chapman Catt and Dr. Anna Howard Shaw, both already in Washington. Three special train cars—"manless specials"[29]—carrying members of

Official program of the March 3, 1913, Woman Suffrage Procession in which Jones and her suffrage pilgrims were to receive top billing (Printed Ephemera Collection, Library of Congress).

NAWSA and the New York state association were already en route in what was described as an "invasion of the capital."[30]

Trains arrived at the rate of one every five minutes into Washington's Union Station, with more than 150,000 passengers arriving on March 3 alone.[31] Of the 250,000 expected for the inauguration, an estimated 100,000 had come to town for the national suffrage parade.[32] Five to ten thousand of those would march through the streets of the capital. The stationmaster of Washington's Union Station told reporters that he had hired four times the usual amount of help to deal with the record crowds streaming into his city, and an additional force of 44 men under the command of Captain Robert Cusick had been installed with the modest goal of keeping the passageways clear.[33] A public comfort committee had been organized to direct visitors arriving by rail to 4,000 pre-inspected rooms that would house more than 40,000 people. Fifteen thousand cots would accommodate still more.

Visitors in a festive mood surged up and down Pennsylvania Avenue on the evening of March 1, greeted by "all varieties of fakers and vendors of everything" who hoped to match the visitors' political enthusiasm with their own commercial exuberance. On the streets of the capital, suffrage souvenirs vied with Woodrow Wilson novelties for top sales. At 9 p.m. hawkers appeared selling mortarboard hats and "fierce and false" moustaches to revelers eager to pay homage to Wilson's previous career as an academic and college president.[34] The moustaches and mortarboards sold like hotcakes, but they were not more popular than the pro-suffrage hat bands and bright yellow votes-for-women pennants waved in high-spirited support of the cause.

The sheer size and enthusiasm of the inaugural crowds streaming into Washington owed much to Rosalie's Army. Inspired by Jones and her pilgrims, world champion distance bicyclist Margaret Gast had pedaled all the way from New York City to Washington to arrive in time for the March 3 suffrage procession.[35] Like her inspiration, Gast had been forced to wallow on foot down the mud road between Elkton and Perryville, Maryland. The route had been more trying, Gast reported, than the 2,500 miles she had ridden to become world champion.

Summing up the influence of General Jones, the *New York Post* wrote:

> Washington did not need the spectacular entrance of "General" Rosalie Jones and her dauntless band of hikers to arouse its interest in the suffrage demonstrations, but there can be no doubt that their descent upon Washington and the tremendous crowd of both the curious and the sympathizing which packed Pennsylvania Avenue ... made a great impression upon the city as a whole. The bright yellow balloons and "Votes for Women" flags have speckled the city ever since.[36]

Increasingly, as the national press sought comment on votes-for-women in the days leading up to the suffrage procession, they sought out the charismatic Jones and her band of pilgrims in lieu of parade organizer Alice Paul or NAWSA President Dr. Anna Howard Shaw. The sympathies of the people were particularly clear in a votes-for-women meeting held the afternoon of March 2 at Poll's Theater in Washington, D.C. The suffrage-friendly auditorium could seat upwards of 1,500, and while the erudite Dr. Shaw presided, the real stars of the show were the marching suffragettes. "The speaker in whom the audience...[was] most interested," one newspaper reported, "was 'Gen.' Rosalie Jones, her pilgrims being clad in their marching costumes."[37]

For its Sunday, March 2, edition the *Sunday Star* in Washington solicited Jones to debate the definition of true womanhood, responding to the president of the National Association Opposed to Woman Suffrage (NAOWS), Josephine Jewell Dodge. Among the items Jones listed on behalf of empowered women everywhere were those that might have served as manifesto for her march for social justice:

- A womanly woman is not too concerned with her own life and duties to remember the rights of other women.
- The willingness to fight for that which is right is womanly.
- The womanly woman, when she hears that ... the road she must travel is stony and tiresome, prays in her heart to be shown the way to make it less hard and stony and tiresome for those who come after.
- She who is truly womanly cannot be harmed by contact with the world. She goes out in the world and labors to convert the world to the standards of true womanliness.[38]

• • •

In her letter to the *Brooklyn Daily Eagle*, hiker Phoebe Hawn complained bitterly of the placement of Rosalie's Army in the March 3 national suffrage procession, where the hikers would be tucked away in the seventh section. She and the rest of the pilgrims viewed the near-to-last placement as yet another attempt by Paul and her committee to diminish the role of the famous suffragettes lest they steal the show.[39] The national heroes of the On-to-Washington march now found themselves stuck behind even the men's league for women's suffrage state car, near the end of the procession.[40]

On the morning of March 3 the army waited for more than an hour while the divisions in front of them, led by parade herald Inez Milholland mounted atop a white horse named Gray Dawn, attempted to process down Pennsylvania Avenue. The weather proved ideal—cloudless skies, nicely warming temperatures, and diminishing southwesterly winds that "left no ground for anything by satisfactions on the part of the women who have arranged for their great demonstration."[41] Despite what should have been the

Suffragist Phoebe Hawn, the "Brooklyn Baby," stands in front of onlookers and admirers, most likely between February 28 and March 3, 1913, in Washington, D.C. (Harris and Ewing Collection, Library of Congress, Prints and Photographs Division).

calming effects of nearly ideal marching conditions, drunk and disorderly crowds attempted to climb atop many of the floats before the parade entered its second city block. Insults were shouted at the women's marchers, and the police once more proved unable to keep the rowdyism in check. Finally, a voluntary force of Army soldiers and Marines cleared the way, aided by Milholland herself, who rode into the throngs in an improvised attempt at crowd control.

The *New York Times* singled out "two New York women"—Milholland and Jones—as central in the honors of the day. Jones, her army clad in their trademark brown pilgrims' cloaks, marched with the New York suffrage contingent near the back of the parade. "Everyone wanted to see the hikers and General Jones," the *Times* reported. "'Which is General Jones?'" was the question that was asked a thousand times by curious ones before "the parade was over."[42] Marching alongside her general, Hawn reported that she had "never seen such a seething mass of people."[43] Adoring crowds showered the pilgrims with bouquets of flowers, with Jones holding six to eight bunches in her arms at once.

National Suffrage Procession herald Inez Milholland, atop Gray Dawn, March 3, 1913. Milholland, a New York lawyer and activist, was the first of four mounted heralds (Bain Collection, Library of Congress, Prints and Photographs Division).

German actress Hedwig Reicher as Lady Columbia in an allegory performed in front of the Treasury Building as part of the Woman Suffrage Procession held in Washington, D.C., March 3, 1913.

Elsewhere the crowd pushed and jostled, and Hawn found herself indignant at the police's ineffectual attempts to protect the safety of the marchers, saying, "Our police 'protecting' would have been a disgrace to any rural town." Jones, Hawn reported, endured it all with a beatific smile. At the end of the parade the six divisions preceding them waited to honor Rosalie's Army with a round of applause, with the *Pittsburgh Post-Gazette* confirming that the "greatest ovation was probably given to 'General' Rosalie Jones."[44] The *Press and Sun-Bulletin* concurred, noting that "to General Jones was given the greatest ovation of the day."[45] The paper described crowds on tiptoe to "get a glimpse of the little woman who led her little band from New York to Washington through rain and snow and almost impassable roads." Genevieve Clark, now reporting for the *Washington Herald*, observed, "No section of the parade was received with more enthusiasm than the suffrage pilgrims led by their faithful commander 'General' Rosalie Gardiner Jones. She answered the cheers of the crowd by bowing to the right and left and by waving her pilgrim staff crowned with flowers."[46] Clark noted an especially satisfying irony: Students from the Maryland Agricultural College scorned for their rough treatment of Jones and her followers only days before now escorted the army through the unruly streets in a gesture Clark called a "frank and manly act." Jones, the *Post* remarked, looked "radiant," the roses she carried offering a "splash of scarlet" against the humble brown of her pilgrim's cloak.

At the conclusion of the procession Jones delivered a farewell speech to her army, thanking them for their cooperation and loyalty. For Hawn, the

Jones poses in her suffrage pilgrim's cloak with a bouquet of roses, most likely in Washington, D.C., between February 28 and March 3, 1913 (Harris and Ewing Collection, Library of Congress, Prints and Photographs Division).

feeling proved mutual. "Now that it is all over I can but pay my respects to General Rosalie Jones and Colonel Ida Craft, and my co-soldiers," she offered, "and say that they have indeed succeeded in the carrying out of a great plan." Hawn continued, "I am very glad that I joined General Jones and her brave little band of pilgrims, for until you yourself have tried walking 250 miles in two weeks under the same conditions, you cannot know what it all means. But I would undergo it all again if I could feel that I had helped along the cause of woman suffrage."[47]

14

Winning the Vote

By March 6, the members of Rosalie's Army had mostly left Washington, D.C., after the March 3 national suffrage parade in which marchers had felt both triumph and terror. The suffrage letter for Wilson that had originally been given to Jones was now reported to be locked in a safe box controlled by Alice Paul, and it was widely doubted whether it would ever be delivered. News reports had surfaced briefly that a conciliatory Dr. Anna Howard Shaw had offered to return the suffrage letter to Rosalie's Army for delivery to Wilson, but there existed no official corroboration of the rumor. In its March 3 edition, the *Evening Star* reported Jones felt the letter had already caused enough trouble and that she wanted nothing more to do with it.[1]

Paul had all but declared the case closed, saying that no one would deliver the letter to President Wilson unless it was delivered by her personally or one of her representatives. "Jealousy at the success achieved by 'General' Jones and her party" was the most oft-cited reason for the curious treatment of the letter, a theory lent greater credence when Jones and her troops were left off the guest list at the Continental Hall reception that followed the grand suffrage procession of March 3.[2] "Rumor had it," one newspaper later wrote of Jones's quiet slipping away from the capital, "that Alice Paul and the pilgrims did not foregather cordially."[3]

Jones herself showed little interest in wresting the letter from Paul's keeping, leaving Washington shortly after the conclusion of the triumphant suffrage parade that had nevertheless been marred by a rowdyism from which Rosalie's Army—exiled by Paul to the end of the parade and guarded both by the students of Maryland Agricultural College and by a troop of Boy Scouts—had felt little direct impact. While national suffrage leaders called for a congressional inquiry into the lack of police control, Jones stayed mostly silent on the mob mentality she had experienced multiple times on her difficult journey. Meanwhile, the pro-suffrage *New York Post* headlined its March 4 coverage "Capital's Shame," alleging that officials had erred by "permitting the great suffrage parade to be all but ruined by a riot of hooliganism due to negligence by reasonable police control."[4] No less than Carrie Chapman Catt urged every woman to "besiege her Senator or Representative" in demanding a full explanation of the day's events on Pennsylvania Avenue. NAWSA's Shaw vowed that she had never seen "such an exhibition of incompetency" as she had by the D.C. police and urged her supporters to likewise demand a congressional investigation. *Woman's Journal and Suffrage News* used the first line of its page-one story to declare, "Washington today has been disgraced."[5] Women, the suffrage mouthpiece alleged, had been "spit upon, slapped up, tripped up, pelted with burning cigar stubs, and insulted by jeers and obscene language too vile to repeat in print." The publication highlighted page-one photos of Jones and Milholland striking triumphant poses, though the coverage overall sounded a note of barely contained indignation. Suffragists widely blamed Antis for instigating the violence, either by their own hands or via proxies. Editor of *Woman's Journal and Suffrage News* Alice Stone Blackwell decried the double standard that allowed Antis to use violent tactics and yet cried foul when votes-for-women activists so much as considered militant methods, writing:

> It will be interesting to see whether some of the publications that have kept up a continual denunciation of militancy in England will have much to say.... Heretofore, when a woman making a suffrage address was knocked down and kicked in Harlem, or when sponges and ... bags of water were dropped on the heads of suffrage speakers in Wall Street, these periodicals have had no rebuke to utter. It is only lawlessness on the other side of ocean, and lawlessness committed by suffragists, that calls out their righteous wrath. It makes a difference whose ox is gored.[6]

Harriet Laidlaw of the New York Woman Suffrage Party joined Blackwell in pointing a finger at a police force that failed to check the rowdyism, reaching the "inevitable conclusion that the police ... deliberately withheld the needed protection." In lengthy comments published in the *New York Post*, President of the Women's Political Union Harriot Stanton Blatch advanced the conspiracy theories one step further, asserting that the "lawlessness was due to the fact that our police knew that the people higher up wished the parade to be failure."[7] Blatch recalled a particularly telling moment when she had implored a policeman to subdue the crowds, only to receive the reply, "Go on home, you old great-grandmother," as policemen nearby laughed at their colleague's jibe. Blatch noted something of a silver lining in the "tide of condemnation now sweeping the country" concerning the rough treatment of the marching suffragists, which she hoped would help sway public opinion to their side. On March 5, just two days after the March 3 rally, the *New York Post* reported that the Senate would indeed hold hearings on police culpability for the "riotous scenes which marked the women's suffrage parade."[8]

While the leaders of the bureaucratic arm of the votes-for-women movement raised a national outcry, Jones left Washington quietly, followed only by rumors of what the now famous leader would attempt next. Reports of a pos-

An unruly crowd breaks up the suffrage procession at Ninth Street in Washington, D.C., March 3, 1913 (Library of Congress, Prints and Photographs Division).

sible trip around the world carrying a suffrage banner surfaced briefly in the *Times Herald*.[9] "Enthused by the 'hike' from New York to Washington," wrote the *Washington Post*, "when 'General' Jones and her army braved the cold … suffragists leaders would now have the banner of 'Votes for Women' carried around the world."[10] As it turned out, Carrie Chapman Catt, not Jones, had floated the idea as a goodwill gesture in the lead-up to the international suffrage convention scheduled for Budapest the following summer.

Craft and Freeman traveled to Harrisburg, Pennsylvania, in the weeks following the national votes-for-women parade, where they appeared before the Senate Committee on Suffrage. In travels throughout the state they intimated a future hike from New York City to Buffalo to be made later that summer.[11] Meanwhile, Corporal Klatschken told the members of a New York suffrage society that newspapers had exaggerated many of the incidents on the hike "to make good stories."[12] It was "the grim battle with the weather and roads and hardships" that had truly characterized the march, she maintained, as well as the hospitality and encouragement the marchers received from the mostly good and helpful people along the way.

Phoebe Hawn continued to garner media attention, filling the auditorium at the headquarters of the *Brooklyn Daily Eagle* to tell her story to a rapt hometown audience. She confessed that she had begun the march merely as a "glorious lark" but that she quickly became "impressed with the serious side of it and … an enthusiastic and sincere disciple of the cause."[13] Hawn claimed that after the luncheon stop in Elizabeth, New Jersey, on the first day of the march, she and Minerva Crowell had been too tired to continue and had been left behind by the rest of the army. The bitter wind chills, the lonely roads, and the hand-numbing temperatures had made them, she recalled, "as blue as any two lone, sad-of-heart girls could be." Hawn further claimed that her rumored engagement to Willie Cator, the Princeton student who had walked with her to Philadelphia, had been exaggerated by the press corps.

In the days following the March 3 votes-for-women procession, reports surfaced suggesting that Jones intended to give up peaceful nonresistance in favor of outright militancy, a rumor that beget at least one impassioned editorial in the pages of the *Washington Herald*. There an anonymous letter writer maintained that the "quiet gracious behavior of the general and her staff" at the suffrage parade in the capital had "allayed suspicion that American women were already militant." Such public relations gains would surely be lost, the letter-writer lamented, if the rumors of Jones's militancy proved true. The letter-writer continued, "'General' Jones's reported defection from the ranks of the regulars to become, so to speak, a 'bushwhacker,' must therefore be deplored for her sake, as well as for her cause's sake."[14]

Content to leave others to speculate about her future, Jones showed little interest in defending her army's 250-mile pilgrimage until March 9, when the *New York Tribune* ran a lengthy piece written by Jones herself, whose contents read:

> In the old days pilgrims walked from town to town preaching their faith. Today we suffrage pilgrims are following their example.
>
> People have criticized because we did not go to…. Washington by train. We answer: "Suffragists have been going to…. Washington by train for fifty years, and the people in the small towns by the way have never heard of them." Would the whole population of the crossroads turn out to see a parlor car go by? Would the people be thinking any more about woman suffrage after that? The people in the small towns don't see suffrage literature. They can't go to great, inspiring suffrage meetings. We had to bring them the message in person.
>
> That was one reason for our pilgrimage. The other reason was the newspapers. People all over the country read of our adventures with cows and snowstorms who never read of our serious meetings. Nothing in the history of suffrage in America has gained so much publicity for the cause as our pilgrimages. We suffragists have learned that to keep a cause alive we must keep people talking about it: that is, we must keep it in the newspapers.
>
> In reply to our anti-suffrage friends who ask why we didn't take advantage of the excellent railroad service, as they did, we ask: "Did their journey attract the interest of the whole country? Did so many New York reporters record their adventures? Did mayors, ministers, colleges, and district schools turn out to welcome them?" The antis had one line in the paper when we had columns.[15]

In late April, Craft stepped forward to make good on exactly that pro-pilgrimage creed, leading 10-mile weekly votes-for-women hikes into the New York City suburbs in what amounted to a suffrage walking club.[16] The colonel commanded a force of 16 activists—most of them veterans of the On-to-Albany or On-to-Washington campaigns—on a march to the borough of Queens that culminated with a stirring speech from Jones. If past patterns held, Craft's temporary promotion to march leader meant Jones would be working behind the scenes on more ambitious projects, and the May 3 suffrage parade up Fifth Avenue in the heart of New York City proved the pattern.

The procession, numbering 10,000 strong, dwarfed the Empire State's previous parades, causing the *New York Times* to call it the "greatest spectacular triumph ever won by women in this country in their pursuit of the ballot."[17] The parade was seen as a chance to remedy the slings and arrows suffered in the Washington, D.C., procession—the disorderliness of the marchers, the unchecked rowdyism of the spectators, and the perceived slight of Rosalie's Army. As she had in Washington, D.C., suffragette lawyer Inez Milholland led the parade up Fifth Avenue on horseback. This time the outcome was different, as police kept crowds estimated in excess of half a million in check throughout an afternoon when temperatures soared to near 90 degrees. At its conclusion, even conservative estimates put the number of marchers at close to 10,000.

As a culminating act, Milholland led participants into a mass meeting at Carnegie Hall where Harriot Stanton Blatch addressed those gathered with unbridled enthusiasm. "For the first time in the history of our movement in this country," she declared, "we find the police deserving of our praise, and I propose to give it to them freely. There was nothing approaching today the terrible indignities of March 3 in Washington." Shortly thereafter Blatch yielded the floor to the Army of the Hudson, who stood for several moments of continuous ovation before Jones gave a short speech in favor of the marches and parades that would take the suffrage sentiment directly to the people via such novel methods as would "set folks to thinking about suffrage."

Just 10 days after Rosalie's Army basked in the applause of fellow activists in Carnegie Hall, the *New York Times* received word that Jones was at it again, this time in her capacity as president of the Nassau County branch of NAWSA. Jones was reportedly organizing another suffrage parade that would truly be "something special" in the town of Mineola on her native Long Island.[18] The May 13 write-up revealed that Jones's parade would "have most of the features of the big New York suffrage parades" but with a rural flavor appropriate to Long Island. Farm wagons would roll alongside fancy automobiles. Craft's walking club would receive a special escort by riders on horseback, and Elisabeth Freeman would lead a group of child marchers. The famous yellow suffrage wagon that Freeman had piloted all the way to Washington would be featured alongside a wagon driven by young women dressed in costumes of the year 1763. As a special treat the oldest suffragist in Nassau County, 85-year-old Rhoda Glover, would ride in a carriage.[19]

The May 24 parade packed the three miles of road between Mineola and Hempstead with crowds of onlookers, and long lines of cars followed the procession of more than 500 participants. Airman Charles Hild thrilled the crowds by piloting an airplane down the marching line at an altitude of 800 feet. Five thousand people gathered at the terminus in Hempstead to hear Jones deliver a speech and award a silver cup for best parade float to a schoolteacher dressed as Lady Liberty. The procession, claimed the *Times*, was "the first event of its kind in the history of Long Island suffrage" and had brought out crowds so large "local police had great difficulty in handling the traffic."[20]

More redemptive news for the faithful followed just four days later when the Senate Committee on the District of Columbia published its report on the alleged lack of police protection during the March 3 suffrage procession in Washington. More than 150 women had testified to the kind of jeering, grabbing, and pushing that might have been prevented by a more engaged, better-prepared police force. Suffragists cheered when, subsequent to the re-

Suffrage parade organized by Jones from Mineola to Hempstead, Long Island, New York, May 24, 1913. Marchers carry placards showing the names of states where women could vote in 1913, including Arizona, California, and Washington (Bain Collection, Library of Congress, Prints and Photographs Division).

The "Flower Girls" of Jones's suffrage parade pose for the camera. The procession went from Mineola to Hempstead, Long Island, New York, May 24, 1913 (Bain Collection, Library of Congress, Prints and Photographs Division).

port, it was announced that District Chief of Police Richard Sylvester would be forced to retire as a consequence of his oversight.

Votes-for-women supporters had reason to cheer again a day after the release of the congressional report when the cause notched yet another breakthrough. On May 30, Jones became the first suffragette to promote the cause from the air, begetting the headline, "woman who led marchers now qualifies as pioneer air pilgrim."[21] Journalists reported no signs of fear from the suffrage general as she took her precarious seat in a Wright biplane decorated with votes-for-women banners, her skirts tied up with a piece of blue string. With her left hand Jones clung to a steel bar; with her right she held tight to a sheaf of yellow votes-for-women leaflets. When a spectator asked the equal rights icon if she was feeling any thrills, Jones quipped, "Would I acknowledge it if I did?" Members of Rosalie's Army turned out in force for the general's landing at the Oakwood Heights, Staten Island, airfield, though most of them had counseled her against the stunt. Thankfully, their worries for her safety turned out to be unfounded, as the flight took off smoothly and made a "pretty entrance" amid a "cloud of yellow leaflets that General Jones let fall fluttering in the air behind."

"You may have thought that suffrage had gone up in the air and that you would never hear of it again," Jones declared once returned to terra firma, "but if you thought that, you are mistaken." The general confessed to reporters that the arrangement of her seat in the biplane, suspended over nothing but air, had caused her considerable consternation. "Today I sat over an open space looking directly down and holding only one [bar]," she reported, "and being told to touch nothing on the right side my position was much less firm. A gust of wind would come from one side and I would find myself adjusting my position to that and then to another coming on the other side." As Jones regaled reporters with tales of her breathless flight, members of the Army of the Hudson fanned out across the grounds; Corporal Klatschken and Colonel Craft made brief statements in favor of votes-for-women while Surgeon General Lavinia Dock from the On-to-Albany march sold suffrage magazines; still more open-air meetings were held just outside the entrance to the airfield.

Several days later on June 2, Jones mustered Craft and Klatschken again along with bugler Milton Wend and his mother Catherine for a three-week auto tour of Upstate New York. The tour stopped first in Newburgh, where on June 4 the town's suffragists held their first-ever votes-for-women parade with an assist from Jones marching at the front. Preceded by police and accompanied by a brass band, 350 women marched through the streets of the Hudson River town 90 miles north of New York City where Jones, Craft, and Klatschken drew crowds estimated in the thousands.[22] From Newburgh, Rosalie's Army traveled on to Albany, Utica, Watertown, Buffalo, Rochester, and Monticello. When complete, the tour demonstrated that the women of Upstate New York were now fully woken in towns that had never before experienced votes-for-women parades. "They have done it once now," Jones said of the towns where suffrage sentiment had been newly stirred, "and we can depend on them to fight for themselves now."[23] By the time she was through, Jones had organized six women's parades while delivering 63 street speeches in the summer heat. This time the army had split up between towns to reach more potential converts. The auto tour proved a success, marked by "large crowds of both men and women waiting for the chance to see and hear the famous suffragist." Increasingly Jones looked like a lock for state suffrage office, with the *Whitesville News* declaring, "Her efficiency as a promoter of suffrage plans combined with the unfailing tact displayed in dealing with discordant element has led to her seriously being considered for the office of state president."

After all the mob violence the Army of the Hudson had encountered, Jones was indeed well-conditioned to deal with opposition elements with tact and strategy; other campaigners, however, felt more extreme measures necessary to protect themselves. Throughout the summer, activists continued to face public ridicule and, especially in evening street meetings, threats to their personal safety. That June, as Jones returned to New York City from what the *Syracuse Herald* described as "twenty-five days' work in the wilds of Central New York," suffrage leader Bertha Elder requested and received permission to carry a revolver from a New York City magistrate; Elder claimed that she needed a firearm in the event she was attacked while returning home from the sort of street meetings Jones had been holding with regularity.[24] Later that summer, Martha Klatschken was waterbombed while giving a soapbox speech in New York City and was forced to leave the rostrum.[25]

Relations between suffragists and Antis in New York deteriorated further later in July when Rosalie ally and fellow suffragette Edna Buckman Kearns drove into the Long Island town of Huntington an antique wagon decorated in accordance with the Spirit of 1776, complete with a banner that read, "If taxation without representation was a tyranny in 1776, why not 1913?"[26] Kearns had been touring the island in the Spirit of 1776 wagon for more than three weeks with fellow suffragette Irene Corwin Davison and Kearns's eight-year-old daughter Serena by the time they reached Main Street in downtown Huntington. Dressed as revolutionaries, the mother-daughter duo and their companion rolled into town accompanied by honking cars draped in yellow votes-for-women banners and a fife and drum corps.[27]

The triumphal march came to an abrupt halt when Rosalie's mother Mary stepped defiantly into the street in front of the wagon, refusing to budge. Mary Jones claimed that the old wagon belonged to her pre–Revolution Tory ancestors on the island and that she would sue if the activists did not immediately cease their unpermitted use of what she insisted was a family heirloom wrongly taken from her cousins, the Hewletts. The controversy caught fire in the New York metropolitan newspapers. Rosalie, likewise campaigning near Huntington at the time while driving her own iconic yellow suffrage wagon, was spared her mother's display in front of the Spirit of '76, but Kearns was not so lucky, telling the *Brooklyn Eagle* that the vehemence of Mary Jones's protestations had made her fear for her safety. A thousand bystanders turned out to witness the warlike skirmish between rival factions, one that ended peacefully when, the following morning, the suffragettes left town to canvas the more hospitable north shore of the island.[28] While headlines in the *Daily Eagle* called her anti-suffragist mother "belligerent," Rosalie emerged from the controversy more popular than ever, with newspapers reporting the general received on average five marriage proposals per day. "If women covet the admiration of men," one Upstate newspaper declared of the moral of the Rosalie Jones story, "suffrage propaganda … is no handicap."[29]

Mary Jones was not the only Anti resentful of the growing popular support of the votes-for-women movement. Further south in Delaware, opposition forces attempted to antagonize other members of the Army of the Hudson. In Wilmington, Elisabeth Freeman was forced to make a public appeal for the recovery of two invaluable rings she claimed had been stolen from her, presumably in retribution for her avowed militancy—one a heavy gold band from India with an opal setting and the other a precious sapphire.[30] The Englishwoman had considered settling down in Wilmington to continue her advocacy work post-march, but now she was not so sure. Later that August, her difficulties mounted as she and British suffragettes Elsie McKenzie and Vera Wentworth—collectively described as "militant suffragists of the deepest hue" by Wentworth—were ordered to police headquarters in Hartford, Connecticut, accused of violating that city's ordinance against "advertising on the streets" through the use of their promotional suffrage wagon.[31] Ida Craft joined Freeman for a portion of the New York-to-Boston campaign, though it was Freeman, McKenzie, and Wentworth who served as mainstays as the horse-drawn cart made its way northward via Stamford, Norwalk Bridgeport, Milford, New Haven, Wallingford, Meriden, New Britain, and Hartford, Connecticut.

Unlike Freeman, Craft had lately met with an unexpected windfall. The colonel who had proudly refused all luxuries on the march to Washington had inherited 100,000 dollars from her mother, Eleanor Vorhees Craft of Brooklyn, generating the headline, "Fortune for Suffragette."[32] Enacting her

Suffragists Elisabeth Freeman, Vera Wentworth, Elsie McKenzie, and Ida Craft in front of the horse-drawn suffrage cart taken on the New York-to-Boston hike in August 1913. The visible portion of the sign at right reads "White slavery, clean streets, wages, and all matters pertaining to the home are women's business" (Bain Collection, Library of Congress, Prints and Photographs Division).

pro-equality creed, Craft took the unusual step of hiring woman attorney Elizabeth Pope for probate.

Elizabeth Aldrich, the young Quaker pacifist suffragette, continued to seek a national platform that summer, offering provocative prophecies of changed relationships between the sexes. In a lengthy op-ed published in both the *Washington Post* and the *Salt Lake Tribune* titled "How Man Will Look When Woman Votes," Aldrich predicted that men of the future would look very unlike the hooligans and hecklers who had disrupted the Washington suffrage procession.[33] The new man would cease to be "ugly, domineering, cruel [and] ruthless" and would finally earn the right to be called a gentleman. Above all, he would "cease being a creature of prey." Men of the future would accept the need for gender equity as an article of faith, being more concerned with helping humanity than in making a profit. He would enjoy more leisure time and an improved mood. He would increasingly eat vegetables rather than meat and would largely eschew hunting.

Post-march, the youthful Mary Boldt, the wealthy financier's wife from New York, channeled her pro-equality stance into the championing of gender-neutral fashions, advocating for trousers of the sort some of the pilgrims had worn on their hike to Washington. "What we need," Boldt told reporters from the *Washington Post*, "is to break the shackles and free these slaves to fashion."[34] Calling for a leader bold enough to wear the new gender-bending fashions rather than merely speak on their behalf, she added, "The trouble with us is that we are many years behind the times in dress. The women of the [Far] East are far more progressive than us in dress. The majority of women in the world today wear trousers—the women of India, Turkey, China, and Japan." For her campaign in favor of the "trouserette," Boldt elicited endorsements from Jones, who lauded Boldt's practical fashion sense as "much-needed dress reform."

In August, just six months removed from the triumphant march of Rosalie's Army into Washington, tragedy struck the Jones family in an event that shook Rosalie to her core. On August 9, Rosalie's father, Dr. Oliver Livingston Jones, took his own life with a pistol in his apartment at 116 West 72nd Street. Coverage of the suicide was splashed across the New York tabloids and in states across the nation where the patriarch of the Jones family had real estate holdings.[35] Dr. Jones was a well-known figure in his own right, though in articles following the incident he was referred to primarily as "the father of Miss Rosalie Jones, the suffrage hiker." Coverage of the suicide dredged up the most painful family memories, including a horrific 1909 fire that burned down the Jones's ancestral mansion on Long Island, a conflagration believed to have been intentionally set by Rosalie's brother, Oliver "Olly" Jones, Jr. The Joneses' eldest son was considered mentally unstable, and New York newspapers of record described Dr. Jones as a "nervous wreck" after the fire and in the years leading up to his tragic suicide.

The tragedy took place in the presence of immediate family. The doctor, his wife Mary, and Rosalie's sister Louise had just returned from a visit on Long Island with Rosalie, who had returned the previous day from speaking at the Greater New York State Fair in Syracuse. Jones had delivered two days' worth of marathon speeches in her suffrage-yellow dress, staving off the heat that rose in waves from the nearby livestock barns.[36] Exhausted by the effort, she stayed behind at Cold Spring Harbor on the fateful day when her father, mother, and sister left for their city apartment on West 72nd Street. Just before noon a pedestrian heard gun shots coming from number 116, and New York City policemen rushed in to find a fully clothed Dr. Jones lying on the tiled floor of the bathroom with blood gushing from a bullet wound above his right ear. Louise ran for help to the nearby offices of a New York City doctor. Simultaneously, the Jones family physician was summoned by telephone. Against the wishes of the privacy-minded family, policemen ordered an ambulance, and the presumed suicide quickly became public.

Oliver Jones was reported to have been in ill health for a prolonged period of time, suffering from an unknown ailment,[37] and yet some in the press used the family's tragedy as an occasion for levity, with the *Washington Post* observing, "Now that 'General' Rosalie Jones's father has left a fortune … she stands a good chance of becoming a duke at least."[38] The reading of the will, in which the doctor left his fortune to his widow Mary E. Jones rather than to Rosalie and her siblings, made the front pages that September, exposing the extent of the wealth of the family patriarch, who was said to own real estate in nearly every state in the nation in addition to valuable holdings in Manhattan.[39]

In October, still grieving over the loss of her father, Jones received nominations from the New York State Woman Suffrage Party in its election for a new president. Once again, however, her distaste for bureaucracy caused her to be passed over by Carrie Chapman Catt, who endorsed Gertrude Foster Brown for the position instead.[40] Brown won handedly on a platform that included the notion that all new suffrage societies in the state should swear allegiance to the New York Woman Suffrage Association—a measure the independent-minded Jones appeared likely to resist.

Against a backdrop of familial loss and personal defeat, Jones's mind increasingly returned to the camaraderie she felt on the On-to-Albany and On-to-Washington marches. And once more in the waning days of 1913, she found herself hearing the pilgrims' call to the open road.

• • •

In late December of 1913 an enticing news item captured the attention of the editors of the *New York Times*: Less than a year after her history-making march from New York to Washington, D.C., Rosalie Jones was in training again, engaging in "trial hikes" to Brooklyn to re-find her marching legs.[41] Not long after the dramatic impeachment of suffrage-friendly New York Governor William "Plain Bill" Sulzer and the installation of Lieutenant Governor Martin H. Glynn in his place, Jones announced a second hike to Albany, New York. This time the suffrage general would not be carrying a votes-for-women message for a governor-elect; instead, she would be conveying something more practical: a petition to the lawmakers of the New York State Assembly to make provision for women poll monitors in the statewide suffrage referendum set for 1915. With widespread corruption alleged in recent votes-for-women referenda in Michigan and elsewhere, Jones was determined that the vote in her home state be fair. Craft and Klatschken signed on to the march immediately, as did other veterans of the On-to-Albany and On-to-Washington hikes, including Elisabeth Freeman, who, to the army's chagrin, would march on the first day only, and bugler Milton Wend. Olive Schultz and Alphonse Major would once again accompany the marchers in support vehicles.

This time, however, there would be changes. A smaller number of war correspondents would march with Rosalie's Army, and then only for the first day or two. Reporters from smaller Hudson Valley and Upstate newspapers such as the *Irvington Gazette* and the *Syracuse Herald* had replaced the national correspondents embedded in the On-to-Washington hike. The army would leave earlier each morning and, when necessary, walk with a lantern by which the rural citizens on their route could identify them. With fewer stops and just three regular "officers" and one "private," Eva Ward, in the ranks, the army would be leaner and nimbler. The second annual march to Albany figured to be significantly more grueling than the first, however, with the army limiting participation to "those who are physically able to stand the strain ... and have enthusiasm enough to last a week under trying conditions."[42] In an attempt to double their hiking speeds, Jones and Craft attempted to improve efficiency with scientific precision, calculating an ideal marching stride of 42 inches and designing special skirts to facilitate ease of movement. The troops would visit new cities and villages, hugging the west shore of the Hudson River rather than the east, with stays planned for Nyack, Highlands, Marlboro, Kingston, Catskill, Ravens, and Albany.[43]

The new private, Eva Ward, was an English organizer with militant leanings. Like Freeman before her, she had been selected for the march both for the international perspective she offered and for her demonstrated abilities as a publicist. As the co-head of the press department of the New York State Woman Suffrage Association, Ward had overseen a veritable publicity machine, sending votes-for-women news items and press releases to 500 newspapers weekly along with countless pages of write-ups and interviews to the major metropolitan dailies in the state.[44] On Ward's watch, the Empire State

Rosalie's Army on the first day of its hike, January 1, 1914, from New York City to Albany. From left to right across the front row are Eva Ward, Martha Klatschken (wearing a messenger bag that reads "The Woman Voter"), Ida Craft and Jones (third from right) with megaphone at the ready. At right are eight-year-old marcher Serena Kearns and Milton Wend. Elizabeth Freeman (second row) is visible between Craft and Jones, as is Edna Buckman Kearns (between Jones and Wend) (Bain Collection, Library of Congress, Prints and Photographs Division).

Campaign Committee had printed 1.4 million leaflets with at least one million of those having already been distributed—many by Rosalie's Army on their pathmaking pilgrimage to Washington. The need for a third mustering of Rosalie's Army, and a second march on Albany, was obviated by the suffrage society's own state-specific canvassing data, which showed what Jones had long known: The votes-for-women gospel had not yet truly penetrated Upstate New York's rural districts. The approximately 134,000 suffrage society members in New York City alone easily outnumbered membership in the entire rest of the state, and many of the Upstate districts were losing money, with only the counties containing the cities of Syracuse, Buffalo and Rochester listed as "self-sustaining."

At 8 a.m. New Year's Day in 1914, Rosalie's Army set out from Broadway and 242nd Street with "a martial air."[45] Broadway was still littered with horns, streamers, and confetti from the New Year's Eve revels when the determined band of activists marched out of the frigid city in the direction of Yonkers.[46] Sixteen hikers, including two men and girl-hiker Serena Kearns, at eight years old the "youngest rebel,"[47] constituted an army described as "fine in quality but small in numbers."[48] Jones held the same oversized American flag she had proudly carried on her previous marches. The Army of the Hudson would call on 10 mayors on their journey to Albany, presenting each with a votes-for-women banner from the New York State Campaign Committee.

The reprise of the march to Albany that first made Jones, Craft, and the rest of the suffrage pilgrims famous in 1912 now gave young reporters who missed the earlier march a second chance to witness history. Among them was Otis Peabody Swift, a first-year student at the Columbia University School of Journalism and a staff correspondent for the *Irvington Gazette*. Rosalie's Army would be marching north on Broadway right through Swift's hometown of Hastings-on-the-Hudson, making this a dream assignment for a cub reporter. Swift had been in high school when the On-to-Albany march of 1912 passed through his home community, and the chance to march alongside those same heroes two years later in 1914 proved enticing.

Early on, however, Swift realized that the two years of near-constant headlines produced by Jones and her army of marching suffragettes had produced a sort of media saturation that all but guaranteed this to be a quieter march than those preceding it. The first indication came when bugler Milton Wend rushed in to say that a police escort had formed just north of march headquarters on Broadway, only to learn shortly thereafter that the supposed escort was meant for the Society of St. Mary parade. Swift was disappointed to report that "the band, police, and members of the society passed by with noses in the air and with never a glance at the footsore army." While the young journalist noted the crowds Eva Ward attracted with her suffrage speech that morning at Getty Square, and the trolley cars and automobiles that stopped to honk their horns in support of Jones and her army, the first leg of the journey struck him as something short of expectations. Swift wrote:

> As we climbed the last hill into Irvington a large body of people were seen advancing down the hill. 'Oh, here comes the reception committee,' cried the general, and for the second time we prepared for a great ovation. Unfortunately, the crowd turned out to be only some schoolgirls going skating, and we sadly tramped on.
>
> I was marching along with general's pack strapped to my back, a yellow ribbon around my hat, and escorting two of the brown-coated pilgrims. At the top of the hill in Irvington some small boys were standing on the corner when they spied me approaching. 'Oh, see the sissy!' they yelled.
>
> At the Tarrytown line we found the first delegation waiting for us and here also was a delegation of Tarrytown suffragettes in automobiles who escorted us into the village. Cold, tired, and hungry we climbed aboard the ferryboat Rockland and soon the Tarrytown shore was lost in the evening mists.[49]

On its first day, the army reached Nyack, New York, approximately 16 miles from its starting point, where, despite badly blistered feet, Jones capped the day's march with a street meeting.[50] Word of Jones's second march on

Albany inspired copycat activists up and down the Eastern Seaboard. Two hundred and twenty miles south in Baltimore, a suffrage army led by Edna Latimer readied itself with cold cream and bandages for a two-day hike to Annapolis, Maryland.[51] Rosalie's Army, meanwhile, would undertake 175 miles for the cause.

By the time the Army of the Hudson reached Albany on January 7, Jones, Craft, and Klatschken had marched over rough roads in bitter temperatures in six and a half days, sleeping only 30 hours in a marathon journey during which they presented 10 mayors with suffrage letters signed by Carrie Chapman Catt. Incredibly, the army had averaged nearly 28 miles per day in rough, snow-covered terrain with Jones carrying a lantern to light the way when the hour grew late.[52] Twice en route Jones had broken down with exhaustion and painfully bruised toes and had been urged to abandon the undertaking altogether, but with several hundred supporters bolstering their ranks as they neared Albany, Jones, Craft, and Klatschken pressed on, hoping to argue their case directly to the new governor, Martin Glynn, and members of the New York State Assembly.

Rosalie's Army marched into Albany on streets buried deep in snow to a crowd made up of "curious, but respectful, thousands" gathered to watch the spectacle of the famous women's rights general marching behind a fife and

Jones smiles broadly as she leads the second On-to-Albany march out of New York City on January 1, 1914. Martha Klatschken (far left) and Milton Wend (holding American flag) look on (Bain Collection, Library of Congress, Prints and Photographs Division).

drum corps.[53] While Jones possessed sufficient energy to march a few paces in front of her platoon, per tradition, other hikers had to lean on newspaper reporters to walk the final leg of the journey. As the crowd neared the Assembly, the commotion was sufficient to derail the proceedings of the newly convened legislature. Milton Wend and Martha Klatschken were dispatched to carry Carrie Chapman Catt's letter to Governor Glynn, who in turn requested a one-on-one meeting with the leader in his executive chambers. Jones reiterated the need for a bill making provision for women poll monitors in future elections while reminding the newly installed governor of the need for "an honest legislature." Rosalie's Army had marched 166 miles in six and a half days to make her emphatic appeal in person.

The march had met its objective, and while the enthusiasm for the on-foot pilgrimage had never waned among the appreciative crowds that greeted the army in Albany, the pilgrims themselves had lost some of their initial zeal for the street meetings and public soapboxes that had sometimes lasted late into the evening on the On-to-Washington hike. The *Syracuse Herald* noted that after days of 25-plus-mile marches, the suffragettes had "little enthusiasm for anything but rest" and that fewer meetings and demonstrations were attempted.[54]

With two separate marches to Albany now in the books and the suffrage message personally delivered to two successive governors, Jones began to set her sights on the Midwestern and Western states where suffrage would soon appear on the ballot. After recuperating for several months from the arduous January march, Jones resurfaced again in the national news in late May of 1914 when she embarked on a campaign that would take her through key Midwestern and Western states were votes-for-women stood a chance of passing in state referenda. Jones traveled first to Chicago, Illinois, where she addressed conventioneers attending the biennial convention of the Federation of Women's Club.[55] President of the Illinois Suffrage Federation Grace Wilbur Trout invited Jones to address a convention attended by more than 3,000 delegates. Mobilized in part by the triumphant march of Rosalie's Army, Illinois had granted partial suffrage to its female citizens in the autumn of 1913.

From Chicago, Jones headed south to Missouri, where a votes-for-women bill had been introduced in the legislature, been referred to committee, reported out favorably, and been put on the legislative calendar, only to be taken off, referred back to committee, and "pigeonholed."[56] Throughout the Show-Me State, Jones rallied cash-strapped suffrage societies with tales of her marches on Albany and Washington. At the time of Jones's visit, the Missouri suffrage society's war chest stood at a paltry 12 dollars before an urgent call to the national committee led to an emergency infusion of cash and in-kind support. National leaders dispatched well-known luminaries to the state, including not just Jones but also Dr. Anna Howard Shaw and Jane Addams. Of all of them, the Missouri Equal Suffrage Society declared in its annual report, Jones had made the most "lasting friends for the cause," injecting new life into a campaign that had been haplessly spinning its wheels.[57] "To appreciate the whole campaign," President Helen Guthrie Miller of the Missouri Equal Suffrage Association wrote, "one must realize that Missouri is larger than any other state east or bordering on the Mississippi River and larger than all the New England states together, counting Rhode Island twice." The state encompassed 114 counties, many with no railroads and "almost impassable" roads. The population, Miller opined, included many who were "racially opposed to universal suffrage."

In Missouri, Jones faced a ground war not dissimilar from the one she had fought in the border state of Maryland during the On-to-Washington march, and here, once more, she proved to be a difference-maker. After visits from the general and other national suffrage icons that summer, 50 women from 50 state suffrage districts filed an incredible 38,000 votes-for-women signatures with the Missouri secretary of state. "And so," Miller wrote, "the fight was on!"[58] The general's visit elicited not just cash and enthusiasm for the cause but also concrete plans for a 200-mile march from St. Louis to Springfield, Missouri.[59]

Leaving Missouri, Jones, accompanied by Craft, headed next for Montana, where votes-for-women stood a fighting chance in the fall election. On July 7, the *Helena Daily Independent* broke the news that the famed suffrage general and her colonel had entered the state, traveling from Yellowstone to Montana's Bitterroot Valley region on their way to a large, open-air demonstration in the state capital of Helena slated for mid–July. The *Daily Independent* hailed the visit by the "two nationally famous women who marched from New York to Albany and Washington," seeking to further introduce the two activist leaders to Montana readers. They described Craft as "a middle-aged woman, very tiny, and radiant with the sincerity of her battle" and a "gentle little lady ... so thoroughly imbued with the ideals of her cause that she long ago gave up the life of leisure."[60] Jones was a "beautiful woman ... from one of the most aristocratic families in Gotham."

In interviews Jones pointed out that a suffrage bill had been pending in the New York legislature for 20 years but that few New Yorkers knew of its existence until Rosalie's Army's first march on Albany in 1912. The march on Washington in 1913 had yielded still greater publicity dividends, Jones told the Montana faithful. "After our earnest army marched on Washington," she told the newspaper, "the people all over the United States knew that we really wanted the right to participate in our own government, and that we were willing to inconvenience ourselves considerably to get it."

On Monday, July 13, Jones and Craft addressed enthusiastic crowds in Livingstone, Montana, having decided to add appearances in the state's smaller towns and cities.[61] On the afternoon of Wednesday, July 15, they reached Butte for a 70-plate luncheon hosted by their friend Jeannette Rankin, the Montana suffragette who had traveled more than 9,000 miles by car to every corner of her home state. Jones surprised attendees of the midday banquet by pointing the finger squarely at "indifferent women" who were, she said, "the greatest menace" to the success of the cause.[62] She urged supporters to actively canvass for votes rather than merely attend fundraisers and lectures; campaigning for votes would require women to grow strong enough to face public criticism. No group of women had been more severely criticized than the suffrage marchers of 1913, she told those gathered for the luncheon, though they had marched on despite the criticism. "After having a baptism of such mud as we found on our marches, we are not afraid of the mud of politics," she told Butte's suffrage faithful. Craft seconded those sentiments, declaring that she and Jones would continue marching until women were emancipated.

Later that evening the two women traveled to their much-anticipated open-air meeting in the state capital of Helena, where crowds filled the city block from Main to Jackson Streets. As in Livingstone and Butte, Craft spoke first, offering listeners a context for the movement while holding up silk flags for each of the major countries in the world where women had won the right to vote. Jones followed with a lengthy speech of her own, tailored to the interests of Montana citizens in particular. Montana, she pointed out, employed more women as county school superintendents than any other state.[63] If citizens trusted women to administer their schools and teach their children, Jones wondered aloud, why would not these same women possess the qualities of an ideal voter? She suggested that women were at least as morally credentialed as men, pointing out early in her speech that women made up only 5.5 percent of the prison population while men made up the remaining 94.5.[64] Women, she concluded, endured taxation without representation, adding, "The right denied by King George in 1776 is the right denied now by American men."[65] At the end of her talk the suffrage general asked all those who were opposed to equal rights to raise their hand; none did, though Jones knew better than to rest on her laurels, urging believers to decide what they might do to aid the movement. "Are you attending meetings?" she asked. "Are you discussing it with your friends? Are you wearing a suffrage button?" From now until election night it would be up to activists to give what time and money they had to help the ballot measure pass.

Most observers agreed that Jones and Craft's Western tour had been an "unquestioned success,"[66] and Jones returned to New York on August 22 riding a wave of momentum, telling the *Sun* in New York City that the trip through the West had been "splendid."[67] All told, she had devoted nearly three months to near-constant votes-for-women campaigning across multiple states, delivering an average of two suffrage speeches a day in an exhausting schedule that had made her "much thinner." "At Miles City, [Montana]," Jones fondly recalled, "the cowgirls carried suffrage banners in spite of the objections of their brothers and sweethearts." After three days in town, even the men had been converted, she noted, adding that the geysers in Yellowstone "came out to look at us."

There would be no rest for the righteous. Building on the momentum generated in Montana, and taking a cue from Rankin's wide-ranging auto tours there, Jones proposed to muster an army of 15 cars to spread the gospel on a route from New York City to Rochester, New York, where the New York Woman Suffrage Convention would be held on October 12. The caravan of suffragists, described as "the firing of the first great gun in the statewide campaign," motored west from Long Island on October 2 with flags flying and bugles blowing, staging 35 open-air suffrage meetings over the course of three days before a scheduled rendezvous in Washington Square Park in New York City.[68] Approximately 13 of the planned 15 cars arrived on time to Washington Square; one of the missing driver-pilgrims had been arrested and ordered to appear in court because a banner inscribed "Victory, 1915" allegedly obscured her license plate from the view of police. Meanwhile, Harriet Laidlaw had been delayed with a flat tire.[69]

Jones and Corporal Martha Klatschken left New York in style, driving a suffrage-yellow car supplied by Chevrolet packed to the gills with 3,000 copies of a publication titled *Woman Voter*. Craft would not accompany Klatschken and Jones this time, as she worked, unsuccessfully, to win a spot in the November 3 election as one of 168 delegates for the upcoming New York State Constitutional Convention of 1915.[70] Trimmed in suffrage yellow and flying banners that read "On to Rochester," Jones and Klatschken's automotive caravan left Washington Square just after 9 a.m. in what was billed as a "statewide pilgrimage." Once beyond New York City, the cars would fan out to cover as much of the state as possible while heading in the direction of Rochester, with Jones focusing on cities—Nyack, Newburgh, Poughkeepsie—in which she had established much goodwill in prior marching campaigns.

Five days and countless street meetings later, Jones and Klatschken arrived in Rochester on Sunday, October 11, first in the cross-state caravan. "General Jones's car holds the honor of having come through from New York without repair or delay," the *Tarrytown Daily News* reported.[71] Passing trains blew their whistle at the general's entry into the city, and groups of men watching from the sidewalk called out, "We're with you—we'll vote for you!" The 46th annual convention—the last before the New York state suffrage referendum scheduled for November of 1915—was viewed as critically important, and Jones and many of her auto pilgrims had arrived early, "desperately business-like" in preparation for several days of executive planning sessions.

Jones had become something of a convert to the auto tour method used so effectively in the West. The earlier marches of Rosalie's Army had been invaluable for publicizing the cause, demonstrating the sacrifice required of true pilgrims, but on foot marchers could only deliver speeches and hold meetings in perhaps three or four cities a day. By contrast, automobiles allowed the most tireless campaigners on the Rochester trip to make as many as 30 speeches in one day and allowed those who could not meet the physical demands of a cross-country march the opportunity to participate more fully. In Nyack, for example, Jones and her fellow activists had convinced the men of that town to form a men's league for equal suffrage[72] before winning still more converts in a street meeting later that same evening in Newburgh. While the long-distance hikes of Rosalie's Army had convinced America that women were physically and emotionally capable of a military-style march, the car caravans served to remind men of a woman's right to pilot her own vehicle and to travel where and when she pleased.

Less than three weeks after the conclusion of the suffrage party convention in Rochester, Jones, Craft, Klatschken and the rest of Rosalie's Army waited anxiously for the early returns from the 1914 suffrage referenda in the battleground states of Missouri and Montana. In Missouri the ballot box corruption and intimidation of which Jones had warned legislators swayed the vote to "no" on the votes-for-women question. Miller blamed "special interests" and the 11th-hour introduction of a "scratch all amendments" order that confused and discouraged would-be voters, suppressing voter turnout in what ended up as a 300,000 vote majority against the votes-for-women measure in Missouri.[73]

In Montana, however, Jones and Craft's remarkable tour had yielded impressive results, helping push votes-for-women over the top. The results were nail-bitingly close for much of the evening and early morning, and Rankin was encouraged to concede the measure's defeat in the hours after midnight on November 3. She refused, pointing out that Helena and Butte—two major Montana cities where Jones and Craft had concentrated their efforts—had yet to report, and Missoula, where the duo had rallied supporters after leaving Helena, had voted firmly in favor.[74] In the end, Rankin's faith in the electorate proved well-placed; with all precincts reporting, Montana voters had approved the votes-for-women measure 52 to 47 percent, a narrow margin that translated into 3,714 votes in the sparsely populated state. Missoula, Livingstone, and Billings—cities in which Jones and Craft had spoken on their tour—had all voted yes.

While Montana and Nevada proudly entered the votes-for-women column on election night 1914, suffrage had been on the ballot in five other states and not passed. The election results proved the pattern; rural Western states where women often homesteaded with men and acted as de facto business partners approved of women's enfranchisement, while the majority of urban men in Western cities voted "no." In Montana, rural counties had carried the day, with support for the measure in Yellowstone, Custer, Rosebud, Stillwater, and Richland Counties at 56 percent or higher.[75]

By January 1915, Jones was ready to take her votes-for-women activism into the public schools. Newspapers throughout New York announced that she would be sponsoring a lucrative series of cash prizes for debaters at 200 pre-selected high schools across the state.[76] The generous cash prizes, open both to young Antis and enfranchisement activists, would be awarded to the young woman who could make the best case for or against votes-for-women. Jones herself pre-set the topic: "What would it mean for New York State to enfranchise women?" Acting as chairperson, Jones set up a board to oversee the competition, whose overall mission was to "demand that the remarkable record made by woman suffrage be recognized for its historical value and that space be given it in the histories that are put into the hands of school-children."[77] To achieve the latter goal, Jones had begun working with textbook publishers to ensure adequate coverage of the movement.

One month later in February, Jones broke gender barriers once again, generating the page-one headline, "Gen. Rosalie Jones Takes Job as Auto Mechanic."[78] On Monday, February 8, Jones began work as a mechanic with Chevrolet Automobile Company in New York City, the same that had sponsored her yellow suffrage car for the auto tour to Rochester in October. In accepting the position, she entered a world populated almost exclusively by men, hoping both to understand the "mysteries of the carburetor" and to achieve greater financial independence from her Anti mother, who controlled the purse strings of the Jones estate. The general had taken up residence at the Hotel Broztell on East 27th Street from whence she telephoned Mary Jones to tell her she was "getting into the automobile business."

In so doing, Jones had followed the lead of her friend Olive Schultz, the intrepid advance scout for the Army of the Hudson during the On-to-Washington campaign who had later been inspired to establish a suffrage taxi service in New York City in cooperation with the Woman's Political Union and Harriot Stanton Blatch. No less than the *New York Times* had praised Schultz for her ability to fix her own vehicle, arguing that she could "do more to improve a peevish carburetor with a hairpin than most mechanics can with a hydraulic drill and an assortment of wrenches."[79] To drive one's own car and possess the know-how to fix it spoke volumes about a woman's self-reliance, and Jones was eager to achieve the kind of fearless independence for which the *Times* had praised Schultz.

While the *Sun* of New York City reported that Jones would work in the auto repair shop, other newspaper accounts suggested she would work in the Chevy salesroom instead, using her oratorical skills to sell cars rather than to fix them. In any case, the motivation for taking the job remained the

Jones pioneers once again, this time as an auto mechanic in the Chevrolet Automobile Company in New York City. She is shown here in her mechanic's apron inflating a tire. While the Library of Congress dates this photograph 1920-1930, headlines from the time point to February 1915 as the proper date (Bain Collection, Library of Congress, Prints and Photographs Division).

same—to gender-diversify a male industry and to achieve for herself the economic independence she advocated for all women.[80] Jones explained to inquiring journalists that she hoped to own her own chauffeuring business one day and that she would proudly drive in the grand suffrage parade when, with luck, the votes-for-women referendum passed in New York in November. When asked if she wore overalls to her new job, Jones replied matter-of-factly,

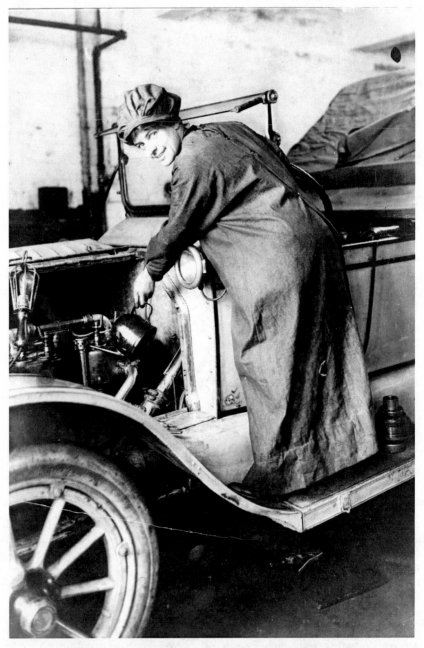

Jones fills the oil in this promotional shot taken at the Chevrolet Automobile Company in New York City. While the Library of Congress dates this photograph 1910, headlines from the time pinpoint February 1915 as the proper date (Bain Collection, Library of Congress, Prints and Photographs Division).

saying, "I wear a big apron, which is better than any masculine attire." Glossy black and white photos showed Jones dressed in a mechanics smock, repairing tires and dutifully oiling engines.

Jones's duties at the auto shop would, it seemed, be as much promotional as practical, as she would still be free to campaign for women's rights at will and travel as often as the cause required. At the behest of New Jersey suffragists, Jones deployed to Newark to serve as a poll monitor or "woman watcher" for the October 19 suffrage referendum there, traveling across the Hudson with Surgeon General Lavinia Dock and other New York suffragists who "came early and stayed late" in an attempt to ensure a fair vote in a city where the "practical politics of the Antis" proved too much for the suffragettes.[81] Headlines declared that the women poll watchers were "worn out" after a day of "discouragements, of fears, of nerve-racking, furious work that seemed as if it was going for nothing." Jones and her army of woman watchers had arranged oversight at all but 25 of the 180 Newark polling sites. The *New York Times* praised Jones in particular as "one of the women most active" during a day that smashed existing records for voter participation in a New Jersey special election.[82] Jones earned special kudos from the newspaper for rushing to replace an election monitor who had been forced to leave her post and staying until the polls closed. The turnout was twice what was predicted, and Jones and her fellow activists put up a "strenuous and unfaltering battle," despite "the great political machines arrayed against them." The votes-for-women referendum, the first of its kind in the East, had given the state of New Jersey "the most unusual election day in its history."

The defeat of votes-for-women in the Garden State dealt Jones and her fellow activists a dispiriting blow, so much so that an exhausted Jones was rumored to be "tiring of the cause."[83] She had shown up well before 6 a.m. at the polling place in Newark, and despite isolated reports from early voters of Anti forces offering bribes and other inducements in return for votes, she nevertheless determined that the election had mostly been a fair one. Though the defeat of the proposed suffrage amendment meant, under New Jersey law, that the proposal could not be resubmitted for a full five years, Jones found solace in the fact that Woodrow Wilson—the president she had marched 250 wintry miles to convert in 1913—had reportedly voted yes on the measure in his home district in New Jersey. There were other bright spots, too, including the many enthusiastic young men and women the general had met in Newark. Early on election day, Jones penned a letter to her friend Rebekah Walters of Cold Spring Harbor. In it she anticipated the proposed amendment's defeat and lamented the few stories she heard of "inducements" offered to bribe voters and isolated reports of "toughs" in the streets attempting to intimidate. While some suffragists cried fraud, Jones's dispatch from Newark the morning of election day described a mostly calm and cordial process:

I personally watched at two polling places and utmost quiet prevailed.... The clerks of election were most polite and considerate, although one could judge that our cause had no interest for them.

The schoolchildren of Newark seemed to be largely our friends, especially the girls, as they took special care to walk past the windows, usually remarking, "I hope the Suffragettes will win."

The boys, too, were not backward, as many times during the day we heard them call out to us "We hope you will beat the crooks." The one remarkable feature of the day was that not an Anti-suffrage pink rose ... was in evidence at the polling booths.

Evidently the members of the New Jersey Association Opposed to Woman's Suffrage knew their interests had been well taken care of by James R. Nugent.

Hastily yours for the cause, Rosalie G. Jones.

Jones's foil in the Garden State, Democratic machine boss James R. Nugent, had predicted the measure's defeat in New Jersey would, domino-like, precipitate its rejection in New York when voters cast their ballots there on the votes-for-women question on November 2. With Nugent's prophecy in mind, Jones hastened back across the Hudson River to renew the fight on her home soil. On October 29, the New York State Woman Suffrage Party enlisted Rosalie's Army to headline a 24-hour speaking marathon on behalf of the cause.[84] The following day, the "Hikers Squad" reprised the marathon speeches, taking the lectern at the peak Saturday evening hours when theater-goers jammed playhouses across the metropolis.[85] Jones and the other around-the-clock suffrage speakers reached a reported 19,800 voters at multiple sites, hoping to make their last best case to New York voters before bringing their whirlwind campaign to a close by midnight of Sunday, October 31. The "women fighters," wrote the New York Times, "were tired but confident of victory" and otherwise "full of hope," though the Antis predicted their side would carry the state by as many as 80,000 votes.

On November 2, 1915, New York men went to the polls to decide the fate of women's enfranchisement. Despite an all-out effort by Jones, Carrie Chapman Catt, Harriot Stanton Blatch and the other tireless activists of the Empire State Campaign Committee, New York suffragists lost a hard-fought battle to become the first state since Colorado in 1893 to pass full suffrage for women, losing by just under 200,000 votes.[86] While there was little consolation for advocates in the defeat, the results of the 1915 ballot validated Jones's particular emphasis on rural counties Upstate, where the tide had turned firmly in favor of suffrage. While a majority of only six counties voted for the suffrage amendment on November 2, those six counties had not been those tightly orbiting around New York City, where suffragists were well-organized, but in counties such as Schenectady (55 percent), Chautauqua (58 percent), and Cortland (61 percent). Meanwhile, the ballot measure had been defeated by a 57 percent vote against in the New York City-area counties: Bronx, Kings, New York, Queens, and Richmond.

The defeat in the 1915 referendum spurred Craft to redouble her efforts, as she participated in monthly "suffrage schools" in preparation for the reappearance of the votes-for-women question on the 1917 ballot in New York. The day-long teach-in events featured morning sessions led by district officials as a prelude to afternoon lectures by votes-for-women headliners, including Craft, who spoke on parliamentary law and efficiency. Publicity for the monthly suffrage schools billed the colonel as "an authority on her subject" and reminded attendees of Craft's status as "the right-hand 'man' of 'General' Rosalie Gardiner Jones, who led the famous 'hike' up the Hudson way back in the early days of local suffrage activity."[87] The "early days" mention proved telling; though Rosalie's Army's march on Washington was less than four years distant, the imminent entry of the United States into World War I coupled with the advent of votes-for-women picketing of the Woodrow Wilson White House by Alice Paul's Silent Sentinels in January of 1917 made the suffrage marches of 1912 and 1913 feel like distant history to some.

Jones, Craft, and their fellow Empire State suffragists would ultimately have to wait until November of 1917 for suffrage to pass in New York on its second consecutive appearance on the ballot. This time, votes-for-women advocates were better funded, boosted by strategic allies in the federal government supporting the idea that women's suffrage should be considered a war measure to support American troops fighting in Europe. Importantly, pro-enfranchisement forces managed to flip the numbers in the New York City metro, where nearly 60 percent voted for the referendum in 1917. New York became the first state east of the Mississippi River to grant full women's suffrage. The state of Illinois had granted its female citizens partial suffrage in 1913, inspired in part by the march of Rosalie's Army that same year, though women in the Land of Lincoln could not vote for governor, state representatives, or members of Congress.

Nearly five years had passed since Rosalie's Army marched triumphantly into Washington, D.C., with bugles blaring. In victory, the *Sun* in New York City ran a full-page spread under the headline, "Names of Suffrage Pioneers Not Forgotten," picturing Inez Milholland, Carrie Chapman Catt, Harriot Stanton Blatch, Alva Belmont, and Rosalie Jones as the originators of the long-awaited triumph. Written by former *New York Tribune* writer Eleanor Booth Simmons, the lengthy paean sought to highlight the work of suffrage greats who had passed away or otherwise been sidelined or marginalized. In her honor roll listing of more recent pioneers, Simmons lauded Jones and the 1913 On-to-Washington marchers in particular, conjuring stirring images of the general "setting her teeth and struggling over the Jersey flats and through the Maryland mud, and breaking into the columns of the New York papers, and the papers of the country for that matter, as suffrage had never broken before."[88] As a newspaperwoman, Simmons lamented the advent of the new suffrage organization woman—the de facto bureaucrat "shut away in their offices and protected by secretaries." She wondered aloud if women "so inclined to the militancy that they couldn't resist" had been cast aside by the desk-bound powers-that-be that had since assumed control of the movement. Activists more inclined to direct action, she implied, had been pushed out. The list of pioneering suffragettes who fell into this category read like a roll call of Rosalie's Army. Excepting Jones—who endured as a figure of national prominence despite her public split with Alice Paul—Ida Craft, Elisabeth Freeman, and Martha Klatschken headed Simmons's list of "uncounted figures who in the last ten years rose one after another … did their bit and sank out of sight, perhaps to be forgotten, not even mentioned when victory came." Freeman had taken her whirlwind suffrage campaign to Texas in 1916, where in addition to organizing for the Texas Woman's Suffrage Association she conducted an influential anti-lynching investigation on behalf of the NAACP.[89] Craft, one of the oldest Brooklyn suffragists, had been "present at the birth of the Woman's Suffrage Party [and] gave night and day to its service," Simmons insisted, recalling fondly the many miles she had "hiked in Ida's wake, admiring to see how she never lost a chance to drop a word for suffrage. What had become of her? She was just dropped out."

Elisabeth Freeman had deeply worried American suffrage leaders when first she arrived in New York as a disciple of English militant Emmeline Pankhurst. "I remember the horror that rocked the party when it became known that Mrs. Catt, who had been abroad, was sending over for service with us a militant who threw bricks," Simmons wrote in her recollection. Freeman had thrown no bricks upon her arrival but instead "threw words around very effectively, and was a picturesque campaigner till she dropped out or was dropped out." Freeman had given her heart and soul to win the vote for New York women in 1917, yet, Simmons fairly asked, "who remembers her now?"

Members of the New York establishment had also forgotten the indefatigable Martha Klatschken. "I always thought Martha deserved decoration," Simmons lamented of an activist who had given up a good job to devote her time and money to the cause of women's equity. Out of filial duty, Klatschken had recently moved to Texas to serve as caretaker of her deceased sister's children. "Martha should have been remembered in the hour of victory for she sacrificed more than most in serving suffrage," she insisted. "Surgeon General" Lavinia Dock, the distinguished nurse and author who had accompanied Jones every step of the way on the first pilgrimage to Albany and marched with the On-to-Washington Army on its first day in New Jersey, belonged in the same category of unrecognized greats as a woman who had "toiled night and day for suffrage" but who had since retired to Pennsylvania to take care of an ailing mother.

In her homage, Simmons failed to mention the underappreciated newspaperwomen who shared her profession, those who had likewise helped immortalize the names of Rosalie Jones, Ida Craft, and the rest of Rosalie's Army. There had been Constance Leupp, the reformer, war correspondent, and hiker who had gone on to author several important pro-labor investigative pieces in magazines ranging from *McClure's* to *The Survey*. There had been hiker-journalist Ethel Lloyd Patterson, whose poignant and poetic accounts of the On-to-Washington hike had been read with such relish by suffragist readers of the *Evening Star* and whose coverage of Rosalie's Army propelled her to a career contributing features to glossy magazines. War correspondent and marcher Emilie Doetsch of the *Baltimore News*, meanwhile, had grown into a noted advocate for newspaperwomen nationwide and just the second woman to pass the Maryland state bar.

Inez Milholland Boissevain, the New York suffrage lawyer and herald of the 1913 national suffrage procession in Washington, D.C., deserved special mention as a martyr for the cause. Milholland, who had married Dutchman Jan Boissevain several months after the suffrage parade, collapsed in October 1916 while delivering a votes-for-women speech in California on behalf of Alice Paul's new National Woman's Party and passed away less than one month later after a series of failed blood transfusions. "Of all the figures of the … rapidly receding past," Simmons wrote, Inez Milholland Boissevain's star should be counted among the brightest. Jones and Milholland Boissevain had been the stars of the national suffrage parade of 1913, and Simmons and other New York City suffragists were determined that, in celebrating the passage of votes-for-women in New York state, "their great names will not die."

15

Life After Generaling

Even before the passage of the New York suffrage amendment in November of 1917, Rosalie Jones had effectively hung up her marching boots in favor of hitting the books. The fight for equality was far from over on a national level, but for reasons both personal and professional, she wanted to change the locus of the battle. Jones had long considered suffrage to be an intellectual argument, and in seeking an advanced degree she hoped to gain the tools by which to win it. "She has been brought up in a home where intellectual attainment is recognized," Ethel Lloyd Patterson had said of Jones on the long march to Washington. "Miss Jones has the advantage of a broad and comprehensive education added to that of a naturally good mind."

Now, in the midst of the negative headlines that had accompanied her father's suicide, Jones prioritized her education with renewed vigor, moving to Washington, D.C., in pursuit of a law degree and to continue her advocacy in closer proximity to the seat of government. She had already completed a Bachelor of Arts degree at Adelphi College in Brooklyn, and now, like suffrage lawyer and martyr Inez Milholland, she sought a credential to make herself an even more formidable advocate for international peace and women's rights.

In the interim the Jones name had received a surfeit of negative press. In July of 1916, the *New York Times* ran the damaging headline, "Warrants Out for 46 Residents, Including Rosalie Jones's Brother, Heir to Millions."[1] No less than Theodore Roosevelt, the Jones's longtime Long Island neighbor, had singled out Charles Jones for unsanitary conditions, and a warrant had been issued for his arrest. Unsanitary conditions in rental tenements of the kind owned by Charles Jones were thought to be contributing factors in an outbreak of infantile paralysis, and conditions were found to be "unusually bad" on the rental properties occupied by the mostly Italian immigrants living in Jones's tenements. Rosalie's brother had been cited for similar violations just the year before, and the public censor of a former president further embarrassed a family whose ancestors had lived on Long Island since the Revolutionary War.

Jones's wholehearted pursuit of her graduate education was also likely influenced by her old nemesis, Alice Paul, whose Silent Sentinels had filled the public relations vacuum left by the general's dramatic marches. Four years earlier in 1913, it had been Jones's idea to confront President Wilson directly—via the visual symbolism of the march on Washington and the dramatic delivery of the suffrage letter. Now it was Paul's activists, picketing six days a week in front of the White House, who seemed to have appropriated that mission and its dramatic appeal while borrowing heavily from Jones's message and method. Much like Jones's On-to-Washington marchers, the Silent Sentinels created powerful images of resistance ready-made for dissemination in the mass media. Unlike her friend and fellow pilgrim Elisabeth Freeman, who eagerly joined Paul's militant National Woman's Party (NWP), Jones continued to side with NAWSA's Carrie Chapman Catt, who preferred a less militant, state-by-state strategy for winning women the vote.

Meanwhile, Jones's powerful personal allies in the House of Representatives, including congresswoman Jeannette Rankin and Speaker of the House Champ Clark, proved instrumental in winning legislative victories that moved the country ever closer to full enfranchisement for women. Jones rejoiced on January 10, 1918, when the House passed a constitutional amendment guaranteeing women the right to vote by a count of 274 to 136.[2] Rankin, Jones's long-time suffrage ally from Montana, had become the first woman elected to Congress in 1915 and was now leading the charge, demanding of her male colleagues, "How shall we answer their challenge, gentlemen: how shall we explain ... the meaning of democracy if the same Congress that voted for war to make the world safe for democracy refuses to give this small measure of democracy to the women of our country?"

One again, in the midst of a historic victory, Simmons reminded the nation's readers of the importance of the women activists whose tireless work had made the great victory possible. Simmons, who had been on Capitol Hill that day to bear personal witness to the momentous achievement, conjured Jones specifically in the deep wellspring of memories drawn up by the occasion:

> They came trooping into my mind, those Great Days, as I sat in the gallery of the House of Representatives waiting for speaker [Champ] Clark to open the proceedings on January 10. Again, I marched, my boots red with the clay of Maryland roads, into Washington with Gen. Rosalie Jones's Suffrage Pilgrims the next day, but one before President Wilson's first inauguration, and saw the curious crowds regard the little band which did so much to break the bonds of conservatism that had retarded the votes-for-women movement.[3]

Regrettably, the movement's moment in the sun did not last long, as a year that had begun with such promise quickly turned tragic on both political and personal fronts. The House bill whose passage Jones, Simmons, and activists all around the nation had initially celebrated ultimately failed to pass the Senate, where, as Simmons feared, the measure lacked the necessary 60 votes despite assurances from Mary Garrett Hay and others that it would "go through with votes to spare."

With the constitutional amendment for which she had marched languishing in the Senate, Jones was dealt another crushing blow later that winter with the death of her brother, Oliver "Olly" Jones, whose ill health was said to have driven their father to "nervous wreck" status and was thought to have been a factor in Dr. Jones's suicide. Having been troubled his whole life and eventually institutionalized,[4] Ollo had not yet reached 40 years of age when he passed away in March of what the *New York Times* listed as pneumonia.[5] Rosalie and family buried Oliver Jr., in the family plot in Cold Spring Harbor. Months later in October of 1918, Rosalie lost her mother, Mary, to hemiplegia[6] and her brother Phillip to pneumonia nine days after the death of their mother.[7] The woman Rosalie had endeavored to please her entire life—her arch-conservative and anti-suffragist mother—was gone.

With the passing of Mary Jones, Rosalie made national news again, this time as an heiress. On October 26, 1918, the *Evening World* in New York City ran the headline, "Worth $5,000,000 Gen. Rosalie Jones Is Socialist Now."[8] Jones would serve as co-executor of her mother's estate along with her sister Louise and her brother Charles. Almost immediately legal trouble began, with the *Long-Islander* printing excerpts of a letter from Rosalie to Charles in which she refused to sign checks written to meet the expenses of the estate, including insurance, which she preferred to allow to lapse on properties to which she might soon become heir.[9] The dispute demonstrated Rosalie's willingness to use knowledge gained in her recent legal studies at George Washington University to challenge traditional patriarchal control, but the courts ultimately ruled against her, ordering that any of the three executors be allowed to draw funds from the estate. Rosalie did not lack for money, but already she was demonstrating a marked tendency to fight fiercely for even the smallest penny, even when it meant defying her family.

"Meet again General Rosalie Jones of ... suffrage memory, who whipped through the news columns as leader of militant suffrage 'hikes'...but now appears with the tinkling of cymbals and sounding brass of socialism," observed the *Evening World*.[10] Jones, the paper claimed, intended to "obtain a super-education so that she may be prepared to cope with the great changes she believes will occur through the revolutionizing of the world after the war." The *Evening World* reporter had found Jones at a study table in the public library where she had been preparing a map to illustrate a research article she had authored on the British Labor Party. Jones planned to submit her scholarship in partial fulfillment of her degree requirements at George Washington University in Washington, D.C., where she went on to earn her LLB degree in 1919—the year in which both houses of Congress finally passed the 19th Amendment constitutionally guaranteeing women the right to vote.[11] Three years later in 1922, Jones earned a Doctor of Civil Law degree from that same university, publishing her doctoral dissertation in 1923 under the title *The American Standard of Living and World Co-operation*. Jones dedicated the book in memory of her brother, Phillip, and listed among her credentials her status as a new member of the New York Bar.

"'General' Rosalie Jones, the very one who gained her title 'hiking' at the head of a suffragist battalion ... from New York to Albany and then to Gotham to the gates of the White House itself, just to prove that woman can be an all-around sort of person, has turned from athletics to the pursuit of literature," observed the *Berkeley Daily Gazette* in a story

Jones is shown in profile in this undated graduation photograph. She earned five academic degrees in her lifetime (Marc Watkins Collection. Used by permission of Marc Watkins).

headlined, "Suffragette Is Authoress."[12] The book's publisher, Boston-based Cornhill, claimed that Jones's tome "solved any number of questions that the average American cannot answer," though the *Daily Gazette* found the 329-page book sufficiently daunting in its scholarship as to call it "terrifying." In the first chapter, Jones acknowledged the complexity of interdisciplinary research requiring in-depth economic, political, and sociological analysis, opining that "in a short, popular treatise it would be impossible" to adequately develop her thesis, which she summarized as "The American standard of living and its influence on international relations."[13] Calling the American standard of living a "byword and a catchphrase" that had been manipulated by political orators and had never, prior to her book, been "satisfactorily defined," she argued in favor of internationalism over nationalism and against protectionist tariffs and immigration policies that overheated competition among nations and often served as a precursor to war. The most effective economic policy, Jones concluded, was "a universal world policy of understanding, tolerance, and cooperation."[14]

Jones's evolving socialism coupled with her emphasis on global cooperation led her to follow fellow equal rights advocates Jeanette Rankin, Elisabeth
Freeman, Carrie Chapman Catt, and Jane Addams into the peace movement,
joining the Women's International League for Peace and Freedom in the
years following World War I. Founded in 1915 by suffragist Jane Addams,
who served as its first president, the league worked to achieve world peace via
disarmament and the cultivation of equal rights across the globe. The American headquarters of the organization had moved to New York City in 1920,
and in 1924, its biennial international congress would be held in America
for the first time. Slated to begin May 1 in Washington, D.C., the "New International Order" theme of the convention closely paralleled the topic of
Jones's dissertation and book.[15] Along with delegates from across the nation
and the world, Jones descended on the capital to hear firsthand reports from
Europe on the prospects of lasting peace there and a keynote address given by
Addams to open a conference otherwise marred by protest. Activists from an
organization called Daughters of 1812 hissed and screamed "traitor" at Jones
and her fellow peace delegates, accusing the league of pledging its members
to nonviolence without a compensatory pledge to "support and defend the
United States against all enemies, foreign and domestic."[16] The Daughters of
1812 agitated for a congressional investigation into the alleged anti–American
activities of the pacifist organization.

Meanwhile, Jones took advantage of the trip to Washington to engage in
some lobbying of her own, arranging for a side meeting with Senator Clarence Dill, a "hardboiled senator from the West" who in the past had appeared
sympathetic to women's rights issues but who had recently been dragging his
feet on support of key legislation.[17] Dill kept Jones and her fellow delegates
waiting for over an hour, angering Jones in what quickly became a "stormy
conference" from which she left disenchanted with the Western senator who
considered himself something of a maverick but who had responded to her
inquiries with what she viewed as the timidity of a mainstream politician.

In September of 1924, Jones's ongoing dissatisfaction with cowardly bureaucrats and the corruption of the two-party system led her to abandon the
Democratic Party altogether in favor of Wisconsin's Robert M. La Follette in
his third-party bid for the presidency.[18] A supporter of peace, women's rights,
and labor, La Follette closely matched Jones in his politics, so closely, in fact,
that the one-time suffrage general announced in September that she would be
campaigning personally for the Progressive Party candidate in battleground
Midwestern states. The planned sojourn would employ a modus operandi very
much like the marches of Rosalie's Army; Jones would be accompanied by two
women lieutenants from her home state of New York—labor activists Helen
Todd and Jeannette Schiener—and men would be "absolutely tabooed in the
party." Footwear ranging from "walking boots to dancing pumps" would be

packed and worn to suit whatever occasion the campaigners encountered on a trip wherein they intended to "meet all classes of people." Like the hikers on the marches to Albany and Washington, the wide-ranging campaigners would be compelled to leave home, office, and loved ones to "hie themselves to the Middle West to beard the political lions in their dens wherever they can find them." Like Jones's peaceful march on Washington, D.C., of 1913, the fight for Fightin' Bob La Follette would be a "bloodless battle"; Jones and her new army would arrive by car in each passing city by 4 p.m., parking in the most prominent spot in town, at which time Schiener would ring a replica Liberty Bell affixed to the front of Jones's vehicle. After listening to the general and others deliver informational speeches, voters willing to sign to support La Follette would be allowed to ring the imitation Liberty Bell in anticipation of the open-air street meetings to be held later that same evening. The advent of a viable third party, and the inherent weakness of incumbent Republican Calvin Coolidge and Democratic nominee Al Smith, had caused Jones to declare the ensuing political landscape "the most mixed up I ever knew." Radical democrats disenchanted with Smith were expected to vote for La Follette, while conservative Democrats threatened to cross party lines to vote for Coolidge.[19]

Jones believed that the spike in youth interest in third-party politics offered a chance for true political sea change. She claimed that young voters "really know how to vote better than the older people" while relaying one particularly revealing story of an aged voter who had always voted Republican but now, influenced by his sons' passionate interest in the "new movement," would vote Progressive. Jones told reporters that she had thrown her support behind the former Wisconsin governor because he alone seemed "to have an understanding of the economic needs of the people and … remedies that are perfectly logical and that are easy to carry out." Populist signs reading "We want our country back" and "What will you do to elect La Follette?" decorated Jones's campaign automobile, along with a broom affixed to the back symbolizing a shared desire to clean up the corruption of the ineffectual two-party system and to end business-as-usual in Washington.

Jones, Todd, and Schiener left La Follette's Manhattan headquarters at West 43rd Street on Tuesday, September 16, 1924, at 10 a.m. following a send-off the night before at the Hotel Astor at which the candidate's son, Robert, had lauded Jones's upcoming journey.[20] Photos of a beaming general standing atop the running board of her car as it prepared to leave Union Square ran in newspapers across the country, including in eastern Iowa, where Jones and company hoped to visit on their way to Nebraska after first spreading the La Follette gospel to New York, Ohio, and Illinois voters.

"Miss Rosalie Jones, former militant suffrage leader of New York City, now on a cross-country speaking trip in a high-powered automobile, invaded Waterloo Saturday evening," announced the *Waterloo Evening Courier*.[21] In

Seated in the driver's seat, Jones on a campaign tour for Robert M. La Follette, September 24, 1924 (Bain Collection, Library of Congress, Prints and Photographs Division).

Jones speaks from the running board of her touring car as Helen Todd, Mrs. Gordon Norrie, and Art G. Hays look on. While the photograph is undated, similar dated photographs as well as headlines of the time strongly point to September 1924 as the proper date. The small bell held by Todd is almost certainly a replica of the Liberty Bell Jones would ring to signal a street meeting (Bain Collection, Library of Congress, Prints and Photographs Division).

Iowa, Jones "flayed President Coolidge and the Democratic candidate for president impartially and lauded 'Fightin' Bob' as the ... pure Progressive of the age."

Even before she left on her auto tour through the Midwest, rumors had begun to swirl that Jones might be seeking marriage. The general's hometown newspaper had asked her point-blank prior to departure whether there was any truth to the gossip that she would be looking for a husband on the trip; Jones responded to the query with polite laughter, saying she was "too busy to think of a husband." Until recently, Jones told the *Long-Islander*, she had been completely occupied with what she called "the business of her mother's estate" but had now resolved matters such that she could leave without worry. Since completing her doctorate in 1922, Rosalie had been living off and on with her sister Louise, a recluse,[22] in the family's concrete mansion, Jones Manor, in Cold Spring Harbor, Long Island, while traveling periodically to Washington, D.C., to engage in peace work and women's rights lobbying. It was from these trips that the rumors of incipient romance had sprung, as Jones had indeed acquired a romantic interest—ironically the very senator, Clarence Dill of Spokane, Washington, whom she first met while attending the Women's International League for Peace and Freedom.

Dill had been a newspaper reporter for the *Cleveland Plain Dealer* and had passed the bar in the state of Washington in 1910. Just 40 years old when he took his seat in 1924, Dill had been dubbed the "boy senator" by his congressional colleagues for his youthful appearance.[23] When Jones accompanied her fellow women-for-peace delegates to Dill's office, she had "ask[ed] him some important questions." Dill answered evasively, and Jones "raked him over the coals" for what she perceived to be his obfuscation. Dill held his ground, however, and Jones left his office in a huff. For weeks after Jones's abrupt Cinderella-like departure from his office, the senator's secretary sought the identity of the mysterious "lady in pink." It had been love at first sight, at least for Dill.[24]

By the spring of 1927, the Jones-Dill long-distance relationship had blossomed into an impending marriage trumpeted in newspapers across the country as both a Cinderella story and "A Capital Romance."[25] Jones announced the engagement publicly on Tuesday, March 8, on returning to New York after a visit with Dill in Washington; the wedding would follow a week later on March 15. "Never, until Miss Jones bawled me out for thwarting her committee had I met a woman who, for me, combined charm and political acumen," Dill explained to a press corps eager for news of the nuptials, adding that Jones's "keenness of intellect" had impressed him most.[26] "She thought of more things to argue about in fifteen minutes in my office, and more way of calling me a dodo, in a nice way, than a male political opponent would have conceived in a couple of days," Dill recalled of their first meeting.

Jones, however, took issue with the love-at-first sight narrative promulgated by the press, confessing that she had been "too angry to feel any such sentiments that day he turned down my committee." Jones's sudden willingness to wed shocked many who knew her. "Pretty, financially independent, and politically-minded, she found that she was quite sufficient unto herself," observed the *Galveston Daily News*, "and thought of men as interruptions and distractions." She was, the newspaper went on to say, "nationally prominent in half a dozen women's organizations" in 1924 and continued to find her "greatest thrill in working for peace ... labor, and other social reforms." The idea of a marriage between a woman who had "never spoken of matrimony without a slight touch of derision" and a man who, at 40, had remained one of Congress's few bachelors fascinated the media, with one newspaper claiming that "such romances are almost always a little peppier, and spicier, and more exciting than the prosaic mating of humans." Another declared that news of the pending nuptials had so enthused Washington that "the 'town crier' had gone to bed with a sore throat."[27] The would-be Mrs. Dill was "a personality to be reckoned with, socially, and politically," causing even the "dear old gossips... [to] agree that Senator Dill picked a great combination when he picked Rosalie Gardiner Jones of Long Island and Washington DC for his helpmate."

Fourteen years after the completion of her historic march, Jones's nom de guerre followed her into marriage in the *New York Times* headline, "'Gen.' Rosalie Jones, Suffragette Leader, Betrothed to United States Senator Dill."[28] Jones found herself forced, once more, to defend her feminist views, even in indulging her basic desire for companionship. "There's no reason for me to change," she was quoted as saying.[29] "No more cause for me to give up my convictions because I'm in love with a man than there is for him to change his party or his stand on a public question because he's married a wife who has convictions as strong as his own." The bottom line, Jones told her friends in the movement, is that she was interested in Dill's political and social work and he was interested in hers. "Mutual interest was the basis of lasting love," she declared.

The wedding, held in the Syosset, Long Island, church Jones's grandfather had helped build, attracted high-profile guests, including former New York Governor William Sulzer and former secretary of the Navy Edwin Denby.[30] While the story of the union landed in newspapers across the country, the most revealing account may well have appeared in the *Long-Islander*, whose description of the nuptials read in part:

> Miss Rosalie Jones, so well-known about Huntington and Cold Spring Harbor for the reason that she usually gets her own way, is now the wife of Clarence C. Dill, United States Senator from Spokane Washington, and at the wedding held Tuesday morning at St. John's Episcopal Church at Cold Spring Harbor, she still carried that idea. In the first place she said that she was not going to say the word "obey." It is an Episcopal marriage ceremony, but it is optional and Miss Jones had her way.[31]

"It is not a word a self-respecting woman of this century likes to give a man," Jones said of excising the word "obey" from her vows, adding, "Mutual understanding, affection, and consideration govern the affections of husbands and wives."[32] On her refusal to be "given away," Jones told the press, "I'm solely responsible for what I'm doing…. I'm independent and my own boss. How ridiculous for a brother or somebody to hand me over to my new lord and master, like a woman of a harem! I'll give myself away." The *Long-Islander* claimed Jones "got her way" in the wedding, including her insistence that she march up the center aisle alone and without attendants and that Dill do the same.[33] Dill, the newspaper reported, was "a very quiet, unassuming man and did not want any big splurge. The fact that the wedding was planned to be held in the quiet little church in Cold Spring Harbor, rather than in some big church in New York City … was … pleasing to him." While the hometown newspaper felt no need to flatter Jones, it did pause to comment on the remarkable number of people from all walks of life that filled the church for the ceremony. "While Miss Jones is a heiress to a large estate, she is one of the most democratic persons that one could care to meet," the article conceded. "She thinks just as much of stopping to give a pleasant word to the working man or woman as she does to those that have climbed to the highest rung of the ladder of success. It was these people who saw Miss Jones married, and her pleasant smile and her handshake showed that she appreciated it."

International newsreel photos captured the "noted suffragette leader" resplendent in white gown with a veil and orange blossoms leaving the little Episcopal Church of St. John at Cold Spring Harbor. Jones surprised many in announcing that she would be called "Mrs. C.C. Dill" and would officially take her husband's name. "I'm not a member of the Lucy Stoner League," she told reporters, "and the only time I shall sign myself 'Rosalie G. Jones' is in connection with the administration of my mother's estate, which my brother and sister share."[34] Still, Jones made it clear that she would be making her own choices henceforth. "The senator hasn't got me in his pocket," she insisted. "Mine is the one vote he will have to get in every election."

The Dills quickly became one of Washington's most influential couples, with Jones continuing her activism in both Washington, D.C., and in Washington state, from whence she published a short monograph titled *Women's Influence Through the Ballot* under her married name, Rosalie Jones Dill. In the slim, 20-page volume, Jones provided women practical advice on public speaking—the very art she had found so trying in her salad days as a suffragette in New York City. "A cause needs supporters who have knowledge, not merely opinions," Jones observed in the book's foreword. "Its helpers should understand the voters' problems and be prepared to answer perplexing questions during the campaign."[35] Frequent mention of the word "campaign" in the small speechmaking manual caused some to wonder whether Jones was

Rosalie Jones and Senator Clarence Dill pose for their wedding photograph in March of 1927. Dill and Jones married at the Syosset, Long Island, church Jones's grandfather helped build (Marc Watkins Collection. Used by permission of Marc Watkins).

in essence distilling what she had learned working for her husband, to whose campaign she had donated generously, or whether she might be foreshadowing a future run for political office of her own. In the short chapter "Women and the Law," Jones, who had been admitted to the bar in New York but had never served as a practicing attorney, reflected on the Seneca Falls Convention of 1848. Modern women, she observed, were now looking back on "the long weary struggle begun by.... Elizabeth Cady Stanton, Lucretia Mott, and Susan B. Anthony, with ever increasing pride." Such pioneers were not "the hard, insensitive women who are sometimes decried" but women "whose brains, energies, and hearts were afire to right injustices against all women." Jazz Age feminists who joined the movement during "its picturesque days of victory" must know that "without the zeal and sacrifice of ... early crusaders" such as Mary Lyons, Belva Lockwood, and Dr. Anna Shaw, the vote would never have been achieved. For women wishing to further develop their thinking on the subject of women and law, Jones concluded her chapter with a handful of suggested speech topics, including "Domestic relations, court, and women," "divorce laws," "property laws," and "American pioneer suffragists."[36]

In 1930, Jones broadened the reach of her advocacy still further, agreeing to serve as the moderator of an NBC Radio program airing on Saturday nights. The broadcast, partially underwritten by the Women's International League for Peace and Freedom for which Jones served as chair of the radio committee, would be broadcast by 75 stations.[37] Jones used her influence within the movement to book "an imposing array of speakers" ranging from Jane Addams to U.S. senators William Borah and Thomas Walsh. She also parlayed her growing influence in Washington into a presidency of the Congressional Club, an influential organization consisting of wives of representatives and senators that in 1933 celebrated its 25th anniversary. Jones seized the opportunity to arrange for a White House visit to mark the group's silver anniversary as well as to honor the women who, contrary to stereotype, had been much more than idle cheerleaders for their

The back of the undated photograph reads "Rosalie Jones Dill, 1026 16th Street NW, Washington DC," suggesting that the photograph captures Rosalie in newlywed years spent in the nation's capital (Marc Watkins Collection. Used by permission of Marc Watkins).

husbands' legislative careers.[38] Crossing party lines, Jones commissioned one of the founding members of the club, representative Florence Kahn, as a featured speaker. Elected as a Republican in 1925, Kahn earned distinction as the first Jewish woman to serve in Congress and only the fifth woman overall. Like congresswoman Mae Nolan, Kahn had won a special election to fill the seat left vacant after the death of a husband. Despite their political differences, Jones admired Kahn, a passionate recruiter of gifted women who no doubt encouraged Jones to consider a future run for office.

As Jones began to wield her political influence in the mid–1930s, her relationship with her senator husband began to suffer, and their marital difficulties deepened when Dill opted not to run for re-election for his Senate seat in 1934, a move Jones, ever the general, considered a cowardly retreat.[39] Shortly after Dill announced his decision, Jones moved back to New York while Dill maintained his residence in Washington, D.C. By 1935, gossip columnists dished that a divorce between the Dills was imminent. However, formal dissolution remained the stuff of tabloids until the headline "Dill Divorce, Eastern Rumor" ran in the *Spokesman-Review* in early January of 1936. "Washington society," the article reported, was "speculating on the prospects of a divorce."[40] This time, the page-one article, originating in Dill's hometown of Spokane, Washington, and run next to stories filed by the Associated Press, carried the weight of real news. Attributed to a special correspondent in Washington, and offered with the caveat "to date it is nothing more than rumor," the story publicly divulged to Dills' immediate constituency the estrangement of the State of Washington's quintessential power couple.

Three months later, the *New York Times* announced the split in its headline, "Ex-Senator Dill Sues for Divorce." The story appeared to glory in the failure of a relationship once described as "love-at-first-sight."[41] From the beginning, Jones had considered herself Dill's equal, holding her husband to the same high standard to which she held all men. Now Jones appeared to be paying dearly for her refusal to live the compliant life expected of a senator's wife. Dill's suit for divorce lodged salacious claims, citing "inhumane treatment" and "personal indignities" that began as early as 1928. In addition to accusing her husband of political cowardice, the complaint alleged she had spread false rumors that Dill had refused to run for re-election because he was losing his mind. The suit further accused Jones of everything from "slovenly habits of dress in her home, on the street and elsewhere" to the charge that she buried dead dogs in the backyard of the couple's Spokane residence and refused to serve sufficient food to guests. The incidents cited in the divorce case struck many as a trumped up pretext, but among those who knew Jones best, the sensational accusations may have held at least a kernel of truth—she had grown notoriously thrifty in her business and real estate dealings after her mother's death and, dating back to her days at the helm of the most famous suffrage army in America, had never been one to conform to norms of feminine dress or behavior.

News of what figured to be a contentious divorce trial quickly spread across the nation, landing in newspapers as far away as New Mexico, where the *Evening News-Journal* in Clovis carried a story datelined July 1, Spokane, in the heart of a heated divorce trial in which Jones was expected to take the witness stand to "attempt to prove she knows how to keep house and to treat a husband."[42] The *Albuquerque Journal* devoted an entire page spread to the debacle, complete with the subheading, "Now he's suing his militant missus for divorce because she ran their house on a feminist basis."[43] Calling a dozen witnesses, former senator Dill cited as grounds his wife's "filthy" habits of dress while recounting specific instances of how she had "embarrassed" him by criticizing his political beliefs and his ability to "make a living."[44] Dill further complained that Jones wrote to his mother falsely alleging that he "drank like a fish" and was losing his eyesight as well as his mind.[45] "She decided that if she couldn't rule me she would ruin me," Dill said in cross-examination. "I wouldn't change my views. Principles mean more to me than votes." The former senator charged Jones with vehement opposition to his political views, including her particular disapproval of his support of Franklin D. Roosevelt at the 1932 Democratic National Convention in Chicago.[46]

In fact, "marked dislike" and "open criticism" of FDR had been the original cause of their marital strife, the Long Island *Manhasset Press* reported in a story headlined, "Suffrage Head Splits Home by Political Views."[47] Dill testified that "he couldn't face the people of this state with them thinking Mrs. Dill is a Progressive." The ex-senator had previously thought his wife to be an admirer of FDR but had since learned that she "didn't like the Theodore Roosevelt family." "She thought Franklin D. was all right until sometime before the convention when she invited him to make a speech over a national radio hook-up she was arranging for the Peace League." After FDR politely declined, Dill reported, "she had no use for him."

On July 6, Jones took the witness stand to tell her side of the story. During a day and a half of cross-examination, she testified to the kind of behavior—melancholy, bouts of inexplicable crying—that suggested her husband's mental instability while insisting that he had once threatened to kill her, though reporters covering the trial noted that particular charge did not appear in Jones's original answer to Dill's divorce complaint.[48] Jones, the *New York Times* reported, consistently "matched wits on the witness stand with Dill's attorney."[49] However, she refused to bring countersuit, insisting that she still loved Dill while calling him "a fine man."[50] His erratic behavior, she said, could be explained by a recent illness and the tension it had created.

Three days later, the judge ruled in Dill's favor, dissolving the union at Dill's request and against Jones's wishes. The judge held "incompetent" and "immaterial" the former senator's charges about his wife's poor housekeeping and manner of dress, deeming them "personal idiosyncrasies" for which Dill lacked sufficient proof.[51] However, the judge sustained Dill's allegations that Jones had called her husband "a crook and a coward" at a 1932 political convention and agreed that such words constituted cruelty. Jones had worked tirelessly for her husband's potential nomination as vice president during the 1932 Democratic National Convention and had supported the senator's campaigns with contributions totaling some 40,000 dollars, an amount the divorce court refused to require Dill to repay.

Within days of receiving the crushing verdict, Jones responded by mounting an "aggressive campaign for the Democratic nomination" for Congress in what amounted to her ex-husband's home district headquartered in Spokane.[52] The bitter defeat in court had galvanized Jones's sense of indignation in the face of political and social injustice, and her 11th-hour campaign would return to a familiar playbook—one that had served her well in her years as America's suffrage general. She would roam far and wide into rural Washington's countryside, personally ringing doorbells in districts where voters were too often forgotten. Simultaneously, she opened a Spokane headquarters where she wooed would-be urban supporters with cultural refinements, including classical music and high tea. And just as she had in the On-to-Albany and On-to-Washington campaigns, the now 53-year-old Jones dressed for the diverse roles required of her, preferring modest clothes for campaigning in the countryside and "a new dress ... for every occasion" to answer society demands in the city.

A newly divorced, recently declared congressional candidate in the summer of 1936, Jones displays her calling cards, which read "Miss Rosalie Jones, Candidate for Congress, 5th District, Spokane, Wash" (Marc Watkins Collection. Used by permission of Marc Watkins).

As she had in the votes-for-women campaign, Jones attempted to win naysayers and fence-sitters in Washington state's 5th District by distributing an abundance of leaflets proclaiming her belief in "the greatest good for the greatest number."[53] Jones touted her educational achievements: a B.A. from Adelphi College, an M.A. from George Washington University, LLB and LLM degrees from the Washington, D.C. Women's College of Law and, finally, a doctorate of Civil Laws from American University. In addition to her educational attainments, Jones campaigned on her experience as a "country property" owner in the state of Washington and a "dirt farmer" in New York state, where she claimed to have managed a "large chicken ranch" and "owned and operated small farms." In a country of breadlines still reeling from the specter of the Dust Bowl, Jones hoped to feature her lifelong love of animal husbandry as a special appeal to rural Washington voters, though the evidence suggested that most of her experience with livestock had been in a supervisory capacity, as was the case with her role as "overseer" of the Suffolk County Pomona Grange, an organization for animal husbandry in New York. As her campaign literature made clear, Jones had spent most of the prior 15 years living in Washington, D.C., achieving "personal acquaintance" with the "workings of all governmental departments" such that she had become "conversant with committee work of all kinds." While Jones listed her experience as "leader in woman suffrage" in her campaign leaflets, that calling card appeared midway down a long list of credentials she felt would be more convincing to voters in eastern Washington.

While she sought the Democratic nomination for Congress, Jones's campaign literature appealed most directly to progressives of the sort that might earlier have supported her Long Island neighbor and fellow suffrage supporter Theodore Roosevelt. Running as a La Follette–styled progressive with a populist bent, Jones claimed to be "independent" because she had "no political debts to pay off." Like Bull Moose Roosevelt, she wanted to bust trusts and boost agriculture. Like La Follette, Jones disdained the use of the military as "an instrument of national policy," preferring to use the armed forces only to "prepare to resist aggression." By now the ardent pacifism of Jones's World War I-era peace work had softened slightly, and though she declared herself to be "absolutely opposed to war between nations," she allowed for an important exception "if the United States were invaded." If that happened, she "would defy the world in any attempt to make American a captive country." Like La Follette, she favored old-age pensions for the elderly, public works such as the completion of Washington's Grand Coulee Dam, government programs and subsidies for farmers and ranchers, and pro-agricultural trade agreements rather than restrictive tariffs.

While Jones waged a populist, up-with-the people campaign firmly rooted in the progressive tradition, the distant strains of racism that had emerged in her historic march on Washington in 1913 resurfaced in her congressional campaign. Jones claimed to be "one hundred percent American," tracing her family's pedigreed lineage to 1690 and before, lending credence to her claims that she was firmly against "communism, fascism, Nazism, or any other 'ism' of a like character." For some, Jones's nativism bordered on jingoism; for others, such pro–America sentiments called into question Jones's earlier socialist beliefs.[54]

While the candidate deemphasized what the *New York Times* called her "militant suffragist" roots, Jones's women's rights platform influenced receptivity, or lack thereof, to her congressional campaign. For months leading up to the divorce judgment against her, headlines in many major metropolitan dailies not-so-subtly perjured her name, including those run by the *New York Times*, a one-time Jones family ally that now parroted Dill's perceptions of her cruelty. Sexist and chauvinist elements in the press apparently relished the irony of a votes-for-women icon successfully charged with cruelty to a politically prominent husband. Newswire headlines datelined Spokane, Washington, poked at the ironies of the Jones campaign, underscoring to readers the irony that the "wealthy Rosalie Jones Dill" now fancied herself a "dirt farmer."[55] Other articles subtly undermined her would-be populism in making specific reference not just to her wealth but to her "elaborate wardrobe."[56]

Despite strong support from women, Jones's campaign struggled to get off the ground, hampered in part by local authorities loyal to her ex-husband. In Wenatchee, Washington, her campaign ran afoul of police chief Carl Hansen, who charged that Jones had violated the city's anti-poster ordinance in tacking campaign signs to "practically every telephone pole in the city."[57] The City of Wenatchee billed the candidate for the two full days it had taken volunteers to remove the signs, though the thrifty Jones refused to pay, countering that it had been her supporters, not she, who had posted the signs. Hansen and the city answered by denying Jones a permit to use a city park for a campaign rally, and the candidate, with her characteristic pluck, threatened to speak in the streets instead. Calling on the stubborn strength that had fueled her On-to-Washington march, Jones vowed that she would "demand [the] right of free speech and hold the meeting on public property."

Throughout the fall of 1936, Jones battled what increasingly seemed like an organized media campaign intended to derail her election. Barely one month after word of her feud with the city of Wenatchee appeared on the United Press newswire, the *New York Times* of September 30 carried the story of a 38,000-dollar court judgment against Jones for unpaid loans to two New York banks.[58] The family image had suffered in New York City, where the Joneses were locked in several bitter land disputes. Already, the city had condemned family-owned property in Queens. When reporters showed up at Rosalie Jones's office at 90 West Street to record her reaction to the latest judgment against her, they found it closed up tight, with Jones presumed to be campaigning in Washington state.

Crippled by media bias and dogged by the lingering effects of an embarrassing divorce, Jones fared poorly in the crowded field in the September 1936 primary in Washington, losing in a landslide to Democrat lawyer Charles Leavy and finishing seventh in a field of nine candidates in her adopted home county of Spokane.[59] Bitter defeats in divorce court and in the court of public opinion further weakened her allegiance to her adopted home state of Washington. Honoring the citizenry of the state as "courteous and friendly," she nevertheless announced that she would be returning to her "Eastern home" in New York.[60] Washington voters had found her campaign claims unconvincing. Perhaps to show the electorate that she was at heart the dirt farmer her campaign literature had promised, Jones returned to her native Long Island to maintain her family's estate.

Once home, Jones "lived a mostly private life"[61] shepherding goats at Jones Manor while allowing her herd to roam freely despite the objections of nearby property-owners. She found herself in nearly continuous legal disputes with her increasingly suburban neighbors on Long Island as she carved up what remained of the family lands into small rental units seen as threatening the island's historically rural character. Tragedy continued to dog the family, too, including the death by suicide of Rosalie's aunt, Louise Livingston Jones Rutherford, who, allegedly battling depression, was reported to have leapt to her death from the window of her apartment. The collective losses suffered by the family were so great that the *New York Journal-American* ran a lengthy article headlined, "Tragedies of Society—Suicides Stalk the Joneses of Long Island."[62] The publication was left to conclude that a "black cloud" of "scandal and divorces" hung over the clan.

Jones's devotion to the goats she grazed on the family land and to her carefully cultivated image as a dirt farmer and real estate developer occupied much of her later years. By September of 1948, when she agreed to an interview with Ruth Schier of the *Long-Islander*, the 65-year-old suffrage general had been back home on Long Island for a dozen years, though she remained a mystery to many of her neighbors. "Rosalie Jones is an enigma," Schier wrote to open her profile of the votes-for-women icon. "She has been puzzling, startling, and dismaying her fellow men ever since the day she stood ... making her maiden speech."[63]

While Jones continued to vex her neighbors with various lawsuits in defense of her property rights and ambitious real estate proposals, her return to the more agrarian lifestyle she had known as a young woman appeared to Schier to have calmed her:

> Miss Jones, so critical when she is dealing with man-made laws, is full of a quiet, refreshing calm when she is abiding by nature's laws. Peace surrounds her as she stands on the good earth of her farm, and she imparts a deep feeling of kinship with nature. No matter that her farm buildings are old and weather-beaten, or that

her fences look frail and unconvincing. So strong an atmosphere of ... productivity permeates her farm that absence of show recedes to unimportance. A quiet, natural poetry creeps into her words as she explains how her land is cleared naturally, as God intended it to be, by putting the goats into the area to be cleared.... The moment Miss Jones comes back to her man-made struggles, her calm deserts her. Our educational system annoys her—It regiments and presses the child into a common form—It ignores the fact that we are individuals and that therein lies our only value. Mothers and the little two-room schoolhouses did a much better job of bringing up children than our great modern public school factories ever could, and the sooner we get back to the old fundamentals, the better it will be for us.

As she aged, Jones's progressive politics turned increasingly libertarian, expressing an agrarian disdain for assembly-line education, assembly-line commercialism, and assembly-line local government that demanded conformity or else. While she was known to speak her mind at local meetings, Jones's flock of goats served as the locus of her fierce defense of nonconformist, free-range thinking. A friend of the family, Cate Ludlam, later recalled of her occasional visits to see the aging "Aunt Rosalie" in Jones Manor:

We would sit in her parlor. I was terrified of the bearskin rug in that room. "Aunt Rosalie" said, I think, that her brother had shot it in Alaska with a bow and arrow, and that it was a Kodiak bear. Finally, after a number of visits and much coaching, I was persuaded to sit on the bear's head. I did it, but I still never really felt comfortable about it! Outdoors, Aunt Rosalie would take me to the barn and introduce the goats to me by name, and one time they followed me all the way around her big house, as though I were the lead goat! I remember how she [Rosalie] dressed. Always a long sort of housedress with a cardigan over it, with pockets, from which she would offer me candy. A scarf wrapped around her head closely in the way women used to when they were cleaning house, and black-high cut men's basketball sneakers![64]

Though she was of no blood relation to her "Aunt Rosalie," Ludlam came to know the aging leader better than some of the general's own nieces and nephews, whose parents still harbored grudges against Jones for what they felt was her obstinate, reckless treatment of the family's finances and reputation for sensible conservatism. "She was unique, and although I understand she angered and irritated some of the locals, all I ever knew of her was kindness," Ludlam recalled. "I knew she was a suffragette known as 'General Jones' when I was a child. But I had to be a mature woman before I really understood fully what that meant, in her day. And what it meant to the women who came after her." Cate's grandfather, Robert Ludlam of Oyster Bay, owned a gas station in nearby Pine Hollow, and when Jones and her "Uncle Bob" would go on casual drives together, Robert Ludlam would tether the goats to his pumps to discourage gas thieves. Hours later, Robert would circle back to his petrol station, untether the anxious animals, load them into the car, and return Jones to her family home in Laurel Hollow.

Rosalie's goats made news in 1940, generating the macabre headlines

"Rosalie's Goat Commits Suicide" and "Dead Goat Found Hanging by Chain."[65] The accident had occurred at Jones's cottage at Lloyd's Harbor, Long Island, where police sergeant Benjamin Smith responded to a gruesome report of a goat hanging by a rope. The officer surmised that the tragedy had occurred when the animal, tethered inside the home, attempted to leap from the window of the cottage. Jones had entrusted the care of her beloved goats to the property's caretaker, only to have the caretaker later confess to neglecting his duties. In her memoir, Rosalie's niece, Mary Gardiner Jones, recalls an anecdote illustrating both Jones's love of her animals and her invocation of the law to defend her flock. During the winter the goats traveled south by rail to more lush grazing grounds. When railroad officials threatened to delay their return to Long Island one spring, Jones, citing the Interstate Commerce Act, insisted to authorities that her goats would have to be milked every day they were delayed en route. On another occasion the far-ranging herd ate a neighbor's dahlia crop.[66] Neighbors once again pursued legal recourse, though to their chagrin Jones won the ensuing lawsuit by citing English Common Law, which put the onus on complaining property owners to fence off land rather than restrict the open range of animals.

Increasingly, Jones saw in her suburban and exurban neighbors signs of the herd mentality, a conformity reinforced by stringent zoning laws that, as she saw it, prevented citizens from earning a living from their own land in the way they saw fit. Of her outsized reputation for individualism, Schier wrote:

> Miss Jones knows that many of her fellow citizens consider her a maverick. As she watches them become more and more entangled in their desperate attempts to conform to artificial herd standards, she's glad she has courage enough to be a rugged individual. It amuses her to know that people keep saying, "Oh Lord. That Rosalie Jones again! What's she up to now?"[67]

Among her fellow Long Islanders, Jones's willfulness sometimes made her the object of ridicule. Long Island resident Barbara Resler Weeks recalls how, when she was a Syracuse University student working summers for local architect Al Graeser in the late 1940s, Rosalie would come to the office seeking consultation on her many building projects. "Mr. Graeser joked about how she kept goats and thus smelled like them," Weeks recalled of a woman known in her old age as a local eccentric.[68] While Jones's zeal for animal husbandry may have crossed the line into obsession, the retired suffrage general took care of her flock with the fierce loyalty she had displayed at the helm of Rosalie's Army some 40 years earlier. Interspersed with reports of the fickle Long Island weather, growing health ailments, and occasional visits from a family increasingly disgruntled with her stewardship of their assets, Jones recorded long, often emotional accounts of the life-and-death cycles of her animals in a typed personal journal titled "Daily Records of RGJ."[69] Assigning each of her goats a name, she painstakingly recorded the birth of their kids, lamented their still-borns, and watched over her flock in constant fear of attack. "Dogs lurk in the bushes. Goats run up and stand watching and saw dogs creeping away...." she noted in one particularly foreboding entry. "They had one because I heard it whimper. I could do nothing but shriek and scream and call to the goats to come to me." Jones reported confronting a pack of wild dogs as an aged woman, alone, with little more than a stick with which to protect her flock.

By the early 1950s, Jones's health had begun to decline along with that of her sister Louise, who passed away in 1952, leaving Rosalie living without family in Jones Manor for the first time in decades. Charles Jones, who along with Louise and Rosalie had served as an executor of his mother's estate, had also passed away. Of the immediate family, only Rosalie and her brother Arthur, who was institutionalized, still survived.[70] In losing Louise, Jones had lost not just her sister but also a housemate of many years and a woman, like Rosalie, "of strong personal convictions and the courage and energy to uphold them." Like her mother, Louise Jones had been a passionate anti-suffrage conservative and a member of the Daughters of the American Revolution.

Louise's death left Rosalie more alone than ever, though she took solace in several nieces and nephews. Among them, Mary Gardiner Jones, the daughter of Charles Herbert Jones and the former Anna Livingston Short, belatedly found inspiration in the figure of her suffragette aunt. Mary Gardiner Jones graduated with a law degree from Yale in 1948, and in 1953, just a year after Louise's death, accepted a position in the antitrust division of the Justice Department as a trial lawyer.[71] A strong advocate for women's rights in the workplace, Mary established a track record as a fierce opponent to monopolies and corporate greed, much like her Aunt Rosalie before her. Mary Gardiner Jones would go on to become the first woman Federal Trade commissioner.

Increasingly, Rosalie Jones's typed diary recorded the signs and symptoms of old age, drifting away from descriptions of her high-spirited, often contrarian public engagement on local issues to more somber reflections on her gradually declining health. Her weight, she noted, had dwindled to a mere 106 pounds by the time she was taken by ambulance from the family mansion to the hospital in 1952. A series of poor financial decisions made by Jones as executor had left the once wealthy estate so badly depleted that her diary entries record selling family jewelry to pay for hospitalization and medical bills. Jones was nearly 70 years old that winter, and age had caught up with her indomitable spirit; her personal journals registered a litany of medical interventions—x-rays, photos, needles, colonics, pills, vitamins. "I am to be a new woman," she noted in journal entries made from her hospital bed, adding wryly, "some will be glad."

Though she had been discouraged from a close relationship with her obstinate and willful aunt, Mary Gardiner Jones went to visit her shortly before her death, an event she later shared with her nephew, Marc Watkins:

> The old fire was still there and I remember her telling me, 'You have to include the men, Mary.' She died soon after, so I never had the chance to visit her again and make up for so much lost time. But I felt a kinship with her nevertheless because of all the causes she stood for and her activist role at a time when it must have been enormously difficult.[72]

Jones's diaries from the time make little mention of her years of international fame as a suffrage general or of visits to her beside seeking her wisdom or her blessing, but for a brief passing reference to a particular visitor to her bedside: Manhattan lawyer and women's rights activist Dorothy Frooks had come bearing flowers. "A friend since suffrage days—she has never failed me since she wrote from her school ... want[ing] to join our suffrage march to Washington in 1913," Jones wrote of Frooks. "She is younger than I but such a life-long friend." The day of Frooks's visit, Jones reported, had been a "beautiful day."

Jones would return to live in the family home for years after her hospital stay, but her ill health and the increasing isolation of Jones Manor would ultimately lead her back to her home-away-from-home in New York City, where she would pass away in Brooklyn at 94 years of age on January 12, 1978.

One of Jones's three surviving nieces, Ann Crooker of Laurel Hollow, Long Island, painstakingly collected the obituaries that ran in Long Island newspapers on the occasion of Jones's death, obituaries that unfailingly mentioned her foundational role as a women's rights advocate. Crooker recalled for the *Long-Islander* that her aunt proclaimed "strongly-held views publicly very early in her life, and was always ready and willing to put up a fight in their defense. She believed that women had much to give to the business of running the government ... and to do so, she felt they be must be allowed to vote."[73] She added that while her aunt's point of view was "not always popular or practical," she was nevertheless "admired and respected for her energy and even for her pugnacity." *Newsday* cited friends and acquaintances who described Jones as "an eccentric, a character, a genius, a thinking person, and, above all, a fighter."[74] In memoriam, the paper dubbed Jones an "early feminist." The *Oyster Bay Guardian* honored Jones as "a forerunner of those in today's women's liberation movement" and ran a photo of Rosalie's Army from 1913, proudly holding their walking sticks as they posed for photos in Central Park.[75] The *Syracuse Post-Standard* remarked on the cruel irony that Jones had lived "long enough to be nearly forgotten."[76]

Jones was laid to rest in a private burial ceremony January 20 in the cemetery at St. John's Episcopal Church in Cold Spring Harbor—the church where in the spring of 1927 she had emerged a blushing bride on land that had once belonged to her ancestors.[77] For her final resting place she had selected a spot less than a mile from Jones Manor in Laurel Hollow. Located firmly within the family plot but outside the family crypt where her mother was interred, her burial site seemed especially symbolic—suffragist and anti-suffragist, mother and daughter, close yet distinct, engaged in eternal debate.

At the close of a decade when Gloria Steinem chose Wonder Woman for the inaugural cover of *Ms. Magazine*, America had missed a chance to mark one of the most charismatic links to the feminist movement's past: a real-life, raven-haired wonder woman who had marched against impossible odds and faced down bigotry and tyranny again and again while speaking truth to authority from New York to Washington, D.C. Here was a patriotic superwoman who, in addition to leading America's longest and most arduous women's rights marches, had barnstormed her way into gubernatorial inaugurations, met with presidents, earned five degrees, published multiple books, and run for Congress. Had her early exploits occurred in the radio or television era, Jones's star would surely have shone forever in the pantheon of social justice greats; as it was she chose to live out her remaining decades quietly invested in the local dramas of her native Long Island and New York City homes, a passionate witness to perceived injustice in neighborhood, district, and borough.

In the penultimate chapter of her 1928 book *Women's Influence Through the Ballot*, Jones considers the legacy of women like Elizabeth Cady Stanton and Lucretia Mott and, in so doing, comments indi-

A poignant photograph of Jones from her early days as America's most beloved suffrage general. The Library of Congress dates the photograph 1910 to 1915, though similar photographs strongly suggest 1912 to 1913 as a more precise date range.

rectly on her own legacy. She cautions fair-weather feminists against the ridicule of pioneers who were far from the "hard insensitive women who were sometimes decried." They were misunderstood women for whom perceived hardness of heart was an unfortunate misnomer for "hearts ... afire to right injustices against all women."[78]

From the beginning to the end of her pilgrim's journey on Earth, Rosalie Gardiner Jones, pioneer suffragette and proto-feminist, marched with courage and purpose, forever and always to her own drummer.

Chapter Notes

Chapter 1

1. "Women in Rally for Hike to Washington," *New York Tribune*, January 10, 1913, 3.

2. "Encyclopedia 1914," Model T. Ford Club of America, accessed May 30, 2018, http://www.mtfca.com/encyclo/1914H.htm

3. "The Suffragist Demonstration," *Brooklyn Daily Eagle*, January 10, 1913, 6.

4. "50,000 Suffragettes in London Parade," NAWSA Suffrage Scrapbooks, Library of Congress, accessed July 8, 2019, https://cdn.loc.gov/master/rbc/rbcmil/scrp7009701/001.jpg

5. "Women Prepare to March to Washington," *New Castle News* (New Castle, PA), January 10, 1913, 16.

6. "The Suffragist Demonstration," *Brooklyn Daily Eagle*, January 10, 1913, 6.

7. "Who's Who in Ranks," *Evening Star* (Washington, D.C.), February 26, 1913, 2.

8. "Will Lead Her Army Here," *Washington Post*, January 10, 1913, 2.

9. "Leading Suffragists' Activities for Monster Parade," *Washington Times*, January 10, 1913, 1.

10. "Will Lead Her Army Here," *Washington Post*, January 10, 1913, 2.

11. "Making a New Record," *Press and Sun-Bulletin* (Binghamton, NY), January 9, 1913, 6.

12. Ruth Schier, "Rosalie Jones Has Spent Most Of Life Clashing With Authority," *The Long-Islander* (Huntington, NY), September 16, 1948, 1.

13. Antonia Petrash, *Long Island and the Woman Suffrage Movement* (Charleston, SC: The History Press, 2013).

14. "Joy of Suffragists Tempered by Fear," *New York Tribune*, January 9, 1913, 7.

15. "Smallpox Found Raging in New Jersey," *New Castle News* (New Castle, PA), January 10, 1913, 16.

16. "Getting Ready for 'Hike,'" *New York Times*, January 12, 1913, 2.

17. "Hiker Leader Visits the Capital," *Washington Herald*, January 12, 1913, 3.

18. "Suffrage Marchers Decide on Costumers," *New York Times*, January 12, 1913, 8.

19. "Just When Women Vote in Each State," *New York Tribune*, January 11, 1913, 6.

20. "'Gen.' De Forest Beats 'Gen.' Jones in Seeing Sulzer," *The Sun* (New York, NY), December 29, 1912.

21. "Just When Women Vote in Each State," *New York Tribune*, January 11, 1913, 6.

22. "All to Wear Hikers," *New York Tribune*, January 11, 1913, 6.

23. "Suffrage Marchers Decided on Costumes," *New York Times*, January 22, 1913, 8.

24. "All to Wear Hikers," *New York Tribune*, January 11, 1913, 6.

25. "5000 at Suffrage Ball," *New York Times*, January 12, 1913, 33.

26. "Hiker Leader Visits the Capital," *Washington Herald*, January 12, 1913, 3.

27. E. S. Fitch, "The Hiking Suffragettes: He Shes," song lyrics, Washington, D.C.: Marks-Goldsmith Company, Inc., 1914, accessed July 5, 2019, https://lccn.loc.gov/2017562286

28. Peg Johnston, *Faithfully Yours, Elisabeth Freeman*, "Overview," accessed May 30, 2018, http://www.elisabethfreeman.org/overview.php

29. "Suffragists' Long Walk," *The Times of London*, October 11, 1912, 8.

30. Antonia Petrash, *Long Island and the Woman Suffrage Movement* (Charleston, SC: The History Press, 2013).

31. Peg Johnston, *Faithfully Yours, Elisabeth Freeman*, "1911–1916: Media Stunts for Suffrage," accessed June 27, 2019, http://www.elizabethfreeman.org/suffrage.php

32. "Leave Mansfield in Yellow Wagon," *Mansfield Ohio News-Journal*, July 22, 1912, 4.

33. "Yellow Wagon and Occupants Arrive," *Chronicle-Telegram* (Elyria, OH), August 30, 1912, 1.

34. "Amendments to the Ohio Constitution," Supreme Court of Ohio, accessed May 30, 2018, http://www.sconet.state.oh.us/Legal Resources/LawLibrary/resources/appendix.pdf

35. "Ohio Women's Suffrage, Amendment 23," Ballotopedia, accessed April 22, 2018, https://ballotpedia.org/Ohio_Women%27s_ Suffrage,_Amendment_23_(September 1912)

36. "Hiker Leader Visits the Capital," *Washington Herald*, January 12, 1913, 3.

37. "Outdo South, in Pageant, Is Women's Plan," *Washington Times*, January 12, 1913, 2.

38. "Left Stockport This Morning," *Hudson Evening Register* (Hudson, NY), December 27, 1912.

39. "Hiker Leader Visits the Capital," *Washington Herald*, January 12, 1913, 3.

40. "Suffrage Women Are 'Marriageable,' Says General Jones," *Washington Times*, January 12, 1913, 1.

41. "Some Suffrage Definitions," *Morning News* (Wilmington, DE), January 18, 1913, 7.

42. "Romance Stirs Suffrage Ranks," *Middletown Daily Times-Press* (Middletown, NY), December 26, 1912.

43. "Suffrage Women Are 'Marriageable,' Says General Jones," *Washington Times*, January 12, 1913, 1.

44. "Suffragettes Plan," *Washington Times*, January 12, 1913, 2.

45. "18-Day March to the Capital," *New York Times*, January 13, 1913, 22.

46. "Motive for Pageant," *Washington Post*, January 13, 1913, 2.

47. "Woman Suffrage Parade Pledge Card," NAWSA Suffrage Scrapbooks, Library of Congress, accessed July 8, 2019, https://cdn.loc.gov/master/rbc/rbcmil/scrp7006502/001.jpg

48. "General Jones Wins 'Em," *Baltimore Sun*, January 14, 1913, 3.

49. "General Jones, Leader of Suffragettes, Here," *Morning News*, January 14, 1913, 1.

50. "Editorial," *Morning News* (Wilmington, DE), January 15, 1913, 6.

51. "Editorial," *News Journal* (Wilmington, DE), January 16, 1913, 4.

52. "Plans for the Hike," *Morning News* (Wilmington, DE), January 17, 1913, 4.

53. "Will Lead Suffrage Hikers to the Capitol," *Washington Times*, January 23, 1913, 7.

54. "Hike or Pay for Substitute," *Washington Herald*, January 19, 1913, 1.

55. "Miss Delafield a Bride," *New York Times*, January 19, 1913, 21.

56. "Suffrage Bill Held Up," *New York Tribune*, January 16, 1913, 7.

57. "Women Win in South Dakota," *New York Tribune*, January 16, 1913, 7.

58. Untitled News Item, *Baltimore Sun*, January 19, 1913, 22.

59. "Antis Denounce Hike," *New York Tribune*, January 16, 1913, 7.

60. "Question of Minorities," *New York Post*, February 14, 1913.

61. "Disorder at Women's Debate," *Chicago Daily Tribune*, January 19, 1913, 7.

62. "Suffragists Hear Arguments of Antis," *New York Times*, January 21, 1913, 8.

63. "The Suffrage Campaign Here," *News Journal* (Wilmington, DE), January 18, 1913, 2.

Chapter 2

1. "Here's General Jones' General Order Number 1," *New York Times*, January 21, 1913, 8.

2. "Will Lead Suffrage Hikers to the Capitol," *Washington Times*, January 23, 1913, 7.

3. "Here's General Jones' General Order Number 1," *New York Times*, January 21, 1913, 8.

4. "Suffrage Marchers Decide on Costumes," *New York Times*, January 22, 1913, 8.

5. "Men to March in Suffrage Parade," *Washington Herald*, January 14, 1913, 2.

6. "Suffrage Passes Senate, *New York Times*, January 23, 1913, 8.

7. "Many Unique Features Will Be Seen in Great Suffrage Parade," *Frederick Post* (Frederick, MD), January 23, 1913, 4.

8. "Suffragettes Get Permit to Use Treasury Building," *Washington Times*, January 23, 1913, 6.

9. "Suffragists in Golden Cars," *Baltimore Sun*, January 24, 1913, 4.

10. "Many Unique Features Will Be Seen in Great Suffrage Parade," *Frederick Post* (Frederick, MD), January 23, 1913, 4.

11. "Women Plan Plane Swoop," *New York Tribune*, January 16, 1913, 7.

12. "Women Practice Marches for Big Suffrage Parade," *Washington Times*, January 24, 1913, 2.

13. "Won't Parade on March 4," *New York Times*, January 25, 1913, 1.

14. "Women Hold Debate at Republican Club," *New York Times*, January 26, 1913, 7.

15. "Artistic Long Island Home on Cold Spring Estate," *New York Times*, January 26, 1913, 34.

16. "Suffragists to Hear Bugler," *Baltimore Sun*, January 27, 1913, 7.

17. "Foss for Equal Suffrage," *Baltimore Sun*, January 27, 1913, 7.

18. "Suffragists Test Living in the Open," *Lock Haven Express* (Lock Haven, PA), January 30, 1913, 1.

19. "Suffrage Marchers Pose for Movies," *New York Tribune*, January 30, 1913, 1.

20. "Members of the 'On to Washington' Band," *Washington Post*, January 31, 1913, 2.

21. "Suffrage Marchers Pose for Movies," *New York Tribune*, January 30, 1913, 2.

22. *Ibid.*, 1.

23. *Ibid.*, 2.

24. "Suffrage Pioneers Not Forgotten in Victory," *The Sun* (New York, NY), December 9, 1917, 5.

25. *Ibid.*, 1.

26. "Wagon to Go with Hikers," *Baltimore Sun*, January 30, 1913, 7.

27. "Suffrage Marchers Pose for Movies," *New York Tribune*, January 30, 1913, 2.

28. "Editorial," *Morning News* (Wilmington, DE), January 30, 1913, 4.

29. "Suffragists Brave Police," *Washington Post*, January 30, 1913, 3.

30. "Real Winter Is Coming," *New York Times*, February 1, 1913, 1.

31. "Weather Man Fears Ice Shortage Here," *New York Times*, January 26, 1913, 7.

32. "Gloom in Suffrage Camp," *New York Times*, February 1, 1913, 1.

33. "Suffrage Hiker Suffers Collapse," *Washington Times*, January 31, 1913, 1.

34. "Sat on Mr. Payne's Lap," *Washington Post*, February 1, 1913, 2.

35. "Suffragettes War on Golf," *Washington Post*, February 1, 1913, 2.

36. "Dublin Castle Bombarded by English Suffragettes," *Washington Post*, January 30, 1913, 3.

37. "Suffragist Assails Tower Treasures," *New York Times*, February 2, 1913, 1.

38. "Suffragettes War on Golf," *Washington Post*, February 1, 1913, 2.

39. "Suffragettes to Jail," *Baltimore Sun*, January 30, 1913, 7.

40. "Suffragettes Raise Racket Over Asquith," *Press and Sun-Bulletin* (Binghamton, NY), January 30, 1913, 1.

41. "British Labor Party Declares for Suffrage," *Press and Sun-Bulletin* (Binghamton, NY), January 30, 1913, 1.

42. "Gen. Rosalie Will Outdo Washington," *Press and Sun-Bulletin* (Binghamton, NY), January 30, 1913, 1.

43. "Will Ride as Heralds," *Washington Post*, January 27, 1913, 2.

44. "Mice May Cause Tumult During Suffrage Parade," *Washington Post*, February 1, 1913, 2.

45. "Mice to Daunt Suffragists," *New York Times*, February 2, 1913, 1.

46. "Mice May Cause Tumult During Suffrage Parade," *Washington Post*, February 1, 1913, 2.

47. "Dr. Walker Arrested Again," *New York Times*, February 2, 1913, 1.

48. "Rosalie Jones Not Ill," *New York Times*, February 2, 1913, 1.

49. "Rehearsing for Hike to Washington," *Baltimore Sun*, February 8, 1913, 2.

50. "Suffrage Parade Cash Given Here," *Philadelphia Inquirer*, February 8, 1913, 4.

51. "Suffragists to Invade Trenton," *Trenton Evening Times*, February 8, 1913, 1.

Chapter 3

1. "Woman's Yell Arouses Gotham," *Press and Sun-Bulletin* (Binghamton, NY), February 12, 1913, 1.

2. "Timetable & Map: Hudson River Tunnels, Hudson and Manhattan Railroad Co., July 1909," Hoboken Historical Museum Online Collections Database, accessed April 23, 2018, http://hoboken. pastperfectonline.com/archive/771B1D96-B4B5-478B-AF33-079990132842

3. "Women's Army on the March," *New York Post*, February 12, 1913, 1.

4. "Suffrage Army Start Delayed by Shiny Nose," *Baltimore News*, February 12, 1913, 1.

5. "Suffragettes Ride Through Town Atop of Fifth Avenue Bus," *Evening World* (New York, NY), February 10, 1913, 8.

6. "Pilgrims Have a Preliminary Taste of Weather," *New York American*, February 11, 1913, 1.

7. "Suffragists Spread Oratory and Tracts," *New York Times*, February 11, 1913, 11.

8. "Women's Army on March," *New York Post*, February 12, 1913, 1.

9. "Suffragists Spread Oratory and Tracts," *New York Times*, February 11, 1913, 11.

10. "Suffrage Hikers Undaunted by Cold," *New York Times*, February 13, 1913, 6.

11. "Suffragists Spread Oratory and Tracts," *New York Times*, February 11, 1913, 11.

12. "On to Washington The Suffragists Cry," *New York American*, February 12, 1913, 1.

13. "Suffrage Army Start Delayed by Shiny Nose," *Baltimore News*, February 12, 1913, 1.

14. "Women's Army on March," *New York Post*, February 12, 1913, 1.

15. "Suffrage Army Start Delayed by Shiny Nose," *Baltimore News*, February 12, 1913, 1.

16. "Suffrage Pilgrims Make Fine Start on Washington Hike," *Brooklyn Daily Eagle*, February 12, 1913, 1.

17. "Suffrage Hikers Undaunted by Cold," *New York Times*, February 13, 1913, 6.

18. "General's Mamma Bound Up State After Daughter," *Brooklyn Daily Eagle*, December 21, 1912.

19. "On to Washington The Suffragists Cry," *New York American*, February 12, 1913, 1.

20. "Women's Army on March," *New York Post*, February 12, 1913, 1.

21. "The Hikers on Their Way," *Daily Republican* (Rushville, IN), February 13, 1913, 7.

22. "Woman's Yell Arouses Gotham," *Press and Sun-Bulletin* (Binghamton, NY), February 12, 1913, 1.

23. "Suffrage Hikers Undaunted by Cold," *New York Times*, February 13, 1913, 6.

24. "Suffrage Hike Starts to Washington with Vim," *Evening World*, February 12, 1913, 4.

25. "Women's Army on March," *New York Post*, February 12, 1913, 1.

26. "Cold Snap Up the State," *New York Post*, February 13, 1913.

27. "Suffrage Hike Starts to Washington with Vim," *Evening World*, February 12, 1913, 4.

28. "Women's Army on March," *New York Post*, February 12, 1913, 1.

29. "Suffrage Hikers Reach This City," *Morning News* (Wilmington, DE), February 19, 1913, 2.

30. "Suffragette Hikers Today One Big Ache," *Baltimore News*, February 14, 1913, 2.

31. *Ibid.*

32. "Witch Hazel to be Suffragist Flag's Symbol," *Baltimore News*, February 16, 1913, 2.

33. "Suffrage Hike Starts to Washington with Vim," *Evening World*, February 12, 1913, 4.

34. "Suffrage Pilgrims Make Fine Start on Washington Hike," *Brooklyn Daily Eagle*, February 12, 1913, 1.

35. "Suffrage Army Start Delayed by Shiny Nose," *Baltimore News*, February 12, 1913, 1.

36. "Suffrage Pilgrims Make Fine Start on Washington Hike," *Brooklyn Daily Eagle*, February 12, 1913, 1.

37. "Hikers Leave on Pilgrimage," *Marion Star* (Marion, OH), February 12, 1913, 1.

38. "Percy Leads March," *Washington Evening Star* (Washington, D.C.), February 13, 1913, 1.

39. "Megaphone Band for Suffragettes," *New York Times*, February 12, 1913, 8.

40. "Suffrage Army Start Delayed by Shiny Nose," *Baltimore News*, February 12, 1913, 1.

41. "Hikers Leave on Pilgrimage," *Marion Star* (Marion, OH), February 12, 1913, 1.

42. "Suffrage Army Start Delayed by Shiny Nose," *Baltimore News*, February 12, 1913, 1.

43. "Suffrage Hikers Undaunted by Cold," *New York Times*, February 13, 1913, 6.

44. "Suffrage Army Start Delayed by Shiny Nose," *Baltimore News*, February 12, 1913, 1.

45. "Quite Personal," *The Practical Druggist*, May 1913.

46. "Megaphone Band for Suffragettes," *New York Times*, February 12, 1913, 8.

47. "Bans Women from Parade," *New York Times*, February 12, 1913, 8.

48. "Suffrage Hikers Undaunted by Cold," *New York Times*, February 13, 1913, 6.

49. "Heflin Stirs Women's Ire," *Chicago Daily Tribune*, February 13, 1913, 3.

50. "On to Washington," *Morning News* (Wilmington, DE), February 13, 1913, 10.

51. "Percy Leads March," *Washington Evening Star*, February 13, 1913, 1.

52. "Blood Flowed Freely in the Streets of Mexico City," *Bradford Era* (Bradford, PA), February 12, 1913, 1.

53. "Quiet After Storm," *Bradford Era* (Bradford, PA), February 12, 1913, 1.

54. "Officials to Try to Avert Clash," *Bradford Era* (Bradford, PA), February 12, 1913, 1.

55. "Rosalie and Her Army Hope to Win in a Walk," *Bradford Era* (Bradford, PA), February 12, 1913, 1.

56. "Give Me Back My Husband or I'll Rout the Army," *New Brunswick Times* (New Brunswick, NJ), February 13, 1913, 1.

57. "Percy Leads March," *Washington Evening Star*, February 13, 1913, 1.

Chapter 4

1. "After Alabaman's Scalp," *Chicago Daily Tribune*, February 13, 1913, 3.

2. "Even Bad Men Love Their Mamas," The Downfall Dictionary, accessed May 30, 2018, http://downfalldictionary.blogspot.com/2013/08/thomas-heflin-even-bad-men-love-their.html

3. "Suffragists Call Mr. Heflin Beau Brummell of the House," *Washington Post*, February 12, 1913, 5.

4. "To Drag Ball and Chain," *Chicago Daily Tribune*, February 13, 1913, 3.

5. "After Alabaman's Scalp," *Chicago Daily Tribune*, February 13, 1913, 3.

6. "Women Burn Down Building," *Chicago Daily Tribune*, February 13, 1913, 3.

7. "Heflin Only Amused," *Washington Post*, February 14, 1913, 3.

8. "Wearied Hikers Plod on in the Dark," *New York Times*, February 14, 1913, 3.

9. "On to Washington," *Morning News* (Wilmington, DE), February 13, 1913, 10.

10. "Women on to the Capital," *New York Post*, February 13, 1913.

11. "Wearied Hikers Plod on in the Dark," *New York Times*, February 14, 1913, 3.

12. "Traditional Songs," Rutgers University, accessed May 30, 2018, https://www.rutgers.edu/about/traditional-songs

13. "Give Me Back My Husband or I'll Rout the Army," *New Brunswick Times* (New Brunswick, NJ), February 13, 1913, 1.

14. "Women on to the Capital," *New York Post*, February 13, 1913.

15. "Wearied Hikers Plod on in the Dark," *New York Times*, February 14, 1913, 3.

16. "Hotel Klein," Rutgers University Repository, accessed May 30, 2018, https://rucore.libraries.rutgers.edu/rutgers-lib/31605/.

17. "Give Me Back My Husband or I'll Rout the Army," *New Brunswick Times* (New Brunswick, NJ), February 13, 1913, 1.

18. "Three Fair Hikers Are Hors de Combat," *Pittsburgh Post-Gazette*, February 14, 1913, 4.

19. "Women on to the Capital," *New York Post*, February 13, 1913.

20. "Wearied Hikers Plod on in the Dark," *New York Times*, February 14, 1913, 3.

21. "Suffrage Marchers Request Audience at Capital," *New York Post*, February 14, 1913.

22. "Three Fair Hikers Are Hors de Combat," *Pittsburgh Post-Gazette*, February 14, 1913, 4.

23. "Wearied Hikers Plod on in the Dark," *New York Times*, February 14, 1913, 3.

24. "Fun with Students," *Evening Star* (Washington, D.C.), February 14, 1913, 2.

25. "Three Fair Hikers Are Hors de Combat," *Pittsburgh Post-Gazette*, February 14, 1913, 4.

26. "Wearied Hikers Plod on in the Dark," *New York Times*, February 14, 1913, 3.

27. "Fun with Students," *Evening Star* (Washington, D.C.), February 14, 1913, 2.

28. "Suffragette Leads Princeton Revel," *New York Times*, February 15, 1913, 6.

29. "Wilson Not at Home When 'Pilgrims' Call," *Brooklyn Daily Eagle*, February 14, 1913, 3.

30. "Suffragette Leads Princeton Revel," *New York Times*, February 15, 1913, 6.

31. "Delaware's New Fame," *New York Post*, February 15, 1913.

32. "Suffragette Hikers Today One Big Ache," *Baltimore News*, February 14, 1913, 1.

33. "Wilson Not at Home When 'Pil-

grims' Call," *Brooklyn Daily Eagle*, February 14, 1913, 3.

34. "Suffragette Leads Princeton Revel," *New York Times*, February 15, 1913, 6.

35. "Fun with Students," *Evening Star* (Washington, D.C.), February 14, 1913, 2.

Chapter 5

1. "Pilgrims Are Jeered at Trenton," *Pittsburgh Post-Gazette*, February 15, 1913, 16.

2. "Suffragette Hikers Today One Big Ache," *Baltimore News*, February 14, 1913, 1.

3. "Valentines for Hikers," *Baltimore Sun*, February 15, 1913, 2.

4. "Suffragette Leads Princeton Revel," *New York Times*, February 15, 1913, 6.

5. "Cupid in Ranks of Suffragettes," *Philadelphia Inquirer*, February 15, 1913, 5.

6. "Romance Thrills Suffragettes on March to Albany," *New York Press*, December 26, 1912.

7. "Romance Stirs Suffrage Ranks," *Middletown Daily Times-Press* (Middletown, NY), December 26, 1912.

8. "Cupid in Ranks of Suffragettes," *Philadelphia Inquirer*, February 15, 1913, 5.

9. Elizabeth Aldrich, "How Man Will Look When Woman Votes," *Washington Post*, May 18, 1913, 5.

10. "Wilson Not at Home When 'Pilgrims' Call," *Brooklyn Daily Eagle*, February 14, 1913, 3.

11. "Suffragette Leads Princeton Revel," *New York Times*, February 15, 1913, 6.

12. "Suffrage Tallyho Carries Valentines," *Baltimore News*, February 14, 1913, 2.

13. "Emilie A. Doetsch," Archives of Maryland, accessed May 30, 2018, http://msa.maryland.gov/megafile/msa/speccol/sc3500/sc3520/013700/013708/html/13708bio.html

14. "Hairpins Fall Along Path of Heroes of 1776," *Baltimore News*, February 13, 1913, 1.

15. "Suffragette Hikers Today One Big Ache," *Baltimore News*, February 14, 1913, 1.

16. "Suffragette Leads Princeton Revel," *New York Times*, February 15, 1913, 6.

17. "Suffragette Hikers Today One Big Ache," *Baltimore News*, February 14, 1913, 1.

18. "Suffragette Leads Princeton Revel," *New York Times*, February 15, 1913, 6.

19. "Pilgrims Are Jeered at Trenton," *Pittsburgh Post-Gazette*, February 15, 1913, 16.

20. "Woman Suffrage," New Jersey Women's History, accessed May 30, 2018, http://www.njwomenshistory.org/discover/topics/woman-suffrage

21. New Jersey Historical Society, *Jersey Journeys*, March 1998, 3, http://essexuu.org/stoneltr.html

22. "Pilgrims Are Jeered at Trenton," *Pittsburgh Post-Gazette*, February 15, 1913, 16.

23. "Suffragette Hikers Today One Big Ache," *Baltimore News*, February 14, 1913, 1.

24. "Witch Hazel to be Suffragist Flag's Symbol," *Baltimore News*, February 16, 1913, 1.

25. "Hiking Pilgrims Hurry to Bed at Burlington," *Philadelphia Inquirer*, February 16, 1913, 17.

26. "Sunday Hike for Army," *Baltimore Sun*, February 16, 1913, 1.

27. "Hike Up Walnut Street," *New York Post*, February 17, 1913.

28. "Hiking Pilgrims Hurry to Bed at Burlington," *Philadelphia Inquirer*, February 16, 1913, 17.

29. "School Expels Girl Eloper," *Baltimore Sun*, February 17, 1913, 7.

30. "Hiking Pilgrims Hurry to Bed at Burlington," *Philadelphia Inquirer*, February 16, 1913, 17.

31. "The Elizabeth Cady Stanton and Susan B. Anthony Papers," Rutgers University, accessed May 30, 2018, http://ecssba.rutgers.edu/docs/seneca.html

32. "Lausanne Takes Hikers Off Route," *The Sun* (New York, NY), February 16, 1913, 12.

33. "Hiking Pilgrims Hurry to Bed at Burlington," *Philadelphia Inquirer*, February 16, 1913, 17.

34. "Sunday Hike for Army," *Baltimore Sun*, February 16, 1913, 1.

35. "Lausanne Takes Hikers Off Route," *The Sun* (New York, NY), February 16, 1913, 12.

36. "Sunday Hike for Army," *Baltimore Sun*, February 16, 1913, 1.

37. "Hiking Pilgrims Hurry to Bed at Burlington," *Philadelphia Inquirer*, February 16, 1913, 17.

38. "Witch Hazel to be Suffragist Flag's Symbol," *Baltimore News*, February 16, 1913, 1.

39. "Hiking Pilgrims Hurry to Bed at Burlington," *Philadelphia Inquirer*, February 16, 1913, 17.

40. "Hike Is Not Funny," *Evening Star* (Washington, D.C.), February 17, 1913, 3.

41. "Calls Back General of Suffrage Army," *New York Times*, December 21, 1912.

42. "Suffrage Hikers Near Death When the Chainless Tires of Their Auto Skidded," *New York Times*, December 29, 1912.

43. "Hike Is Not Funny," *Evening Star* (Washington, D.C.), February 17, 1913.

Chapter 6

1. "Forums," NJPineBarrens.com, accessed May 30, 2018, https://forums.njpinebarrens.com/threads/im-looking-for-pre-1900-maps-of-delran-nj-showing-residences-please-help.6381/

2. "Nearer They Come," *Washington Post*, February 17, 1913, 1.

3. "Hike Up Walnut Street," *New York Post*, February 17, 1913.

4. "Nearer They Come," *Washington Post*, February 17, 1913, 1.

5. "General Lets Hikers Accept Lift on Road," *Baltimore News*, February 15, 1913, 1.

6. "Current Comment," *Lock Haven Express* (Lock Haven, PA), February 17, 1913, 6.

7. "Witch Hazel to be Suffragist Flag's Symbol," *Baltimore News*, February 16, 1913, 2.

8. "General Lets Hikers Accept Lift on Road," *Baltimore News*, February 15, 1913, 1.

9. "Mob Buffets Hikers, Now in Philadelphia," *New York Times*, February 17, 1913, 6.

10. Charlotte Perkins Gilman, *Women and Economics* (Boston: Small, Maynard, and Company, 1898), http://digital.library.upenn.edu/women/gilman/economics/economics.html

11. "Proposals and Orchids Cheer Women Hikers," *Baltimore News*, February 17, 1913, 2.

12. "Mob Buffets Hikers, Now in Philadelphia," *New York Times*, February 17, 1913, 6.

13. "Hooting Crowds Greet Weary Pilgrims," *Pittsburgh Post-Gazette*, February 17, 1913, 1.

14. "Mob Buffets Hikers, Now in Philadelphia," *New York Times*, February 17, 1913, 6.

15. "Hooting Crowds Greet Weary Pilgrims," *Pittsburgh Post-Gazette*, February 17, 1913, 1.

16. "Yes, I Vote, Says Suffragette, One of Army in 1913 Capitol Hike," *Poughkeepsie Journal* (Poughkeepsie, NY), January 8, 1956, 1C.

17. "Hike Is Not Funny," *Evening Star* (Washington, D.C.), February 17, 1913, 3.

18. "Mob Buffets Hikers, Now in Philadelphia," *New York Times*, February 17, 1913, 6.

19. "Hike Is Not Funny," *Evening Star* (Washington, D.C.), February 17, 1913, 3.

20. "Proposals and Orchids Cheer Women Hikers," *Baltimore News*, February 17, 1913, 2.

21. "Suffrage Pilgrims at Phila.," *The News* (Frederick, MD), February 17, 1913, 7.

22. "Rosalie's Army Greeted by Mob," *San Francisco Call*, February 17, 1913, 7.

23. "The Hikers," *Morning News* (Wilmington, DE), February 17, 1913, 6.

24. "Army Limps into City," *Philadelphia Inquirer*, February 17, 1913, 1.

25. "Isn't It Remarkable What Little Things Will Do?" *Pittsburgh Post-Gazette*, February 17, 1913, 1.

Chapter 7

1. "Suffrage Band Adds New Recruits," *Washington Times*, February 17, 1913, 1.

2. "Proposals and Orchids Cheer Women Hikers," *Baltimore News*, February 17, 1913, 1.

3. "Hikers Reach Chester," *Baltimore Sun*, February 18, 1913, 1.

4. "Suffrage Band Adds New Recruits," *Washington Times*, February 17, 1913, 1.

5. "Proposals and Orchids Cheer Women Hikers," *Baltimore News*, February 17, 1913, 1.

6. "Hikers Enjoy Brooklyn Day," *Brooklyn Daily Eagle*, February 18, 1913, 1.

7. William Penn, *Fruits of Solitude* (London: Headley, 1905), 43, https://archive.org/details/somefruitssolit00penngoo

8. "Proposals and Orchids Cheer Women Hikers," *Baltimore News*, February 17, 1913, 1.

9. "Proposals and Orchids Cheer Women Hikers," *Baltimore News*, February 17, 1913, 2.

10. "Suffragette Hikers Enlist Four Recruits While in Quaker City," *Press and Sun-Bulletin* (Binghamton, NY), February 17, 1913, 1.

11. "Suffrage Band Adds New Recruits," *Washington Times*, February 17, 1913, 1.

12. "Suffragette Hikers Enlist Four Recruits While in Quaker City," *Press and Sun-Bulletin* (Binghamton, NY), February 17, 1913, 1.

13. "Pass 100-mile Mark on Washington Hike," *New York Times*, February 18, 1913, 5. Also see: "Mob Buffets Hikers," *New York Times*, February 17, 1913, 6.

14. "Mob Buffets Hikers," *New York Times*, February 17, 1913, 6.

15. "Suffrage Band Adds New Recruits," *Washington Times*, February 17, 1913, 1.

16. "Hikers Reach Chester," *Baltimore Sun*, February 18, 1913, 1.

17. "Hikers Enjoy Brooklyn Day," *Brooklyn Daily Eagle*, February 18, 1913, 1.

18. "Hostile Reception," *Oil City Derrick* (Oil City, PA), February 18, 1913, 1.

19. "Army Is Footsore," *Evening Star* (Washington, D.C.), February 18, 1913, 1.

20. *Ibid.*

21. *Ibid.*

22. "Hikers Reach Chester," *Baltimore Sun*, February 18, 1913, 1.

23. "Rains Coins for Cause at Carnegie Hall," *New York Tribune*, February 18, 1913, 3.

24. Jonathan Miller, "Change Is the Constant in a Century of New York City Real," Estate," 17, accessed May 30, 2018, http://www.millersamuel.com/files/2012/10/DE100yearsNYC.pdf

25. "Rains Coins for Cause at Carnegie Hall," *New York Tribune*, February 18, 1913, 3.

26. "Militants Ruin Golf Links," *Baltimore Sun*, February 16, 1913, 1.

27. "Michigan Girl Goes to Jail," *New Castle News* (New Castle, PA), February 18, 1913, 7.

28. "Suffragists Will Insist on Military Guard in Pageant," *Washington Times*, February 16, 1913, 6.

29. *Ibid.*

30. "Milholland-Heflin Debate," *Washington Post*, February 17, 1913, 6.

31. "Editorial Jottings," *Baltimore Sun*, February 18, 1913, 6.

32. "The Voteless Voters," *New York Times*, February 18, 1913, 12.

33. "Washington House Has Glorious History," *Delaware County Daily Times* (Chester, PA), November 9, 1963, 23.

34. "Hike Is Not Funny," *Evening Star* (Washington, D.C.), February 17, 1913, 3.

Chapter 8

1. "Hikers Slow in Starting," *New Castle News* (New Castle, PA), February 18, 1913, 7.

2. "Suffrage Hikers Reach This City," *Morning News* (Wilmington, DE), February 19, 1913, 1.

3. "Suffragists March to Wilmington," *News Journal* (Wilmington, DE), February 18, 1913, 6.

4. "Hikers Slow in Starting," *New Castle News* (New Castle, PA), February 18, 1913, 7.

5. "Army Enters Delaware," *Baltimore Sun*, February 19, 1913, 1.

6. "Suffragists March to Wilmington," *News Journal* (Wilmington, DE), February 18, 1913, 6.

7. "Hikers Welcomed at Wilmington," *Philadelphia Inquirer*, February 19, 1913, 6.

8. "Doings of Suffragists in Wilmington Today," *News Journal* (Wilmington, DE), February 19, 1913, 6.

9. "Suffrage Hikers Reach This City," *Morning News* (Wilmington, DE), February 19, 1913, 2.

10. *Ibid.*, 1.

11. *Ibid.*, 2.

12. "Hikers Welcomed at Wilmington," *Philadelphia Inquirer*, February 19, 1913, 6.

13. "Army Enters Delaware," *Baltimore Sun*, February 19, 1913, 1.

14. "Hikers Welcomed at Wilmington," *Philadelphia Inquirer*, February 19, 1913, 6.

15. "Suffrage Hikers Reach This City," *Morning News* (Wilmington, DE), February 19, 1913, 1.

16. "Mayor to Welcome Suffrage Pilgrims," *Morning News* (Wilmington, DE), February 17, 1913, 1.

17. "Suffrage Hikers Reach This City," *Morning News* (Wilmington, DE), February 19, 1913, 1.

18. "Doings of Suffragists in Wilmington Today," *News Journal* (Wilmington, DE), February 19, 1913, 6.

19. "Cupid Drummed out of Camp by 'General Jones,'" *Baltimore News*, February 19, 1913, 1.

20. "Suffragette Hikers Today One Big Ache," *Baltimore News*, February 14, 1913, 2.

21. "Army Enters Delaware," *Baltimore Sun*, February 19, 1913, 7.

22. "Suffrage Hikers Reach This City," *Morning News* (Wilmington, DE), February 19, 1913, 2.

23. "Army Enters Delaware," *Baltimore Sun*, February 19, 1913, 1.

24. "Glad Hand for Hikers," *Washington Post*, February 19, 1913, 1.

25. "Hikers Welcomed at Wilmington," *Philadelphia Inquirer*, February 19, 1913, 6.

26. "Glad Hand for Hikers," *Washington Post*, February 19, 1913, 1.

27. "Cupid Drummed out of Camp by 'General Jones,'" *Baltimore News*, February 19, 1913, 1.

28. "Suffrage Hikers Reach This City," *Morning News* (Wilmington, DE), February 19, 1913, 2.

29. "Glad Hand for Hikers," *Washington Post*, February 19, 1913, 1.

30. "Suffrage Hikers Reach This City," *Morning News* (Wilmington, DE), February 19, 1913, 2.

31. "Hard Tack Strays But Suffrage Army Thrives," *New York Tribune*, February 19, 1913, 7.

32. "Suffrage Hikers Reach This City," *Morning News* (Wilmington, DE), February 19, 1913, 2.

33. "Suffrage Army Worried Over Pretty Private," *Baltimore News*, February 18, 1913, 1.

34. "Suffrage Hikers Reach This City," *Morning News* (Wilmington, DE), February 19, 1913, 2.

35. "Out in True Colors," *Evening Star* (Washington, D.C.), February 19, 1913, 2.

36. "Former Brooklyn Boy Joins Hikers to Win a Bride," *Brooklyn Daily Eagle*, February 19, 1913, 1.

37. "Cupid Hits a Pilgrim," *Washington Post*, February 20, 1913, 1.

38. "Former Brooklyn Boy Joins Hikers to Win a Bride," *Brooklyn Daily Eagle*, February 19, 1913, 1.

39. "Cupid Hits a Pilgrim," *Washington Post*, February 20, 1913, 1.

40. "Don't Want March Spoiled by Romance," *Morning News* (Wilmington, DE), February 20, 1913, 10.

41. "Cupid Drummed out of Camp by 'General Jones,'" *Baltimore News*, February 19, 1913, 1.

42. "Doings of Suffragists in Wilmington Today," *News Journal* (Wilmington, DE), February 19, 1913, 6.

43. "Cupid Drummed out of Camp by 'General Jones,'" *Baltimore News*, February 19, 1913, 1.

44. "Suffragette Army Rests at Wilming-ton," *Morning Echo* (Bakersfield, CA), February 20, 1912, 2.

45. "Suffragists Divided Over the Outrage," *Morning News* (Wilmington, DE), February 20, 1913, 10.

46. "Doings of Suffragists in Wilmington Today," *News Journal* (Wilmington, DE), February 19, 1913, 6.

47. "Hikers May Get Mobbed in Baltimore," *Pittsburgh Post-Gazette*, February 20, 1913, 9.

48. "Hard Labor for American Girl in London," *New York Tribune*, February 19, 1913, 7.

49. "Jane Addams Praises Suffragette Hikers," *Washington Herald*, February 19, 1913, 3.

50. "Tell of the Tramp," *Evening Star* (Washington, D.C.), February 20, 1913, 3.

51. "Yes, I Vote, Says Suffragette, One of Army in 1913 Capitol Hike," *Poughkeepsie Journal* (Poughkeepsie, NY), January 8, 1956, 1C.

52. "Pilgrims Draw Big Crowd to Garrick," *Morning News* (Wilmington, DE), February 20, 1913, 10.

53. "Suffragists in an Education Campaign," *Morning Journal* (Wilmington, DE), February 19, 1913, 10.

54. "Suffragists Will Insist on Military Guard in Pageant," *Washington Times*, February 16, 1913, 6.

55. "Don't Want March Spoiled by Romance," *Morning News* (Wilmington, DE), February 20, 1913, 10.

56. "Suffragists Will Insist on Military Guard in Pageant," *Washington Times*, February 16, 1913, 6.

Chapter 9

1. "Hike On, Hike On," *Morning News* (Wilmington, DE), February 19, 1913, 6.

2. "Editorial," *Morning News* (Wilmington, DE), February 19, 1913, 6.

3. "Bids the Suffragists Pause," *Washington Post*, February 19, 1913, 5.

4. "Ask Lawmakers for Votes," *Washington Post*, February 19, 1913, 5.

5. "Gov. Wilson Hides from an Army of Suffragettes," *San Francisco Call*, February 19, 1912, 5.

6. "Wilson Stole Away," *News Journal* (Wilmington, DE), February 18, 1913, 6.

7. "Australian on Suffrage," *Washington Post*, February 19, 1913, 5.

8. "Editorial," *Philadelphia Inquirer*, February 20, 1913, 8.

9. "Equal Suffrage," *Morning News* (Wilmington, DE), February 17, 1913, 6.

10. "Hikers May Get Mobbed in Baltimore," *Pittsburgh Post-Gazette*, February 20, 1913, 9.

11. Treva B. Lindsey, *Colored No More: Reinventing Black Womanhood in Washington, D.C.* (Champaign, IL: University of Illinois Press, 2017).

12. "Mice Scatter Army," *Washington Post*, February 21, 1913, 1.

13. "Unity, Peace, and Concord Is Restored," *Democrat and Chronicle* (Rochester, NY), February 21, 1913, 1.

14. "Hair-Primped Hikers March on Baltimore," *Baltimore News*, February 20, 1913, 1.

15. "Hikers Near Maryland," *Baltimore Sun*, February 20, 1913, 1.

16. "Hair-Primped Hikers March on Baltimore," *Baltimore News*, February 20, 1913, 1.

17. "Cupid Drummed out of Camp by 'General Jones,'" *Baltimore News*, February 19, 1913, 7.

18. "Hikers Near Maryland," *Baltimore Sun*, February 20, 1913, 1.

19. "Hair-Primped Hikers March on Baltimore," *Baltimore News*, February 20, 1913, 1.

20. "Mice Scatter Army," *Washington Post*, February 21, 1913, 1.

21. "Hikers Near Maryland," *Baltimore Sun*, February 20, 1913, 2.

22. "Wellesleyites Welcome Stork," *Cedar Rapids Daily Republican* (Cedar Rapids, IA), December 21, 1912.

23. "Would Let Men Nurse Babies," *Baltimore Sun*, February 22, 1913, 7.

24. "Schools to Be out for Women Parade," *Washington Times*, February 19, 1913, 2.

25. "Marching Pilgrims Sing," *New York Post*, February 21, 1913, 3.

26. "Mice Scatter Army," *Washington Post*, February 21, 1913, 1.

27. "Hikers Near Maryland," *Baltimore Sun*, February 20, 1913, 1.

28. "Antis Planning Campaign," *Baltimore Sun*, February 20, 1913, 2.

29. "Mice Scatter Army," *Washington Post*, February 21, 1913, 1.

30. "Women Colleges Fail," *New York Tribune*, February 19, 1913, 7.

31. "Hair-Primped Hikers March on Baltimore," *Baltimore News*, February 20, 1913, 1.

32. "Marching Pilgrims Sing," *New York Post*, February 21, 1913, 3.

33. "Enter Maryland," *Oil City Derrick* (Oil City, PA), February 21, 1913, 1.

34. "In the Days That Are No More," *Baltimore Sun*, February 21, 1913, 6.

35. "Help, Men, Help!" *Washington Post*, February 21, 1913, 1.

36. "Hikers Near Maryland," *Baltimore Sun*, February 20, 1913, 1.

37. "Fame for Elkton," *Evening Star* (Washington, D.C.), February 21, 1913, 2.

38. "Marching Pilgrims Sing," *New York Post*, February 21, 1913, 3.

39. "Hog and Hominy Put New Life in Hikers," *Baltimore News*, February 21, 1913, 1.

40. "Plans for the Hike," *Morning News* (Wilmington, DE), February 17, 1913, 4.

41. "16½ Miles in 13 Hours," *Baltimore Sun*, February 22, 1913, 1.

42. "Suffrage Marchers Struggle with Mud," *New York Times*, February 22, 1913, 5.

43. "Suffrage Band Near Collapse," *Washington Herald*, February 22, 1913, 3.

44. "To Improve Maryland Roads," *Morning News* (Wilmington, DE), February 22, 1913, 3.

45. "Suffrage Band Near Collapse," *Washington Herald*, February 22, 1913, 3.

46. "Suffragette Army Near Extinction," *Morning Herald* (Uniontown, PA), February 22, 1913, 1.

47. "Suffrage Band Near Collapse," *Washington Herald*, February 22, 1913, 3.

48. "Suffrage Band in Havre de Grace," *Morning News* (Wilmington, DE), February 21, 1913, 1.

49. "Hikers Are Near Collapse," *New Castle News* (New Castle, PA), February 22, 1913, 1.

50. "Suffragette Army Near Extinction," *Morning Herald* (Uniontown, PA), February 22, 1913, 1.

51. "Suffrage Band in Havre de Grace," *Morning News* (Wilmington, DE), February 21, 1913, 1.

52. "16½ Miles in 13 Hours," *Baltimore Sun*, February 22, 1913, 1.

53. "Hiking for Suffrage Is Not Funny," *Akron Beacon Journal* (Akron, OH), February 21, 1913, 1.

54. "Hikers Are Near Collapse," *New Castle News* (New Castle, PA), February 22, 1913, 1.

55. "Hiking for Suffrage Is Not Funny," *Akron Beacon Journal* (Akron, OH), February 21, 1913, 1.

56. "Fame for Elkton," *Evening Star* (Washington, D.C.), February 21, 1913, 2.

57. "Suffrage Band Near Collapse," *Washington Herald*, February 22, 1913, 3.

58. "Hiking for Suffrage Is Not Funny," *Akron Beacon Journal* (Akron, OH), February 21, 1913, 1.

59. "Mired in Maryland Mud Hikers Drop Exhausted," *Press and Sun-Bulletin* (Binghamton, NY), February 22, 1913, 1.

60. "16 ½ Miles in 13 Hours," *Baltimore Sun*, February 22, 1913, 1.

61. "Hikers Are Near Collapse," *New Castle News* (New Castle, PA), February 22, 1913, 1.

62. "16½ Miles in 13 Hours," *Baltimore Sun*, February 22, 1913, 1.

63. "Suffrage Band Near Collapse," *Washington Herald*, February 22, 1913, 3.

64. "Suffrage Marchers Struggle with Mud," *New York Times*, February 22, 1913, 5.

65. "Suffrage Band Near Collapse," *Washington Herald*, February 22, 1913, 3.

66. "16½ Miles in 13 Hours," *Baltimore Sun*, February 22, 1913, 1.

Chapter 10

1. "Hikers Plod in Mud and Reach Belair," *Brooklyn Daily Eagle*, February 23, 1913, 74.

2. "Mired in Maryland Mud Hikers Drop Exhausted," *Press and Sun-Bulletin* (Binghamton, NY), February 22, 1913, 1.

3. "Women Hikers to Bivouac in City Tomorrow," *Baltimore News*, February 22, 1913, 1.

4. "One Martyr Among Pilgrims," *Baltimore Sun*, February 22, 1913, 7.

5. "Suffrage Army to Enter City's Gates Before Nightfall," *Baltimore News*, February 23, 1913, 1.

6. "Welcome to the Hikers," *Baltimore Sun*, February 22, 1913, 7.

7. "Women Hikers to Bivouac in City Tomorrow," *Baltimore News*, February 22, 1913, 1.

8. "Cupid Drummed out of Camp by 'General Jones,'" *Baltimore News*, February 19, 1913, 1.

9. "Urges Women to War," *Washington Herald*, February 22, 1913, 3.

10. "Would Kidnap Cabinet," *Baltimore Sun*, February 22, 1913, 7.

11. "City of Corpses," *Baltimore Sun*, February 19, 1912, 2.

12. "200 from Philadelphia in Suffrage Parade," *Philadelphia Inquirer*, February 22, 1913, 4.

13. "Woman Censures Suffragist Hikers," *Philadelphia Inquirer*, February 22, 1913, 4.

14. "Shoe Shiner Only Man on Suffrage Special," *Philadelphia Inquirer*, February 22, 4.

15. "NY Suffragettes Open Store," *New Castle News* (New Castle, PA), February 22, 1913, 1.

16. "Said Taft Would Die Today," *Baltimore Sun*, February 22, 1913, 7.

17. "Taft Not to See Parade," *Baltimore Sun*, February 22, 1913, 7.

18. "She Is Not a Suffragette," *Baltimore Sun*, February 22, 1913, 7.

19. "Siege of the Fair," *Washington Post*, February 22, 1913, 1.

20. "Would Let Men Nurse Babies," *Baltimore Sun*, February 22, 1913, 7.

21. "Siege of the Fair," *Washington Post*, February 22, 1913, 1.

22. "Suffragists Deny Mud Slinging at Antis," *Press and Sun-Bulletin* (Binghamton, NY), February 22, 1913, 1.

23. "Siege of the Fair," *Washington Post*, February 22, 1913, 1.

24. *Ibid.*

25. "Want 'Anti' Pageant," *Washington Post*, February 25, 1913, 2.

26. "Women Hikers to Bivouac in City Tomorrow," *Baltimore News*, February 22, 1913, 1.

27. "Colonel Craft Walks On, But Hikers Protest," *New York Times*, February 23, 1913, 20.

28. "Women Protest Slight of Flag," *Washington Times*, February 23, 1913, 1.

29. "The Spreading Suffrage," *New York Post*, February 24, 1913, 4.

30. "Root Against Woman Suffrage," *New York Post*, February 24, 1913, 4.

Chapter 11

1. "Colonel Craft's Guard Reaches Baltimore," *Brooklyn Daily Eagle*, February 24, 1913, 3.

2. "Hikers Lost Tribe Rejoins Army," *Baltimore News*, February 24, 1913, 1.

3. "Hikers March In," *Baltimore Sun*, February 24, 1913, 12.

4. "Hike Leader Visits Capital," *Washington Herald*, January 12, 1913, 3.

5. "Suffrage Hikers Reach Baltimore," *Morning News* (Wilmington, DE), February 24, 1913, 1.

6. "Suffrage Army to Enter City's Gates Before Nightfall," *Baltimore News*, February 23, 1913, 1.

7. "Colonel Craft's Guard Reaches Baltimore," *Brooklyn Daily Eagle*, February 24, 1913, 3.

8. "Hikers March In," *Baltimore Sun*, February 24, 1913, 12.

9. "Colonel Craft's Guard Reaches Baltimore," *Brooklyn Daily Eagle*, February 24, 1913, 3.

10. "Hikers March In," *Baltimore Sun*, February 24, 1913, 12.

11. "Suffrage Hikers Reach Baltimore," *Morning News* (Wilmington, DE), February 24, 1913, 1.

12. "Colonel Craft's Guard Reaches Baltimore," *Brooklyn Daily Eagle*, February 24, 1913, 3.

13. "Washington Is Honored Today," *Washington Times*, February 22, 1913, 1.

14. "Hikers' Lost Tribe Joins Main Army," *Baltimore News*, February 24, 1913, 1.

15. "Suffragette Army Took Needed Rest," *Philadelphia Inquirer*, February 25, 1913, 2.

16. "Colonel Craft's Guard Reaches Baltimore," *Brooklyn Daily Eagle*, February 24, 1913, 3.

17. "Colonel Craft Is Angry; Snub for General Jones," *New York Times*, February 25, 1913, 7.

18. "Lebanon Ladies Did Not Desert," *Lebanon Daily News*, February 24, 1913, 6.

19. "Colonel Craft Is Angry; Snub for General Jones," *New York Times*, February 25, 1913, 7.

20. "Colonel Craft's Guard Reaches Baltimore," *Brooklyn Daily Eagle*, February 24, 1913, 3.

21. "Colonel Craft Is Angry; Snub for General Jones," *New York Times*, February 25, 1913, 7.

22. "Pilgrims Not Weary," Washington Post, February 25, 1913, 2.

23. "Colonel Craft Is Angry; Snub for General Jones," *New York Times*, February 25, 1913, 7.

24. "Steel City Women to Be in Parade," *Pittsburg Post-Gazette*, February 27, 1913, 3.

25. "Pilgrims in Sight of National Capital," *Brooklyn Daily Eagle*, February 27, 1913, 5.

26. "Colonel Craft Is Angry; Snub for General Jones," *New York Times*, February 25, 1913, 7.

27. "Colonel Craft's Guard Reaches Baltimore," *Brooklyn Daily Eagle*, February 24, 1913, 3.

28. "Colonel Craft Is Angry; Snub for General Jones," *New York Times*, February 25, 1913, 7.

29. "Shelter Weakens Hikers," *New York Post*, February 26, 1913, 3.

30. "Hikers' Lost Tribe Joins Main Army," *Baltimore News*, February 24, 1913, 1.

31. "Would Entertain Hikers," *Baltimore Sun*, February 20, 1913, 2.

32. "The Army's Schedule," *Baltimore Sun*, February 24, 1913, 12.

33. "Hikers' Lost Tribe Joins Main Army," *Baltimore News*, February 24, 1913, 1.

34. "Big Welcome to Hikers Planned at Washington," *Philadelphia Inquirer*, February 24, 18.

35. "Suffragettes Stroll into Baltimore," *Pittsburgh Post-Gazette*, February 24, 1913, 1.

36. "Women Who Will Play a Prominent Part in the Suffrage Parade," *Washington Herald*, February 23, 1913, 15.

37. "Women Complete Arrangements for Big Washington Parade, March 3," *Oakland Tribune*, February 23, 1913, 1.

38. "Votes for Women," *Washington Post*, February 25, 1913, 2.

39. "Who's Who in Ranks," *Evening Star* (Washington, D.C.), February 26, 1913, 2.

40. "He Disapproves Hikes," *Baltimore Sun*, February 24, 1913, 12.

41. "Blame Her for Bomb," *Washington Post*, February 25, 1913, 2.

42. "Hikers Take Cardinal by Bold Strike," *Baltimore News*, February 25, 1913, 1.

43. "Cardinal Gibbons Receives Pilgrims," *Brooklyn Daily Eagle*, February 25, 1913, 3.

44. "Cardinal Gibbons," Library of Congress, accessed May 30, 2018, https://www.loc.gov/item/today-in-history/july-23#cardinalgibbons

45. "Hikers Take Cardinal by Bold Strike," *Baltimore News*, February 25, 1913, 1.

46. *Ibid.*, 2.

47. "'Mrs.' Title for All Women," *Baltimore Sun*, February 24, 1913, 1.

48. "Why 'Mrs.' for a Miss?" *New York Times*, February 25, 1913, 7.

49. "Hikers Take Cardinal by Bold Strike," *Baltimore News*, February 25, 1913, 2.

50. "Why 'Mrs.' for a Miss?" *New York Times*, February 25, 1913, 7.

51. "Austrian Feminist 'Hikers' Cue Taken from Rosalie Jones," *San Francisco Call*, February 23, 1913, 70.

52. "A Long Journey 'Hiker' Spent Night in this City," *Lock Haven Express* (Lock Haven, PA), February 24, 1913, 4.

53. Elbert Hubbard, *Hearst's Magazine*, 23 (1913): 312.

54. "Pilgrims' Blood Shed for Cause," *Washington Times*, February 24, 1913, 2.

55. "Miss Lucy Burns," *Star-Gazette* (Elmira, NY), February 25, 1913, 1.

56. "Suffragists Plan Big Reception for Pilgrim Army Here Friday," *Washington Post*, February 26, 1913, 3.

57. "Suffrage Army Is Drawing Near," *Washington Times*, February 26, 1913, 1.

58. "Suffrage Army Finishes Plans," *Washington Herald*, February 26, 1913, 2.

59. "Miss Lucy Burns," *Star-Gazette* (Elmira, NY), February 25, 1913, 1.

60. "Shocked by Hikers," *Washington Post*, February 26, 1913, 3.

61. "Current Comment," *Lock Haven Express* (Lock Haven, PA), February 26, 1913, 6.

62. "Where the Suffragettes Score," *Baltimore Sun*, February 26, 1913, 6.

63. "A Boost from North East," *Baltimore Sun*, February 26, 1913, 6.

64. "Measles Halt Mother," *Altoona Mirror* (Altoona, PA), February 25, 1913, 10.

65. "Suffragists Answering Root, Blame Men for All Dangers to Children," *Washington Post*, February 26, 1913, 3.

66. "Color Line in 'Army,'" *Baltimore Sun*, February 27, 1913, 12.

67. "Suffrage Hikers Send Wilson a Flag," *New York Times*, February 27, 1913, 6.

Chapter 12

1. "Hikers Enter on Last Stretch," *Washington Herald*, February 27, 1913, 2.

2. "Pilgrims in Sight of National Capital," *Brooklyn Daily Eagle*, February 27, 1913, 5.

3. "Color Line in 'Army,'" *Baltimore Sun*, February 27, 1913, 12.

4. "Hikers Enter on Last Stretch," *Washington Herald*, February 27, 1913, 2.

5. "Color Line in 'Army,'" *Baltimore Sun*, February 27, 1913, 12.

6. *Ibid.*

7. "Hikers Enter on Last Stretch," *Washington Herald*, February 27, 1913, 1.

8. J. D. Zahisner and Amelia R. Fry, *Alice Paul: Claiming Power* (New York: Oxford University Press, 2019), 137.

9. "Pilgrims in Sight of National Capital," *Brooklyn Daily Eagle*, February 27, 1913, 5.

10. "Picture in Words," *Evening Star*, February 25, 1913, 8.

11. "Hikers Enter on Last Stretch," *Washington Herald*, February 27, 1913, 2.

12. "Suffrage Hikers Send Wilson a Flag," *New York Times*, February 27, 1913, 6.

13. "Hikers Enter on Last Stretch," *Washington Herald*, February 27, 1913, 1.

14. "Hikers Hike Thro' Rain," *New Castle News* (New Castle, PA), February 27, 1913, 12.

15. "Color Line in 'Army,'" *Baltimore Sun*, February 27, 1913, 12.

16. "Hikers Hike Thro' Rain," *New Castle News* (New Castle, PA), February 27, 1913, 12.

17. *Ibid.*

18. "Steel City Women to be in Parade," *Pittsburg Post-Gazette*, February 27, 1913, 3.

19. "Gen. Jones' Army Enters Washington," *Evening Star* (Washington, D.C.) February 28, 1913, 2.

20. "Pilgrims Told to Enter City by Side Streets," *Washington Herald*, February 28, 1913, 1.

21. "Wilson Message Taken from Angry Pilgrims," *New York Tribune*, February 28, 1913, 7.

22. "Pilgrims Told to Enter City by Side Streets," *Washington Herald*, February 28, 1913, 1.

23. "Hiking Beauty Plodding Along in Bare Feet," *Baltimore News*, February 27, 1913, 1.

24. "Wilson Message Taken from Angry Pilgrims," *New York Tribune*, February 28, 1913, 7.

25. "Hiking Beauty Plodding Along in Bare Feet," *Baltimore News*, February 27, 1913, 5.

26. "Pilgrims Told to Enter City by Side Streets," *Washington Herald*, February 28, 1913, 2.

27. "Message to Wilson Taken from Hikers," *New York Times*, February 28, 1913, 3.

28. "Wilson Message Taken from Angry Pilgrims," *New York Tribune*, February 28, 1913, 7.

29. *Ibid.*

30. "Fist Fight Features Suffragettes' March," *Morning News* (Wilmington, DE), February 27, 1913, 10.

31. "Wilson Message Taken from Angry Pilgrims," *New York Tribune*, February 28, 1913, 7.

32. "Hikers Are Brave in the Face of Rain," *Washington Times*, February 27, 1913, 2.

33. "Fist Fight Features Suffragettes' March," *Morning News* (Wilmington, DE), February 27, 1913, 10.

34. "Oh, He Dared Antis," *Washington Post*, February 27, 1913, 5.

35. "'Army' Scout Here," *Washington Post*, February 27, 1913, 5.

36. "Steel City Women to be in Parade," *Pittsburgh Post-Gazette*, February 27, 1913, 3.

37. "'Army' Scout Here," *Washington Post*, February 27, 1913, 5.

38. "Steel City Women to be in Parade," *Pittsburgh Post-Gazette*, February 27, 1913, 3.

39. "Hikers Are Brave in the Face of Rain," *Washington Times*, February 27, 1913, 2.

40. "Message to Wilson Taken from Hikers," *New York Times*, February 28, 1913, 3.

41. "Pilgrims Told to Enter City by Side Streets," *Washington Herald*, February 28, 1913, 2.

42. "Message to Wilson Taken from Hikers," *New York Times*, February 28, 1913, 3.

43. "Gen. Jones' Army Enters Washington," *Evening Star* (Washington, D.C.), February 28, 1913, 9.

44. David Dismore, "Today in Herstory: 'Oh Sisters, My Sisters!': The Trip Is Nearly Done," Feminist Majority Foundation, accessed July 5, 2019, http://feminist.org/blog/index.php/2015/02/27/today-in-herstory-oh-sisters-my-sisters-the-trip-is-nearly-done/

Chapter 13

1. "Public Greeting Is Balm to Hikers on Entry to Capital," *Washington Times*, February 28, 1913, 1.

2. "Suffrage Army Soothed," *New York Tribune*, February 28, 1913, 7.

3. "Many Unique Features Will Be Seen in Great Suffrage Parade," *Frederick Post* (Frederick, MD), January 23, 1913, 4.

4. "Public Greeting Is Balm to Hikers on Entry to Capital," *Washington Times*, February 28, 1913, 1.

5. "Army Ends Its Hike; Gen. Jones Scores," *New York Times*, February 29, 1913, 6.

6. "Hikers Get Ovation at Their Goal," *Baltimore News*, February 28, 1913, 1.

7. "Public Greeting Is Balm to Hikers on Entry to Capital," *Washington Times*, February 28, 1913, 1.

8. "'Army' Takes Capital," *Baltimore Sun*, March 1, 1913, 7.

9. "Gen. Jones' Army Enters Washington," *Evening Star* (Washington, D.C.), February 28, 1913, 1.

10. "Hikers Get Ovation at Their Goal," *Baltimore News*, February 28, 1913, 1.

11. "'Army' Takes Capital," *Baltimore Sun*, March 1, 1913, 7.

12. "Gen. Jones' Army Enters Washington," *Evening Star* (Washington, D.C.), February 28, 1913, 1.

13. "Throngs Greet Pilgrims' Entry," *Washington Post*, March 1, 1913, 1.

14. "'Army' Takes Capital," *Baltimore Sun*, March 1, 1913, 7.

15. "Capital Greets Suffrage Band with Cheers," *Pittsburgh Post-Gazette*, March 1, 1913, 1.

16. "'Army' Takes Capital," *Baltimore Sun*, March 1, 1913, 7.

17. "Hikers Warmly Greeted," *New York Post*, February 28, 1913, 1.

18. "Hikers Get Ovation at Their Goal," *Baltimore News*, February 28, 1913, 1.

19. "Public Greeting Is Balm to Hikers on Entry to Capital," *Washington Times*, February 28, 1913, 1.

20. "Gen. Jones' Triumph," *Chicago Daily Tribune*, March 1, 1913, 6.

21. "Rested Hikers Capture City," *Washington Times*, March 1, 1913, 1.

22. "Gen. Jones' Army Enters Washington," *Evening Star* (Washington, D.C.), February 28, 1913, 2.

23. "Picture in Words," *Evening Star* (Washington, D.C.), February 25, 1913, 8.

24. "Harmony Feast Is Attended by Army of the Hudson," *Washington Herald*, March 2, 1913, 1.

25. "Woman Suffrage Excites House," *Philadelphia Inquirer*, March 2, 1913, 6.

26. "Editorial," *Oakland Tribune*, March 2, 1913, 30.

27. "Women's Cause Moves On," *San Francisco Call*, March 3, 1913, 6.

28. "'Gen.' Jones Lauds Army's Heroism," *Washington Post*, March 1, 1913, 8.

29. "5000 Women to March," *Baltimore Sun*, March 3, 1913, 1.

30. "Suffrage Invasion Is on in Earnest," *New York Times*, March 2, 1913, 15.

31. "250,000 Flock to Wilson's Inauguration," *Press and Sun-Bulletin* (Binghamton, NY), March 3, 1913, 1.

32. "5000 Women to March," *Baltimore Sun*, March 3, 1913, 1.

33. "Record March 1 Crowd Pours Into Capital," *Washington Post*, March 2, 1913, 2.

34. "Vendors of Novelties Greet Surging Crowds," *Sunday Star* (Washington, D.C.), March 2, 1913, 8.

35. "From New York Awheel," *Baltimore Sun*, March 3, 1913, 12.

36. "Woman's Day at the Capital," *New York Post*, March 3, 1913, 1.

37. "Thousands Are Given to Suffrage Cause, *Evening Star* (Washington, D.C.), March 3, 1913, 11.

38. "True Womanliness Defined by Rival Faction Leaders," *Sunday Star*, March 2, 1913, 8.

39. "Is a Bit Homesick Says Phoebe Hawn," *Brooklyn Daily Eagle*, March 3, 1913, 5.

40. "Order of the March," *Women's Journal and Suffrage News*, 44, no. 9 (March 1, 1913): 72.

41. "Woman's Day at the Capital," *New York Post*, March 3, 1913, 1.

42. "5000 Women March Beset by Crowds," *New York Times*, March 4, 1913, 5.

43. "'Baby Pilgrim' Tells of Great Parade," *Brooklyn Daily Eagle*, March 4, 1913, 20.

44. "Suffragists' Parade Is Helped Through Mob," *Pittsburgh Post-Gazette*, March 4, 1913, 3.

45. "Parading Suffragists Fight Way Through Jeering Mob That Spits on Banners and Insults Women," *Press and Sun-Bulletin* (Binghamton, NY), March 4, 1913, 1.

46. "Parade as Seen by Miss Clark," *Washington Herald*, March 4, 1913, 2.

47. "Is a Bit Homesick Says Phoebe Hawn," *Brooklyn Daily Eagle*, March 3, 1913, 5.

Chapter 14

1. "Thousands Are Given to Suffrage Cause," *Evening Star* (Washington, D.C.), March 3, 1913, 11.

2. "Letter Carried By Hikers Is Held Up," *Washington Times*, March 6, 1913, 9.

3. "Spring Doings in Washington Give Society Plenty to Keep 'Up' On," *La Crosse Tribune and Leader-Press* (La Crosse, WI), March 17, 1927, 5.

4. "Capital's Shame," *New York Post*, March 4, 1913, 1.

5. "Parade Struggles to Victory Despite Disgraceful Scenes," *Woman's Journal and Suffrage News*, 44, no. 10 (March 8, 1913): 76.

6. Alice Stone Blackwell, "Whose Ox is Gored," *Woman's Journal and Suffrage News*, 44, no. 10 (March 8, 1913): 76.

7. "Rowdies Help Suffrage," *New York Post*, March 5, 1913, 3.

8. "Woman's Parade Riot Inquiry," *New York Post*, March 5, 1913.

9. "Women Banner to Be Carried around the World," *Times Herald* (Olean, NY), March 8, 1913, 1.

10. "Leaders Plan Globe-Encircling Trip," *Washington Post*, March 9, 1913, 2.

11. "Col. Craft and Capt. Freeman Move on Harrisburg Today," *Lebanon Daily News* (Lebanon, PA), March 17, 1913, 1.

12. "Heard the 'Little' Corporal," *Brooklyn Daily Eagle*, March 15, 1913, 8.

13. "Phoebe Hawn's Story of Washington Hike," *Brooklyn Daily Eagle*, March 13, 1913, 9.

14. "Is 'Gen.' Rosalie a Guerilla?" *Washington Herald*, March 7, 1913, 6.

15. Rosalie Jones, "Value of a Pilgrimage," *New York Tribune*, March 9, 1913, 21.

16. "Suffrage Hikers Out," *New York Times*, April 27, 1913, 4.

17. "10,000 Marchers in Suffrage Line," *New York Times*, May 4, 1913, 1.

18. "Gen. Rosalie Jones Has Organized Something Special at Mineola," *New York Times*, May 13, 1913, 11.

19. "Parade of Suffragists," *South Side Messenger* (Freeport and Belmore, NY), May 30, 1913, 3.

20. "Hempstead Aglow in Suffrage Hues," *New York Times*, May 25, 1913, C7.

21. "General Rosalie Jones Flies for Suffrage," *New York Times*, May 31, 1913, 6.

22. "Newburg Women Parade," *New York Times*, June 5, 1913, 1.

23. "'General' Jones Back from Rural Districts," *Syracuse Herald* (Syracuse, NY), June 26, 1913, 4.

24. "Suffragist, Out Late Nights, Gets Permit to Carry Revolver," *Syracuse Herald* (Syracuse, NY), June 26, 1913, 4.

25. Untitled News Item, *Akron Beacon Journal* (Akron, OH), August 21, 1913, 6.

26. Marguerite Kerns, "The Spirit of 1776," *New York Archives*, Fall 2013, 3.

27. "Gen. Jones' Mother a Belligerent Anti," *Brooklyn Daily Eagle*, July 31, 1913, 4.

28. "Gen. Jones on Long Island," *The Sun* (New York, NY), July 27, 1913, 10.

29. "With the Suffragists," *Whitesville News* (Whitesville, NY), July 17, 1913.

30. "After Lost Rings," *News Journal*, March 6, 1913, 2.

31. "Suffs Put under Ban in Hartford," *Bridgeport Evening Farmer* (Bridgeport, CT), August 20, 1913, 5.

32. "Fortune for Suffragette," *Middletown Daily Times-Press* (Middletown, NY), July 3, 1913, 5.

33. Elizabeth Aldrich, "How Man Will Look When Woman Votes," *Salt Lake Tribune*, June 25, 1913, 47.

34. "Suffragist Beauty in Trousers Leads Dress Reform Campaign," *Washington Post*, July 1, 1913, 3.

35. "Dr. Oliver L. Jones Shoots Himself," August 9, 1913, *New York Times*, 14.

36. "Prize Cow at Fair Is Anti-Suffragist," *The Sun* (New York, NY), August 6, 1913, 4.

37. "Dr. Jones Left $10,000,000," *Washington Post*, September 12, 1913, 1.

38. Untitled News Item, *Washington Post*, September 13, 1913, 6.

39. Dr. Oliver L. Jones Shoots Himself," *New York Times*, August 9, 1913, 14.

40. "Mrs. R. G. Brown Named Head of Suffragists," *Syracuse Herald*, October 16, 1913, 15.

41. "Gen. Jones' Hike Starts," *New York Times*, January 2, 1914, 3.

42. "On Hike to Albany," *Nassau County Review* (Freeport, NY), January 2, 1914, 5.

43. "'General' Rosalie and Band on Way to Albany," *Post-Star* (Glens Falls, NY), January 2, 1914, 7.

44. National American Woman's Suffrage Association, *The Handbook of the National American Woman's Suffrage Association*

(New York: N.W.S. Publishing Company, 1914), 154.

45. "Gen. Jones' Hike Starts," *New York Times*, January 2, 1914, 3.

46. "'Ouch!' Is Hikers' Cry on First March," *The Sun* (New York, NY), January 2, 1914, 14.

47. "Suffragists Off for Albany," *Indiana Gazette* (Indiana, PA), January 2, 1914, 8.

48. "'Gen. Jones' Hike Starts," *Long-Islander*, January 2, 1914, 4.

49. "Marching on Albany with the Suffragette Army," *Irvington Gazette* (Irvington, NY), February 9, 1914, 5.

50. "16 Miles Nearer Albany," *Washington Post*, January 2, 1914, 5.

51. "Women to 'Hike' for Vote," *Washington Post*, January 2, 1914, 5.

52. "Pilgrims Enter Albany," *New York Post*, January 7, 1914, 2.

53. "General Jones Storms Capitol," *Allegany County Reporter* (Wellsville, NY), January 8, 1914, 1.

54. "Suffragists Begin Second Day of Hike," *Syracuse Herald*, January 2, 1914, 1.

55. "Suffrage Live Topic at Women's Meeting," *Anaconda Standard* (Anaconda, MT), June 10, 1914.

56. National American Woman's Suffrage Association, *The Handbook of the National American Woman's Suffrage Association* (New York: N.W.S. Publishing Company, 1914), 132.

57. *Ibid.*

58. *Ibid.*

59. "Missouri Suffrage Hike: Women Inspired by 'Gen.' Jones to March from St. Louis," *New York Times*, June 21, 1914, 3.

60. "Suffrage Leaders Will Speaker Here," *Helena Daily Independent* (Helena, MT), July 7, 1914, 10.

61. "Livingston News," *Helena Independent*, July 13, 1914, 8.

62. "Suffragists Enjoy One Day in Butte," *Anaconda Standard*, July 16, 1914, 14.

63. "Crowds Gather Around 'Hikers,'" *Helena Independent*, July 16, 1914, 2.

64. *Ibid.*, 1.

65. *Ibid.*, 2.

66. *Ibid.*, 1.

67. "Rosalie Jones Back Thinner," *The Sun* (New York, NY), August 23, 1914, 9.

68. "Suffrage Campaign on Long Island," *Nassau County Review* (Freeport, NY), October 2, 1914, 3.

69. "Suffrage Advance to Rochester Is On," *The Sun* (New York, NY), October 8, 1914, 8.

70. "Ida Craft," Her Hat Was in the Ring: U.S. Women Who Ran for Public Office Before 1920, accessed June 27, 2019, http://www.herhatwasinthering.org/biography.php?id=7204

71. "Suffs Arrive at Rochester," *Tarrytown Daily News* (Tarrytown, NY), October 14, 1914, 4.

72. "Suffrage Advance to Rochester Is On," *The Sun* (New York, NY), October 8, 1914, 8.

73. National American Woman's Suffrage Association, *The Handbook of the National American Woman's Suffrage Association* (New York: N.W.S. Publishing Company, 1914), 133.

74. "'Votes for Women' Remembering Montana's Battle for Suffrage Over 100 Years Ago," *Bozeman Daily Chronicle* (Bozeman, MT), March 16, 2014, accessed May 30, 2018, https://www.bozemandailychronicle.com/news/sunday/votes-for-women/article_9b65361e-ac87-11e3-9e3b-0019bb2963f4.html

75. "Celebrate Montana Women's Suffrage Centennial: Vote," *Billings Gazette* (Billings, MT), October 19, 2014, accessed May 30, 2018, http://billingsgazette.com/news/opinion/editorial/gazette-opinion/gazette-opinion-celebrate-montana-women-s-suffrage-centennial-vote/article_65900009-f83c-51b2-bb5a-dec14fb797b4.html

76. "Gen. Jones Offers Prize," *Nassau Post* (Freeport, NY), January 14, 1915, 8.

77. "Equal Suffrage Notes," *South Side Signal* (Bellmore, NY), January 15, 1915, 2.

78. "General Rosalie Jones Takes Job as Auto Mechanic," *The Sun* (New York, NY), February 10, 1915, 1.

79. "Suffragette Now Runs a Taxicab," *New York Times*, October 3, 1913, 3.

80. "Rosalie Jones, Suff 'General' to Sell Autos," *Ogdensburg Journal* (Ogdensburg, NY), February 11, 1915, 4.

81. "Fraud in Newark Is Suffragist Cry," *The Sun* (New York, NY), October 20, 1915, 2.

82. "Women Will Keep up the Fight," *New York Times*, October 20, 1915, 1.

83. "Miss Rosalie Jones Still Militant for Suffrage," *Long-Islander* (Huntington, NY), October 29, 1915, 9.

84. "Suffrage Campaign to End in a Whirl," *New York Times*, October 29, 1915, 5.

85. "Suffrage Campaign Closes at Midnight," *New York Times*, October 31, 1915, 4.

86. Walt Gable, "Women's Suffrage Series, Part 4 'Finally, Triumph in New York!'" *Finger Lake Times* (Geneva, NY), March 26, 2017.

87. "Second Monthly Suffrage School," *Middletown Times-Press* (Middletown, NY), January 23, 1917, 4.

88. "Suffrage Pioneers Not Forgotten in Victory," *The Sun* (New York, NY), December 9, 1917, 5.

89. Peg Johnston, *Faithfully Yours, Elisabeth Freeman*, "1916: NAACP Anti-Lynching Campaign," accessed June 27, 2019, http://www.elizabethfreeman.org/naacp.php

Chapter 15

1. "Oyster Bay Dirty, Colonel Discloses," *New York Times*, June 26, 1916, 5.

2. "Historical Highlights January 10, 1918," History Art and Archives, United States House of Representatives, accessed May 30, 2018, http://history.house.gov/HistoricalHighlight/Detail/35873?ret=True

3. "Suffrage Victory in the House Pleases All But Antis," *The Sun* (New York, NY), January 20, 1918, 8.

4. Judith Adler Spinzia, "Women of Long Island: Mary Elizabeth Jones, Rosalie Gardiner Jones," *The Freeholder*, 11 (Spring 2007): 3–7.

5. "Obituary," *New York Times*, March 22, 1918, 13.

6. "Obituary," *New York Times*, October 23, 1918, 13.

7. "Obituary," *New York Times*, November 2, 1918, 15.

8. "Worth $5,000,000 Gen. Rosalie Jones Is Socialist Now," *Evening World*, October 26, 1918, 5.

9. "Trouble Over Jones' Estate," *Long-Islander* (Huntington, NY), May 23, 1919, 10.

10. "Worth $5,000,000 Gen. Rosalie Jones Is Socialist Now," *Evening World*, October 26, 1918, 5.

11. Judith Adler Spinzia, "Women of Long Island: Mary Elizabeth Jones, Rosalie Gardiner Jones," *The Freeholder*, 11 (Spring 2007): 3–7.

12. "Suffragette Is Authoress," *Berkeley*

Daily Gazette (Berkeley, CA), February 26, 1923, 4.

13. Rosalie G. Jones, *The American Standard of Living and World Co-operation* (Boston: Cornhill Publishing Company, 1923), 3.

14. *Ibid.*, 311.

15. "Three Women's Meetings Open During Week," *Capital Times* (Madison, WI), April 29, 1924, 7.

16. "Women's Peace League Hissed," *Cook County Herald* (Arlington Heights, IL), May 1, 1924, 2.

17. "How Senator Dill Won the Suffragette," *Galveston Daily News* (Galveston, TX), January 16, 1927, 12.

18. "Miss Rosalie Jones Backs Third Party," *Long-Islander* (Huntington, NY), September 19, 1924, 10.

19. "Germans Support La Follette for One Reason Only," *Waterloo Evening Courier* (Waterloo, IA), September 29, 1924, 2.

20. "'General' Rosalie Receives Gift," *Davenport Democrat and Leader* (Davenport, IA), September 23, 1924, 9.

21. "Active Campaign Is Waged Here by La Follette Aids," *Waterloo Evening Courier* (Waterloo, IA), September 29, 1924, 2.

22. "The Mansion of Hope," *Newsday*, March 2, 1961, 1C.

23. "Ex-Senator Dill Sues for Divorce," *New York Times*, March 31, 1936, 14.

24. "How Senator Dill Won the Suffragette," *Galveston Daily News* (Galveston, TX), January 16, 1927, 12.

25. "'Gen.' Jones to Wed U.S. Senator Dill," *Long-Islander* (Huntington, NY), September 11, 1927, 4.

26. "How Senator Dill Won the Suffragette," *Galveston Daily News* (Galveston, TX), January 16, 1927, 12.

27. "Spring Doings in Washington Give Society Plenty to Keep 'up' on," *La Crosse Tribune and Leader-Press* (La Crosse, WI), March 17, 1927, 5.

28. "'Gen.' Rosalie Jones, Suffragette Leader, Betrothed to United States Senator Dill," *New York Times*, March 9, 1927, 27.

29. "How Senator Dill Won the Suffragette," *Galveston Daily News* (Galveston, TX), January 16, 1927, 12.

30. "When the Senator Found One Woman's Place Was Not the Home," *Albuquerque Journal*, May 30, 1936, 17.

31. "Mrs. Rosalie Jones Dill Since Last Tuesday," *Long-Islander* (Huntington, NY), March 18, 1927, 10.

32. "How Senator Dill Won the Suffragette," *Galveston Daily News* (Galveston, TX), January 16, 1927, 12.

33. "Mrs. Rosalie Jones Dill Since Last Tuesday," *Long-Islander* (Huntington, NY), March 18, 1927, 10.

34. "'Not a Lucy Stoner' Declares Mrs. Dill," *New York Times*, March 14, 1927, 29.

35. Rosalie Jones Dill, *Women's Influence Through the Ballot* (Spokane Washington, 1928), 3.

36. *Ibid.*, 17.

37. "W. I. L. Announces Saturday Evening Broadcasts to Begin," *Capital Times*, January 30, 1930, 1.

38. "Invitation from Congressional Club Is Received by Mrs. Cole," *Findlay Morning Republican and Courier* (Findlay, OH), April 3, 1933, 1.

39. "Ex-Senator Dill Sues for Divorce," *New York Times*, March 31, 1936, 14.

40. "Dill Divorce Eastern Rumor," *Spokesman-Review* (Spokane, WA), January 14, 1936, 1.

41. "Ex-Senator Dill Sues for Divorce," *New York Times*, March 31, 1936, 14.

42. "Housekeeping Enters Divorce Row," *Evening News Journal* (Clovis, NM), July 1, 1936, 3.

43. "When the Senator Found One Woman's Place Was Not the Home," *Albuquerque Journal*, May 30, 1936, 17.

44. "Housekeeping Enters Divorce Row," *Evening News Journal* (Clovis, NM), July 1, 1936, 3.

45. "Looking Back from the *Times*' Files," *Portsmouth Times* (Portsmouth, OH), July 11, 1936, 6.

46. "Rosalie Jones Dill Offers Her Defense," *Sandusky Star-Journal* (Sandusky, OH), July 1, 1936.

47. "Suffrage Head Splits Home by Political Views," *Manhasset Press* (Manhasset, NY), July 3, 1936, 6.

48. "Senator's Wife Says He Threatened to Kill Her," *Daily Capital News* (Jefferson, MO), July 7, 1936, 8.

49. "Dill Wins Divorce from Rosalie Jones," *New York Times*, July 10, 1936, 21.

50. "When the Senator Found One Woman's Place Was Not the Home," *Albuquerque Journal*, May 30, 1936, 17.

51. "Dill Wins Divorce from Rosalie Jones," *New York Times*, July 10, 1936, 21.

52. "Mrs. Dill Campaigns," *Portsmouth Times* (Portsmouth, OH), August 3, 1936, 2.

53. "Rosalie Jones Dill Candidate for Congress," Official Campaign Leaflet, 1936.

54. "Ex-Senator Dill Sues for Divorce," *New York Times*, March 31, 1936, 14.

55. "Mrs. Dill Campaigns," *Portsmouth Times* (Portsmouth, OH), August 3, 1936, 2.

56. "Mrs. Dill Will Stick to Name," *Salt Lake Tribune*, July 28, 1936, 2.

57. "Divorced Wife of Senator Dill Is After Congress Seat," *Evening Observer* (Dunkirk, NY), August 28, 1936, 2.

58. "Judgements Granted Against Mrs. Dill," *New York Times*, October 1, 1936, 16.

59. "September 1936 Primary," Washington Secretary of State, https://www.sos.wa.gov//elections/results_report.aspx?e=98&c=&c2=&t=&t2=&p=&p2=&y=

60. "Dill Wins Divorce from Rosalie Jones," *New York Times*, July 10, 1936, 21.

61. "Rosalie Jones," *Post-Standard* (Syracuse, NY), December 6, 2006, E4.

62. "Tragedies of Society—Suicides Stalk the Joneses of Long Island," *New York Journal and American* (New York, NY), April 17, 1936, 1-M.

63. Ruth Schier, "Rosalie Jones Has Spent Most Of Life Clashing With Authority," *The Long-Islander* (Huntington, NY), September 16, 1948, 1.

64. Marc Watkins, e-mail message to the author, August 15, 2019.

65. "Dead goat found hanging by chain," *Nassau Daily Review-Star* (Freeport, NY), July 12, 1940, 20.

66. Judith Adler Spinzia, "Women of Long Island: Mary Elizabeth Jones, Rosalie Gardiner Jones," *The Freeholder*, 11 (Spring 2007): 3–7.

67. Ruth Schier, "Rosalie Jones Has Spent Most of Life Clashing with Authority," *The Long-Islander* (Huntington, NY), September 16, 1948, 1.

68. Barbara Weeks, July 5, 2018 (11:31 a.m.), comment posted on "Votes for Women!" by Robert C. Hughes.

69. "Daily Records of RGJ," unpublished diary, 1945–1955.

70. "Miss Louise Jones of Pioneer Family Dies in New York," *Long-Islander* (Huntington, NY), June 19, 1952, 8.

71. Margalit Fox, "Mary Gardiner Jones, Consumer Advocate, Dies at 89," *New York Times*, January 7, 2010, accessed July 11, 2019, https://www.nytimes.com/2010/01/08/us/08jones.html

72. Marc Watkins, e-mail message to the author, August 15, 2019.

73. "Rosalie Gardiner Jones," *Long-Islander* (Huntington, NY), January 19, 1978, 29.

74. "Rosalie Jones, 95, an Early LI Feminist," *Newsday*, January 13, 1978.

75. "Rosalie Jones Dies at 95," *Oyster Bay Guardian* (Oyster Bay, NY), January 19, 1978, 1.

76. "Rosalie Jones," *Post-Standard* (Syracuse, NY), December 6, 2006, E-4.

77. "Rosalie Jones Dies at 95," *Oyster Bay Guardian*, January 19, 1978, 1.

78. "Rosalie Jones Dill," *Women's Influence Through the Ballot* (Spokane, WA, 1928), 17.

Bibliography

"After Alabaman's Scalp," *Chicago Daily Tribune*, February 13, 1913, 3.

Aldrich, Elizabeth. "How Man Will Look When Woman Votes," *Washington Post*, May 18, 1913, 5.

"All to Wear Hikers," *New York Tribune*, January 11, 1913, 6.

"Antis Denounce Hike," *New York Tribune*, January 16, 1913, 7.

"Army Ends Its Hike; Gen. Jones Scores," *New York Times*, February 29, 1913, 6.

"Army Enters Delaware," *Baltimore Sun*, February 19, 1913, 1.

"Army Is Footsore," *Evening Star* (Washington, D.C.), February 18, 1913, 1.

"Army Limps into City," *Philadelphia Inquirer*, February 17, 1913, 1.

"'Army' Scout Here," *Washington Post*, February 27, 1913, 5.

"'Army' Takes Capital," *Baltimore Sun*, March 1, 1913, 7.

"Artistic Long Island Home on Cold Spring Estate," *New York Times*, January 26, 1913, 34.

"Ask Lawmakers for Votes" *Washington Post*, February 19, 1913, 5.

"'Baby Pilgrim' Tells of Great Parade," *Brooklyn Daily Eagle*, March 4, 1913, 20.

"Bans Women from Parade," *New York Times*, February 12, 1913, 8.

"Bids the Suffragists Pause," *Washington Post*, February 19, 1913, 5.

"Big Welcome to Hikers Planned at Washington," *Philadelphia Inquirer*, February 24, 18.

Blackwell, Alice Stone. "Whose Ox is Gored," *Woman's Journal and Suffrage News*, 44, no. 10 (March 8, 1913): 76.

"Blame Her for Bomb," *Washington Post*, February 25, 1913, 2.

"A Boost from North East," *Baltimore Sun*, February 26, 1913, 6.

"Calls Back General of Suffrage Army," *New York Times*, December 21, 1912.

"Capital Greets Suffrage Band with Cheers," *Pittsburgh Post-Gazette*, March 1, 1913, 1.

"Capital's Shame," *New York Post*, March 4, 1913, 1.

"Cardinal Gibbons," Library of Congress, accessed May 30, 2018, https://www.loc.gov/item/today-in-history/july-23#cardinalgibbons

"Cardinal Gibbons Receives Pilgrims," *Brooklyn Daily Eagle*, February 25, 1913, 3.

"Colonel Craft Walks On, But Hikers Protest," *New York Times*, February 23, 1913, 20.

"Colonel Craft's Guard Reaches Baltimore," *Brooklyn Daily Eagle*, February 24, 1913, 3.

"Color Line in 'Army,'" *Baltimore Sun*, February 27, 1913, 12.

"Cupid Drummed out of Camp by 'General Jones,'" *Baltimore News*, February 19, 1913, 1.

"Cupid Hits a Pilgrim," *Washington Post*, February 20, 1913, 1.

"Cupid in Ranks of Suffragettes," *Philadelphia Inquirer*, February 15, 1913, 5.

"Daily Records of RGJ," unpublished diary.

"Delaware's New Fame," *New York Post*, February 15, 1913.

Dill, Rosalie Jones. *Women's Influence Through the Ballot* (Spokane, WA, 1928), 17.

"Dill Wins Divorce from Rosalie Jones," *New York Times*, July 10, 1936, 21.

Dismore, David. "Today in Herstory: 'Oh Sisters, My Sisters!': The Trip Is Nearly Done," Feminist Majority Foundation, accessed July 5, 2019, http://feminist.org/blog/index.php/2015/02/27/today-in-

herstory-oh-sisters-my-sisters-the-trip-
is-nearly-done/

"Disorder at Women's Debate," *Chicago Daily Tribune,* January 19, 1913, 7.

"Doings of Suffragists in Wilmington Today," *News Journal* (Wilmington, DE), February 19, 1913, 6.

"Don't Want March Spoiled by Romance," *Morning News* (Wilmington, DE), February 20, 1913, 10.

"Dr. Oliver L. Jones Shoots Himself," *New York Times,* August 9, 1913, 14.

"Editorial," *Morning News* (Wilmington, DE), January 15, 1913, 6.

"Editorial," *Morning News* (Wilmington, DE), January 30, 1913, 4.

"Editorial," *Morning News* (Wilmington, DE), February 19, 1913, 6.

"Editorial," *News Journal* (Wilmington, DE), January 16, 1913, 4.

"Editorial," *Philadelphia Inquirer,* February 20, 1913, 8.

"Editorial Jottings," *Baltimore Sun,* February 18, 1913, 6.

"18-Day March to the Capital," *New York Times,* January 13, 1913, 22.

"The Elizabeth Cady Stanton and Susan B. Anthony Papers," Rutgers University, accessed May 30, 2018, http://ecssba. rutgers.edu/docs/seneca.html

"Emilie A. Doetsch," Archives of Maryland, accessed May 30, 2018, http://msa.maryland. gov/megafile/msa/speccol/sc3500/ sc3520/013700/013708/html/13708bio.html

"Equal Suffrage," *Morning News* (Wilmington, DE), February 17, 1913, 6.

"Ex-Senator Dill Sues for Divorce," *New York Times,* March 31, 1936, 14.

"Fame for Elkton," *Evening Star* (Washington, D.C.), February 21, 1913, 2.

"50,000 Suffragettes in London Parade," NAWSA Suffrage Scrapbooks, Library of Congress, accessed July 8, 2019, https://cdn.loc.gov/master/rbc/rbcmil/ scrp7009701/001.jpg

"Fist Fight Features Suffragettes' March," *Morning News* (Wilmington, DE), February 27, 1913, 10.

Fitch, E. S. "The Hiking Suffragettes: He Shes," song lyrics, Washington, D.C.: Marks-Goldsmith Company, Inc., 1914, accessed July 5, 2019, https://lccn.loc. gov/2017562286.

"5000 Women March Beset by Crowds," *New York Times,* March 4, 1913, 5.

"5000 Women to March," *Baltimore Sun,* March 3, 1913, 1.

"Former Brooklyn Boy Joins Hikers to Win a Bride," *Brooklyn Daily Eagle*, February 19, 1913, 1.

Fox, Margalit. "Mary Gardiner Jones, Consumer Advocate, Dies at 89," *New York Times,* January 7, 2010, accessed July 11, 2019.

"Fraud In Newark Is Suffragist Cry," *The Sun* (New York, NY), October 20, 1915, 2.

"From New York Awheel," *Baltimore Sun,* March 3, 1913, 12.

"Fun with Students," *Evening Star* (Washington, D.C.), February 14, 1913, 2.

"'Gen.' De Forest Beats 'Gen.' Jones in Seeing Sulzer," *The Sun* (New York, NY), December 29, 1912.

"Gen. Jones' Army Enters Washington," *Evening Star* (Washington, D.C.), February 28, 1913, 9.

"Gen. Jones' Hike Starts," *New York Times,* January 2, 1914, 3.

"'Gen.' Jones Lauds Army's Heroism," *Washington Post,* March 1, 1913, 8.

"Gen. Jones on Long Island," *The Sun* (New York, NY), July 27, 1913, 10.

"Gen. Jones' Triumph," *Chicago Daily Tribune,* March 1, 1913, 6.

"Gen. Rosalie Jones Has Organized Something Special at Mineola," *New York Times,* May 13, 1913, 11.

"'Gen.' Rosalie Jones, Suffragette Leader, Betrothed to United States Senator Dill," *New York Times,* March 9, 1927, 27.

"General Jones, Leader of Suffragettes, Here," *Morning News,* January 14, 1913, 1.

"General Jones Wins 'Em" *Baltimore Sun,* January 14, 1913, 3.

"General Lets Hikers Accept Lift on Road," *Baltimore News,* February 15, 1913, 1.

"General Rosalie Jones Flies for Suffrage," *New York Times,* May 31, 1913, 6.

"General Rosalie Jones Takes Job as Auto Mechanic," *The Sun* (New York, NY), February 10, 1915, 1.

"General's Mamma Bound Up State After Daughter," *Brooklyn Daily Eagle,* December 21, 1912.

"Getting Ready for 'Hike,'" *New York Times,* January 12, 1913, 2.

Gilman, Charlotte Perkins. *Women and Economics* (Boston: Small, Maynard, and Company, 1898).

"Glad Hand for Hikers," *Washington Post,* February 19, 1913, 1.

"Gloom in Suffrage Camp," *New York Times,* February 1, 1913, 1.

Goodier, Susan, and Karen Pastorello. Women Will Vote: Winning Suffrage in New York State (Ithaca: Cornell University Press, 1917).

"Hairpins Fall Along Path of Heroes of 1776," *Baltimore News,* February 13, 1913, 1.

"Hair-Primped Hikers March on Baltimore," *Baltimore News,* February 20, 1913, 1.

"Hard Tack Strays But Suffrage Army Thrives," *New York Tribune,* February 19, 1913, 7.

"Harmony Feast Is Attended by Army of the Hudson," *Washington Herald,* March 2, 1913, 1.

Harper, Ida Husted. History of Woman Suffrage: 1900–1920 (New York: J. J. Little & Ives, 1922).

"He Disapproves Hikes," *Baltimore Sun,* February 24, 1913, 12.

"Heard the 'Little' Corporal," *Brooklyn Daily Eagle,* March 15, 1913, 8.

"Heflin Only Amused," *Washington Post,* February 14, 1913, 3.

"Heflin Stirs Women's Ire," *Chicago Daily Tribune,* February 13, 1913, 3.

"Help, Men, Help!" *Washington Post,* February 21, 1913, 1.

"Hempstead Aglow in Suffrage Hues," *New York Times* May 25, 1913, C7.

"Here's General Jones's General Order Number 1," *New York Times,* January 21, 1913, 8.

"Hike Is Not Funny," *Evening Star* (Washington, D.C.), February 17, 1913, 3.

"Hike On, Hike On," *Morning News* (Wilmington, DE), February 19, 1913, 6.

"Hike or Pay for Substitute," *Washington Herald,* January 19, 1913, 1.

"Hike Up Walnut Street," *New York Post,* February 17, 1913.

"Hiker Leader Visits the Capital," *Washington Herald,* January 12, 1913, 3.

"The Hikers," *Morning News* (Wilmington, DE), February 17, 1913, 6.

"Hikers Are Brave in the Face of Rain," *Washington Times,* February 27, 1913, 2.

"Hikers Enjoy Brooklyn Day," *Brooklyn Daily Eagle,* February 18, 1913, 1.

"Hikers Get Ovation at Their Goal," *Baltimore News,* February 28, 1913, 1.

"Hikers' Lost Tribe Rejoins Army," *Baltimore News,* February 24, 1913, 1.

"Hikers March In," *Baltimore Sun,* February 24, 1913, 12.

"Hikers May Get Mobbed in Baltimore," *Pittsburgh Post-Gazette,* February 20, 1913, 9.

"Hikers Near Maryland," *Baltimore Sun,* February 20, 1913, 1.

"Hikers Plod in Mud and Reach Belair," *Brooklyn Daily Eagle,* February 23, 1913, 74.

"Hikers Reach Chester," *Baltimore Sun,* February 18, 1913, 1.

"Hikers Take Cardinal by Bold Strike," *Baltimore News,* February 25, 1913, 1.

"Hikers Warmly Greeted," *New York Post,* February 28, 1913, 1.

"Hikers Welcomed at Wilmington," *Philadelphia Inquirer,* February 19, 1913, 6.

"Hiking Beauty Plodding Along in Bare Feet," *Baltimore News,* February 27, 1913, 1.

"Hiking Pilgrims Hurry to Bed at Burlington," *Philadelphia Inquirer,* February 16, 1913, 17.

"Hog and Hominy Put New Life in Hikers," *Baltimore News,* February 21, 1913, 1.

"Hooting Crowds Greet Weary Pilgrims," *Pittsburgh Post-Gazette,* February 17, 1913, 1.

Hubbard, Elbert. *Hearst's Magazine,* 23 (1913): 312.

"In the Days That Are No More," *Baltimore Sun,* February 21, 1913, 6.

"Is a Bit Homesick Says Phoebe Hawn," *Brooklyn Daily Eagle,* March 3, 1913, 5.

"Is 'Gen.' Rosalie a Guerilla?" *Washington Herald,* March 7, 1913, 6.

"Isn't It Remarkable What Little Things Will Do?" *Pittsburgh Post-Gazette,* February 17, 1913, 1.

"Jane Addams Praises Suffragette Hikers," *Washington Herald,* February 19, 1913, 3.

Johnston, Peg. *Faithfully Yours, Elisabeth Freeman,* "1911–1916: Media Stunts for Suffrage," accessed June 27, 2019, http://www.elizabethfreeman.org/suffrage.php

Johnston, Peg. *Faithfully Yours, Elisabeth Freeman,* "1916: NAACP Anti-Lynching Campaign," accessed June 27, 2019, http://www.elizabethfreeman.org/naacp.php

Johnston, Peg. *Faithfully Yours, Elisabeth Freeman,* "Overview," accessed May 30, 2018, http://www.elisabethfreeman.org/overview.php

Jones, Rosalie. "Value of a Pilgrimage," *New York Tribune,* March 9, 1913, 21.

Jones, Rosalie G. *The American Standard of*

Living and World Co-operation (Boston: Cornhill Publishing Company, 1923).

"Joy of Suffragists Tempered by Fear," *New York Tribune,* January 9, 1913, 7.

"Judgements Granted Against Mrs. Dill," *New York Times,* October 1, 1936, 16.

"Just When Women Vote in Each State," *New York Tribune,* January 11, 1913, 6.

Kearns, Marguerite. "The Spirit of 1776," *New York Archives,* Fall 2013, 3.

"Lausanne Takes Hikers Off Route," *The Sun* (New York, NY), February 16, 1913, 12.

"Leaders Plan Globe-Encircling Trip," *Washington Post,* March 9, 1913, 2.

"Leading Suffragists' Activities for Monster Parade," *Washington Times,* January 10, 1913, 1.

"Letter Carried By Hikers Is Held Up," *Washington Times,* March 6, 1913, 9.

Lindsey, Treva B. *Colored No More: Reinventing Black Womanhood in Washington, D.C.* (Champaign, IL: University of Illinois Press, 2017).

"The Mansion of Hope," *Newsday,* March 2, 1961, 1C.

"Marching Pilgrims Sing," *New York Post,* February 21, 1913, 3.

"Mayor to Welcome Suffrage Pilgrims," *Morning News* (Wilmington, DE), February 17, 1913, 1.

"Megaphone Band for Suffragettes," *New York Times,* February 12, 1913, 8.

"Members of the 'On to Washington' Band," *Washington Post,* January 31, 1913, 2.

"Men to March in Suffrage Parade," *Washington Herald,* January 14, 1913, 2.

"Mice May Cause Tumult During Suffrage Parade," *Washington Post,* February 1, 1913, 2.

"Mice to Daunt Suffragists," *New York Times,* February 2, 1913, 1.

"Milholland-Heflin Debate," *Washington Post,* February 17, 1913, 6.

"Missouri Suffrage Hike: Women Inspired by 'Gen.' Jones to March from St. Louis," *New York Times,* June 21, 1914, 3.

"Mob Buffets Hikers, Now in Philadelphia," *New York Times,* February 17, 1913, 6.

"Motive for Pageant," *Washington Post,* January 13, 1913, 2.

"'Mrs.' Title for All Women," *Baltimore Sun,* February 24, 1913, 1.

National American Woman's Suffrage Association. *The Handbook of the National American Woman's Suffrage Association* (New York: N.W.S. Publishing Company, 1914).

Naylor, Natalie A. *Women in Long Island's Past: A History of Eminent Ladies and Everyday Lives* (Charleston, SC: The History Press, 2012).

"Nearer They Come," *Washington Post,* February 17, 1913, 1.

"Newburg Women Parade," *New York Times,* June 5, 1913, 1.

"Oh, He Dared Antis," *Washington Post,* February 27, 1913, 5.

"On to Washington," *Morning News* (Wilmington, DE), February 13, 1913, 10.

"On to Washington The Suffragists Cry," *New York American,* February 12, 1913, 1.

"One Martyr Among Pilgrims," *Baltimore Sun,* February 22, 1913, 7.

"Order of the March," *Women's Journal and Suffrage News,* 44, no. 9 (March 1, 1913): 72.

"'Ouch!' Is Hikers' Cry on First March," *The Sun* (New York, NY), January 2, 1914, 14.

"Out in True Colors," *Evening Star* (Washington, D.C.), February 19, 1913, 2.

"Outdo South, in Pageant, Is Women's Plan," *Washington Times,* January 12, 1913, 2.

"Oyster Bay Dirty, Colonel Discloses," *New York Times,* June 26, 1916, 5.

"Parade as Seen by Miss Clark," *Washington Herald,* March 4, 1913, 2.

"Parade Struggles to Victory Despite Disgraceful Scenes," *Woman's Journal and Suffrage News,* 44, no. 10 (March 8, 1913): 76.

"Pass 100-mile Mark on Washington Hike," *New York Times,* February 18, 1913, 5.

Penn, William. *Fruits of Solitude* (London: Headley, 1905).

"Percy Leads March," *Washington Evening Star* (Washington, D.C.), February 13, 1913, 1.

Petrash, Antonia. *Long Island and the Women's Suffrage Movement* (Charleston, SC: The History Press, 2013).

"Phoebe Hawn's Story of Washington Hike," *Brooklyn Daily Eagle,* March 13, 1913, 9.

"Pilgrims Are Jeered at Trenton," *Pittsburgh Post-Gazette,* February 15, 1913, 16.

"Pilgrims' Blood Shed for Cause," *Washington Times,* February 24, 1913, 2.

"Pilgrims Draw Big Crowd to Garrick," *Morning News* (Wilmington, DE), February 20, 1913, 10.

"Pilgrims Enter Albany," *New York Post,* January 7, 1914, 2.

"Pilgrims Have a Preliminary Taste of Weather," *New York American,* February 11, 1913, 1.

"Pilgrims Told to Enter City by Side Streets," *Washington Herald,* February 28, 1913, 1.

"Plans for the Hike," *Morning News* (Wilmington, DE), January 17, 1913, 4.

"Prize Cow at Fair Is Anti-Suffragist," *The Sun* (New York, NY), August 6, 1913, 4.

"Proposals and Orchids Cheer Women Hikers," *Baltimore News,* February 17, 1913, 2.

"Public Greeting Is Balm to Hikers on Entry to Capital," *Washington Times,* February 28, 1913, 1.

"Question of Minorities," *New York Post,* February 14, 1913.

"Rains Coins for Cause at Carnegie Hall," *New York Tribune,* February 18, 1913, 3.

"Record March 1 Crowd Pours Into Capital," *Washington Post,* March 2, 1913, 2.

"Rehearsing for Hike to Washington," *Baltimore Sun,* February 8, 1913, 2.

"Rested Hikers Capture City," *Washington Times,* March 1, 1913, 1.

"Romance Stirs Suffrage Ranks," *Middletown Daily Times-Press* (Middletown, NY), December 26, 1912.

"Romance Thrills Suffragettes on March to Albany," *New York Press,* December 26, 1912.

"Root Against Woman Suffrage," *New York Post,* February 24, 1913, 4.

"Rosalie Jones, 95, an Early LI Feminist," *Newsday,* January 13, 1978.

"Rosalie Jones Back Thinner," *The Sun* (New York, NY), August 23, 1914, 9.

"Rosalie Jones Not Ill," *New York Times,* February 2, 1913, 1.

"Rosalie's Army Greeted by Mob," *San Francisco Call,* February 17, 1913, 7.

"Rowdies Help Suffrage," *New York Post,* March 5, 1913, 3.

Schier, Ruth. "Rosalie Jones Has Spent Most Of Life Clashing With Authority," *The Long-Islander* (Huntington, NY), September 16, 1948, 1.

"Schools to Be out for Women Parade," *Washington Times,* February 19, 1913, 2.

"She Is Not a Suffragette," *Baltimore Sun,* February 22, 1913, 7.

"Shocked by Hikers," *Washington Post,* February 26, 1913, 3.

"Shoe Shiner Only Man on Suffrage Special," *Philadelphia Inquirer,* February 22, 1913, 4.

"Siege of the Fair," *Washington Post,* February 22, 1913, 1.

"16 Miles Nearer Albany," *Washington Post,* January 2, 1914, 5.

"16½ Miles in 13 Hours," *Baltimore Sun,* February 22, 1913, 1.

"Some Suffrage Definitions," *Morning News* (Wilmington, DE), January 18, 1913, 7.

Spinzia, Judith Adler. "Women of Long Island: Mary Elizabeth Jones, Rosalie Gardiner Jones," *The Freeholder,* 11 (Spring 2007): 3–7.

"The Spreading Suffrage," *New York Post,* February 24, 1913, 4.

"Steel City Women to be in Parade," *Pittsburg Post-Gazette,* February 27, 1913, 3.

Stovall, James G. *Seeing Suffrage: The 1913 Washington Parade, Its Pictures, and Its Effects on the American Political Landscape* (Knoxville: University of Tennessee Press, 2013).

"Suffrage Advance to Rochester Is On," *The Sun* (New York, NY), October 8, 1914, 8.

"Suffrage Army Finishes Plans," *Washington Herald,* February 26, 1913, 2.

"Suffrage Army Is Drawing Near," *Washington Times,* February 26, 1913, 1.

"Suffrage Army Soothed," *New York Tribune,* February 28, 1913, 7.

"Suffrage Army Start Delayed by Shiny Nose," *Baltimore News,* February 12, 1913, 1.

"Suffrage Army to Enter City's Gates Before Nightfall," *Baltimore News,* February 23, 1913, 1.

"Suffrage Band Adds New Recruits," *Washington Times,* February 17, 1913, 1.

"Suffrage Band in Havre de Grace," *Morning News* (Wilmington, DE), February 21, 1913, 1.

"Suffrage Band Near Collapse," *Washington Herald,* February 22, 1913, 3.

"Suffrage Bill Held Up," *New York Tribune,* January 16, 1913, 7.

"Suffrage Campaign Closes at Midnight," *New York Times,* October 31, 1915, 4.

"The Suffrage Campaign Here," *News Journal* (Wilmington, DE), January 18, 1913, 2.

"Suffrage Campaign to End in a Whirl," *New York Times,* October 29, 1915, 5.

"Suffrage Hike Starts to Washington with Vim," *Evening World* (New York, NY), February 12, 1913, 4.

"Suffrage Hiker Suffers Collapse," *Washington Times,* January 31, 1913, 1.

"Suffrage Hikers Near Death When the

Chainless Tires of Their Auto Skidded," *New York Times*, December 29, 1912.

"Suffrage Hikers Out," *New York Times*, April 27, 1913, 4.

"Suffrage Hikers Reach This City," *Morning News* (Wilmington, DE), February 19, 1913, 2.

"Suffrage Hikers Undaunted by Cold," *New York Times*, February 13, 1913, 6.

"Suffrage Invasion Is on in Earnest," *New York Times*, March 2, 1913, 15.

"Suffrage Marchers Decide on Costumers," *New York Times*, January 12, 1913, 8.

"Suffrage Marchers Pose for Movies," *New York Tribune*, January 30, 1913 1.

"Suffrage Marchers Struggle with Mud," *New York Times*, February 22, 1913, 5.

"Suffrage Parade Cash Given Here," *Philadelphia Inquirer*, February 8, 1913, 4.

"Suffrage Passes Senate," *New York Times*, January 23, 1913, 8.

"Suffrage Pilgrims Make Fine Start on Washington Hike," *Brooklyn Daily Eagle*, February 12, 1913, 1.

"Suffrage Pioneers Not Forgotten in Victory," *The Sun* (New York, NY), December 9, 1917, 5.

"Suffrage Tallyho Carries Valentines," *Baltimore News*, February 14, 1913, 2.

"Suffrage Victory in the House Pleases All But Antis," *The Sun* (New York, NY), January 20, 1918, 8.

"Suffrage Women Are 'Marriageable,' Says General Jones," *Washington Times*, January 12, 1913, 1.

"Suffragette Hikers Today One Big Ache," *Baltimore News*, February 14, 1913, 2.

"Suffragette Leads Princeton Revel," *New York Times*, February 15, 1913, 6.

"Suffragette Now Runs a Taxicab," *New York Times*, October 3, 1913, 3.

"Suffragettes Get Permit to Use Treasury Building," *Washington Times*, January 23, 1913, 6.

"Suffragettes Plan," *Washington Times*, January 12, 1913, 2.

"Suffragettes Ride Through Town Atop of Fifth Avenue Bus," *Evening World* (New York, NY), February 10, 1913, 8.

"Suffragettes Stroll into Baltimore," *Pittsburgh Post-Gazette*, February 24, 1913, 1.

"Suffragist Beauty in Trousers Leads Dress Reform Campaign," *Washington Post*, July 1, 1913, 3.

"The Suffragist Demonstration," *Brooklyn Daily Eagle*, January 10, 1913, 6.

"Suffragists Brave Police," *Washington Post*, January 30, 1913, 3.

"Suffragists Call Mr. Heflin Beau Brummell of the House," *Washington Post*, February 12, 1913, 5.

"Suffragists Divided Over the Outrage," *Morning News* (Wilmington, DE), February 20, 1913, 10.

"Suffragists Hear Arguments of Antis," *New York Times*, January 21, 1913, 8.

"Suffragists in an Education Campaign," *Morning Journal* (Wilmington, DE), February 19, 1913, 10.

"Suffragists in Golden Cars," *Baltimore Sun*, January 24, 1913, 4.

"Suffragists' Long Walk," *The Times of London*, October 11, 1912, 8.

"Suffragists March to Wilmington," *News Journal* (Wilmington, DE), February 18, 1913, 6.

"Suffragists' Parade Is Helped Through Mob," *Pittsburgh Post-Gazette*, March 4, 1913, 3.

"Suffragists Plan Big Reception for Pilgrim Army Here Friday," *Washington Post*, February 26, 1913, 3.

"Suffragists Spread Oratory and Tracts," *New York Times*, February 11, 1913, 11.

"Suffragists to Hear Bugler," *Baltimore Sun*, January 27, 1913, 7.

"Suffragists to Invade Trenton," *Trenton Evening Times*, February 8, 1913, 1.

"Suffragists Will Insist on Military Guard in Pageant," *Washington Times*, February 16, 1913, 6.

"Sunday Hike for Army," *Baltimore Sun*, February 16, 1913, 1.

"Taft Not to See Parade," *Baltimore Sun*, February 22, 1913, 7.

"Tell of the Tramp," *Evening Star* (Washington, D.C.), February 20, 1913, 3.

"10,000 Marchers in Suffrage Line," *New York Times*, May 4, 1913, 1.

"Thousands Are Given to Suffrage Cause," *Evening Star* (Washington, D.C.), March 3, 1913, 11.

"Three Fair Hikers Are Hors de Combat," *Pittsburgh Post-Gazette*, February 14, 1913, 4.

"Throngs Greet Pilgrims' Entry," *Washington Post*, March 1, 1913, 1.

"To Drag Ball and Chain," *Chicago Daily Tribune*, February 13, 1913, 3.

"To Improve Maryland Roads," *Morning News* (Wilmington, DE), February 22, 1913, 3.

"Tragedies of Society—Suicides Stalk the Joneses of Long Island," *New York Journal and American* (New York, NY), April 17, 1936, 1-M.

"200 from Philadelphia in Suffrage Parade," *Philadelphia Inquirer*, February 22, 1913, 4.

"Urges Women to War," Washington Herald, February 22, 1913, 3.

"Valentines for Hikers," *Baltimore Sun*, February 15, 1913, 2.

"Vendors of Novelties Greet Surging Crowds," *Sunday Star* (Washington, D.C.), March 2, 1913, 8.

"The Voteless Voters," *New York Times*, February 18, 1913, 12.

"Votes for Women," *Washington Post*, February 25, 1913, 2.

"Wagon to Go with Hikers," *Baltimore Sun*, January 30, 1913, 7.

Walton, Mary. *A Woman's Crusade: Alice Paul and the Battle for the Ballot* (New York: St. Martin's Griffin, 2010).

"Want 'Anti' Pageant," *Washington Post*, February 25, 1913, 2.

"Wearied Hikers Plod on in the Dark," *New York Times*, February 14, 1913, 3.

"Welcome to the Hikers," *Baltimore Sun*, February 22, 1913, 7.

"Where the Suffragettes Score," *Baltimore Sun*, February 26, 1913, 6.

"Who's Who in Ranks," *Evening Star* (Washington, D.C.), February 26, 1913, 2.

"Why 'Mrs.' for a Miss?" *New York Times*, February 25, 1913, 7.

"Will Lead Her Army Here," *Washington Post*, January 10, 1913, 2.

"Will Lead Suffrage Hikers to the Capitol," *Washington Times*, January 23, 1913, 7.

"Will Ride as Heralds," *Washington Post*, January 27, 1913, 2.

"Wilson Message Taken from Angry Pilgrims," *New York Tribune*, February 28, 1913, 7.

"Wilson Not at Home When 'Pilgrims' Call," *Brooklyn Daily Eagle*, February 14, 1913, 3.

"Wilson Stole Away," *News Journal* (Wilmington, DE), February 18, 1913, 6.

"Witch Hazel to be Suffragist Flag's Symbol," *Baltimore News*, February 16, 1913, 2.

"Woman Censures Suffragist Hikers," *Philadelphia Inquirer*, February 22, 1913, 4.

"Woman Suffrage Excites House," *Philadelphia Inquirer*, March 2, 1913, 6.

"Woman Suffrage Parade Pledge Card," NAWSA Suffrage Scrapbooks, Library of Congress, accessed July 8, 2019, https://cdn.loc.gov/master/rbc/rbcmil/scrp700 6502/001.jpg

"Woman's Day at the Capital," *New York Post*, March 3, 1913, 1.

"Woman's Parade Riot Inquiry," *New York Post*, March 5, 1913.

"Woman's Yell Arouses Gotham," *Press and Sun-Bulletin* (Binghamton, NY), February 12, 1913, 1.

"Women Complete Arrangements for Big Washington Parade, March 3," *Oakland Tribune*, February 23, 1.

"Women Hikers to Bivouac in City Tomorrow," *Baltimore News*, February 22, 1913, 1.

"Women Hold Debate at Republican Club," *New York Times*, January 26, 1913, 7.

"Women in Rally for Hike to Washington," *New York Tribune*, January 10, 1913, 3.

"Women on to the Capital," *New York Post*, February 13, 1913.

"Women Plan Plane Swoop," *New York Tribune*, January 16, 1913, 7.

"Women Practice Marches for Big Suffrage Parade," *Washington Times*, January 24, 1913, 2.

"Women Protest Slight of Flag," *Washington Times*, February 23, 1913, 1.

"Women to 'Hike' for Vote," *Washington Post*, January 2, 1914, 5.

"Women Who Will Play a Prominent Part in the Suffrage Parade," *Washington Herald*, February 23, 1913, 15.

"Women Will Keep up the Fight," *New York Times*, October 20, 1915, 1.

"Women Win in South Dakota," *New York Tribune*, January 16, 1913, 7.

"Women's Army on the March," *New York Post*, February 12, 1913, 1.

"Won't Parade on March 4," *New York Times*, January 25, 1913, 1.

"Worth $5,000,000 Gen. Rosalie Jones Is Socialist Now," *Evening World* (New York, NY), October 26, 1918, 5.

"Would Kidnap Cabinet," *Baltimore Sun*, February 22, 1913, 7.

"Would Let Men Nurse Babies," *Baltimore Sun*, February 22, 1913, 7.

"Yes, I Vote, Says Suffragette, One of Army in 1913 Capitol Hike," *Poughkeepsie Journal* (Poughkeepsie, NY), January 8, 1956, 1C.

Zahniser, J. D., and Amelia R. Fry. *Alice Paul: Claiming Power* (New York: Oxford University Press, 2019).

Index

267